INSPIRE / PLAN / DISCOVER / EXPERIENCE

PACIFIC NORTHWEST

OREGON, WASHINGTON AND BRITISH COLUMBIA

DK EYEWITNESS

PACIFIC NORTHWEST

OREGON, WASHINGTON AND BRITISH COLUMBIA

CONTENTS

DISCOVER 6

EXPERIENCE 62

NEED TO KNOW 300

Left: Astoria-Megler Bridge in the fog, Oregon
Previous page: Strolling along Oregon's Cannon Beach
Front cover: Cabins reflected in Lake O'Hara, BC

DISCOVER

The Space Needle and Seattle's skyline

WELCOME TO THE PACIFIC NORTHWEST

Home to a perfect blend of pristine wilderness and vibrant cosmopolitan cities, the Pacific Northwest is as diverse as it is breathtaking. Whatever your dream trip to this enormous, rich region includes, this DK Eyewitness travel guide will prove the perfect companion.

1 The bright lights of Downtown Vancouver.

2 Cocktails in Portland.

3 Brewing the perfect cup of coffee in Portland.

4 The spectacular Mount Hood rising behind the trees in Oregon.

Crossing both the US and Canada, the Pacific Northwest marries the best of both nations: Indigenous traditions, pioneer history, and multicultural cuisine fill every corner of Oregon, Washington, and British Columbia. But beyond this, the one quality that characterizes the region is its natural beauty, its lengthy coastline encircling a landscape of lofty mountains, deep gorges, and rolling vineyards. It's no wonder that the call of the wild is the draw for many, with white-water rafting awaiting summer adventurers and skiing calling winter lovers.

All this natural allure provides an immense backdrop for the urban sophistication of the region's three major cities, where residents have preserved charming old quarters while accommodating new growth. Portland has retained its small-town atmosphere, Seattle continues to pay tribute to its musical legacy, and Vancouver leads the way in farm-to-table dining methods. The region's smaller cities and towns are equally charismatic, each with their own unique character, from Victoria's island appeal to Bend's outdoor recreational spirit.

With so much to pack in, any visit to the Pacific Northwest requires thoughtful planning. We've broken the region down into easily navigable chapters, with detailed itineraries, expert local knowledge, and comprehensive maps to help plan the perfect trip. Whether you're staying for the weekend or longer, this Eyewitness travel guide will ensure that you see the very best of the region. Enjoy the book, and enjoy the Pacific Northwest.

REASONS TO LOVE THE PACIFIC NORTHWEST

Mesmerizing natural beauty, cities pulsing with energy, and deliciously fresh cuisine washed down with local brews: there are endless reasons to love the Pacific Northwest, but here are some of our favorites.

1 SPECTACULAR JOURNEYS

Whether you're marveling at glacier-clad peaks from glass-domed trains, driving along lush coastal highways, or embarking on an epic cruise, every journey is a scenic one.

SIP AND SAVOR 2

Rich wine produced in bountiful vineyards; coffee roasted to perfection; organic huckleberry beer crafted with precision: libations are a serious art form in this region *(p50)*.

3 FOOD-TRUCK SCENE

The last decade has seen a dramatic rise in the number of food carts *(p38)*, especially in Portland. Succulent beef ribs, savory pakora waffles, and fluffy steamed buns await.

COASTAL CHARM 4

Craving a surf break, quaint seaside towns, or an island-hopping adventure? The seemingly endless coast plays a huge role in recreational living in the Pacific Northwest.

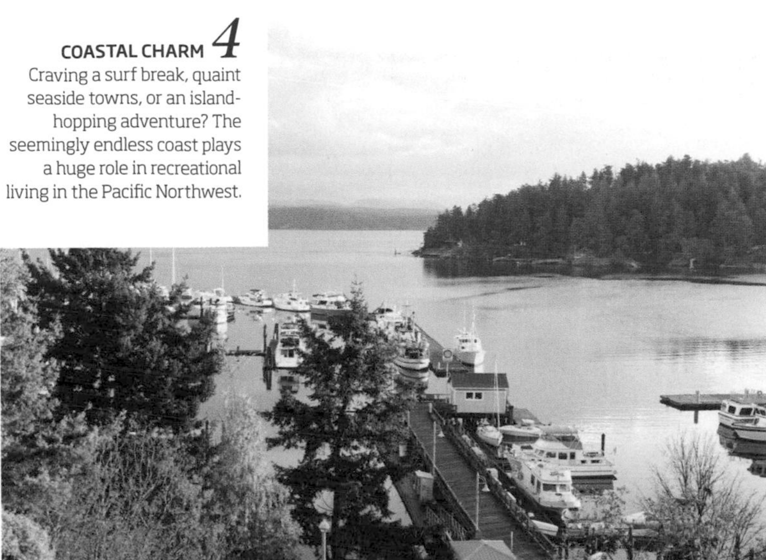

HIKING THE NATIONAL PARKS 5

From the astonishing beauty of Yoho National Park *(p284)* to the pristine wilderness of Crater Lake *(p116)*, the region's vast national parks are all calling out to be explored.

FRESH SEAFOOD 6

Tide to table is the apt motto when it comes to the region's seafood cuisine *(p39)*. Grilled salmon fillets, freshly shucked oysters, and seared scallops - it's all local, and it's all delicious.

GLITTERING CITIES 7

Three of North America's coolest cities - Portland, Seattle, and Vancouver - anchor this region, all offering a vibrant mix of urban activity against a backdrop of natural beauty.

PIKE PLACE MARKET 8

Surround yourself in a flurry of the senses at Seattle's multi-level, buzzing farmers' market *(p166)*, where stands overflow with fine mushrooms, creamy cheeses, and ripe strawberries.

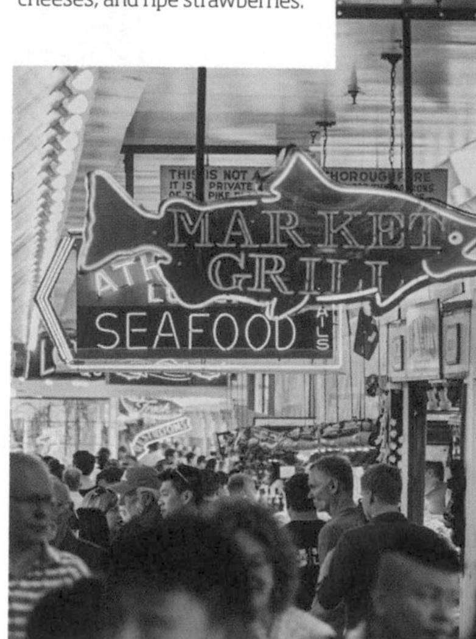

9 TOWERING TOTEMS

The phenomenal skills of Indigenous artists can be seen in intricately carved cedar poles *(p32)*. They retell ancient sagas and are found only in the Pacific Northwest.

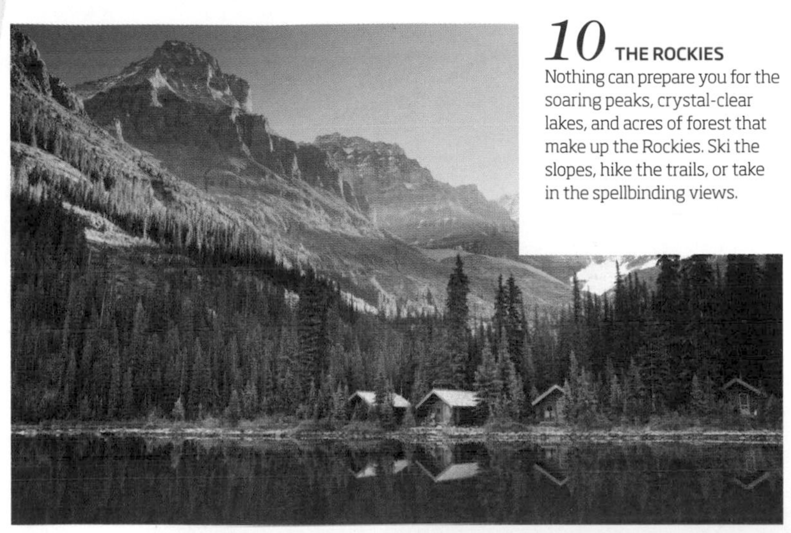

10 THE ROCKIES

Nothing can prepare you for the soaring peaks, crystal-clear lakes, and acres of forest that make up the Rockies. Ski the slopes, hike the trails, or take in the spellbinding views.

INNOVATIVE MUSIC SCENE 11

The Pacific Northwest's musical legacy is second to none. Whether hitting a summer blues festival or tracing grunge origins at MoPOP *(p176)*, music is at the core of this region.

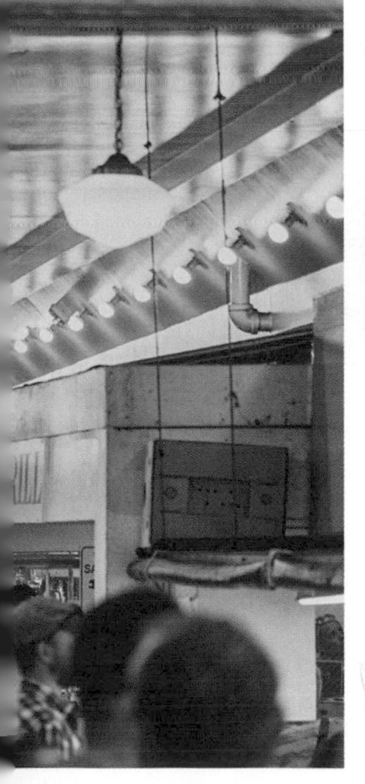

WILDLIFE SPOTTING 12

The thrill of spotting a rare spirit bear in Haida Gwaii *(p280)*, a whale breaching the Olympic Peninsula *(p212)*, or the predatory bald eagle soaring city skies never gets old here.

Pacific Ocean

EXPLORE THE PACIFIC NORTHWEST

This guide divides the Pacific Northwest into six color-coded sightseeing areas, as shown on the map to the right. Find out more about each area on the following pages.

0 kilometers 250
0 miles 250
N

NORTHWEST TERRITORIES
Fort Nelson
Smithers
Rocky Mountains
CANADA
Prince George
Edmonton
BRITISH COLUMBIA
p264
Coast Mountains
ALBERTA
Calgary
Kamloops
Kelowna
Vancouver Island
VANCOUVER
p216
Victoria
Olympic Peninsula
SEATTLE
p142
Spokane
Missoula
Tacoma
Olympia
WASHINGTON
p192
Astoria
Cascades
PORTLAND
p64
Pendleton
IDAHO
OREGON
p106
Eugene
Bend
Boise
UNITED STATES OF AMERICA
Burns Junction
Twin Falls
Medford
CALIFORNIA
NEVADA
Wells
CANADA
PACIFIC NORTHWEST
UNITES STATES OF AMERICA
Pacific Ocean
Atlantic Ocean
MEXICO
CUBA
NORTH AMERICA

GETTING TO KNOW THE PACIFIC NORTHWEST

Straddling two nations - the US and Canada - the Pacific Northwest is an area of contrasts, characterized by its natural beauty and anchored by vibrant, sophisticated cities. From the imposing mountain ranges of British Columbia to the evergreen forests that carpet Oregon, each region has a history and essence distinctly its own.

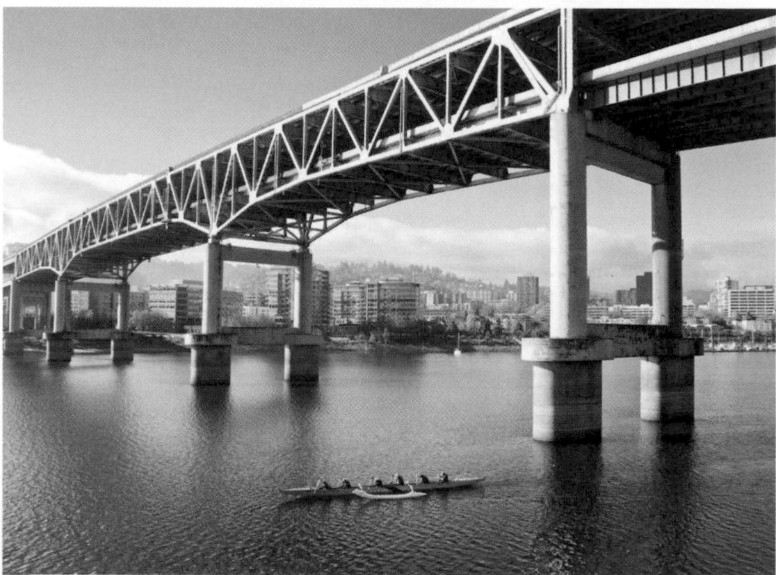

PAGE 64

PORTLAND

Oregon's largest city enhances its beautiful natural surroundings with a healthy dose of urban vitality and a relaxed lifestyle. Lush green spaces and miles of bicycle lanes, not to mention its leading farm-to-table produce, organic wineries, and superb microbreweries, make Portland a leading city in the eco-friendliness category. Beyond its mix of individualistic culture and cuisine, the city's historic landmarks and fascinating museums show off its commitment to preserving its rich past. If you're itching to get moving, the sparkling Willamette River offers serene paddling opportunities in the midst of this convivial metropolis.

Best for
Craft beer, scenic park trails, and food trucks

Home to
Washington Park, Sauvie Island

Experience
Sipping a coffee and perusing the aisles of literary treasures at Powell's City of Books

PAGE 106

OREGON

Snowcapped mountains piercing the clouds; waves breaking on rocky shores; dense forests clinging to ravines: opportunities for adventures draw lovers of the great outdoors to Oregon. Hells Canyon – the deepest gorge in North America – and the mighty Columbia River are the main draws but this easygoing rural state offers much more, from the snow-covered slopes of Mount Hood to cosmopolitan pleasures in the shape of Ashland's Shakespeare Festival. Wherever you go, the glimmer of a distant mountain peak and the scent of pine in the air will add an extra zest.

Best for

Beach towns, backcountry adventures, and epic road trips

Home to

Salem, Eugene, Bend, Crater Lake National Park, Columbia River Gorge, Mount Hood

Experience

Driving around the panoramic perimeter of the deep-blue Crater Lake in the summer

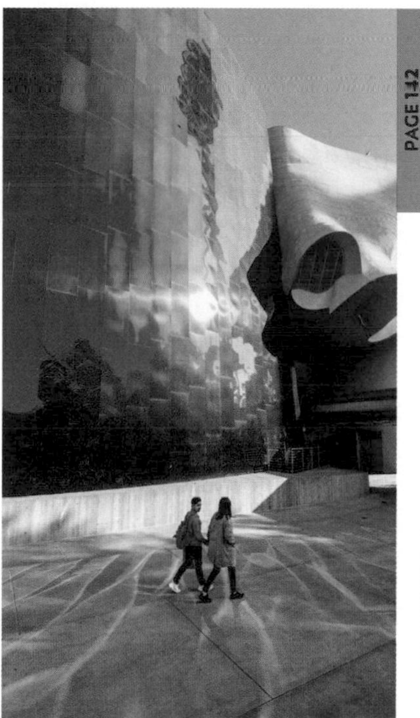

PAGE 142

SEATTLE

Innovative, daring, and modern, the largest of the area's three main cities still holds firmly on to its industrious past. Pioneer Square indulges in Seattle's pivotal role during the Gold Rush days, while the once-futuristic Space Needle remains an architectural icon that dominates the imposing skyline. Thanks to its waterfront location on the Puget Sound, seafood cuisine thrives here, with plenty of its ocean bounty proudly displayed at Pike Place Market. Top art exhibits, chic rooftop lounges, and an iconic music scene complete the picture of Washington's most vibrant city.

Best for

Seafood restaurants, intriguing museums, and live music

Home to

Seattle Art Museum, Pike Place Market, Museum of Pop Culture (MoPOP), Space Needle

Experience

Dining on fresh local oysters, scallops, and crab at a Pike Place Market eatery

→

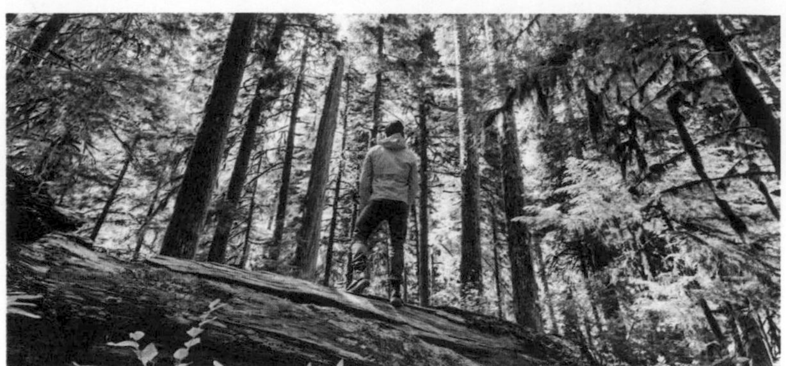

PAGE 192

WASHINGTON

Miles of scenic coastline, expansive lakes, and towering moss-draped trees are sprinkled liberally throughout this forested and mountainous state, which shares a border with Canada. The remote Olympic Peninsula in the coastal region offers serene beachcombing and whale-watching opportunities, while the islands in the west are home to charming towns that let you slip into "island time" for a day or two. A drive to the eastern region – at its best in late spring to mid-fall – leads to the wine country and breathtaking peaks.

Best for
Island hopping, mountain trails, and fine wines

Home to
Port Townsend, San Juan Islands, Mount Rainier National Park

Experience
Touring the San Juan Islands by boat, spotting seals and whales along the way

PAGE 216

VANCOUVER

Cosmopolitan Vancouver, nestled between BC's Coast Mountains and the Strait of George, arguably enjoys the best setting of the Pacific Northwest's cities. The glass skyscrapers of its buzzing downtown sit alongside trendy restaurants, flourishing art galleries, and independent boutiques in the historic Gastown district. Adding to its creative dining scene is Canada's largest Chinatown, where mouthwatering eateries can be found on every corner. Throw in abundant parks, outstanding Indigenous art, and a lively LGBT+ nightlife scene, and it's easy to see why this eclectic, laid-back city attracts so many visitors.

Best for
Indigenous culture, international dining, and park strolls

Home to
Stanley Park, Vanier Park, Granville Island, Museum of Anthropology at UBC

Experience
Cycling along the Seawall in Stanley Park, taking in the magnificent city views as you go

PAGE 264

BRITISH COLUMBIA

BC's exceptionally beautiful coast, mountain ranges, forests, and lakes offer a relaxed pace of life and play host to some unmissable experiences. In contrast, the towns on the southeastern corner buzz with their lively food and arts scene, and the pretty, provincial capital of Victoria has fine museums packed with the works of indigenous artists, plus a charming harbor. Inland, the interior's many lakes provide glistening vistas and sunny playgrounds for water sports of all kinds. In sharp contrast, the dramatic wilderness of the northern national parks includes volcanic terrain, ice fields, and historic mining towns. The remote, misty archipelago of Haida Gwaii is the epitome of this northern majestic back country, where ancient rainforest is preserved.

Best for

Mountain treks, hot springs, wildlife spotting, and summer fruits

Home to

Victoria, Haida Gwaii, Whistler, Yoho National Park, Tofino

Experience

Feeling the refreshing mist of Yoho National Park's Takakkaw Falls in the Rockies

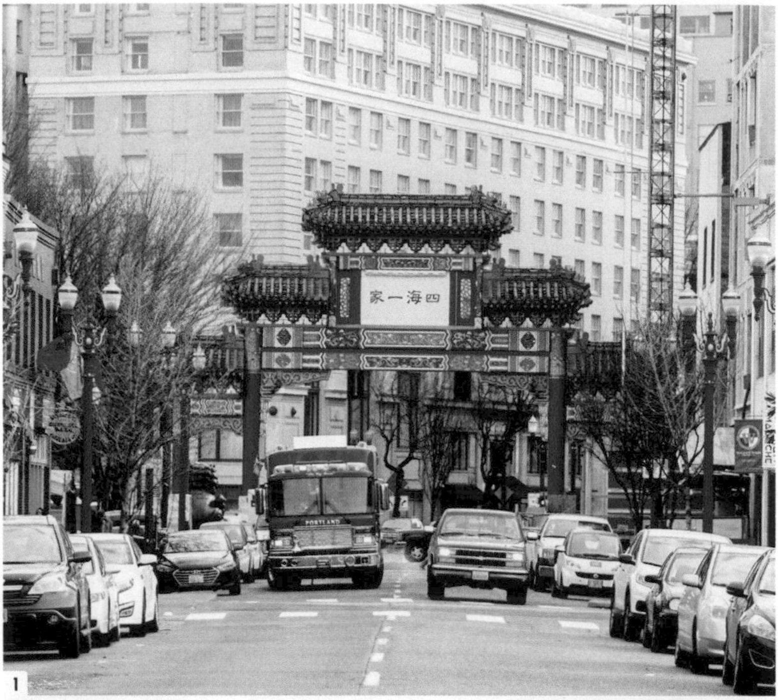

1

2

3

4

←

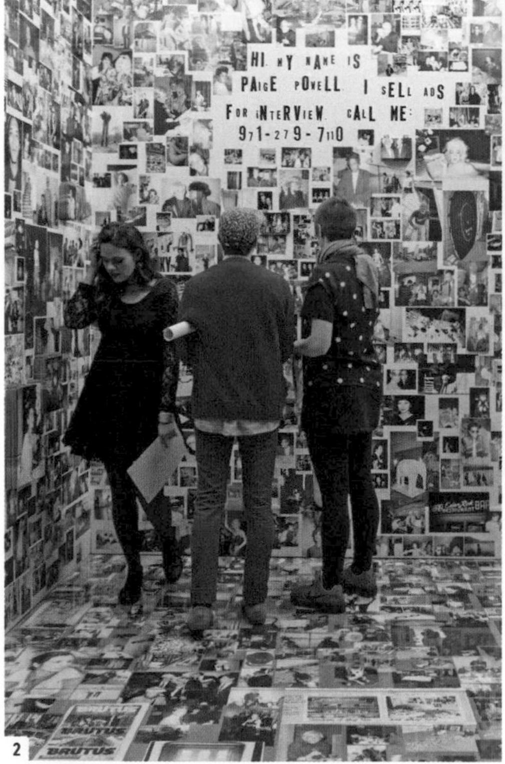

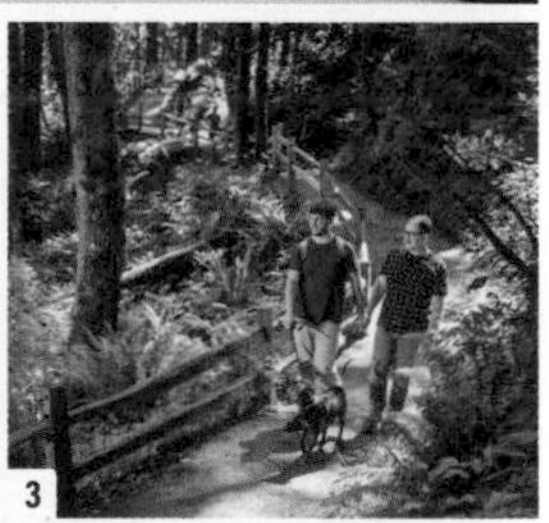

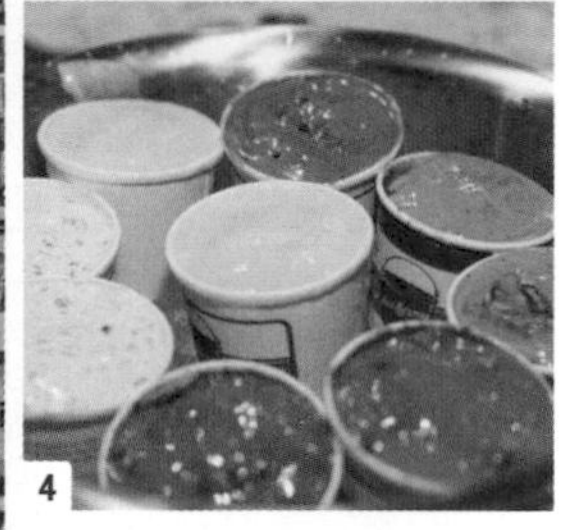

1 Old Town Chinatown.

2 Admiring art in the Portland Art Museum

3 Walking through Washington Park

4 Ice cream at Salt & Straw.

The Pacific Northwest brims with travel possibilities, from exciting tours around the big cities to epic road trips along vast forested landscapes. These itineraries will help you to chart your own course through this vibrant and varied region.

2 DAYS

in Portland

Day 1

Morning Begin your trip to Portland with a nourishing breakfast at Mother's Bistro & Bar *(p76)*, fueling up for a browse in the stores and boutiques that populate the trendy Pearl District. When you've picked up some souvenirs, continue through the city's original namesake port, Old Town Chinatown. The breathtaking Lan Su Chinese Garden *(p74)* makes a wonderful stopping-off point, with stone paths winding through Chinese pavilions. It's a short walk south to the historic Burnside Bridge, from which you can snap a photo of the White Stag Sign, Portland's iconic neon symbol since the 1940s.

Afternoon Tuck into a healthy lunch at Bamboo Sushi *(p76)*, then hop aboard one of the streetcars that link Old Town Chinatown to downtown. Idle the afternoon away at the fantastic Portland Art Museum *(p87)*, the oldest art museum in the region. Whittle its 42,000 treasures down by focusing on its core European collection, looking out for *The Ox-Cart* by Vincent van Gogh. As the late afternoon approaches, head to Pioneer Courthouse Square *(p84)* to people-watch commuters during the after-work rush.

Evening Snag a happy-hour beverage to wash down Vietnamese food at Luc Lac Vietnamese Kitchen *(p88)*, one of the finest drinking dens in the city. Still thirsty? Move on to the cosy lounge of the Multnomah Whiskey Library *(p88)*.

Day 2

Morning The Fifth Avenue Food Cart Pod *(SW 5th Ave and SW Oak and Stark sts)* is your best bet for a fast and filling breakfast. Once satiated, take the light rail to reach the sprawling Washington Park *(p94)*. Start at the poignant Oregon Holocaust Memorial, taking in the objects left behind by Holocaust victims, then recoup and reflect while strolling through the Japanese Garden. This beautiful landscape is a tranquil spot no matter the season, with its well-tended plants surrounding ponds and streams.

Afternoon Embark on a stroll through the charming Nob Hill *(p100)* neighborhood, located at the base of Washington Park. Its pretty streets are lined with Victorian-era homes and independent boutiques to dip into. Break at the St. Honoré Bakery *(p101)* for fine French baked goods, both sweet and savory. A 15-minute bus ride south brings you to Powell's City of Books *(p75)*, the world's largest independent bookstore. With more than a million volumes on hand, there's plenty to keep you occupied and work up an appetite for dinner.

Evening Head downtown to enjoy a movie at the vintage 1920s McMenamins Bagdad Theater & Pub *(p102)*, complete with an elegant interior. Procure a balcony spot for dinner and drinks delivered to your seat. End the day with an unusual ice-cream treat from Salt & Straw *(p101)*.

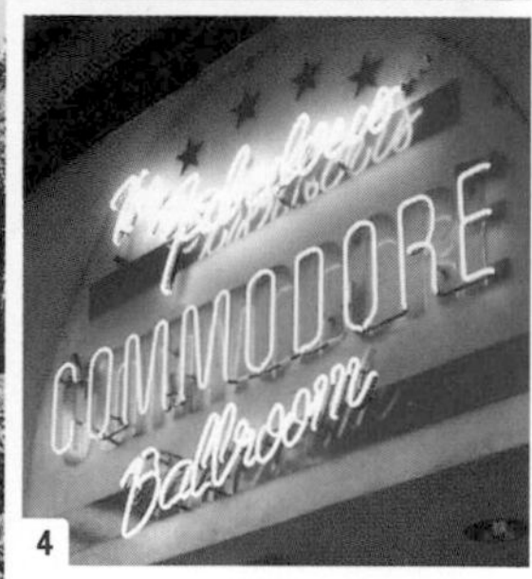

←

1 False Creek and the skyline of downtown Vancouver.

2 The serene Dr. Sun Yat-Sen Classical Chinese Garden.

3 Coffee brewing at Revolver on Cambie Street.

4 Neon sign for the Art Deco Commodore Ballroom.

2 DAYS

in Vancouver

Day 1

Morning Start the day with a leisurely latte at Revolver *(325 Cambie St)* and people-watching on Robson Street, then head to the lovely Stanley Park *(p238)*. The Seawall here is flat and easily circumnavigated in an hour; you can book an e-bike and a tour guide to cycle it or, if you're feeling less energetic, board the hop-on-hop-off bus. Don't miss the totem poles near Brocton Oval or the Vancouver Aquarium, which is worth going to for its mesmerizing jellyfish tank alone. Afterward, head down to False Creek to take an Aquabus across to Granville Island *(p252)*, a small peninsula dominated by a huge food market brimming with fresh produce, fishmongers, cheesemakers, and bakers.

Afternoon After a hearty lunch at the market, take a 20-minute bus ride from Granville Loop Park to Mount Pleasant, a vibrant neighborhood filled with boutiques, galleries, coffee shops, and craft breweries. Nearby Brassneck Brewery *(2148 Main St)* is a favorite with thirsty locals sporting hipster beards and plaid shirts. When you've had your fill of craft beers, take another short bus ride up to Chinatown and enjoy a stroll around the tranquil Dr. Sun Yat-Sen Classical Chinese Garden *(p230)*.

Evening Work up an appetite browsing aromatic apothecary and grocery stores on Keefer and East Pender streets before having dinner at Bao Bei *(p230)*. If you have to join a waiting list for a table, enjoy a cocktail at The Keefer Bar *(p230)*.

Day 2

Morning Take the SeaBus across Burrard Inlet to North Vancouver and bus or hike to Grouse Mountain *(p261)* for a panoramic view of the city. Take the same bus to the spectacular Capilano Suspension Bridge *(p260)* and visit the Indigenous Peoples cultural center, located in the same park, to see demonstrations of weaving, beadwork, and carving. Before jumping back on the SeaBus, check out Lonsdale Quay *(p260)*, a market selling beautiful handcrafted items.

Afternoon Drive or catch a bus west, and amble along Jericho Beach Park's trails, keeping an eye out for bald eagles in the sky and bunnies in the brambles. Pause for a refreshing beer and juicy salmon burger at the beach-side Galley Patio & Grill *(1300 Discovery St)*. Continue westward toward UBC *(p263)* and peek around the Museum of Anthropology *(p258)*, filled with totem poles, masks, and other Indigenous artifacts from around the globe. Be sure to take in the ocean views from the exterior of the museum before heading back to the city center and trendy Gastown, Vancouver's oldest neighborhood.

Evening Gastown's restaurants range from funky to fine dining. Join the after-work crowd at Cardero's Restaurant *(p229)* before taking in a show at the Commodore Ballroom *(p48)*, an Art Deco venue known for its sprung dance floor. If you want to party the night away afterward, Granville Street is definitely the place to be.

1

2

3

4

5

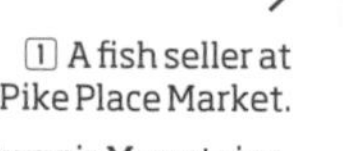

1 A fish seller at Pike Place Market.

2 Olympic Mountains.

3 General Porpoise cafe.

4 Dish from The Walrus and the Carpenter.

5 Bainbridge Island ferry.

4 DAYS

in Seattle

Day 1

Get in the Seattle spirit with a caffeine fix with a twist at the original Starbucks® in Pike Place Market *(p168)*, the city's most popular attraction. Browse local delicacies throughout the market, snacking as you go. Once satiated, wander toward the waterfront and the Seattle Great Wheel; a spin on this goliath offers unparalleled panoramas over Elliott Bay. Catch a harbor boat tour with Argosy Cruises *(www.argosy cruises.com)*, before feasting on succulent shellfish at Ivar's Acres of Clams *(p170)*. Stroll toward Pioneer Square, where you can browse independent shops and galleries, before finishing your day with cocktails and a lofty view from the bar at Smith Tower *(p157)*.

Day 2

Indulge in a heavy breakfast of filled doughnuts and fancy coffee at General Porpoise *(www.gpdoughnuts.com)* before heading to the iconic Museum of Pop Culture *(p176)*, a must for music fans. After you've had your fill of Nirvana memorabilia, check out the world-famous Space Needle *(p178)*, where you'll be rewarded with breathtaking views of the city and beyond. Pass through Belltown for lunch – try sustainable eatery Local 360 *(www.local360.org)* – before heading eastward to Capitol Hill, Seattle's hippest neighborhood and an LGBT+ epicenter packed with independent shops and fun bars. Capitol Cider *(www.capitolcider.com)* – with over 200 ciders and live music – makes for a great night out.

Day 3

Start the day in historic-meets-hipster Ballard *(p190)*. Breakfast at Hattie's Hat *(www.hatties-hat.com)*, an institution since 1904 that specializes in stacks of hotcakes, then browse the independent retailers around NW Market Street. Pick up one of the city's dockless bikes and take the Burke-Gilman Trail to Golden Gardens Park for beach strolls, forest trails, and views of the Olympic Mountains. Sip suds in the brewery district at Peddler Brewing *(www.peddlerbrewing.com)*, before tucking into freshly shucked oysters at in-demand The Walrus and the Carpenter *(p190)*. If you've still got some energy left over, hit the Tractor Tavern *(p190)* to watch live rock bands until the early hours.

Day 4

A 35-minute inexpensive ferry ride will get you from downtown Seattle to Bainbridge Island *(p202)*, a postcard-perfect excursion. Disembark and head to the downtown area for coffee and a cream scone at Blackbird Bakery *(www.blackbirdbakery.com)*, then spend the rest of the morning exploring the quaint town. Take a return ferry to town and spend the afternoon exploring the light-filled galleries of Seattle Art Museum *(p154)*. To continue your glorious waterfront views, book a table at Aerlume *(www.aerlumeseattle.com)* for dinner, where you can sit around a cosy fire-pit table and dine on the finest Pacific Northwest cuisine, including Dungeness crab wraps. End your trip with fancy cocktails alongside Seattle's cool crowd.

1

2

7 DAYS
in Southern BC

Day 1

After spending a couple of days in vibrant Vancouver *(p22)*, make the long drive east to the Okanagan Valley on the scenic Trans-Canada Highway 1. The route follows spectacular deep valleys cut by the Fraser river, but the gem of this area is Bridal Falls. Stop off to stretch your legs and snap some photos of this iconic waterfall, then continue east along the Crowsnest Highway 3. It's a three-hour stretch to the beautiful resort town of Osoyoos along the Okanagan Valley, so once you've arrived, unwind with a glass of Riesling at Nk'Mip Cellars *(p289)*. End your day in a hot tub at the nearby Spirit Ridge Resort *(1200 Rancher Creek Rd)*.

Day 2

Line your stomach with a salmon eggs benedict at the resort's main restaurant, then embark on a day sampling amazing wines in Canada's second-largest wine region. Take the hop-on-hop-off Ok Wine Shuttle *(www.okwineshuttle.ca)* for a day off from driving and indulge in award-winning varietals and gorgeous views at the Burrowing Owl Estate Winery *(p289)*, one of the many stops. Head back to Osoyoos to enjoy a casual dinner at Sofia Mexican Food Truck *(9910 Crowsnest Hwy)*.

Day 3

Back in the driver's seat, begin the long trip east toward the West Kootenays *(p276)* along Highway 3, which winds through spectacular mountains and verdant farmlands. You'll also pass some of BC's most historic towns, including tiny Greenwood, a great place to stop for a coffee break. Once rejuvinated, follow the spectacular road as it climbs into the Monashee Mountains before descending into the West Kootenays and into Nelson *(p276)*. You've earned a fabulous, farm-to-table dinner at Pitchfork Eatery *(518 Hall St)*, so tuck in before bedding down at the sophisticated Hume Hotel & Spa *(p276)*.

Day 4

It's easy to see why Nelson is called the Queen City of the Kootenays, settled right up the side of a hill overlooking the West

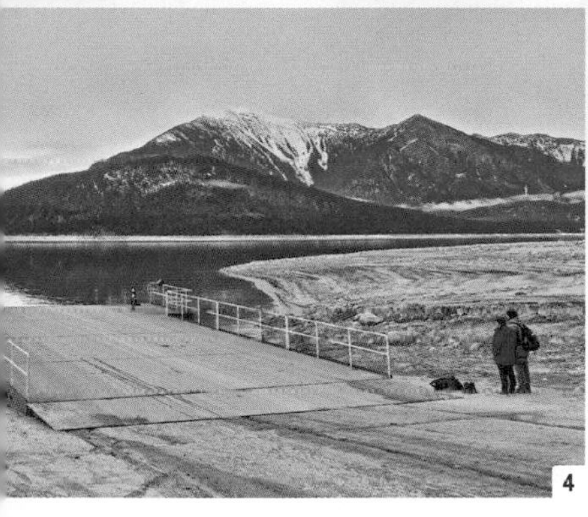

1 The tumbling Bridal Falls. ↑

2 Backroads Brewing in Nelson.

3 A cocktail at Pitchfork Eatery.

4 Touring the Columbia River by the Monashee Mountains.

5 Canoes in Yoho National Park.

Arm of the glacier-fed Kootenay Lake Pick up a self-guided tour map at the Nelson Visitor Centre to explore this proud gem of a town, brimming with rows of preserved heritage buildings alongside timber frame homes. In the afternoon, take a tour of Nelson's breweries, starting at the renowned Backroads Brewing *(www.backroadsbrewing.com)*, then dig into awesome pizza at Thor's Pizzeria *(www.thorspizza.ca)*.

Day 5

Pick up organic picnic supplies for your drive north to Kaslo *(p277)*, a scenic mountain village that, like the others in the region, once prospered in silver mining. Enjoy the divine views of the Purcell Mountains while you tuck into your picnic lunch, then continue north through Nakusp *(p276)*. The highlight of this small town is the Halcyon Hot Springs Resort, so have a swim in the mineral-rich pools that overlook the Upper Arrow Lake below. The excellent onsite Kingfisher Restaurant is the perfect spot for dinner before picking a luxury chalet for the night.

Day 6

Rise early and head north to board the free Upper Arrow Lake Ferry *(www.arrowlakeferry.com)* to Revelstoke, the gateway city to some of Canada's most spectacular national parks. Fill up on poutine, a Canadian take on fries smothered in cheese curds and gravy, at the rustic ski pub The Village Idiot *(www.thevillageidiot.ca)*, then drive east along the Trans-Canada Highway 1 to Glacier National Park *(p295)*, with a tent in tow. It's a good idea to set up your bed for the night at one of the three campgrounds here before embarking on one of the many breathtaking trails.

Day 7

The jagged snowy peaks of the Canadian Rockies provide the incredible backdrop to the conclusion of this epic road trip. About an hour after exiting Glacier, Yoho National Park *(p284)*, to the east, comes into view. A majestic alpine paradise with gem-colored lakes awaits, so rent a canoe at Emerald Lake for a perfect and peaceful end to the tour before heading back to Vancouver.

1

2

3

7 DAYS
in Western Washington and Western Oregon

Day 1

Once you've had your fill of Seattle *(p24)*, hop on a ferry to Bainbridge Island *(p202)*, from where you can begin the drive to Port Townsend *(p196)*. This charming seaport is bejeweled by lovingly restored Victorian-era buildings, but focus on the Jefferson County Courthouse and the Rothschild House for the morning. When hunger strikes, enjoy a fitting coastal lunch at Doc's Marina Grill *(141 Hudson St)*, fueling up for an afternoon immersed in military history at Fort Worden State Park *(p196)*. End your history-filled day in a chic room at the colonial-style Ravenscroft Inn *(p197)*.

Day 2

Port Townsend is the perfect base from which to explore the Olympic Peninsula *(p212)*, where glaciers, subalpine meadows, dense rainforest, and wild coastlines await. Begin driving west and stop off for a home-style brunch at Granny's Cafe *(www.grannyscafe.net)*, then walk off your meal with the short trail through old-growth forest to Marymere Falls by Lake Crescent, where spotted owls nest. Continue west to Rialto Beach and beachcomb among the driftwood. Stay at the vintage Lake Quinault Lodge *(345 S Shore Rd, Quinault)* for the night, dining on classic comfort foods and sipping a fire-side digestif.

Day 3

Rise early and head south to Astoria *(p124)*, the oldest American settlement west of the Rocky Mountains. Climb atop the Astoria Column for scenic views of the region, then tuck into tender seafood served on a converted boat at Bowpicker *(www.bowpicker.com)*. Once satiated, carry on south to Cannon Beach *(p125)*, one of the Oregon coast's most well-known beach towns. Choose a luxury oceanfront room at the Ocean Lodge *(p125)* and take the lodge's '57 Chevy Bel Air shuttle service to dinner along South Hemlock Street.

Day 4

After breakfast at the lodge, make your way south, stopping in Tillamook *(p129)* to visit its famous Creamery and sample

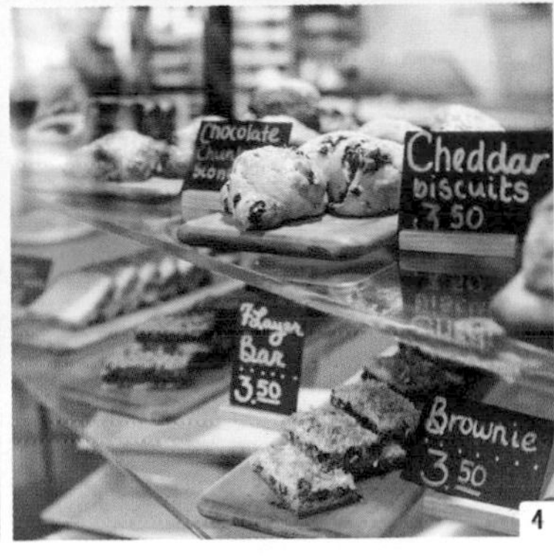

[1] Boats in Port Townsend. ↑

[2] Following the trail to Marymere Falls.

[3] The lush sea stacks reflected at Cannon Beach.

[4] Baked goods at Tillamook's Creamery.

[5] Tower Theatre in Bend.

award-winning cheeses. Keep heading south until you reach Lincoln City *(p128)*, where you can ramble around the steep cliffs and misty rainforests of the Cascade Head Preserve. A 30-minute drive further south takes you to Newport *(p126)*, an atmospheric fishing town full of convivial bars and seafood restaurants. Local Ocean Seafoods *(p127)* is one of the best spots for a meal, so tuck into a fresh fish dinner overlooking the marina before bedding down for the night.

Day 5

Set off from Newport and drive south to the incredible Oregon Dunes National Recreation Area *(p128)*, the epitome of the dry desert-like landscapes that define this region. Take it all in from the scenic overlook point, then embark on the long drive east to another natural wonder: Crater Lake National Park *(p116)*. The 33-mile (53-km) Rim Drive *(p118)* is the best way to experience the deepest lake in the US, and offers incredible vistas. Unwind with a quiet evening at the rustic Crater Lake Lodge *(p118)* on the route.

Day 6

Start the day in style with a rich coffee overlooking the lake, then head to Bend *(p114)*, a two-hour drive north. Bend is an active city where the focus is heavily on outdoor recreation, healthy dining, and good beer. You can tick all of these off the list by starting with a delicious lunch at Spork *(p115)*. Take an extra snack to go for the walk along the Deschutes River Trail *(p114)*, then reward yourself with a tasting flight and an elk burger at the Deschutes Brewery *(p115)*. For some evening entertainment, check to see what's on at the Tower Theatre *(p114)*.

Day 7

End your trip with sophistication by journeying to the heart of the Wine Country of the North Willamette Valley *(p136)*, a three-hour drive northwest. Tour the wonderful wineries (which offer plenty of delicious soft drinks for the designated driver) and tuck into a local varietal before making the short drive north to rugged Portland *(p20)* to tag on a couple of extra cultural days to your trip.

On the Road

The vast wilderness of the Pacific Northwest makes it a prime road-trip region, with long highways skirting rocky headlands. The US Route 101 is the best road for a cliff-hugging coastal drive through Washington and Oregon, while the BC portion of the Trans-Canada Highway 1, the world's longest national road, slices through lush forests.

The winding Rowena Crest Curve Road in Oregon, with sweeping views of the hills

THE PACIFIC NORTHWEST FOR SCENIC JOURNEYS

With an endless supply of stunning coastal, mountain, and city landscapes to marvel at, the Pacific Northwest is the perfect canvas for an array of impressive journeys. Whether you discover the unspoiled scenery by train, car, or ferry, you'll be fueled with epic stories to tell for a lifetime.

CRUISE TO ALASKA

Continuing a tradition that began in 1880, cruise ships ply the Inside Passage, a protected waterway that runs along the BC coast to the inlets of Alaska. The waters are calmer than those of the open Pacific Ocean, so porpoises and whales can often be sighted. Along the way you'll also be rewarded with views of glaciers, mountains, and scenic ports of call. The highly popular cruises, many of which are combined with shore excursions, start from Canada Place and Ballantyne Pier cruise-ship terminals in Vancouver, and attract over one million passengers a year.

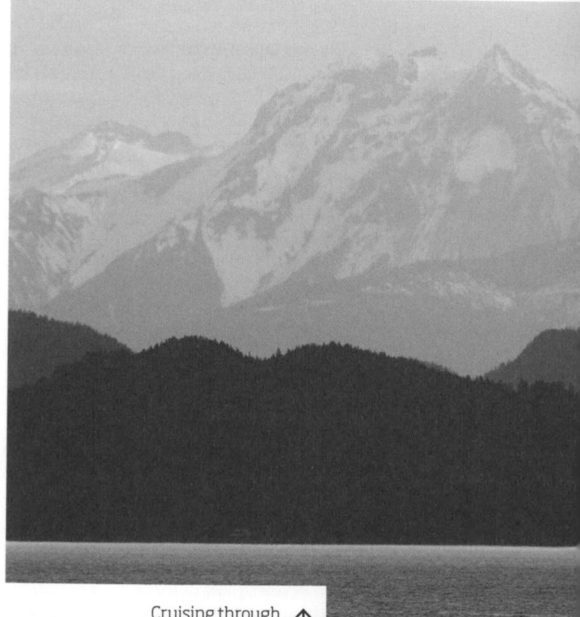

Cruising through Vancouver, and *(inset)* approaching Seattle ↑

Train Touring

With an endless supply of breathtaking tours, the enduring allure of train travel is well-founded in the Pacific Northwest. Cross the border in style on an Amtrak train *(p304)*, which skirts around the Cascade Range and offers gorgeous views of Mount Rainier. If you're looking for luxury, slow down and indulge in a gourmet meal aboard a Via Rail sleeper train *(p304)* as BC's remote mountain towns unfold around you.

→

Traveling along dense, verdant forests on a Via Rail train in Canada

INSIDER TIP
Pack a Picnic

Pick up local snacks for your journeys at Trader Joe's *(www.traderjoes.com)* in Washington and Oregon, and Choices Markets *(www.choicesmarkets.com)* in BC.

Ferry Forays

Hundreds of miles of pristine coastline and multiple forest-clad islands provide the perfect excuse to embark on a scenic voyage. A cruise through the San Juan Islands is a top choice for spotting the whales and orcas that inhabit the frigid seas here, while taking an Aquabus in Vancouver or a Washington State Ferry in Seattle affords priceless cityscape views that don't break the bank. Want to captain your own ship? Rent a boat and zip around your choice of waters, whether it's the mighty Columbia River or the peaceful Okanagan Lake.

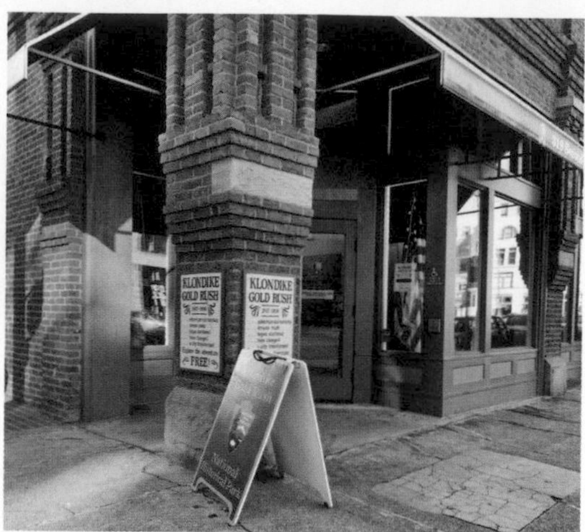

Panning for Gold

Gold fever first gripped the Pacific Northwest in 1848, when the precious metal was discovered in California *(p59)* and soon fueled the growth of the region's cities. Sense the fever, comprehend the perils, and master gold-panning yourself at the Klondike Gold Rush National Historical Park *(p159)* or be transported back to the gold boom days on a historical trolley tour in Jacksonville *(p135)*.

The rustic Klondike Gold Rush National Historical Park visitor center

THE PACIFIC NORTHWEST FOR HISTORY BUFFS

Intrepid prospectors have done much to shape the character of the Pacific Northwest, but the region's history is not all about the pioneers: scandalous stories of a hidden past await discovery. Walk in the footsteps of explorers, amble through ghost towns, and find old opium dens in this colorful land.

SACAGAWEA

Born in Idaho in 1788, Sacagawea is well known for being the sole female member of the Lewis and Clark Expedition. She joined in 1804, when she was just 16 years old and pregnant, and helped establish contacts with Indigenous populations the group encountered. Her language skills and knowledge of the land made her contributions to the expedition invaluable. She died around 1812.

Along the Oregon Trail

In 1804, American explorers Meriwether Lewis and William Clark *(p58)* set out on a 2,000-mile (3,218-km) trail from Missouri to Oregon City to find an overland route to the Pacific Ocean. Early pioneers yearning for fertile land soon followed, and you can discover more about this famed wagon road - much of which can be driven by car - at the End of the Oregon Trail Interpretive Center *(p104)*. Take a guided walk along part of the trail before getting immersed in craft workshops that bring hardships to life.

→

The entrance to the famed End of the Oregon Trail Interpretive Center

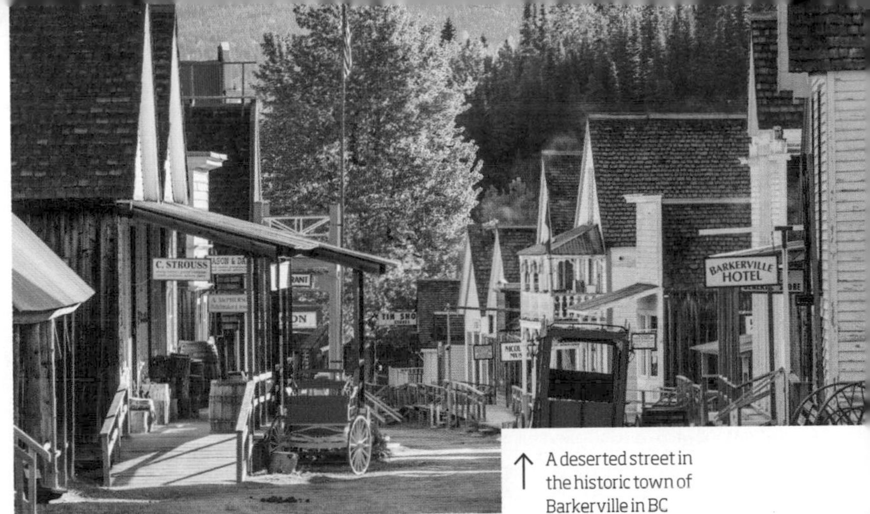

A deserted street in the historic town of Barkerville in BC

Mostly Ghostly

When the gold ran out, so did the people. The Pacific Northwest is home to countless abandoned settlements in various states of ruin that invite you to relive the mining-boom past, imagine the promised riches, and see authentic frontier-style storefronts. The ghost town of Barkerville *(p293)* in BC is now a wonderfully restored, hands-on village exhibit, while the eerie-looking town of Molson in Washington is home to lovely vintage pioneer buildings and rusty farming equipment to explore.

INSIDER TIP
Visit Victoria

Victoria, BC, is one of the most haunted cities in the region. If you dare, embark on a Ghostly Walks tour *(www.discoverthepast.com)*, passing by such sites as Bastion Square, known for its many executions.

Hidden Secrets

Though literally paved over and concealed for decades, the dark history of the early 1900s Prohibition-era crimes rears its head again in alluring underground tours. Amble past dusty subterranean storefronts and uncover Seattle's vibrant past on Bill Speidel's Underground Tour *(p156)*, or weave through back alleys full of illicit stores (opium dens and bordellos, to name a few) on Vancouver's Forbidden Tour *(www.forbiddenvancouver.ca)*.

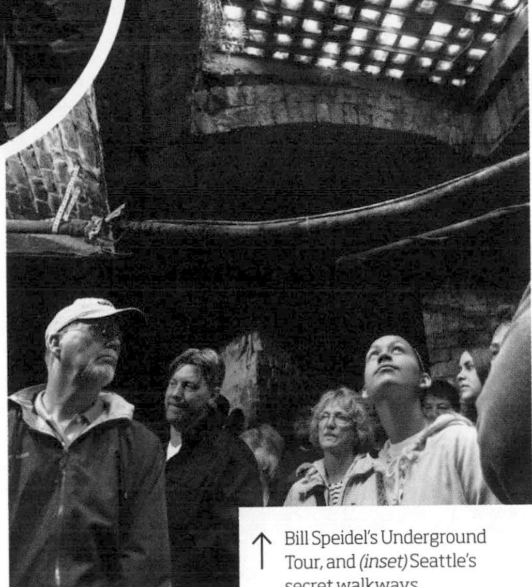

Bill Speidel's Underground Tour, and *(inset)* Seattle's secret walkways

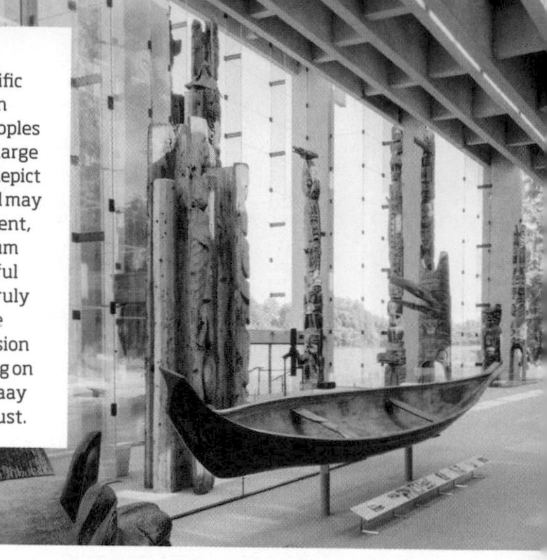

Traditional Totems

Totem poles, utterly unique to the Pacific Northwest, are among the best-known artifacts created by the Indigenous Peoples of this region. Intricately carved from large cedar trees, the brightly painted poles depict sacred animals and human figures and may recount a legend, commemorate an event, or record ancestry. Vancouver's Museum of Anthropology *(p258)* holds wonderful examples of Haida totems, but to get truly immersed, watch artists at work at the carving studio of the Capilano Suspension Bridge Park *(p260)*. For totems standing on their original sites, a visit to SGang Gwaay (Ninstints) *(p281)* in Haida Gwaii is a must.

→

Totem poles with stylized carvings at the Museum of Anthropology, Vancouver

THE PACIFIC NORTHWEST FOR INDIGENOUS CULTURE

Despite the toll that European colonization took on Indigenous communities in the 18th century, Indigenous Peoples have given the Pacific Northwest a rich cultural heritage. Immerse yourself in impressive art, ancient sites, and powwow celebrations to get a feel for this enduring legacy.

Ceremonial Splendor

Powwows are energetic celebrations of Indigenous culture, with spectacular displays of ceremonial regalia, drumming, dancing, singing, storytelling, and traditional crafts. Widely held throughout the Pacific Northwest and attended by Indigenous Peoples across North America, they are a great, fun way to celebrate local culture. Don't miss one of the biggest, the Kamloopa Powwow, held each summer in the Kamloops *(p292)* in BC.

Elaborately costumed dancers at the Kamloopa Powwow in BC

Indigenous Immersion

Many Indigenous Peoples have established illuminating cultural tours that invite visitors to immerse themselves in traditions. The informative Tillicum Village tour *(p204)*, located in Blake Island State Park, is one of the most welcoming experiences. Hear historical stories, visit wood-carvers, and feast on fire-roasted salmon and venison stew before enjoying a performance of traditional song and dance. In Haida Gwaii *(p280)*, amble through lush rainforests, home to longhouses that once belonged to ancient Indigenous villages.

← Serving up tempting dishes on the Tillicum Village tour

TOP 3 **NOTEWORTHY INDIGENOUS CHIEFS**

Chief Seattle (1786-1866)
The city's namesake and an ecologist who urged peaceful coexistence with settlers.

Chief Joseph (1840-1904)
A warrior from Oregon's Wallowa Valley, known for his bravery to protect his Nez Perce peoples from invaders.

Chief Joe Capilano (1850-1910)
Born on what is now Vancouver's North Shore, this Squamish leader petitioned for rights for his people.

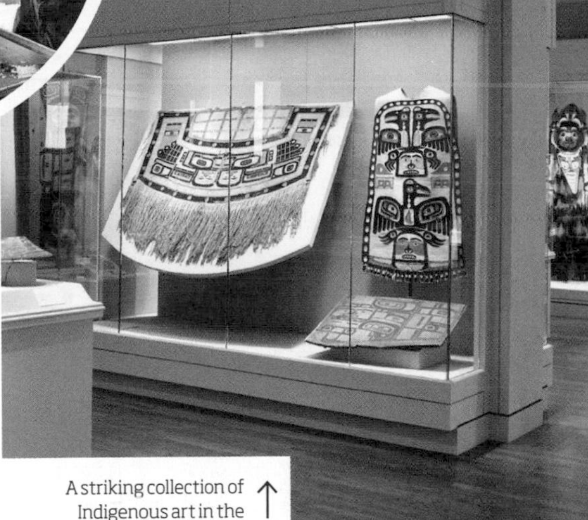

A striking collection of Indigenous art in the Portland Art Museum ↑

SHOP

Eighth Generation
This excellent Indigenous-owned gift shop, located in Seattle's Pike Place Market, sells beautiful wool blankets, colorful jewelry, and limited-edition prints, all created locally by Indigenous artists.

B3 93 Pike St eighthgeneration.com

Contemporary Art

While rooted in tradition, contemporary Indigenous art is bold, exciting, and often political. Look for the vibrant multimedia works of Wendy Red Star at the Portland Art Museum *(p87)*, and the powerful sculptures of Haida artist Bill Reid, a collection of which can be seen at the Museum of Anthropology *(p258)*. Reid's *The Raven and the First Men* is one to check off the bucket list.

In Search of the Spirit Bear

The remote parts of BC provide the only dwelling for the Kermode bear, better known as the spirit bear. This rare subspecies of the black bear (with a recessive gene that gives them near-white fur) is even believed to have supernatural powers, making them the official provincial mammal of BC and protected by law. Spend a night at the Spirit Bear Lodge *(www.spiritbear.com)*, located in the Great Bear Rainforest on BC's north and central coast, for a chance to spot these unique omnivorous creatures in their natural habitat.

THE PACIFIC NORTHWEST FOR WILDLIFE ENCOUNTERS

Lush river valleys, harsh desert landscapes, and dense old-growth forests provide rich habitats for a great diversity of wildlife in the Pacific Northwest. Grab a pair of binoculars and keep a watchful eye out for ocean dwellers and creatures of the Rockies – it will prove to be a rewarding part of any visit.

Eye an Elk

The subalpine forests of the Rockies and eastern Oregon mountains make the perfect home for the regal-looking Elk, part of the deer family. For your best chance to spot these dominating species, head to the Oak Creek Wildlife Area in Washington or the Dean Creek Elk Viewing Area in Oregon in the winter. If you're visiting during mating season in the fall, you'll want to keep a safe distance, as both male and female elk can exhibit aggressive behavior.

Elk roaming the snow-dusted landscape at the Oak Creek Wildlife Area

INSIDER TIP
Keep a Distance

Wildlife needs to remain wild, so feeding wild animals is illegal, as well as dangerous. Whether driving or trekking through wild-life corridors, always exercise caution and be prepared. Carry bear spray and do not get too close to wildlife.

←

The imposing spirit bear hunting for fish in BC's Inside Passage

Whale-Watching

The thrill of seeing an orca gushing out of the water or a humpback plying the waves is incredible. Migrating whales regularly pass Vancouver Island, the Olympic Peninsula, and the Oregon coast from December to January and March to June. The San Juan Islands, Tofino, and Newport are some of the best areas to view these animals. Hop on a tour boat stationed at a local marina or take a kayak tour to ensure your trip minimizes disturbing these mammals.

→

An orca whale performing for canoeists in the waters of Washington

Bald Eagle Viewing

No trip to the region is complete without spotting a bald eagle: the national bird of the US, now mainly found in the Pacific Northwest's coastal areas or near large inland lakes. Head to Sauvie Island *(p98)* to see this beautiful predator year-round, or take part in the annual Bald Eagle Count *(p54)* in Brackendale in January, where you'll be witness to the largest number of wintering bald eagles in North America.

←

The majestic bald eagle, a symbol of strength and independence

Food Cart Culture

In the Pacific Northwest, delightful fast bites from a street vendor are the way to do lunch. Portland's food-cart scene is particularly legendary, so join the locals and dig in at one of the city's 600 tiny kitchens. Try Wild North *(930 SE Oak St)* for stellar wood-fired dishes, or head to Fifth Avenue "pods" for Indian and Thai offerings.

A food cart serving authentic local delicacies in Portland

THE PACIFIC NORTHWEST FOR FOODIES

Blessed with fertile valleys and an impressive coastline, it's little wonder the Pacific Northwest is renowned for its fresh, local flavors and down-to-earth food. Farmers' markets proudly showcase these bountiful riches, while talented chefs shape ingenious creations, leaving diners in foodie paradise.

Markets Galore

Stalls overflowing with artisanal goods, freshly harvested greens, and hand-picked orchard bounties are a year-round sight in the region's farmers' markets, offering a wonderful opportunity to savor local flavors. Whether it's the large covered markets of Pike Place *(p166)* or Granville Island *(p252)*, or open-air gems such as the Portland Saturday Market *(p74)*, shopping at a market is a quintessential part of a local weekend here. The larger markets often have amazing tasting tours available, too, ensuring you don't miss a thing.

International Influence

The Pacific Northwest is indebted to its multicultural citizens for the plethora of world cuisines on offer here. Eateries serving everything from Russian comfort food to Hawaiian delights are thriving and have given rise to a fusion cuisine unique to the West Coast. For close-to-authentic dim sum, hit up Seattle's International District *(p157)*. Vancouver may have two Chinatowns, but *bibimbap*, a Korean rice dish, is the star cuisine here. More of a Mexican fan? Portland is chockful of affordable restaurants serving homestyle dishes.

→ Picking up delectable Russian pastries in a market in Seattle

Fruit of the Sea

As a coastal region, it's no surprise that sockeye salmon fillets, Dungeness crab cakes, and freshly shucked oysters feature heavily on menus here. Seattle is famed for its seafood, and Taylor Shellfish Oyster Bar *(p159)* has the best offerings – and even a shellfish happy hour. If you're in Tofino, Tacofino *(p287)* serves up fresh catches of the day in tasty tacos.

← A fresh shellfish platter at Taylor Shellfish Oyster Bar in Seattle

What's Cooking?

Unlock the secrets of the region's classic, seasonal foods and enrich your recipe repertoire with a culinary workshop. Grab a bucket and head to Lincoln City *(p128)* for free crabbing and clamming lessons from late spring to early fall, or excel at searing maple-glazed scallops at The Dirty Apron *(www.dirtyapron.com)* in Vancouver.

→ Learning the tricks of the pasta trade at The Dirty Apron in Vancouver

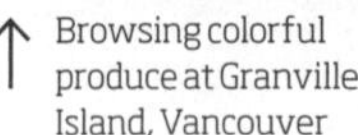

↑ Browsing colorful produce at Granville Island, Vancouver

Paddle Time

Vast coastlines, monumental rivers, and picture-perfect alpine lakes invite endless opportunities for exploration. Spectacular kayaking trips await at Desolation Sound, BC, where orcas breach the waters as you glide amid the forest-cloaked fjords. For something a bit different, hop on a stand-up paddleboard on Lake Chelan *(p207)*, which offers lessons and rentals.

Kayaks lined up on the pretty West Curme Island in Desolation Sound

THE PACIFIC NORTHWEST FOR OUTDOOR ADVENTURES

Lovers of the great outdoors will find the Pacific Northwest's vast landscape of untamed coastline, placid lakes, and tempting mountain peaks an indisputable natural playground. With surfing, mountain biking, caving, and kayaking on offer, thrill-seekers and adventurers are spoiled for choice.

TOP 3 HIKING TRAILS IN THE REGION

Rialto Beach, Olympic National Park, WA
A two-hour beach trail with views of sea stacks and tidal pools.

Misery Ridge Trail, Smith Rock State Park, OR
A demanding 4-mile (6.5 km) loop trail touring an arid canyon floor.

Lyle Lakes, West Kootenays, BC
Ascend three hours through grizzly country toward three mineral-blue subalpine lakes.

On Your Bike

In summer, sleds are swapped for sturdy bikes as ski slopes turn into splendid mountain biking trails throughout the region. Hit the dirt tracks of the West Kootenays *(p276)* in BC, where endless routes crisscross the forested peaks, or enjoy breathtaking views of the Columbia River Gorge *(p120)* on rolling, freeride trails near the serene river in Oregon.

Jumping off a rock on a challenging trail by the Columbia River Gorge

Delve into Caves

Whether you're a serious caver or simply interested in venturing into lava tubes, there are thousands of caving opportunities in the region. Descend into a subterranean labyrinth of crystals at Horne Lake Caves *(www.hornelake.com)* in BC, or opt for a candle-lit tour at the Oregon Caves National Monument *(p131)*.

INSIDER TIP

Up High

Embrace your inner Tarzan and zip along steel cables suspended high among the tree-tops and rivers in Whistler *(p282)*. Check out ZipTrek Ecotours *(www.ziptrek.com)*.

↑ Entering the moss-covered Horne Lake Caves in BC

In the Mountains

Ascending the region's great ridges isn't limited to experienced climbers. The clamber up Oregon's highest peak, Mount Hood *(p122)*, is made easier with Timberline Mountain Guides *(www.timberlinemtguides.com)*, who provide all the gear (and encouragement). Prefer to go solo? Tackle the tricky Mount Loki in the Purcell Mountains *(p296)* in the summer. You won't need equipment, but you will need a comfortable fitness level.

← Beginning the icy climb up to the monumental Mount Hood in Oregon

Hit the Waves

You'll want to don a wetsuit to withstand the cool waters of the Pacific, but prime surfing conditions are a welcome reward. Rent a board, suit up, and ride the big blue waves off the wild coast of Tofino *(p286)*, between the sea stacks of Cannon Beach *(p125)*, and among the playful harbor seals of the idyllic Whidbey Island *(p202)*.

→ Approaching an incoming wave in the waters of a beach in Tofino, BC

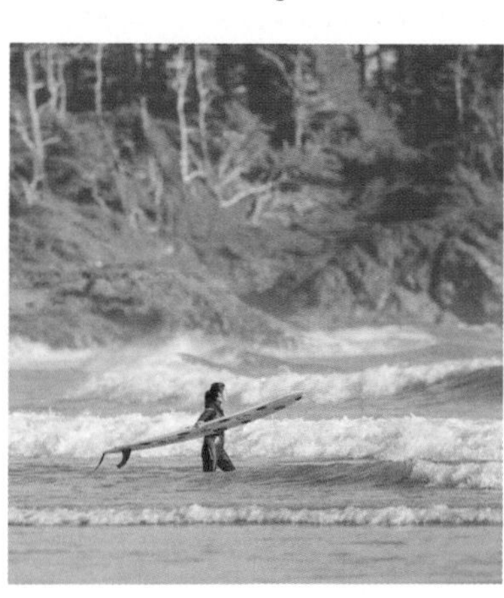

Dry Desert

East of the mountain and coastal regions, the terrain tends to be more barren, with little precipitation. Get a feel of this vastly different landscape by following the scent of sagebrush and wildflowers through the remote wilderness of Hells Canyon *(p140)*, the deepest river gorge in North America. If you'd rather avoid thirsty work, learn more about these unique environments at the High Desert Museum *(p114)* in Bend.

→ Trekking through the wild terrain of Hells Canyon in Oregon

THE PACIFIC NORTHWEST FOR NATURAL BEAUTY

From glacier-clad volcanic peaks bubbling with natural hot springs to ancient coastal rainforests, the Pacific Northwest is imbued with an abundance of dramatically varied landscapes. The call of the wild is strong here, so get out there and experience it for yourself.

LIMIT YOUR IMPACT

As Chief Seattle once said, "Take nothing but memories, leave nothing but footprints". The pristine wilderness in the Pacific Northwest relies on its custodians to keep it in that state, so take all trash with you, leave wildflowers for all to enjoy, and stay on designated trails to lessen disturbances to natural areas. Many companies, such as Evergreen Escapes *(www.evergreenescapes.com)*, organize ecotours, allowing you to enjoy the beauty of the land while respecting local communities and the environment.

Deep in the Forest

Lush, misty, and primeval, the Pacific Northwest's rainforests are the ultimate way to disconnect from modern life. In parts of Haida Gwaii *(p280)* and the Pacific Rim National Park Reserve *(p290)*, you can get your fill of thousand-year-old cedar trees. For an accessible adventure (both buggy and wheelchair friendly), try the Hemlock Grove Boardwalk trail in Glacier National Park *(p295)*, where Western Red Cedar dominates the thick canopy.

Embarking on a walking trail through the Pacific Rim National Park ↑

Wonderful Waters

From exploding lava-filled mountaintops to retreating glaciers, eons of geological activity have sculpted an incredible landscape of water features in the Pacific Northwest. The mesmerizing blue waters of Crater Lake *(p116)* reach depths further than any other lake in the US, while the glistening Emerald Lake in Yoho National Park *(p284)* is a photographer's delight. The show-stopper at Yoho National Park, however, is the thundering Takakkaw Falls. A total drop of 1,260 ft (384 m) makes these falls some of the highest on the continent – see them at their best in early summer.

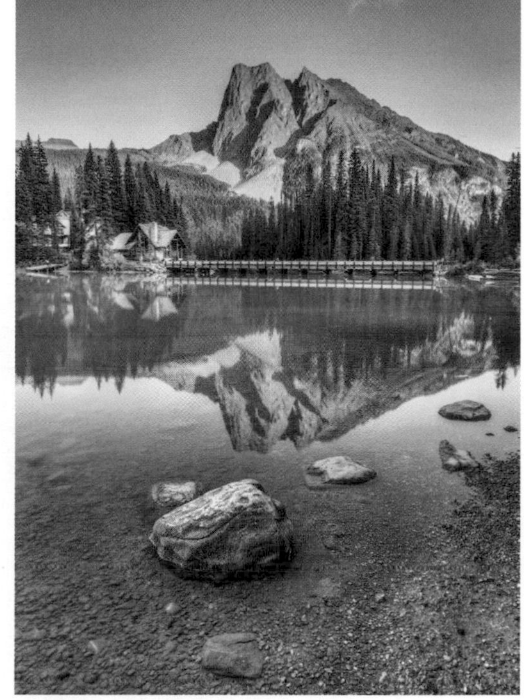

→ Mountains reflected in Emerald Lake, Yoho National Park

Ring of Fire

Though dangerous when spewing lava, volcanoes have been central to the landscape here since they began erupting 55 million years ago. Explore the lunar landscape and bat-filled lava tubes at the Newberry National Volcanic Monument *(p133)*, or enjoy the volcanic vista of Mount St. Helens *(p210)*, which has thankfully recovered from its 1980 eruption.

← Marveling at the mighty Mount St. Helens in Washington

Geothermal Pools

Nothing brings you closer to nature quite like therapeutic bathing in hand-made stone pools. There are plenty of developed, mineral-fed hot springs around the region, but Halcyon Hot Springs *(p276)* in BC and Cougar Hot Springs in Oregon are the best spots to relax while admiring the surrounding forest.

→ Relaxing in lush hot springs in the middle of a forest in Oregon

City Thrills

Keeping kids entertained in the city is easy thanks to an array of awesome activities. Let the little ones loose at fun-filled Stanley Park *(p238)* in Vancouver, where they can explore the aquarium, take a miniature train ride, and splash about in its outdoor pool. Traveling with water babies in Oregon? The Wings & Waves Waterpark in McMinnville *(p127)* will thrill adrenaline junkies of all ages. If the little ones are tired out in Washington, a ride on the vintage carousel at Spokane's Riverfront Park *(p206)* is the perfect lazy afternoon activity.

→ Embarking on a water-slide thrill at the pool in Stanley Park

THE PACIFIC NORTHWEST FOR FAMILIES

The Pacific Northwest has it sorted when it comes to families. For inclement weather days, museums hold a treasure trove of discoveries to keep boredom at bay, while the region's spectacular landscape is a never-ending playground, offering adventures from fossil hunting to little hikes.

TOP 3 KID-FRIENDLY HIKES

Cooper Mountain Loop, Cooper Mountain Nature Park, Beaverton, OR
Prairie and wetlands meet oak forests home to plenty of birds on this easy trail.

Gibson Lake Loop, Kokanee Glacier Provincial Park, BC
Crowned by sky-high ridges, this short loop is flat and scenic.

Wolf Tree Natural Trail, Discovery Park, Seattle, WA
With gorgeous views of Puget Sound, this toddler-friendly trail can easily be extended.

Rainy Days

While drizzly days are to be expected, there's plenty to keep the kids enthralled indoors. Museums abound, so head to Seattle's Burke Museum of Natural History and Culture *(p188)* to see dinosaur bones, or check out interactive exhibits at Vancouver's Science World *(p242)*. Alternatively, treat the whole family to a movie: Portland's retro movie theaters often have special matinees for families, and the Academy Theater *(www.academytheaterpdx.com)* even offers babysitting services.

Follow the Fossils

Little archaeologists are in for a treat in the Pacific Northwest. Take them to the Stonerose Interpretive Center & Eocene Fossil Site *(www.stonerosefossil.org)* in Washington, where they can dig for their very own fossil specimens and take them home as souvenirs. Not up for getting your hands dirty? Admire the John Day Fossil Beds National Monument *(p135)* in Oregon, riddled with 40-million-year-old fossils. The Painted Hills landscape here will wow the whole family with its vivid red, pink, and tan hues.

← Painted Hills at the John Day Fossil Beds National Monument

EAT

The Dane

This sleek, modern Scandinavian cafe has excellent coffee for the adults as well as a kid's nook and story time to entertain the little ones on Tuesdays and Thursdays.

B3 8000 15th Av NW, Seattle, WA
thedaneseattle.com

$$

Rocky Mountain Flatbread Co.

A long-standing family favorite where kids can make their own delicious and healthy pizzas.

F5 1876 W 1st Av, Vancouver, BC
rockymountainflatbread.ca

$$

Overlooking Lake Okanagan and its lush surrounds in the summer ↑

↑ Observing specimens in the Burke Museum

Into the Wild

Out in the country, outdoor space is practically limitless, impromptu picnics are set up in a pinch, and there's little chance of getting stuck in traffic with tired little ones. In summer, Lake Chelan *(p207)* and Lake Okanagan *(p288)* are pleasant enough for a swim. If you'd rather stay on dry land, the verdant valleys in the region also make for great u-pick farms. The Bella Organic Farm *(p99)* on Portland's Sauvie Island offers picking options year-round, from berries in summer to pumpkins in fall.

Hit the Slopes

Sublime white-powder slopes, thrilling runs, and breathtaking scenery make for some of the world's best snowboarding and downhill and cross-country skiing conditions. Calling snow enthusiasts from all over the globe each season, the lofty Mount Hood *(p122)* offers six ski and snowboard areas, from absolute beginner bunny hills to terrifyingly steep double black diamond runs. Whistler Blackcomb *(p283)*, North America's largest resort, also has year-round snow on its Horstman Glacier, as well as over 200 runs and a fantastic après-ski scene. Almost all of the region's resorts offer lessons and rentals, and discounts are often available for hitting the runs in the evening.

→

Making a graceful turn on the spotless powder at the Whistler Blackcomb ski resort

THE PACIFIC NORTHWEST FOR WINTER FUN

Guaranteed snow and dramatic terrain make the Pacific Northwest a haven for winter-sports lovers. Brave the chilly temperatures and dive into this stunning winter wonderland, whether that means racing down ski slopes, exploring the woods on snowshoes, or enjoying a thrilling snowmobile ride.

Don Your Snowshoes

As a resplendent, easier alternative to skiing, snowshoeing has become a winter favorite in the region. With an array of wilderness areas, parks, and ski resorts blanketed in snow, there's a walking trail to suit every need here. Join the curious ravens on the trails up at Grouse Mountain *(p261)* where snow-heavy tree tops curl into magical shapes, or head up to Crystal Mountain *(p209)* for a Snowshoe & Sip tour: after you've worked up a sweat, you'll be rewarded with a group dinner and a local beverage.

Working through a thick blanket of pristine snow in Oregon

TOP 3 FAMILY SKI RESORTS

Mount Bachelor, OR
mtbachelor.com
Snow tubing and snowshoe tours in addition to skiing are offered for kids.

White Pass, WA
skiwhitepass.com
Around 30 percent of the runs are dedicated to beginners.

Revelstoke Mountain Resort, BC
revelstokemountain resort.com
Drop the kids off for half- or full-day lessons and lunch while you take to the slopes.

Skate Away

Lace up a pair of skates and take a twirl on the ice. There are indoor and outdoor skating rinks, often with music, at parks and plazas across the region. Robson Square *(p241)* in Vancouver offers free ice skating from early December to late February, while the Lloyd Center *(p101)* in Portland lets you hit the rink all year.

→

Skating in Portland's Lloyd Center

At Full Speed

Nothing beats the thrill of whizzing through white powder on a high-speed snowmobile. Many resorts offer tours that provide the snowmobile and all the gear, as well as a cosy cabin to warm up in afterward. If you're looking for exhilirating backcountry scenery, opt for a tour of the vast Mount Hood area with Mt. Hood Outfitters *(www.mthoodoutfitters.com)*.

←

Snowmobiling down open terrain on Mount Hood in Oregon

Fantastic Festivals

The Pacific Northwest hosts an array of exceptional music festivals throughout the year. Once the warm weather arrives in July, you can relax to amazing blues performances at the Waterfront Blues Festival *(www.waterfrontbluesfest.com)* in Portland, or hear blues, world music, and pop mingle harmoniously at the Vancouver Folk Music Festival *(www.thefestival.bc.ca)*. September welcomes over 100 acts from every genre to the annual Bumbershoot at the Seattle Center.

→

Freshlyground performing at the Vancouver Folk Music Festival

THE PACIFIC NORTHWEST FOR MUSIC LOVERS

Home to a wealth of talent and a rich musical history, the Pacific Northwest caters for all tastes. Enjoy indie-rock bands reliving the grunge days in a lively dive bar, follow the footsteps of the region's most famed artists, and soak up soulful sounds in the great outdoors.

Classic Venues

Atmospheric, legendary, and historic venues oozing old-world charm are in abundance in the Pacific Northwest, and offer shows to suit every taste. Listen to Grammy award-winners at the Art Deco Commodore Ballroom *(www.commodoreballroom.com)* in Vancouver, or discover underground indie bands at Portland's McMenamins Crystal Ballroom *(p75)*, which has a "floating" dance floor.

←

The Washboard Union playing at Commodore Ballroom

Revived Record Shops

A rarity in today's digital world, vinyl record stores have managed to keep a stronghold in the Pacific Northwest. Portland is well known to LP collectors, where Crossroads Records *(www.xro.com)* and Music Millennium *(www.musicmillennium.com)* are two of over a dozen shops filled with boxes of turntable music, both old and new. Independent record label Sub Pop, which signed Nirvana's debut single in the 1980s, still sells records from this iconic band and many more at its Seattle Mega Mart store *(www.megamart.subpop.com)*.

←

Rows of old and new jazz records at Georgetown Records in Seattle

THE LEGEND

Born in Seattle, Jimi Hendrix (1942–70) had a phenomenal career as a singer, rock guitarist, and songwriter. As a young boy, Hendrix spent time at his grandmother's home in Vancouver. He began playing guitar at the age of 15, released many classics, and headlined the iconic Woodstock Festival in 1969. Seattle has a statue of the influential star at the intersection of E Pine St and Broadway, while the city of Vancouver hopes to erect a new shrine after closing the one at Union and Main Streets for redevelopment.

Smells like Grunge Spirit

The soul of the Seattle Sound – the grunge music scene that emerged during the 1980s – is still felt strongly in the region. Pivotal to the scene was the iconic rock band Nirvana, and it's easy to retrace their steps. See Kurt Cobain's guitar at the MoPOP *(p176)*, take in a live show at The Crocodile *(www.thecrocodile.com)* – where Nirvana have played – then bed down at The Edgewater Hotel *(www.edgewaterhotel.com)*, where the band spent many restless nights.

→

Gerhard Trimpin's *Roots and Branches* at MoPOP

Did You Know?

The Edgewater Hotel in Seattle offers a Beatles and a Pearl Jam suite, decked out in memorabilia.

Get in the Spirit

A highly creative, new generation of craft distilleries is causing a stir in the region, using locally grown ingredients to produce small-batch spirits. If you're in Vancouver, pop into Odd Society *(www.oddsocietyspirits.com)* to taste their smooth single malt vodka, or shock your taste buds with the cinnamon Vulcan's Fire liqueur at Monashee Spirits *(www.monasheespirits.com)* in Revelstoke. Portland even has an entire area devoted to spirits aptly called Distillery Row *(www.distilleryrowpdx.com)*, where you can sample more than 80 unique spirits between 12 distilleries.

INSIDER TIP
Distillery Discounts

Pick up the Distillery Row Passport *(www.proofpdx.com)* for tastings and discounts, as well as events and classes, at the unique producers on Distillery Row in Portland.

THE PACIFIC NORTHWEST
RAISE A GLASS

Lofty alpine hikes are thirsty work, but with famed wines, organic ales, and rich coffees on offer, the Pacific Northwest promises to rejuvenate you. Drive through blossom-scented valleys with ribbons of vineyards, refresh your soul with a great espresso, and indulge freely in this region's libations.

Coffee Culture

How do you prefer your caffeine elixir: pour-over, classic drip, French press? While the bean can't be grown here, roasting and extracting coffee is a serious business practiced to perfection. Seattle was the first home to the famous Starbucks® chain *(p169)*, so it's no surprise its residents apparently consume more coffee than in any other US city. Stumptown *(p102)* coffee is one of the best in Oregon, and for BC, try No6 Coffee (*www.no6coffee.co*).

→ Rich coffee varieties at No6 Coffee, roasted in Nelson, BC

The stylish, smart interior of Odd Society in Vancouver

STAY

Black Walnut Inn & Vineyard
Bed-and-breakfast with views of the vines.

A4 9600 NE Worden Hill Rd, Dundee, OR blackwalnut vineyard.com

$$$

The Inn at Abeja
Farmstead suites on a winery estate.

D4 2014 Mill Creek Rd, Walla Walla, WA abeja.net

$$$

Unwind with a Local Wine

This may be a densely forested region, but plenty of valleys are tucked in between, with balmy temperatures and fertile soils - the perfect environment to grow wonderful grape varieties. Picturesque and verdant, Oregon's Willamette Valley *(p136)*, Washington's Walla Walla Valley *(p211)*, and BC's Okanagan Valley *(p288)* produce some of the world's top wines, from delectable Cabernet to aromatic Pinot Noir.

Ideal soil conditions at the lush, wine-producing Walla Walla Valley

Craft Creations

Hops and barley grow well in the cool and temperate climate of the region, where some of the purest water on earth flows. This combination, plus the innovative nature of its residents, has led the way for outstanding beer breweries. Refreshing blonde ales, bourbon barrel-aged stouts, and seasonal varieties such as pumpkin ale are a sample of what's available. Check out Deschutes Brewery *(p115)* in Bend and the eco-friendly Hopworks *(p102)* in Portland - one of the city's 75 plus breweries - to savor the best.

Getting crafty with the brewing process at Deschutes Brewery

Into the Night

There's a bar or club for every taste in the Pacific Northwest's big cities, which come alive after dark. Seattle has the most diverse nightlife, with legendary jazz clubs and grunge-era taverns in the Belltown district, as well as wine bars and breweries by the waterfront. If you're looking for more sophisticated drinking dens, Portland has you covered, with fine spirits served at the cosy Multnomah Whiskey Library *(p88)* and swanky cocktails with a view at Departure *(p88)*. Looking to dance the night away? Vancouver's West End has a host of iconic, fun LGBT+ bars and clubs *(p254)* to check off the list.

Seattle's buzzing Belltown district in the evening

THE PACIFIC NORTHWEST'S COOL CITIES

Defining the region are three of the continent's most sophisticated cities: Portland, Seattle, and Vancouver. Shoppers will love Portland's unique boutiques, aficionados of craft libations should head to Seattle's chic bars, and Vancouver is a delight for those seeking outstanding local art.

Go Green

From innovative architecture to supporting home-grown businesses, the region's major cities have proved their commitment to sustainability. Portland may be one of the greenest cities in the US, but Vancouver and Seattle are also home to a network of bike lanes and a locavore culture. Wherever you are, check out bike-sharing systems for the easiest way to ensure a green stay. Enjoy the ride!

Did You Know?

Greenpeace, the global environmental organization, was founded in Vancouver in 1971.

↑ Cycling through Vancouver on a Mobi bike, one of the city's rental companies

Shop Til You Drop

Top brands, local designers, and funky boutiques will spoil shoppers in the big cities. One of the pleasures of shopping in Portland is the fact that no state sales tax is levied, allowing you to indulge in its eclectic mix of chic and trendy shops. Among these is the world's largest independent bookstore, Powell's City of Books *(p75)*, which you could spend an entire day perusing. Seattle offers the best of everything: dedicate the morning to browsing the iconic Pike Place Market *(p166)* for vintage treasures before window-shopping your way around 5th Avenue's ritzy boutiques. To take home one-of-a-kind Indigenous crafts, head to Vancouver's gallery shops.

← Scanning the richly stocked shelves in Powell's City of Books

SEATTLE PRIDE MARCH

What began as a huge protest in 1970 to commemorate the first anniversary of the Stonewall Riots in New York (which sparked the gay rights movement) has become a day of celebration, music, and pageantry in Seattle. Held in Capitol Hill *(p189)* until 2006, the PrideFest rally now takes place in Seattle Center over Pride Weekend in late June, and sees sponsors, performers, and over 100 vendors take part. Although Capitol Hill can no longer accommodate the large numbers that come to participate, it remains an important and welcoming neighborhood for Seattle's LGBT+ community.

Catch Some Culture

It wouldn't be a city break without soaking up local culture in world-class spaces. Portland's ever evolving art scene brims with inventive and visionary works, and one of the best ways to immerse yourself is on the first Thursday of each month, when galleries around the Downtown area stay open late and debut new, exciting exhibitions. There's also complimentary wine and appetizers to take advantage of. Over in Washington, the Seattle Art Museum *(p154)* is renowned for its brilliant historical and contemporary collection, and also honors first Thursdays with free admission. Meanwhile, get your fix of Canadian art and the work of one of the country's best-loved artists, Emily Carr, at the well-curated Vancouver Art Gallery *(p241)*.

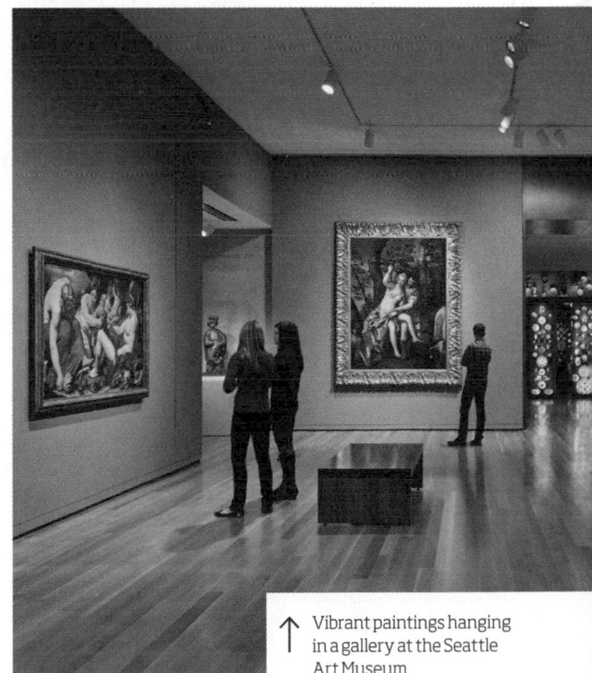

↑ Vibrant paintings hanging in a gallery at the Seattle Art Museum

A YEAR IN THE PACIFIC NORTHWEST

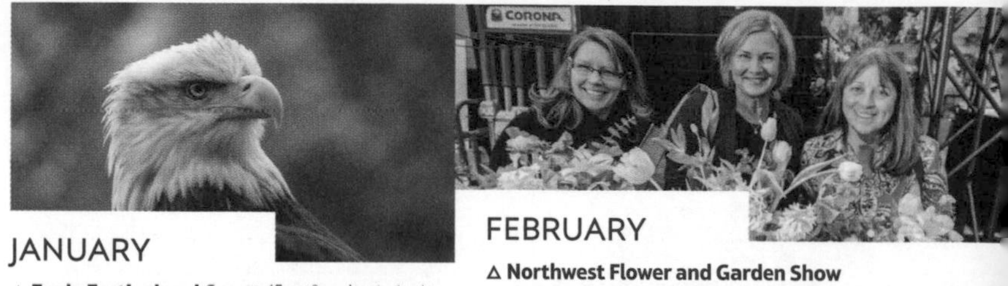

JANUARY

△ **Eagle Festival and Count** *(first Sunday in Jan).* Annual celebration in Brackendale, BC, to count the number of bald eagles settling for the winter.

Chinese New Year *(late Jan/early Feb).* Portland, Seattle, and Vancouver all have thriving Chinese communities who celebrate New Year in style.

FEBRUARY

△ **Northwest Flower and Garden Show** *(early Feb).* This five-day show in Seattle is the second-largest garden festival in the US.

Newport Seafood and Wine Festival *(mid–late Feb).* Featuring over 150 wines to taste and pair with Oregon's wonderful seafood, this four-day event draws foodies from all over the state and beyond.

MAY

△ **Cinco de Mayo Fiesta** *(early May).* Three days of Mexican food, art, music, and dance on the Portland waterfront.

Northwest Folklife Festival *(Memorial Day weekend).* Since 1972, Seattle has hosted one of the largest free events in the US, with music, dance, exhibits, and workshops.

JUNE

Fremont Fair *(late Jun).* Seattle's biggest summer market brings together live music, art, and over 400 vendors selling crafts, and food and drink over the course of one busy weekend.

△ **Bard on the Beach Shakespeare Festival** *(Jun–Sep).* This annual celebration of Shakespeare's work takes place overlooking the waterfront in Vanier Park, Vancouver, BC.

SEPTEMBER

△ **Washington State Fair** *(early Sep).* A 17-day state fair in Puyallup with rides, exhibits, a rodeo, and live music.

Oktoberfest *(mid-Sep).* Enjoy Bavarian food, and of course plenty of beer, at this fun event held over four days in Mount Angel, Oregon.

Autumn Leaf Festival *(last weekend).* One of Washington's oldest festivals celebrating the arrival of fall in Leavenworth.

OCTOBER

△ **Okanagan Wine Festival** *(early Oct).* Enjoy vineyard tours and wine tastings, as well as gourmet food, at grape harvest time in BC's lush Okanagan Valley.

OysterFest *(early Oct).* A weekend of oyster shucking, wine tastings, and cooking contests takes place in Shelton, Washington.

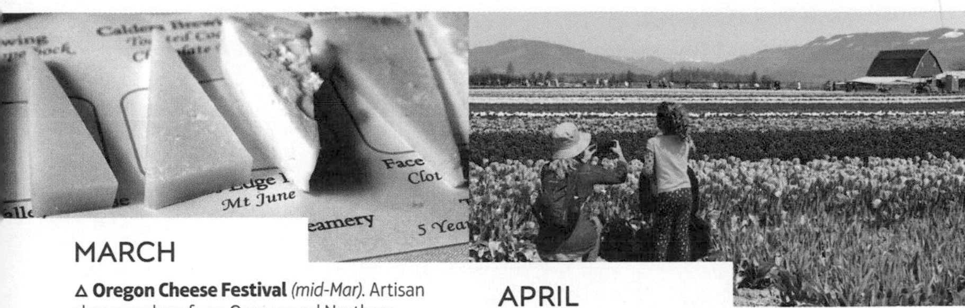

MARCH

△ **Oregon Cheese Festival** *(mid-Mar).* Artisan cheesemakers from Oregon and Northern California dairies show their wares, along with local wines, in Central Point.

Portland International Film Festival *(early–mid-Mar).* The biggest film event in Oregon lasts two weeks and includes film viewings, workshops, talks, and visiting directors.

Taste Washington *(late Mar).* Four-day event at CenturyLink Field, Seattle, featuring over 230 wineries and 60 restaurants from the area.

APRIL

△ **Skagit Valley Tulip Festival** *(Apr).* A month-long festival of crafts fairs, barbecues, and walking tours amid thousands of tulips in Washington.

Washington State Apple Blossom Festival *(late Apr–early May).* Parades, concerts, and a carnival all celebrate the arrival of spring in Wenatchee, Washington.

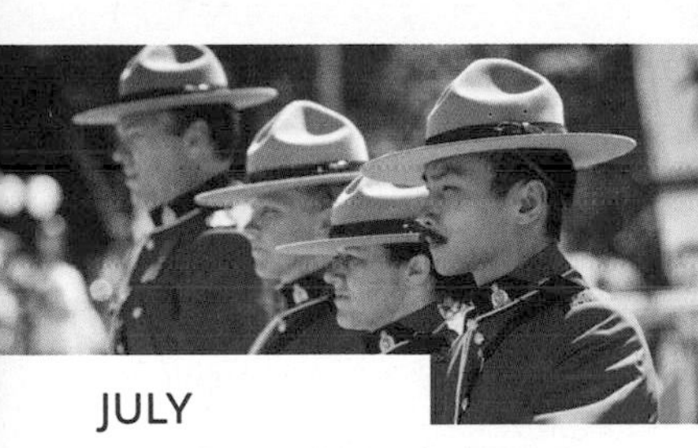

JULY

△ **Canada Day** *(Jul 1).* Parades, live music, and evening fireworks are held all across BC in celebration of the nation's birthday.

Independence Day *(Jul 4).* A spectacular fireworks display takes place over Gas Works Park in Seattle to celebrate US independence.

Oregon Brewers Festival *(late Jul).* Craft brewers bring their best beers to Governer Tom McCall Waterfront Park in Portland.

AUGUST

△ **Kaslo Jazz Etc Summer Music Festival** *(early Aug).* Kaslo Bay Park in BC hosts this long weekend of local and international acts, the "etc" encompassing blues, folk, world music, and more.

Pacific National Exhibition *(mid-Aug–early Sep).* Entertainment, rides, pavilions, and agricultural exhibits take place every summer in Vancouver.

Evergreen State Fair *(late Aug–early Sep).* Arts and crafts, rides, races, and rodeo events, all in Monroe in Washington.

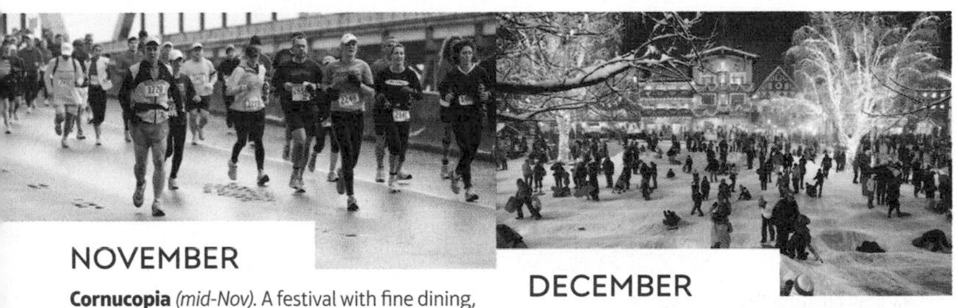

NOVEMBER

Cornucopia *(mid-Nov).* A festival with fine dining, wine tastings, and seminars in Whistler, BC.

△ **Seattle Marathon** *(Sun after Thanksgiving).* More than 10,000 participants run off their Thanksgiving excesses in this annual race which ends in the Memorial Stadium.

Vancouver Christmas Market *(late Nov–Christmas Eve).* Enjoy shopping, and festive food and drink at Jack Poole Plaza.

DECEMBER

△ **Christmas Lighting Festival** *(first three weekends).* Visitors to Leavenworth, Washington, can enjoy roasted chestnuts, bratwurst, strolling carolers, and twinkling lights against the snow-capped Cascade Mountains.

Portland's Christmas Ships Parade *(Dec).* Beautifully decorated illuminated boats sail down the Willamette and Columbia rivers.

A BRIEF HISTORY

Indigenous Peoples lived in harmony with the land for thousands of years before explorers started opening up the territory that straddles two nations. After settlers began to arrive in the early 19th century, the modern Pacific Northwest was born. Today the area thrives on agriculture and tourism.

Earliest Inhabitants

Nomadic hunter-gatherers are thought to have entered North America around 15,000 to 25,000 years ago, having crossed a land bridge across the Bering Strait from Russia. Indigenous cultures flourished in all corners of the land, with tribes having their own languages and customs, establishing complex trade routes, and building towns. Many lived in well-established settlements, fished the rivers for salmon, and, in long dugouts, set out to sea in search of whales. Tribes living in the harsher landscapes east of the mountains had fewer resources at hand and migrated across high-desert hunting grounds in search of game.

1 A map of the Pacific coast of North America from 1778. ↑

2 Petroglyph of a deer in eastern Oregon.

3 Early Indigenous groups fishing in a river.

4 Sir Francis Drake, who claimed land in the region for the British.

Timeline of events

23,000–13,000 BC
Nomadic hunters arrive in North America across a land bridge from Russia.

1492
Christopher Columbus arrives in America.

1543
Juan Rodriguez Cabrillo, a Spaniard, sails from Mexico to the coast of southern Oregon.

1579
British explorer Sir Francis Drake sails up the west coast of North America.

1592
Juan de Fuca sails to Vancouver Island and is the first to navigate the strait later named for him.

2

3

4

Arrival of Explorers

In the 16th century, Europeans began exploring the Pacific Northwest in search of the Northwest Passage, a sea route that would provide a passage between Europe and the Far East. Once the Spanish had gained a stronghold in the so-called New World, a succession of vessels arrived from Britain, America, France, Russia, and Portugal. Some of the most impactful expeditions came in the 1790s, when Captains George Vancouver and Peter Puget charted what are now Vancouver and Puget Sound in 1791, followed a year later by the discovery of the mighty Columbia River by Captain Robert Gray.

Community Upheaval

For the Indigenous Peoples of the Pacific Northwest, 15,000 years of a bountiful life and rich cultural tradition were abruptly upset when these European settlers began arriving. Diseases such as smallpox, measles, and influenza introduced by these newcomers all but obliterated many local groups, and those who survived were forced to surrender their lands and ways of life, and move to government-designated reservations.

THE ROLE OF WOMEN

Although tribal villages were governed by bodies of men, women did have a large say in decision-making processes. They also had the important responsibility of running each household, including the making of tools and the harvesting of medicinal plants to cure ailments.

1663

France proclaims Canada a French colony.

1765

Military commander Robert Rogers maps the territory of "Ouragon."

1763

Canada becomes a British Crown colony.

1778

Captain James Cook explores the Pacific coast.

1792

Captain Robert Gray is the first non-Indigenous person to navigate the Columbia River.

1

2

Lewis and Clark Expedition

In 1801, US president Thomas Jefferson called on his former secretary, Meriwether Lewis, and Lewis's friend, William Clark, to find an overland route to the Pacific Ocean from the eastern half of the continent. Along with an entourage of 32 men and one woman, Sacagawea, the pair set out from Missouri in May 1804. The group walked, rode horseback, and canoed to the Oregon coast, which they reached six months later. The famed expedition set the stage for the rapid settlement of the region.

1 Lewis and Clark. ↑

2 Explorer Sacagawea with Lewis and Clark.

3 Astoria in 1811.

4 The first 1886 transcontinental train of the Canadian Pacific Railway.

A Battle for the Spoils

Lewis and Clark opened up the region to US fur traders, and in 1811, the fur-trading post Astoria was established at the mouth of the Columbia River. However, the British-owned Hudson's Bay Company continued to rule the region until the mid-19th century. Territorial tensions between Britain and the US erupted in the War of 1812, and in 1846, the two divided up the Pacific Northwest using the 49th parallel as the new boundary. Land to the north (BC) was claimed by Britain, and to the south (Oregon) by the US; in 1852, lands north of the Columbia River formed the Washington

Did You Know?

It was quipped that the initials "HBC" for the Hudson's Bay Company stood for "Here Before Christ."

Timeline of events

1804–1805
Expedition of Meriwether Lewis and William Clark

1811
John Jacob Astor establishes Astoria, a trading post at the mouth of the Columbia River.

1846
The Washington and Oregon areas are claimed by the US, BC by Britain.

1848
Oregon Territory is established.

1852
Washington Territory is formed.

3

4

Territory. Indigenous groups suffered greatly as a consequence: already decimated by diseases introduced by settlers, they were forcibly removed from their lands, too.

Gold Rushes

Many of the new settlers who had staked land claims in Oregon began to head south in 1848, lured by the hope of making their fortune after gold was discovered in California. The Gold Rush moved north in 1851 when prospectors found gold in Oregon, and north again, to BC's Fraser River, in 1858. The Klondike, in Canada, was the stage for the next frenzy. Over 100,000 miners flooded into the Klondike gold fields, and Vancouver and Seattle prospered by housing the explorers and banking their finds.

Arrival of the Railroads

By the 1870s, transcontinental railroads arrived in the US and Canada, making the region accessible to more settlers. The railroad was especially beneficial to the tiny settlement of Alki-New York in Washington, which soon burgeoned into Seattle, and eventually outstripped Portland as the region's major port.

↑ A pair of miners in the Klondike, panning for gold in 1897

1867
Dominion of Canada is created under the British North America Act.

1871
BC joins the Dominion of Canada.

1886
Canadian transcontinental railroad completed; fire destroys a large part of Vancouver.

1889
Washington becomes the USA's 42nd state.

1897
The Klondike Gold Rush brings prosperity to Seattle and Vancouver.

1

2

3

Industry and Technology

By the early 20th century, the Pacific Northwest was celebrating its prosperity. The World Wars ushered in a wave of economic fortune, starting with the founding of the Boeing Airplane Company in Seattle in 1916, which created tens of thousands of jobs. As a center for military aircraft contracts, the region continued to prosper during World War II (1939–45), with factories producing aircraft, weapons, and warships for the Allies' war effort. In the late 20th century, high-tech businesses introduced an economic shift when Seattle-based Microsoft took off in the 1980s, followed by the launch of Amazon in 1995.

The Natural World

For all the fortunes that trade brought the major cities, the vast landscapes of the Pacific Northwest and the inhabitants that lived outside of the cities suffered greatly in the 20th century. The construction of dams along many rivers destroyed traditional fishing grounds and diminished salmon runs that Indigenous groups depended upon. Beyond the damage caused by industrial growth, the region has seen a succession

1 Boeing aircraft, 1960s. ↑

2 Bill Gates, co-founder of Microsoft, in 1985.

3 The eruption of Mount St. Helens in 1980.

4 Seattle's Amazon Spheres at Amazon HQ.

Did You Know?

Women were granted the right to vote in Washington ten years before the rest of the US, in 1910.

Timeline of events

1916

Boeing Airline Company is founded in Seattle.

1919

USA's first General Strike occurs when 60,000 workers mobilize in Seattle.

1962

Seattle's Century 21 Fair and the opening of the Space Needle.

1926

Seattle elects its first female mayor, Bertha Knight.

of natural disasters, forcing irreversible damage. Washington's Mount St. Helens erupted violently in 1980, and the accompanying earthquake triggered the largest avalanche in recorded history, killing 57 people as well as millions of wildlife species.

The Pacific Northwest Today

Keeping the landscape pristine continues to be both a source of pride and an ongoing bone of contention. Conservationists fight to curtail lumbering operations and limit growth, while loggers and ranchers often resist intervention. This conflict between the need to protect the environment and interests in capitalizing on the region's natural resources shows no sign of slowing. Despite this, Portland, Seattle, and Vancouver are among the fastest-growing cities in North America, and tend to be liberal in their politics. While other areas in the region are more conservative, Oregon has become especially progressive in recent years, being among the first in the US to have approved assisted suicide for the terminally ill, followed by Washington. Over in BC, Vancouver continues to flourish economically as the third largest center for the film industry in North America.

THE MINDS BEHIND MICROSOFT

Seattle is home to two of the world's wealthiest and most accomplished entrepreneurs. Bill Gates and Paul Allen met at a prestigious prep school and were both fascinated with technology. The pair co-founded Microsoft in 1975, which went on to become the leader of the computer software industry. Today, Microsoft employs over 144,000 people in 135 countries.

1980

Irreversible damage is caused by the eruption of Mount St. Helens, Washington.

1995

Entrepreneur Jeff Bezos launches Amazon.com from his Seattle home.

2000

The Nisga'a Treaty awards land in northern BC to the Nisga'a Nation.

2018

Canada becomes the first G7 country to legalize the use of recreational marijuana.

EXPERIENCE

Strolling in Vancouver's Downtown

PORTLAND

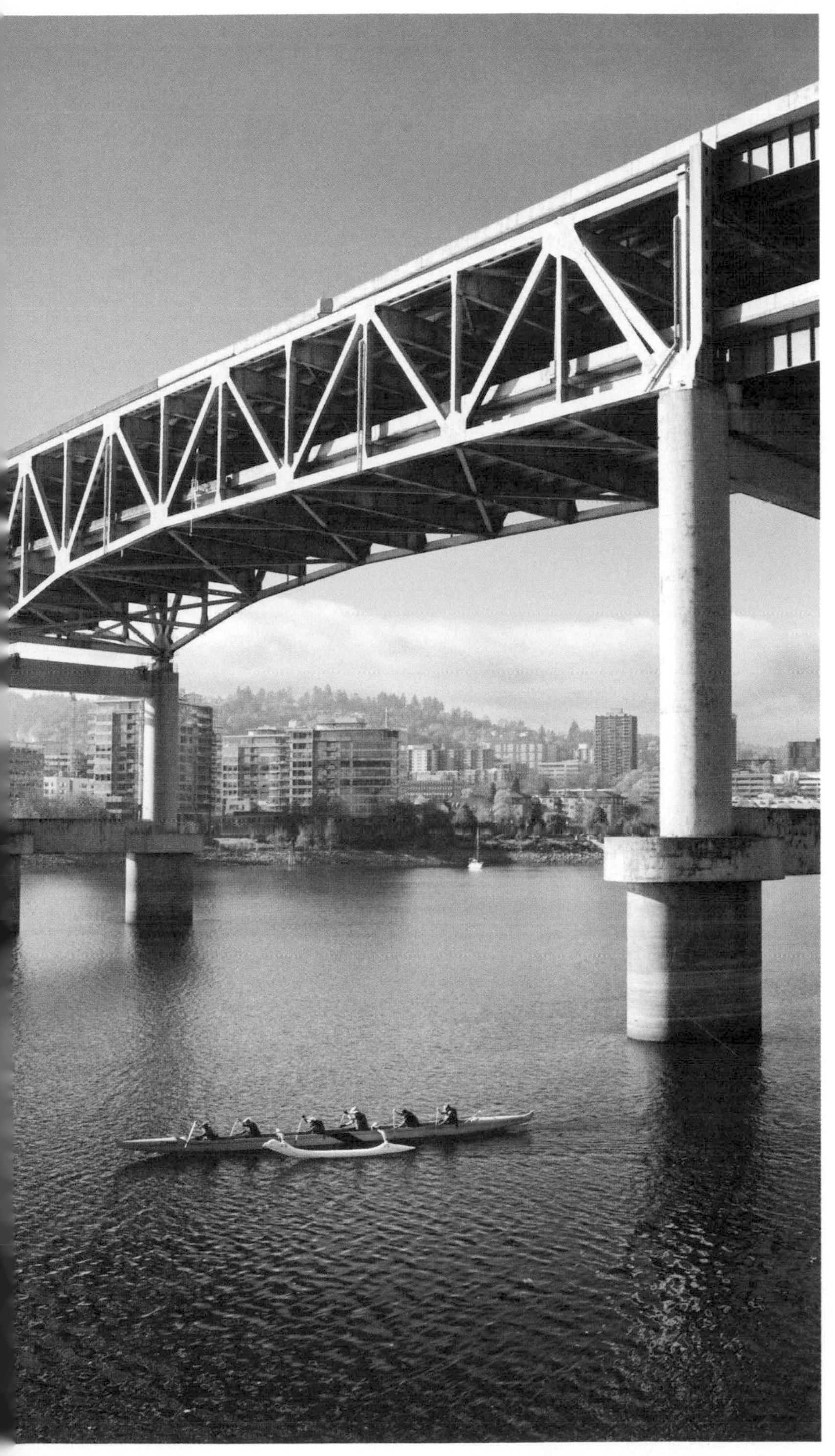

Kayaking on the Willamette River under Portland's Marquam Bridge

EXPLORE PORTLAND

This guide divides Portland into three sightseeing areas: the two on this map and one for sights beyond the city center. Find out more about each area on the following pages.

Freemont Bridge
Willamette River
NW NAITO PARKWAY
ELIOT
ROSE QUARTER
The Moda Center
PACIFIC HWY W
North Broadway Bridge
Union Station
NW NAITO PARKWAY
Oregon Convention Center
NW 12TH AV
NW 11TH AV
NW 10TH AV
NW 9TH AV
NW HOYT ST
North Steel Bridge
NW GLISAN ST
NW FLANDERS ST
Lan Su Chinese Garden
PACIFIC HWY
PEARL DISTRICT
NW EVERETT ST
OLD TOWN CHINATOWN AND THE PEARL DISTRICT
p70
NW DAVIS ST
CHINATOWN
NW COUCH ST
Powell's City of Book
W BURNSIDE ST
Burnside Bridge
NW ANKENY ST
OLD TOWN
SW OAK ST
Governor Tom McCall Waterfront Park
SW 11TH AV
SW HARVEY MILK ST
SW WASHINGTON ST
SW ALDER ST
SW 10TH AV
SW 9TH AV
SW PARK AV
SW MORRISONS ST
Pioneer Courthouse
Morrison Bridge
DOWNTOWN
p80
SW SALMON ST
SW 4TH AV
SW 3RD AV
SW 2ND AV
SW 1ST AV
PACIFIC HWY
SW MAIN ST
SW MADISON ST
Governor Tom McCall Waterfront Park
Willamette River
SW BROADWAY
SW JEFFERSON ST
SW COLUMBIA ST
SW CLAY ST
SW MARKET ST
Hawthorne Bridge
SW HARRISON ST
0 meters 400
0 yards 400
N

GETTING TO KNOW PORTLAND

Compact and easy to navigate, Portland is made up of numerous quadrants, all of which have their own distinctive character. The Willamette River divides the city into east and west, while the green spaces of the outlying neighborhoods offer a tranquil retreat from the ceaseless bustle.

PAGE 70

OLD TOWN CHINATOWN AND THE PEARL DISTRICT

Made up of the city's oldest neighborhood and a former industrial district, this area brings together cultural legacy and sophisticated urban living. Old Town Chinatown buzzes with dynamic eateries and colorful shops and markets, while the authentic Lan Su Chinese Garden offers peaceful respite from the bustling streets. In the Pearl District, renowned art galleries, chic boutiques, and cool coffee shops housed in former warehouses become social hubs in the day, while fine restaurants, endless breweries, and trendy clubs deliver a lively ambience after dark.

Best for
Historical architecture, eclectic eateries, and iconic landmarks

Home to
Portland Saturday Market, Powell's City of Books, Lan Su Chinese Garden

Experience
Kayaking on the Willamette River

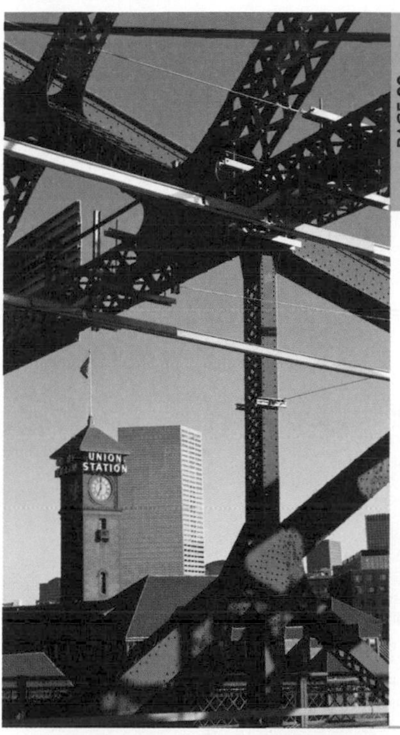

PAGE 80

DOWNTOWN

The downtown portion of the city is without question the bustling arts district, home to the oldest museum in the Pacific Northwest – the Portland Art Museum – and a thriving theater scene thanks to the Portland'5 Centers for the Arts and its Keller Auditorium. Culinary culture here is centered on the city's famed food trucks, and the delicious aromas of Korean tacos and Latin American dishes drifting out from tiny kitchens draw hungry crowds at lunchtime. At the center of downtown is Pioneer Courthouse Square, a welcoming expanse of brick paving where Portlanders gather, come rain or shine.

Best for

Museums, people-watching, and food trucks

Home to

Portland Art Museum, Governor Tom McCall Waterfront Park

Experience

Tucking into lunch from a food truck pod in Pioneer Courthouse Square

PAGE 92

BEYOND THE CENTER

Few places in Portland require much effort to get to, even those beyond the city center. Old and new come together in the attractions here: tuck into a warming coffee at an independent roaster in the neighborhoods around Reed, Hawthorne, and the Southeast Division, or head to the end of the historic Oregon Trail just south of Portland's city center. The west side opens into the city's favorite green retreat, Washington Park, where you can relax after browsing the high-end boutiques of Nob Hill.

Best for

Walking trails, eating out, tranquil gardens, and shopping

Home to

Washington Park, Sauvie Island

Experience

Window-shopping for vintage treasures along Southeast Division Street

ONE WAY
NW 11th Av
NO TURN ON RED

Cycling past Powell's City of Books in the stylish Pearl District

OLD TOWN CHINATOWN AND THE PEARL DISTRICT

Portland grew up along the west bank of the Willamette River when settlers began to arrive in the 1930s, traveling on The Oregon Trail. Following its establishment in 1843, and its naming after Portland, Maine, in 1845, it became a major port. Its location on the river gave it easy access to the Pacific Ocean for trading, and to the rich agricultural land upriver to provide the goods to trade. Docks in the riverfront quarter now known as Old Town Chinatown were often lined with schooners that sailed across the Pacific Ocean to China and around Cape Horn to the east coast of the US. Old Town Chinatown was the city's commercial center and home to many Asian immigrants who came to work at the port. It also attracted Gold Rush miners and sailors, and became one of the most dangerous ports in the world.

The city center moved inland in the late 19th century, when the arrival of the railroad reduced river trade. Declared a National Historic Landmark in 1975, Old Town Chinatown is now once again a popular part of the city. Many 19th-century buildings have been restored, and a Chinese-American business community still operates here. The Pearl District, an early 20th-century industrial area west of Old Town Chinatown, has also been transformed into a trendy neighborhood.

PEARL DISTRICT
Pearl District
Union Station
Greyhound Bus Terminal
Customs House
Oregon Jewish Museum
North Park Blocks
Roseland Theater
Powell's City of Books
McMenamins Crystal Ballroom
Portland Institute for Contemporary Art
O'Bryant Square
DOWNTOWN
p80
Pioneer Courthouse Square
Pioneer Courthouse
Portland's Centers for the Arts
Tanner Park
Jamison Sq
OLD TOWN CHINATOWN AND THE PEARL DISTRICT
NW MARSALL ST
NW LOVEJOY ST
NW KEARNEY ST
NW JOHNSON ST
NW IRVING ST
NW HOYT ST
NW GLISAN ST
NW FLANDERS ST
NW EVERETT ST
NW DAVIS ST
NW COUCH ST
W BURNSIDE ST
SW OAK ST
SW WASHINGTON ST
SW ALDER ST
SW HARVEY MILK ST
SW YAMHILL ST
SW SALMON ST
SW TAYLOR ST
NW STATION WAY
NW BROADWAY
NW 6TH AV
NW 5TH AV
NW PARK AV
NW 9TH AV
NW 10TH AV
NW 11TH AV
NW 12TH AV
NW 13TH AV
NW 14TH AV
NW 15TH AV
STADIUM FREEWAY
SOUTHWEST 4TH AV
SOUTHWEST 6TH AV

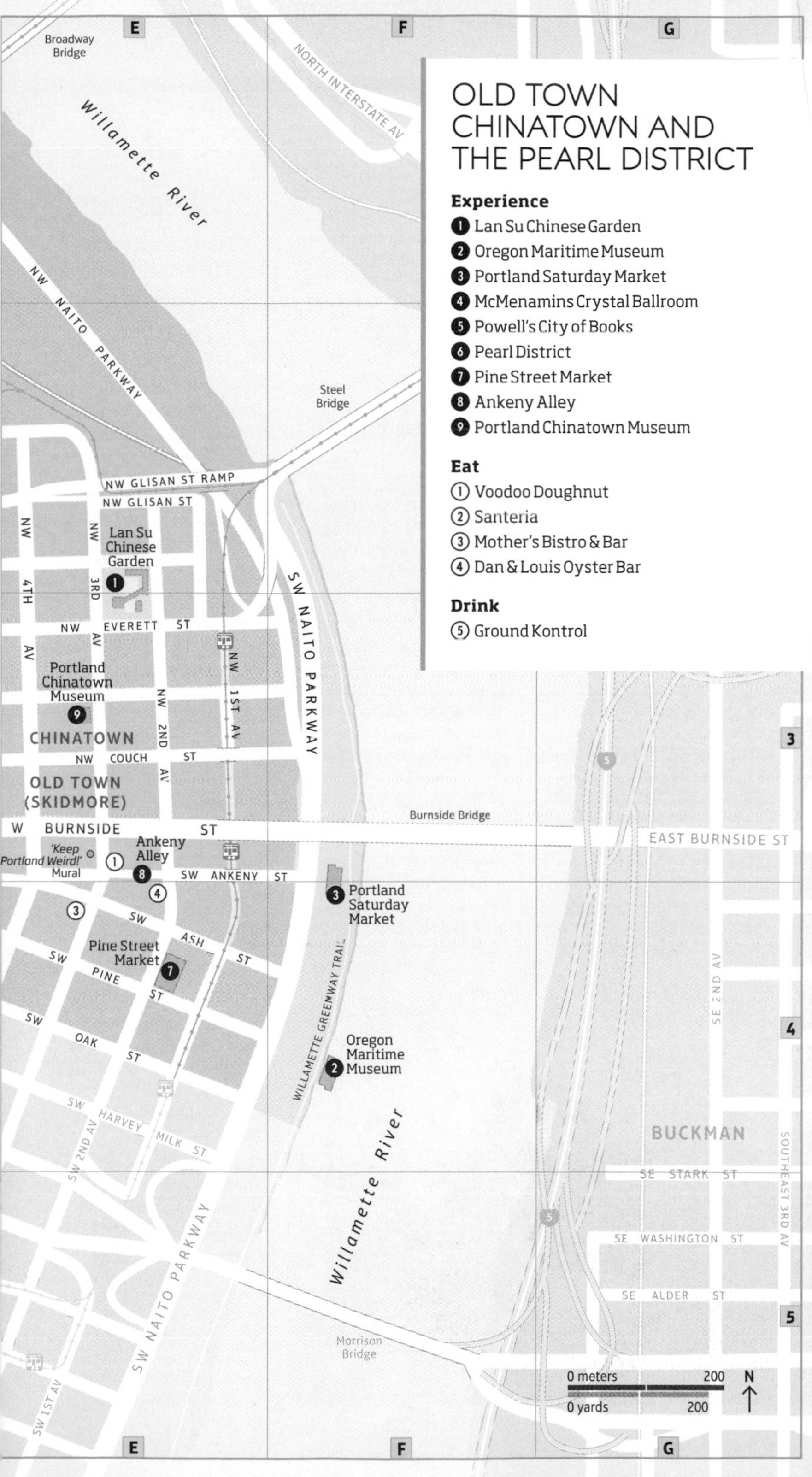
OLD TOWN CHINATOWN AND THE PEARL DISTRICT
Experience
1 Lan Su Chinese Garden
2 Oregon Maritime Museum
3 Portland Saturday Market
4 McMenamins Crystal Ballroom
5 Powell's City of Books
6 Pearl District
7 Pine Street Market
8 Ankeny Alley
9 Portland Chinatown Museum
Eat
① Voodoo Doughnut
② Santeria
③ Mother's Bistro & Bar
④ Dan & Louis Oyster Bar
Drink
⑤ Ground Kontrol
Broadway Bridge
Willamette River
NORTH INTERSTATE AV
NW NAITO PARKWAY
Steel Bridge
NW GLISAN ST RAMP
NW GLISAN ST
Lan Su Chinese Garden
NW 4TH AV
NW 3RD AV
NW EVERETT ST
SW NAITO PARKWAY
Portland Chinatown Museum
CHINATOWN
NW 2ND AV
NW 1ST AV
NW COUCH ST
OLD TOWN (SKIDMORE)
Burnside Bridge
W BURNSIDE ST
EAST BURNSIDE ST
'Keep Portland Weird!' Mural
Ankeny Alley
SW ANKENY ST
Portland Saturday Market
SW ASH ST
Pine Street Market
SW PINE ST
SW OAK ST
WILLAMETTE GREENWAY TRAIL
Oregon Maritime Museum
SW HARVEY MILK ST
SW 2ND AV
SE 2ND AV
BUCKMAN
SE STARK ST
SOUTHEAST 3RD AV
SE WASHINGTON ST
SE ALDER ST
Morrison Bridge
SW 1ST AV
0 meters 200
0 yards 200
N
E
F
G
3
4
5

EXPERIENCE

1    

Lan Su Chinese Garden

E2 239 NW Everett St Old Town/Chinatown 10am-4pm daily (mid-Mar-mid-May: to 6pm; mid-May-mid-Oct: to 7pm) Jan 1, Thanksgiving, Dec 25 lansugarden.org

Artisans and architects from Suzhou, Portland's sister city in China, built this walled garden in the late 1990s. The serene garden, which covers one entire city block, or 40,000 sq ft (3,716 sq m), is located in Portland's Chinatown.

The landscape of pavilions, waterfalls, lily pads, bamboo, a bridged lake, and stone paths is classic Ming Dynasty style and provides a tranquil glimpse of nature amid urban surroundings. Hundreds of plants grow in the garden, many of which are indigenous to China. Traditional Taihu rocks mimic mountain peaks, while the mirror-like surface of the central Lake Zither reflects the plants and architecture of the garden. Mosaic-patterned footpaths lead to several pavilions intended to be places for rest and contemplation. The ornate Tower of Cosmic Reflection pavilion houses a traditional teahouse that serves tea and Chinese delicacies. Throughout the garden, poems and literary allusions are inscribed on rocks, entryways, plaques, and above doors and windows.

2  

Oregon Maritime Museum

F4 Moored in the Willamette River, at the end of SW Pine St Skidmore Fountain 11am-4pm Wed & Fri-Sat Major hols oregonmaritime museum.org

This small but colorful museum is housed aboard the *Portland*, a stern-wheel, steam-powered tugboat – the last to be in operation in the US when it was decommissioned in 1982. The ship is now permanently moored alongside Governor Tom McCall Waterfront Park *(p89)*, where docks once bustled with seafaring trade.

Visits include a climb up to the captain's quarters and the wheelhouse, which provides a captivating view of the river, the downtown waterfront, and the bridges that span the Willamette River. You can also descend into the huge below-decks engine room.

In the main cabin, paintings, photographs, models of ships, navigation instruments, and other marine memorabilia record the pre-railroad days when Portland, with its key position at the confluence of the Willamette and Columbia rivers, flourished as a major seaport. You also get a glimpse of maritime life in 20th-century Portland, when the city was an important shipping center and its shipyards were some of the largest in the world. Portland continues to be a major port today.

Did You Know?

Portland is nicknamed "Stumptown" for the tree stumps left after its rapid development in the 1850s.

3 

Portland Saturday Market

F4 2 SW Naito Pkwy Skidmore Fountain Mar-Dec 24: 10am-5pm Sat, 11am-4:30pm Sun portlandsaturday market.com

Founded by craftspeople Sheri Teasdale and Andrea Scharf, the bustling Portland Saturday Market is the largest weekly open-air arts and crafts market in the US.

A lakeside pavilion offering a spot for contemplation in Lan Su Chinese Garden

CITY OF BRIDGES

Portland, the City of Roses, is also called the City of Bridges because the east and west banks of the Willamette River *(above)* are linked by 12 bridges. The first to be built was the Morrison, in 1887, though the original wooden crossing has long since been replaced. Pedestrian walkways on many of the bridges connect the Eastbank Esplanade with Governor Tom McCall Waterfront Park on the west side. The Steel Bridge affords the most dramatic crossing: when a ship needs to pass, the entire lower deck is lifted into the bottom of the roadway above. The latest addition is the striking Tilikum Crossing, which is for pedestrians, cyclists, and public transportation only.

Operating since 1974 and located in Governor Tom McCall Waterfront Park and Ankeny Plaza, the market features handcrafted goods made by the people who sell them, local and international food, and entertainment ranging from live music to colorful street performances. Every participating member is chosen by a jury, and each item is reviewed to ensure it meets the market's standards.

With a variety of products on offer, including clothes, art, jewelry, and ceramics, this is a great place to buy gifts and souvenirs. It is open only on weekends, except in the week before Christmas, when it holds its "Festival of the Last Minute."

4  

McMenamins Crystal Ballroom

B3 1332 W Burnside St Times vary, check website crystalballroompdx.com

Located across the street from the iconic McMenamins Crystal Hotel, the Crystal Ballroom, which is listed on the National Register of Historic Places, was built as a ballroom in 1914. Though it is now mainly a live music venue, it also hosts poetry readings and seasonal events.

The musical acts that perform here cater to a range of tastes, from blues and jazz to country, pop, hip-hop, and big-band swing. Talented musicians that have played here over the years include the Grateful Dead, Buffalo Springfield, and James Brown. The ballroom also hosts the popular Portland Folk Festival every January.

5 

Powell's City of Books

C3 1005 W Burnside St 9am-11pm daily powells.com

The largest independent bookstore in the world houses more than one million volumes, including new, old, used, rare, and out-of-print books, on a wealth of subjects. The store welcomes 6,000 shoppers each day, and has become one of Portland's most beloved cultural institutions since its establishment in 1971.

Despite its size, Powell's is easy to browse in: the 3,500 sections are divided into nine color-coded and well-marked rooms, and knowledgeable staff at the information desks possess the remarkable ability to lay their hands on any book in the store. The in-store coffee shop allows browsers to linger for hours, making Powell's a popular hangout any day of the year. Indeed, it's open all 365 of them. Visit on a Sunday to explore the store and learn about its history on a free guided tour, which begins at 10am.

PICTURE PERFECT

The Studious Staircase

With more than a million books on its shelves, Powell's City of Books relies on color-coded staircases to guide visitors. Witty words inscribed on the steps make for distinctive photos.

EAT

Voodoo Doughnut
Over 100 varieties of doughnuts - including vegan options - are available 24/7 here.
E3 22 SW 3rd Av
voodoodoughnut.com

Santeria
This ordinary-looking Mexican place serves extraordinarily good food, with plenty of choice for vegetarians and vegans.
D3 703 SW Ankeny St (503) 956-7624
For dinner

Mother's Bistro & Bar
Homey French bistro serving down-to-earth and hearty US favorites.
E4 121 SW 3rd Av
mothersbistro.com

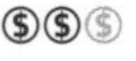

Dan & Louis Oyster Bar
A lively and historic oyster bar that has been shucking Oregon's tasty oysters since 1907.
E4 208 SW Ankeny
danandlouis.com

DRINK

Ground Kontrol
A futuristic arcade for pinball fans offering a good beer and cocktail selection.
D3 115 NW 5th Av
groundkontrol.com

Pearl District

C2 W Burnside St to the Willamette River (N), from NW 8th to NW 15th avs To NW Glisan St

One of Portland's most desirable neighborhoods occupies an old industrial district on the north side of Burnside Street, between Chinatown to the east and Nob Hill *(p100)* to the west. Galleries, shops, design studios, breweries, cafes, restaurants, and clubs occupy former factories, warehouses, and garages.

One of the most enjoyable times to visit is during a First Thursday event (the first Thursday of every month), when the many art galleries in the area remain open late to show the latest pieces. The collections feature a range of contemporary art and artists. Gallery receptions are open to the public free of charge.

Art galleries have played such an important role in the development of the Pearl District that Jamison Square Park is named after William Jamison, the first art dealer to set up shop in the area. The park includes a water feature that fills and recedes over a central plaza. When the fountain is not in use, the plaza is used as an amphitheater for small performances. The park also features a wooden boardwalk, lawns, and colorful public art. It is an excellent place to begin a walk around the area, taking in the fine contemporary and historical buildings, and the district's ongoing regeneration.

The name of the district itself is said to have been coined by a local gallery owner, Thomas Augustine. He suggested that the buildings in the Warehouse District were like gray, dull oysters, and that the galleries within were like pearls.

Pine Street Market

E4 126 SW 2nd Av SW Oak and 1st Times vary, check website pinestreetpdx.com

Pine Street Market opened in 2016 in the historic Carriage and Baggage Building. It features nine open-plan eating places that serve a range of cuisines made by some of the city's top chefs, including Korean-style street food, Japanese food, tapas, pizza, burgers, and much more.

Ankeny Alley

E3 SW Ankeny St, between 2nd and 3rd avs W Burnside and NW 5th

A block from Pine Street Market, this "alley" is actually a pedestrianized stretch of SW Ankeny Street, which has become an attractive spot for people to meet, have a bite to eat, and drink anything from a coffee to a cocktail. Part of its appeal is the great variety of eating options, including an oyster bar, the popular Voodoo Doughnut, a creperie, a speakeasy, live music at Valentine's, sushi, tacos, and several more to choose from.

Portland Chinatown Museum

E3 127 NW 3rd Av NW 5th and Couch MAX Station Noon-5pm Thu-Sun portlandchinatownmuseum.org

Opened in 2018, this museum tells the fascinating story of Portland's Chinese community and the development of the city's two Chinatown neighborhoods. The Chinese were the largest immigrant group, and by 1900 Portland's Chinatown was the second-biggest in the United States, with an estimated 10,000 people. Exhibits include a re-created Chinatown store, Bow Yuen & Co, just as it was when it closed in 1929. It is more than just a museum, though, as it features art installations, movies, talks, and changing exhibitions highlighting Chinese arts and crafts. Tours of the museum operate Monday through Wednesday, but be sure to reserve ahead.

←

Enjoying a coffee outside a cafe in the Pearl District, and *(inset)* cooling off in Jamison Square Park's fountain

PORTLAND STREETCAR

Horse-drawn streetcars began running in the 1870s. By the early 20th century, electric streetcars were rumbling all across Portland, bringing downtown within reach of newly established residential neighborhoods. Cars had replaced streetcars by the 1950s but, in the late 1990s, city planners turned to them again to reduce congestion and ensure the vitality of the central business district. The streetcars still travel along three lines today.

A SHORT WALK
OLD TOWN CHINATOWN

Distance 0.6 miles (1 km) **Time** 15 minutes
Nearest station Old Town/Chinatown

Elegant brick facades and quiet streets belie Old Town Chinatown's raucous 19th-century frontier-town past, when the district hummed with traders, dockworkers, shipbuilders, and sailors from around the world. While the saloons and bordellos that once did a brisk business are long gone, Old Town Chinatown is still known for harboring some of the city's wilder nightlife. You'll encounter a colorful street life as you walk through the area, too, especially on weekends, when the Saturday Market takes over several blocks, as well as during the festivals held year-round on the nearby waterfront.

The multicolored, five-tiered, dragon-festooned Chinatown Gate is the official entryway to **Chinatown**.

The popular **Pine Street Market** (p77), *Portland's modern food hall, features several big-name cafes, restaurants, bars, and more. It spans the ground floor of a historic building, built in 1886, located at 126 SW 2nd Avenue.*

↑ Water falling from the elegant Skidmore Fountain

New Market Block, *a group of Italianate buildings, is typical of the cast-iron and brick structures built after fire destroyed much of Portland in the 1870s.*

Built in 1888 as a place for citizens and horses to quench their thirst, the **Skidmore Fountain** *and the adjacent plaza are at the center of Old Town Chinatown.*

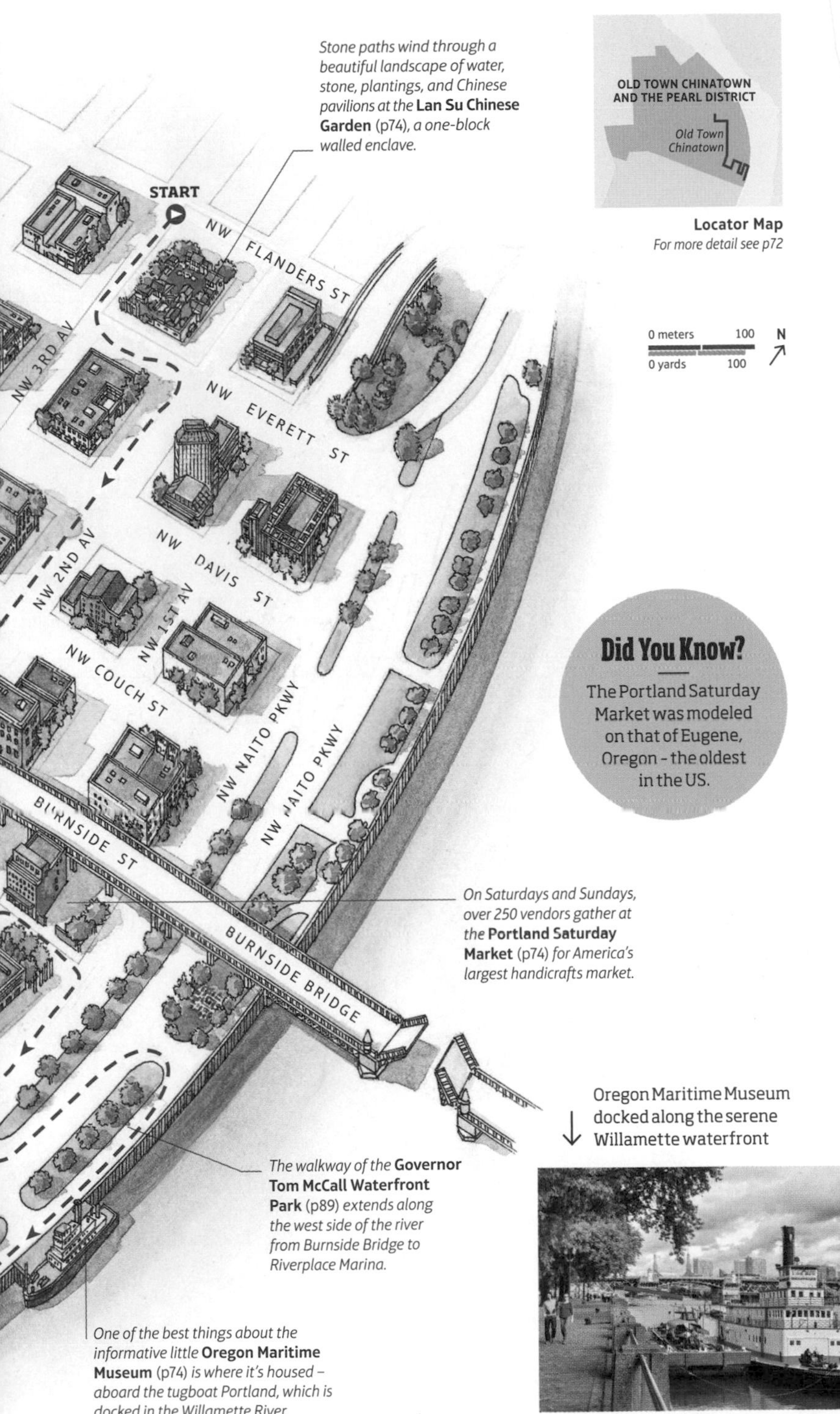

Locator Map

For more detail see p72

Stone paths wind through a beautiful landscape of water, stone, plantings, and Chinese pavilions at the **Lan Su Chinese Garden** (p74), *a one-block walled enclave.*

On Saturdays and Sundays, over 250 vendors gather at the **Portland Saturday Market** (p74) *for America's largest handicrafts market.*

The walkway of the **Governor Tom McCall Waterfront Park** (p89) *extends along the west side of the river from Burnside Bridge to Riverplace Marina.*

One of the best things about the informative little **Oregon Maritime Museum** (p74) *is where it's housed – aboard the tugboat Portland, which is docked in the Willamette River.*

Did You Know?

The Portland Saturday Market was modeled on that of Eugene, Oregon - the oldest in the US.

↓ Oregon Maritime Museum docked along the serene Willamette waterfront

UNION
STATION

Union Station rising up behind the steel Broadway Bridge

DOWNTOWN

With the decline of river traffic in the late 19th century, Portland's center moved inland to the blocks around the intersection of Morrison Street and Broadway. The 1905 Lewis and Clark Exposition, the 100th anniversary of the expedition *(p58)*, brought new prosperity and new residents to the city: downtown became a boomtown. Steelframe buildings with facades of glazed, white terra-cotta tiles (the Meier & Frank Building is a fine example) began to rise and they continue to give the downtown area a bright, distinctive look.

By 1930, Portland's population had jumped to over 300,000, leading to a steep rise in housing developments. The city's urban landscape today is still defined by its narrow streets and houses and short city blocks, in among the later high-rise buildings. The mid-20th century saw the atmosphere of downtown shift greatly, with organized crime bosses prevalent in the 1930s. The 1960s saw the introduction of a hippie counterculture scene to rival San Francisco's.

Since the 1970s, urban planning efforts have earned Portland's downtown a reputation as one of the most successful city centers in the US. The area around Pioneer Courthouse Square is the city's commercial and cultural hub, while many government offices are housed in innovative new buildings to the east, near historic Chapman and Lownsdale squares.

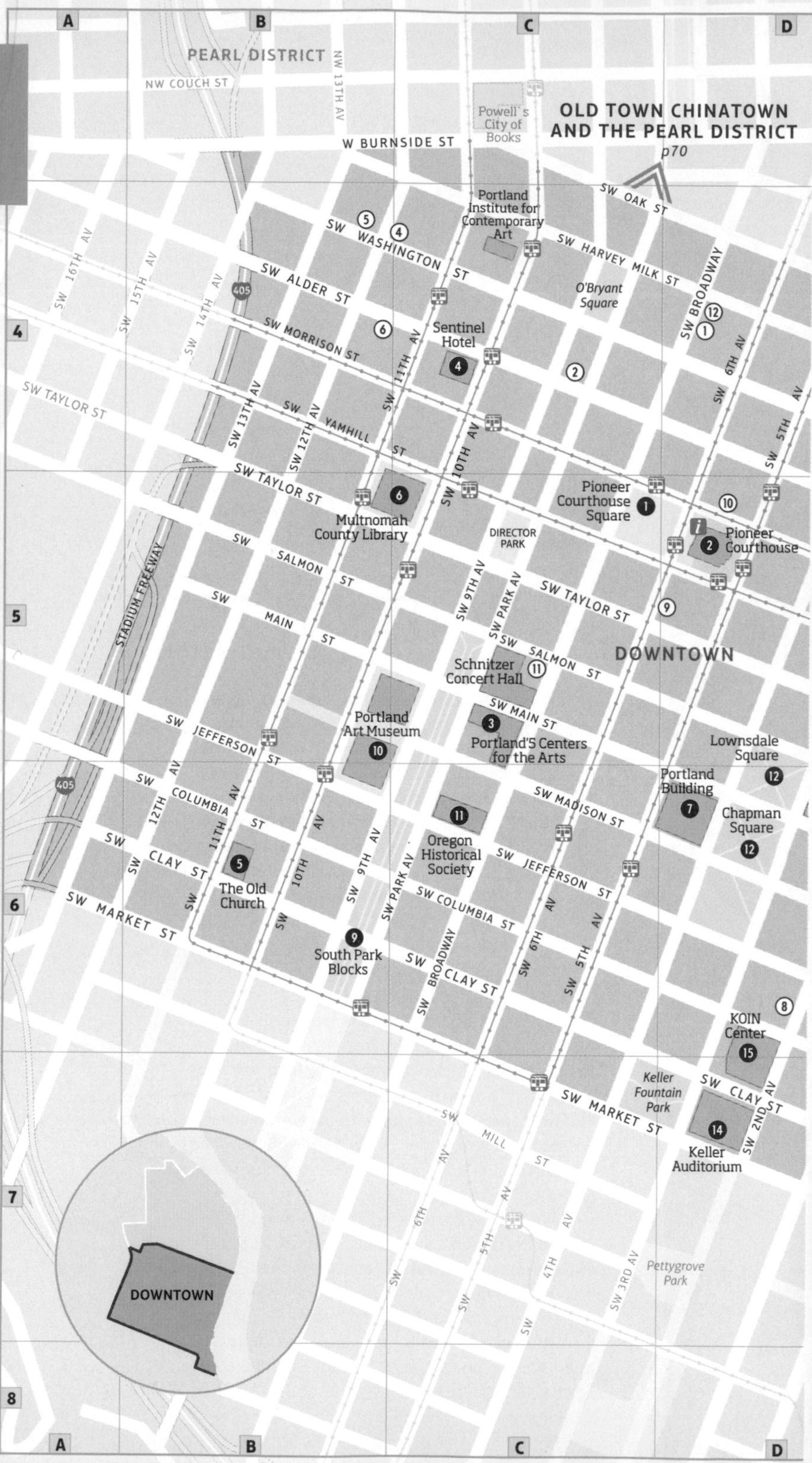

PEARL DISTRICT
NW COUCH ST
NW 13TH AV
Powell's City of Books
W BURNSIDE ST
OLD TOWN CHINATOWN AND THE PEARL DISTRICT
p70
SW OAK ST
Portland Institute for Contemporary Art
SW WASHINGTON ST
SW HARVEY MILK ST
SW ALDER ST
O'Bryant Square
SW BROADWAY
SW MORRISON ST
Sentinel Hotel
SW 16TH AV
SW 15TH AV
SW 14TH AV
SW 6TH AV
SW 5TH AV
SW TAYLOR ST
SW 13TH AV
SW 12TH AV
SW YAMHILL ST
SW 11TH AV
SW 10TH AV
Pioneer Courthouse Square
Multnomah County Library
DIRECTOR PARK
Pioneer Courthouse
SW SALMON ST
SW 9TH AV
SW PARK AV
STADIUM FREEWAY
SW MAIN ST
DOWNTOWN
Schnitzer Concert Hall
Portland Art Museum
Portland'5 Centers for the Arts
SW JEFFERSON ST
Lownsdale Square
Portland Building
SW COLUMBIA ST
SW MADISON ST
Chapman Square
Oregon Historical Society
SW CLAY ST
The Old Church
SW MARKET ST
South Park Blocks
KOIN Center
Keller Fountain Park
SW 2ND AV
Keller Auditorium
SW MILL ST
SW 4TH AV
SW 3RD AV
Pettygrove Park

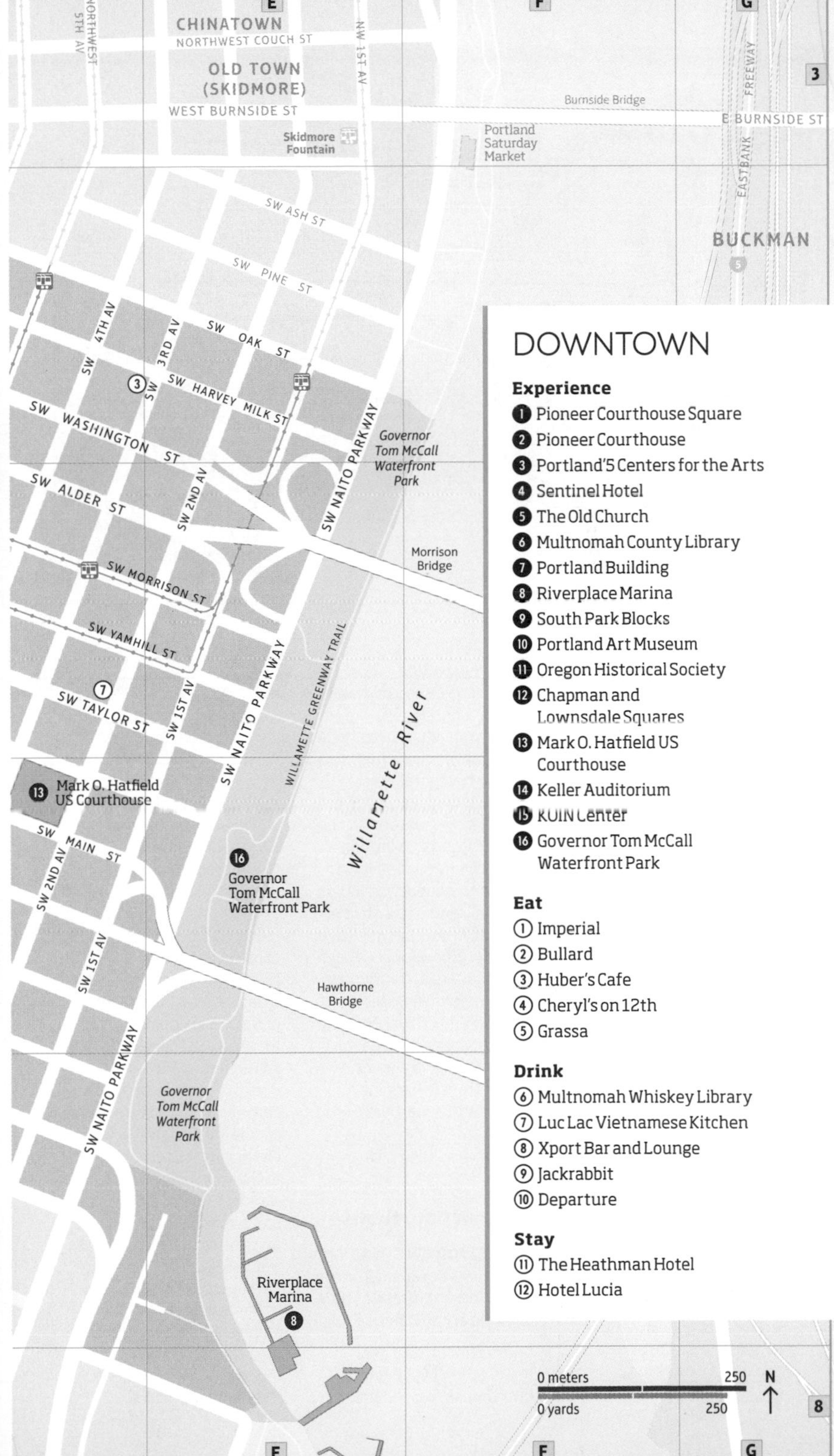

DOWNTOWN

Experience

1. Pioneer Courthouse Square
2. Pioneer Courthouse
3. Portland'5 Centers for the Arts
4. Sentinel Hotel
5. The Old Church
6. Multnomah County Library
7. Portland Building
8. Riverplace Marina
9. South Park Blocks
10. Portland Art Museum
11. Oregon Historical Society
12. Chapman and Lownsdale Squares
13. Mark O. Hatfield US Courthouse
14. Keller Auditorium
15. KOIN Center
16. Governor Tom McCall Waterfront Park

Eat

(1) Imperial
(2) Bullard
(3) Huber's Cafe
(4) Cheryl's on 12th
(5) Grassa

Drink

(6) Multnomah Whiskey Library
(7) Luc Lac Vietnamese Kitchen
(8) Xport Bar and Lounge
(9) Jackrabbit
(10) Departure

Stay

(11) The Heathman Hotel
(12) Hotel Lucia

EXPERIENCE

Pioneer Courthouse Square

C5 SW Broadway & Yamhill St Pioneer Square thesquarepdx.org

City planners designed this pedestrian-only square in the mid-1980s to resemble the large central plazas of many European cities. The square stands on hallowed Portland ground: the city's first schoolhouse was erected on this site in 1858, and the much-admired Portland Hotel stood here from 1890 to 1951, when it was demolished to make way for a parking lot.

The square has become the center of the city, a friendly space where locals gather to enjoy a brown-bag lunch or free outdoor concert. Architectural flourishes include amphitheater-like seating, a fountain that resembles a waterfall, and a row of 12 columns crowned with gilt roses.

Underground spaces next to the square accommodate offices and businesses, including the Travel Portland Visitors Information Center, Portland Walking Tours, Trimet Transit Planning Center, and a Starbucks®.

HIDDEN GEM

Portland Police Museum

An 8-minute walk from Pioneer Courthouse, this fantastic free museum is housed inside the Department of Justice Building *(1111 SW 2nd Av)* and exhibits historic photos and early arrest records.

Pioneer Courthouse

D5 700 SW 6th Av Pioneer Square 9am-4pm Mon-Fri Major hols pioneercourthouse.org

Completed in 1873 and restored in 2005, Pioneer Courthouse was the first federal building to be constructed in the Pacific Northwest and is the second-oldest federal building west of the Mississippi River. The trees planted here in 1873 are still standing. The Italianate structure, faced with freestone and topped by a domed cupola, houses the US Court of Appeals. As part of a visit to the courthouse, you can wander the grand hallways and public areas, where fascinating exhibits explore the building's history. There are superb panoramic views of Portland from the cupola, and historic photographs next to each window show the same view as it was in the city's early years.

↑ Pioneer Courthouse Square, and *(inset)* a courtroom in the Court of Appeals

Portland'5 Centers for the Arts

C5 1111 SW Broadway To SW Broadway portland5.com

Portland'5 Centers for the Arts has been the city's major venue for theater, music, and dance since the mid-1980s. The complex consists of the Arlene Schnitzer Concert Hall, on Broadway, and the Keller Auditorium *(p88)*, a few blocks east at Southwest 3rd Avenue and Clay Street. In the Antoinette Hatfield Hall, the Newmark Theatre, the Brunish Theatre, and the Dolores Winningstad Theatre open off a dramatic, five-story, cherry-paneled rotunda capped by a dome designed by glass artist James Carpenter.

The Arlene Schnitzer Concert Hall occupies a former vaudeville house and movie palace built in 1927. Its ornate, Italian Rococo Revival interior has been restored, and it is now the home of the Oregon Symphony. The marquee continues to illuminate Broadway with 6,000 lights, and it now props up an unmissable 65-ft- (20-m-) high sign that screams "Portland" in bright white lights.

Sentinel Hotel

C4 614 SW 11th Av Galleria/SW 10th Av To SW Alder St sentinelhotel.com

Originally opened as the Seward Hotel in 1909, and later the Governor Hotel in 1991, this extensively renovated hotel now bears the moniker of the Sentinel. The expedition of Meriwether Lewis and William Clark *(p58)*, whose 1804–1806 journey across the US and down the Columbia River put Oregon on the map, figures prominently in the hotel. A mural in the restaurant shows a map of the expedition and depicts scenes from their journey.

The hotel incorporates the ornate former headquarters of the Elks Lodge as its west wing, built in the luxuriant style of the pre-Depression early 1920s to resemble the Palazzo Farnese in Rome. Mahogany detailing, leather chairs, fireplaces, and warm tones create an atmosphere of old-fashioned opulence.

The Old Church

B6 1422 SW 11th Av To SW Clay St 11am-3pm Tue-Fri theoldchurch.org

Built in 1882, this church reflects a Victorian Gothic Revival style, also known as Stick or Carpenter Gothic style, with exaggerated arches, a tall steeple, and sleek windows. The rough-hewn wood exterior lends it a distinctly Pacific Northwestern flavor. On Wednesdays at noon, you can catch free classical concerts here.

The Arlene Schnitzer Concert Hall of Portland'5 Centers for the Arts

STAY

The Heathman Hotel

This charming 1927 institution with city views and old-world charm is a magnet for visiting musicians and writers.

C5 1001 SW Broadway heathmanhotel.com

Hotel Lucia

A stylish hotel with acclaimed artworks, luxurious beds, and even a pillow menu.

D4 400 SW Broadway hotellucia.com

Multnomah County Library

C5 801 SW 10th Av Library/SW 9th Av To SW Taylor St 10am-8pm Mon, noon-8pm Tue & Wed, 10am-6pm Thu-Sat, 10am-5pm Sun Major hols multcolib.org

Alfred E. Doyle, the architect whose work in Portland includes the Meier and Frank department store, and the drinking fountains that grace downtown streets, chose limestone and brick for this distinctive Georgian structure. The building, completed in 1913, is the headquarters of the county library system, established in 1864 and the oldest library system west of the Mississippi.

The library's most valuable possession, worth millions, is *The Birds of America* by John James Audubon, in a full-size multi-volume folio edition.

7

Portland Building

D6 1120 SW 5th Av
Gallery: (503) 823-5252
Transit Mall For renovations, scheduled to reopen late 2020/ early 2021

The Portland Building, designed by Michael Graves, has been controversial ever since it was completed in 1982. This first large-scale post-modern office building in the US has been hailed as a major innovation in contemporary urban design. It has also been denounced as just plain ugly. There is a playfulness to the exterior, while the modest height and rows of small square windows suggest practicality and a lack of pretension, as befits the home of government offices. More ostentatious is *Portlandia*, a 36-ft- (11-m-) tall statue above the main doors, by sculptor Raymond Kaskey (1985) and modeled on Lady Commerce, the symbolic figure that appears on the city seal and supposedly welcomed traders into the port.

A gallery on the second floor displays public art of the region, and plans and models related to the design and construction of the building and the *Portlandia* statue.

TOP 3

PORTLAND BOAT CRUISES

Portland Spirit Cruises
110 SE Caruthers St
portlandspirit.com
Sail the Columbia River Gorge on a dining cruise.

Willamette Jetboat Excursions
1945 SE Water Av
willamettejet.com
Take in Portland and the Willamette Falls.

BrewBarge Cruise
1425 NW Flanders St
brewgrouppdx.com
Bring your own beer on this floating vessel that you pedal yourself.

8  

Riverplace Marina

E7 SW Clay St & Willamette River
RiverPlace

Riverplace Marina is located on the west bank of the Willamette River, at the southwest end of Governor Tom McCall Waterfront Park. Amenities include upscale shops, several restaurants, including Portland's only floating restaurant, and one of the city's higher-end hotels, Kimpton RiverPlace Hotel. The complex also has sloping lawns, riverside walks, and a large marina. Sea kayaks are available for rental, providing a different way to view the river and city.

South Park Blocks

B6 Bounded by SW Salmon St & I-405, SW Park & SW 9th avs To stops between SW Salmon & SW Mill sts

In 1852, frontier businessman and legislator Daniel Lownsdale set aside the blocks between Park and 9th avenues as park-land, and landscape designer Louis G. Pfunder planted 104

The copper *Portlandia* statue watching over the street from the Portland Building

Paintings hanging in a stylish gallery in the Portland Art Museum ↑

Lombardy poplars and elms between Salmon and Hall. The so-called South Park Blocks continue to form a 12-block ribbon of tree-shaded lawns through the central city.

In 1917, lumber baron Samuel Benson commissioned architect A. E. Doyle to design distinctive, four-bowled drinking fountains. He placed 20 of them throughout the South Park Blocks and the rest of downtown to quench the thirst of residents who might otherwise be tempted to visit saloons.

Portland Art Museum

B5 1219 SW Park Av Library/SW 9th Av To Jefferson St 10am-5pm Tue-Sun (to 8pm Thu & Fri) Major hols portlandartmuseum.org

The oldest art museum in the Pacific Northwest opened in 1892, introducing citizens to classical art with a collection of plaster casts of Greek and Roman sculpture. Today, the superb 42,000-piece collection is housed in a building designed by modernist architect Pietro Belluschi.

A sizable collection of European paintings, including works by Van Gogh and Picasso, hang in the galleries. Works by Rodin and Brancusi fill the sculpture court; further galleries house works by Frank Stella and Willem de Kooning; and there is a wing devoted to historical and contemporary art by local artists. The Grand Ronde Center for Native American Art displays masks, jewelry, totem poles, and works by artists from 200 American Indian groups.

Oregon Historical Society

C6 1200 SW Park Av Library/SW 9th Av To Jefferson St Museum: 10am-5pm Mon-Sat, noon-5pm Sun; Library: 1-5pm Tue, 10am-5pm Wed-Sat ohs.org

Eight-story murals by Richard Haas on the west and south facades of the Oregon Historical Society depict the Lewis and Clark expedition *(p58)*, fur trading, and other events that have shaped the history of Oregon. On display in the galleries are some of the 85,000 objects that make this museum the largest repository of Oregon historical artifacts. The exhibits, which include maps, paintings, photographs, and historical documents, change frequently. On permanent display is "Oregon My Oregon," a remarkable exhibition that includes 50 separate displays recounting the history of the state, and the original Portland Penny, the coin that decided the name of the town after two New Englanders established a joint land claim.

EAT

Imperial

Hotel Lucia's restaurant, run by acclaimed chef Vitaly Paley, serves classic Pacific Northwest cuisine.

D4 410 SW Broadway imperialpdx.com

$$$

Bullard

Bullard is exceptional, with mouthwatering Tex-Mex dishes like slow-smoked beef ribs.

C4 813 SW Alder St bullardpdx.com

$$$

Huber's Cafe

This place has been serving American food since 1879, with turkey a staple.

D4 411 SW 3rd Av hubers.com

$$$

Cheryl's on 12th

Tuck in to gourmet New American cuisine at this light and busy corner brunch spot. Try the local hot sauce Secret Aardvark here.

C4 1135 SW Washington St cherylson12th.com

$$$

Grassa

An Italian restaurant with industrial decor serving impeccable pasta dishes.

B4 1205 SW Washington St grassapdx.com

DRINK

Multnomah Whiskey Library
This brick-walled cocktail bar serves not just whiskies, but spirits from around the world.
B4 1124 SW Alder St Times vary, check website mwlpdx.com

Luc Lac Vietnamese Kitchen
This is one of the best drinking spots in town, with a good cocktail list, beer on tap, and wine.
D5 835 SW 2nd Av luclac kitchen.com

Xport Bar and Lounge
Enjoy a wine, beer, or imaginative cocktail at this smart-casual rooftop bar/restaurant with impressive mountain views.
D6 1355 SW 2nd Av Times vary, check website xport portland.com

Jackrabbit
This bar/restaurant showcases local beers and wines, and creative options include a gin or tequila coin-toss cocktail.
D5 830 SW 6th Av gojackrabbitgo.com

Departure
Sip a cocktail or sake by the glass atop the Meier and Frank Building at this pan-Asian lounge with a view.
D5 15th Floor, 525 SW Morrison St Times vary, check website departure portland.com

Chapman and Lownsdale Squares

D6 Bounded by SW Salmon & SW Madison sts, SW 3rd & SW 4th avs Mall/SW 4th Av, City Hall/SW Jefferson St

It is only fitting that Daniel Lownsdale should have a one-block-square park named for him. The tanner, who became one of Oregon's early legislators, had the foresight to set aside a parcel of downtown for the South Park Blocks *(p86)*, and he did much to encourage trade on the nearby waterfront by building a wood-plank road into the countryside so that goods could be transported to the Portland docks.

Judge William Chapman, for whom the adjoining square is named, was one of the founders of the *Oregonian* newspaper. Along with Terry Schrunk Plaza – a third, adjacent park-like block – the squares provide a soothing stretch of greenery in Portland's quiet courthouse and government-building district. The neighborhood was not always so sedate, though: anti-Chinese riots broke out here in the 1880s, and the area was particularly raucous in the early 20th century.

Mark O. Hatfield US Courthouse

D6 1000 SW 3rd Av (503) 326-8000 Transit Mall 8:30am-4:30pm Mon-Fri Major hols

Completed in 1997, this courthouse defies any notion that a government building is by definition unimaginative, with its handsome and bold facade of glass, aluminum, and limestone. A ninth-floor sculpture garden provides excellent views of both the river and Portland's beloved Elk Fountain, which stands across the street. When automobile traffic began to increase in the early 20th century, the Elk Fountain stood in the path of a proposed extension of Main Street. Angry citizens protested plans to move the fountain; it now stands in the middle of the street.

Did You Know?
In the 1920s, Chapman Square was off-limits to men so that women could enjoy the space in safety.

Keller Auditorium

D7 222 SW Clay St Transit Mall portland5.com

When a big production comes to Portland, the 3,000-seat Keller Auditorium often plays host. Built in 1917 on the former site of an exhibition hall and sports arena known as the Mechanics' Pavilion, the auditorium was completely remodeled in the late 1960s.

Water flowing down the Ira Keller Memorial Fountain, opposite the Keller Auditorium

The space is part of the Portland'5 Centers for the Arts *(p85)* and is home to the Portland Opera, the Oregon Ballet, and sometimes the Oregon Children's Theatre.

Across the street is the Ira Keller Memorial Fountain, a waterfall cascading over 18-ft (5.5-m) concrete cliffs into a pool crisscrossed with platforms laid out like stepping stones, and enclosed by a delightful garden. It is dedicated to Ira Keller, a longtime Portland Development Commission (PDC) chairman.

KOIN Center

D6 222 SW Columbia St Transit Mall

The postmodern KOIN Center incorporates a plurality of architectural styles in one structure. Completed in 1984, the 35-story blond-brick tower capped by a pyramidal blue steel roof was designed by the Portland firm of Zimmer Gunsul Frasca, and is considered a model urban complex. The building houses shops, residences, offices – including those of the television station for which it is named – and a popular steakhouse.

Governor Tom McCall Waterfront Park

E6 Bounded by SW Harrison & NW Glisan sts, SW Naito Pkwy & Willamette River Skidmore Fountain, Morrison/SW 3rd Av, Yamhill District

This 1.5-mile- (2.5-km-) long park on the west bank of the Willamette River covers land that once bustled with activity on the Portland docks and which, from the 1940s to the 1970s, was buried beneath an expressway. The city converted the land to a park as part of an urban renewal scheme and named it for the environmentally minded Tom McCall, Oregon's governor, 1967–75.

The park is a much-used riverside promenade and the locale for many festivals. One of its most popular attractions is Salmon Street Springs, a fountain that has 185 jets splashing water directly onto the sidewalk.

A block away, at the foot of Southwest Taylor Street, is Mill Ends Park, measuring only 452 sq inches (0.3 sq m). The park is the former site of a telephone pole, removed in the late 1940s. Local journalist Dick Fagan began planting flowers on the patch of earth and writing articles about what he dubbed the "World's Smallest Park," which it officially became when the city adopted it as part of the park system in 1976.

The Battleship Oregon Memorial, built in 1956, honors an 1893 US Navy ship. A time capsule sealed in its base in 1976 is due to be opened in 2076.

GREEN PORTLAND

Portland's parks are often described in superlatives. The city is home to one of the largest forested city parks in the US - 8-sq-mile (21-sq-km) Forest Park - and the smallest park in the world - 452-sq-inch (0.3-sq-m) Mill Ends Park. The city has some of the nation's largest and most extensive rose test gardens *(p97)*, one of the world's most renowned rhododendron gardens *(p101)*, one of the finest Japanese gardens outside Japan *(p96)*, and the largest classical Chinese garden outside China *(p74)*.

A SHORT WALK
DOWNTOWN

Distance 1 mile (1.6 km) **Time** 20 minutes
Nearest bus stop SW Jefferson & Broadway

One of the most appealing characteristics of Portland is the way the city combines cosmopolitan sophistication with a relaxed, low-key ambience. Nowhere is this more in evidence than on a walk through the attractive downtown blocks that surround Pioneer Courthouse Square. Broadway and the streets that cross it here are lined with department stores and boutiques, office complexes, hotels, restaurants, theaters, and museums, many occupying well-restored century-old buildings. The route is short in length, so take your time, stopping to sit in one of the many open spaces that offer glimpses of distant mountains.

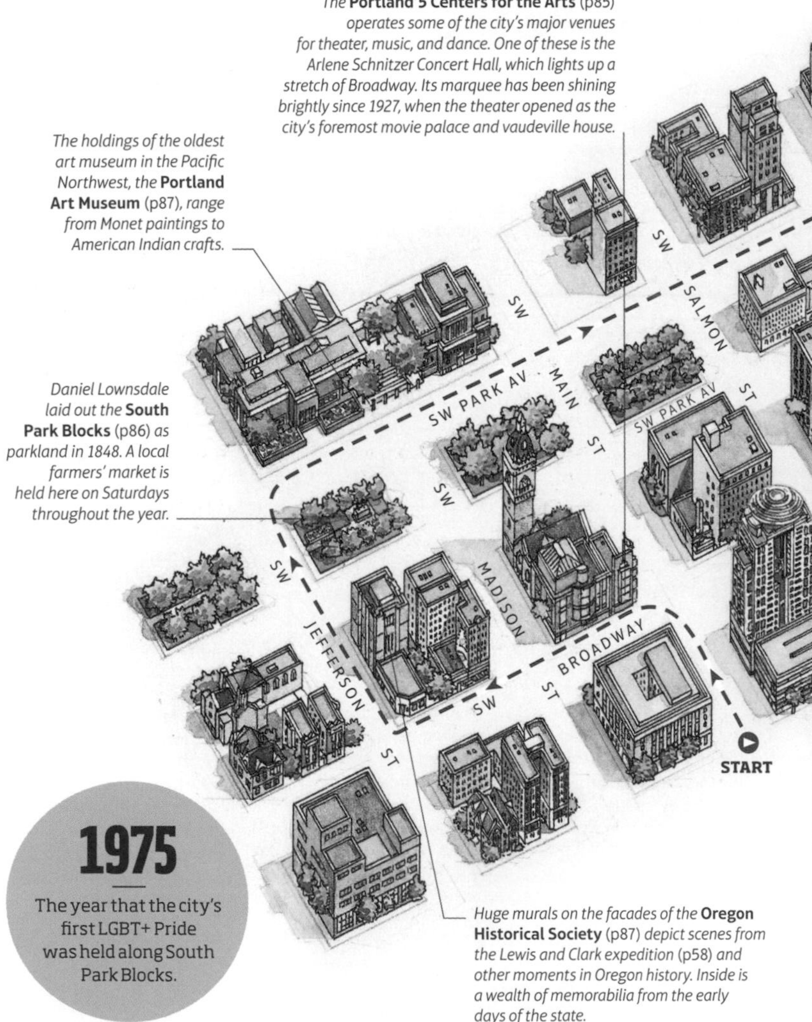

The **Portland'5 Centers for the Arts** (p85) *operates some of the city's major venues for theater, music, and dance. One of these is the Arlene Schnitzer Concert Hall, which lights up a stretch of Broadway. Its marquee has been shining brightly since 1927, when the theater opened as the city's foremost movie palace and vaudeville house.*

The holdings of the oldest art museum in the Pacific Northwest, the **Portland Art Museum** (p87), *range from Monet paintings to American Indian crafts.*

Daniel Lownsdale laid out the **South Park Blocks** (p86) *as parkland in 1848. A local farmers' market is held here on Saturdays throughout the year.*

1975

The year that the city's first LGBT+ Pride was held along South Park Blocks.

Huge murals on the facades of the **Oregon Historical Society** (p87) *depict scenes from the Lewis and Clark expedition* (p58) *and other moments in Oregon history. Inside is a wealth of memorabilia from the early days of the state.*

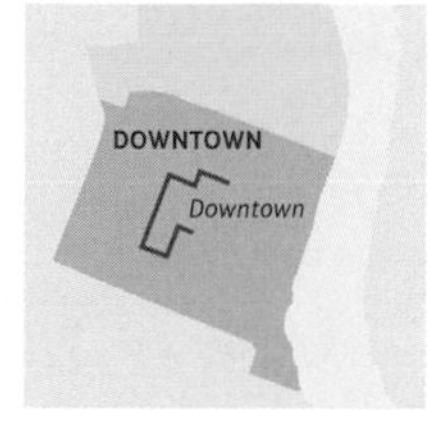

Locator Map
For more detail see p82

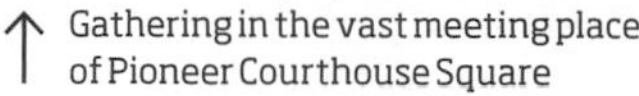

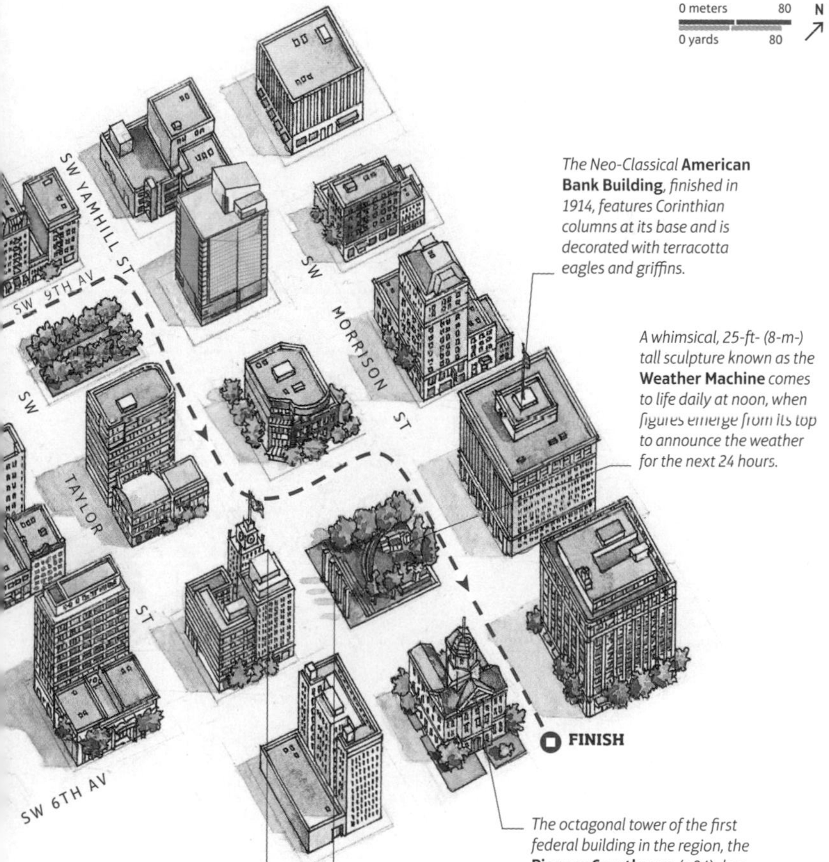

↑ Gathering in the vast meeting place of Pioneer Courthouse Square

0 meters 80
0 yards 80
N

SW YAMHILL ST
SW 9TH AV
SW MORRISON ST
SW TAYLOR ST
SW 6TH AV

The Neo-Classical **American Bank Building**, *finished in 1914, features Corinthian columns at its base and is decorated with terracotta eagles and griffins.*

A whimsical, 25-ft- (8-m-) tall sculpture known as the **Weather Machine** *comes to life daily at noon, when figures emerge from its top to announce the weather for the next 24 hours.*

FINISH

The octagonal tower of the first federal building in the region, the **Pioneer Courthouse** (p84), *has been a fixture of the Portland skyline since 1873.*

Jackson Tower *was built by the Reid brothers for a newspaper magnate in 1912. It features glazed terra-cotta as a decorative element and a steel frame.*

The open space of **Pioneer Courthouse Square** (p84) *is the heart of Portland, where fountains splash and Portlanders gather for free lunchtime concerts, flower shows, and other events, or simply for a chance to sit and enjoy their city.*

The tranquil Japanese Garden in Washington Park

BEYOND THE CENTER

By the late 19th century, Portland was fast growing from a small riverfront settlement surrounded by forests into an important port city. It expanded westward into Nob Hill, where wealthy merchants settled, and eastward across the Willamette River. Many interesting sights lie outside of the city center, and numerous key events in Oregon's history transpired south of Portland. Oregon City was the site of the first meeting of the territory's provisional legislature, in 1843, and a Utopian society once thrived at Aurora.

Must Sees

1. Washington Park
2. Sauvie Island

Experience More

3. Pittock Mansion
4. Eastbank Esplanade
5. Nob Hill
6. Rose Quarter
7. Crystal Springs Rhododendron Garden
8. Sellwood District
9. Southeast Division Street
10. Oregon Museum of Science and Industry
11. Hawthorne District
12. End of the Oregon Trail Interpretive Center
13. Reed College
14. Oregon City
15. Aurora

1

WASHINGTON PARK

Located between Burnside St & US 26 Washington Park 5am-10pm daily (not all sights) explorewashingtonpark.org

Whether hiking on a forest trail beneath a canopy of pine trees, or coming upon a meadow filled with wildflowers, you may find it hard to believe that Washington Park is surrounded by the city. Today, the park is one of Portland's most popular outdoor playgrounds.

Though a park first took shape in the western hills of downtown Portland in 1871, it was not until 1903 that Washington Park acquired much of its present appearance. This was the year Boston landscape architect John Olmsted came to Portland to help plan the Lewis and Clark Exposition and lay out a parks plan for the young city. Reflecting Olmsted's suggestions, Washington Park has developed, over the years, to encompass large expanses of manicured lawn, great groves of evergreens, and recreational facilities. Wild as the hilly terrain is in places, however, the park also contains some of the city's best tended gardens and the always busy zoo. Scenic roadways, an extensive trail system, and even a miniature railway make it easy to explore the park and enjoy its diverse experiences. With a different story to tell each season, this park is a delight no matter when you visit.

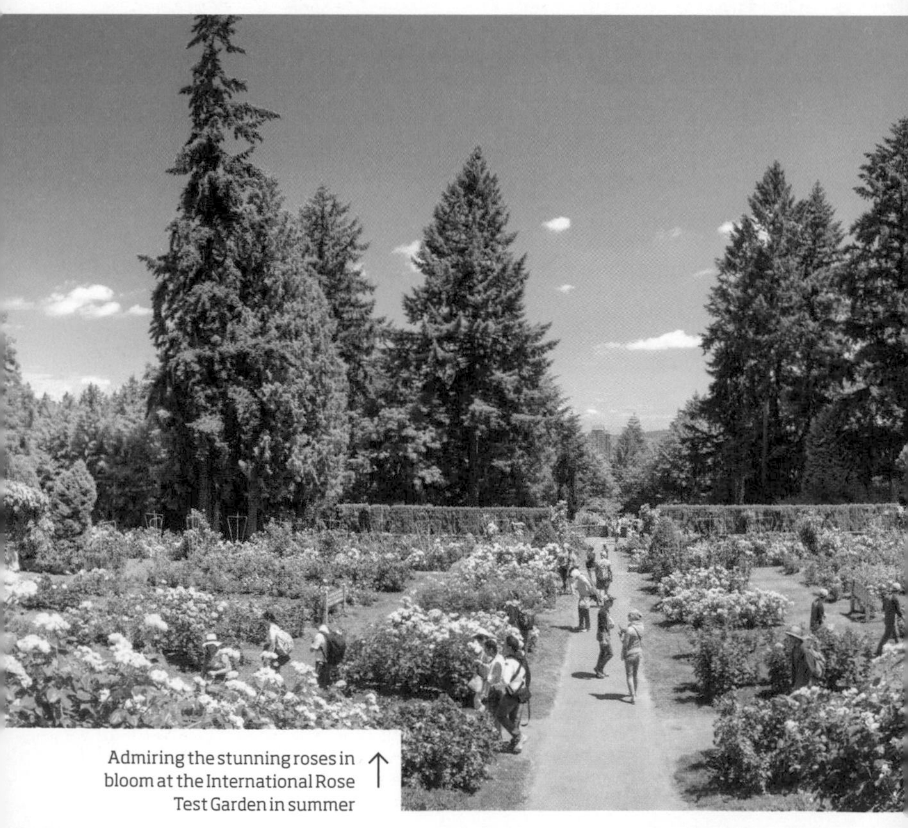

Admiring the stunning roses in bloom at the International Rose Test Garden in summer ↑

INSIDER TIP
Shuttle Along

A free way to get around the park and see as much of it as possible is the Explore Washington Park shuttle. This runs a loop every 15 minutes inside the park throughout the year. From May till October it runs daily, 9:30am–7pm; from November till April it runs on weekends only, 10am–4pm.

Seasonal Guide

Spring

▶ Washington Park awakes from its slumber in spring, with birds chirping on their spring migration and lush gardens coming into bloom in an array of glorious colors. March is a good time to visit the Japanese Garden to see the cherry blossom trees in their bright pink hues, while in May the International Rose Test Garden *(right)* starts to come into its own, with roses from all over the world flowering right through into September. Magnolias, bell-shaped Oregon plum flowers, and blossoming dogwood color the Hoyt Arboretum, too.

Summer

While summer is not assuredly sunny in Portland, the warm weather offers the perfect opportunity for entertainment in the splendid open spaces. The Washington Park Festival takes place every summer (generally over a weekend, typically in July or August) and is the highlight of the season, with art and crafts, dance, and a series of free music concerts put on in the Rose Garden Amphitheater. It's also a good chance to cherish the garden's 1,000 roses, which are in full bloom, and provides the perfect soundtrack to a picnic. Summer also sees the park's sporting facilities getting the most use, with its soccer pitches, tennis courts and archery range always heaving with locals and visitors.

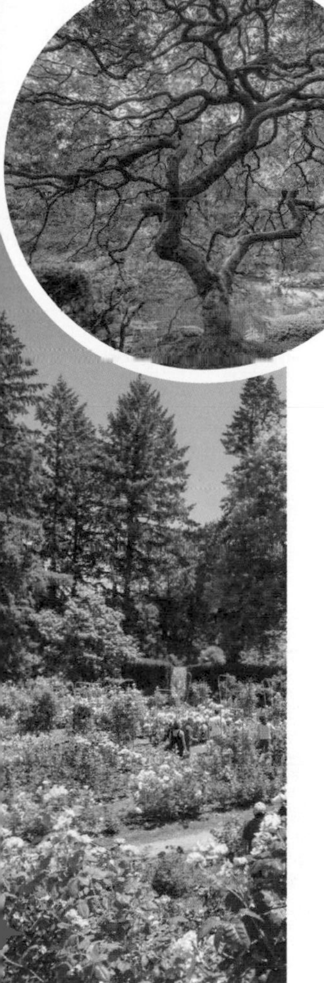

Autumn

◀ Fall foliage is spectacular in the park, as brilliant reds and yellows stand out against evergreens. Milder temperatures and crisp autumn air shape the perfect season for leaf crunching hikes. Leaf-peepers will love the Hoyt Arboretum, where the trees burst into their vivid autumnal colors. The best way to explore the garden is with a map, helping you to spot the likes of holly, fir, and magnolias as you amble along any of the 21 trails. This is also the most breathtaking time to visit - and photograph - the Portland Japanese Garden *(left)*, when the bright crimson, fiery shades of Japanese maples reflected in the glistening ponds inaugurate a foliage spectacle.

Winter

▶ Though short days tend to meet with rainy weather in winter, Christmas celebrations and white snow blanketing the landscape provide a cheerful glow in the park. A stroll through Hoyt Arboretum's Winter Garden will prove enchanting in the day, with the bare bones of trees and ornamental plants providing a unique topography and winter colors. Evenings are especially stunning, though. Families should check out the ZooLights, where more than 1.5 million lights bring the zoo to life. There's also an illuminated train and carousel, carolers, and local food carts, and little ones can even get a photo with Santa. For the adults, the zoo also puts on a BrewLights evening, where local cider and beer provide the perfect antidote to a cold winter night.

① 

World Forestry Center Discovery Museum

4033 SW Canyon Rd
10am-5pm daily
Thanksgiving, Dec 25
worldforestry.org

Trees steal the show at this museum devoted to the world's forests. On the main floor is a grove of trees native to the area. Upstairs, photographs explore old-growth forests. The Global Forest exhibit, featuring the sights, sounds, and smells of each world forest, is worth a visit.

②

Oregon Holocaust Memorial

95205 SW Washington Way 5am-midnight daily ojmche.org

This powerful and moving memorial includes shoes, a teddy bear, and a suitcase to represent the everyday objects Holocaust victims often left behind when they were removed from their homes. There's also a panel with remarks from Holocaust survivors, beneath which are soil and ashes taken from six concentration camps.

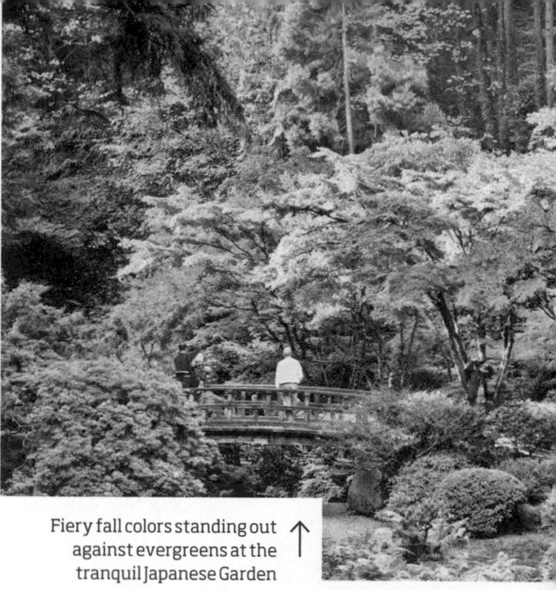

Fiery fall colors standing out against evergreens at the tranquil Japanese Garden

③  

Oregon Zoo

4001 SW Canyon Rd
9:30am-4pm daily (Jun-Aug: to 6pm daily) Dec 25
oregonzoo.org

More than 1,800 mammals, reptiles, invertebrates, and birds live in the zoo, many in spacious, naturalistic habitats. Home to the largest breeding herd of elephants in captivity, Oregon Zoo is noted for its efforts to perpetuate some 19 endangered and 9 threatened species. The Cascade exhibit provides a look at the animals that roam the Pacific Northwest wilds.

④    

Japanese Garden

611 SW Kingston Dr
Apr-Sep: 10am-7pm daily; Oct-Mar: 10am-4pm daily (Mon: from noon year-round) Jan 1, Thanksgiving, Dec 25 japanesegarden.org

This lovely, manicured landscape is one of the most authentic Japanese gardens outside of Japan and is one of the most tranquil spots in Portland. Designed by noted Japanese landscape architect Takuma Tono, meticulously tended plantings surround ponds, streams, and pavilions.

TOP 3 TRAILS IN THE PARK

Wildwood Trail
This 30-mile (48-km) trail runs the length of the park.

Hoyt Arboretum Trail
Appreciate more than 8,000 trees and shrubs along 12 miles (19 km) of hiking trails.

Washington Park Loop Trail
A family-friendly 3-mile (5-km) trail linking many attractions.

Climbing on large marble sculptures by Jim Gion at the park's Oregon Zoo

Paths wind through five distinct landscapes: the Flat Garden, a typical urban garden; the Tea Garden, built around a ceremonial teahouse; the Strolling Pond Garden, where bridges cross carp-filled pools; the Natural Garden, where shrubs, ferns, and mosses grow in their natural state; and the Sand and Stone Gardens, in which raked gravel simulates the sea and plantings depict a sake cup and gourd.

---

5   

Portland Children's Museum

4015 SW Canyon Rd
9am-5pm daily
portlandcm.org

When it was established in 1949, the Portland Children's Museum was one of the first of its kind in the US. Today the museum offers a wide range of exhibits geared to kids under the age of 10. "Play" is the operative word here, as youngsters turn cranks to send water cascading through Water Works, use their nurturing instincts at the Pet Hospital, and learn about herbs, fruit, and vegetables in the Zany Maze.

6 

Hoyt Arboretum

4000 SW Fairview Blvd
5am-10pm daily **hoyt arboretum.org**

Home to more than 6,000 trees and plants from around the world, this living museum is an oasis year-round. It aims to conserve the vulnerable and endangered species that live in its groves and meadows. The visitors' center provides maps of walking trails and routes in the arboretum and detailed lists of the trees and plants to see along the way.

EAT

Umami Café

Located inside the Japanese Garden, this cafe has a very relaxing feel. Experience a Japanese tea-tasting paired with a range of tasty snacks.

SW Kingston Drive
japanesegarden.org

7

International Rose Test Garden

400 SW Kingston Dr
(503) 823-3636
7:30am-9pm daily

A magnificent treat for all those who love flowers, this is the oldest continuously operated rose test garden in the US, established in 1917. Today, 10,000 bushes and 650 species come into bloom in a spectacle of color every June. In the All-American Rose Test Garden, new varieties of roses are carefully observed for two years and evaluated for color, form, and other criteria to determine the best roses.

2

SAUVIE ISLAND

17 NW 21st Av/St. Helens Rd Sauvie Island Wildlife Area: 4am-10pm daily 18330 NW Sauvie Island Rd; www.sauvieisland.org

Just 10 miles (16 km) from Portland's lively downtown, at the confluence of the Willamette and Columbia rivers, is Sauvie Island. At an expanse of 26,000 acres (10,522 ha), it's one of the largest river islands in the US, and a wildlife-filled oasis away from the city.

With rich soil that supports many berry farms and orchards, the southern half of the island is primarily agricultural. Farms offer hayrides and other recreational activities that are great for families, as well as pick-your-own opportunities for a huge array of crops including peaches, strawberries, raspberries, blueberries, and herbs. The northern half is set aside as the Sauvie Island Wildlife Area, managed by the Oregon Department of Fish and Wildlife. Bird-watchers come to see some of the estimated quarter of a million birds – including swans, ducks, and cranes – that stop here on their spring and fall migrations.

During the summer, swimmers and sunbathers enjoy beaches on the island's Columbia River side, and anglers fish for sturgeon and salmon in nearby channels. There are also a number of excellent hiking trails. The Oak Island Nature Trail skirts around the Oak Island peninsula, while the Wapato State Greenway, a circular walk around Virginia Lake, is terrific for bird-watching as you go. With its ripe berry crops, Sauvie Island is a prime spot for wine tasting, too. Cherry wines and ciders provide the perfect complement to a hot summer's day, and can be tasted and bought at the Bella Organic Farm, along with delicious jams.

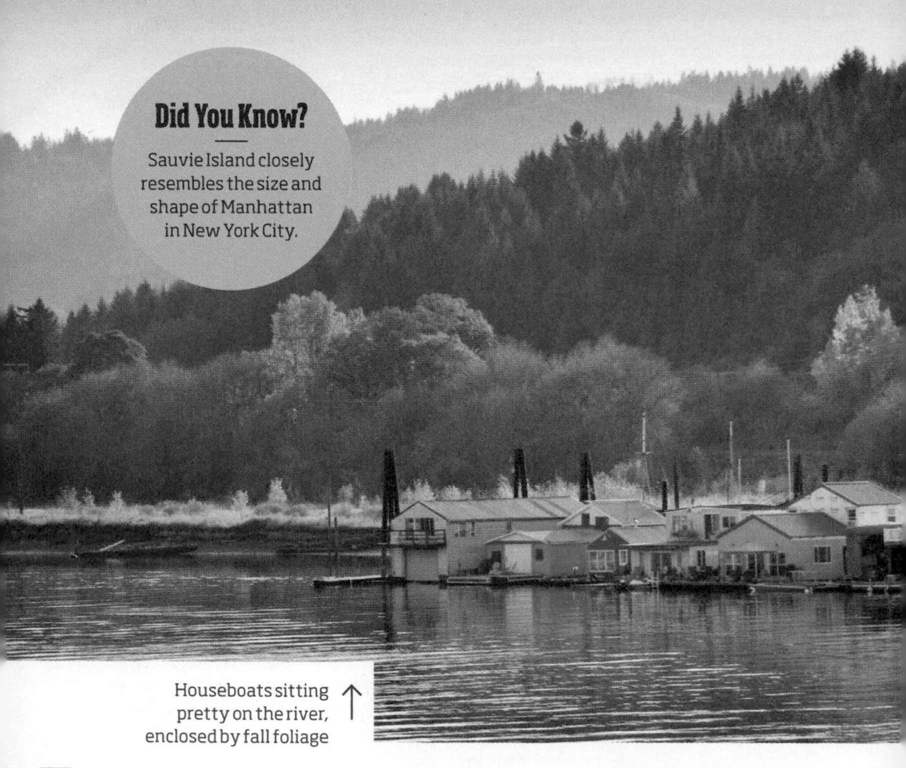

Did You Know?

Sauvie Island closely resembles the size and shape of Manhattan in New York City.

Houseboats sitting pretty on the river, enclosed by fall foliage

A towhee, one of the many birds who migrate here, perched on a branch

Harvesting crops on a charming, small organic farm in the early morning on leafy Sauvie Island

TOP 3 U-PICK FARMS ON SAUVIE ISLAND

Bella Organic Farm
16205 NW Gillihan Rd
bellaorganic.com
A family-run farm featuring a corn maze, a pumpkin patch, and a winery. U-picking for various berries runs from June to August.

Blue Bee Farm
20541 NW Sauvie Island Rd
bluebeefarm.net
This blueberry farm grows six varieties that extend the picking season from early July to the fall.

Douglas Farm
15330 NW Sauvie Island Rd
douglasfarmu-pick.com
There's almost always something you can pick here as the farm grows a wide range of crops including apples, pears, and many vegetables.

EXPERIENCE MORE

3   

Pittock Mansion

3229 NW Pittock Dr ■ 10am–4pm daily (Jun–Aug: to 5pm) Jan, Thanksgiving, Dec 25 & major hols pittock mansion.org

Henry Pittock, who came west on the Oregon Trail *(p32)* as a young man and published the *Oregonian* newspaper, commissioned this mansion in 1909. Designed by San Francisco architect Edward T. Foulkes, the house is still the grandest residence in Portland. Perched on a 1,000-ft (305-m) summit in the West Hills, it commands superb views of the city and snowcapped mountain peaks.

Guided tours, including self-guided tours, show off the mansion's remarkable embellishments, including a marble staircase, elliptical drawing room, and circular Turkish-style smoking room. The furnishings, though not original to the house, reflect the finest tastes of Pittock's time.

A good time to visit is in the build-up to Christmas when the house is spectacularly decorated, with trees in many of the rooms and a themed exhibition. There are also special events throughout the year, including regular "Behind the Scenes" tours.

Did You Know?

The Pittock Mansion took five years to build and had luxuries that included a walk-in fridge.

4

Eastbank Esplanade

Bounded by Willamette River & I-5, Steel & Hawthorne bridges Rose Quarter 

This pedestrian and bicycle path following the east bank of the Willamette River between the Hawthorne and Steel bridges was part of a massive riverfront redevelopment. While its unobstructed views of downtown Portland and the opportunity to enjoy the river make it worth a visit, the walkway is an attraction in its own right. A 1,200-ft (365-m) section floats on the water, and a cantilevered portion is suspended above one of the city's original commercial piers.

The esplanade provides access to four of the city's major downtown bridges, linking the walkway to Governor Tom McCall Waterfront Park *(p89)* on the west bank of the river.

5

Nob Hill

W Burnside to NW Pettygrove sts, from NW 17th to NW 24th sts To NW 23rd St

Also known as Northwest 23rd in reference to its main business street, Nob Hill is a gracious, late 19th-century neighborhood of leafy streets, apartment

↑ The imposing Pittock Mansion surrounded by lush grounds

→ Flowers in bloom beside a lake at Crystal Springs Rhododendron Garden

buildings, and large wooden houses. With its proximity to downtown and its inherent charms, Nob Hill has become one of the city's most popular commercial and residential neighborhoods. A slightly bohemian atmosphere, together with upscale shops and restaurants, make Nob Hill a pleasant place to stroll.

Northwest 23rd Street from West Burnside to Northwest Lovejoy streets is the neighborhood's commercial core. The side streets are lined with lovely old houses. The 1892 Victorian gingerbread Pettygrove House *(2287 Northwest Pettygrove Street)* was the home of Francis Pettygrove, the city founder who won a coin toss against fellow founder Asa Lovejoy to determine the city's name (Lovejoy preferred "Boston").

Rose Quarter

1 Center Ct Rose Quarter rosequarter.com

Portland's major venues for sports, conventions, and big-ticket entertainment events are clustered in the Rose Quarter, a commercial riverside area on the east bank of the Willamette River. Locals come in droves to the otherwise quiet neighborhood to attend Portland Trail Blazers basketball games, Portland Winterhawks ice hockey games, and major pop and rock concerts at the fantastic Moda Center.

The smaller, nearby Veterans Memorial Coliseum *(300 N Winning Way)* once hosted these events. Its glass-fronted hall is now used for trade shows and conventions, and is the primary home for the Winterhawks WHL team.

The Lloyd Center, east of the Rose Quarter, is recognized as the USA's first covered shopping center. The Lloyd Center has an old-fashioned charm, with nearly 200 shops and restaurants lining handsome, well-planted walkways that radiate from a skating rink that is open year-round.

Crystal Springs Rhododendron Garden

SE 28th Av & SE Woodstock Blvd (503) 771-8386 6am-10pm daily (Oct-Mar: to 6pm)

This garden is laced with trails that cross streams, pass beneath misty cascades, and circle a spring-fed lake attracting ducks, geese, herons, and other waterfowl. The garden erupts into a breathtaking blaze of color during spring through to early summer, when hundreds of species of rare rhododendrons and azaleas – one of the world's leading collections of these woodland plants – are in bloom. Entry to the garden is free on Mondays and October through March.

EAT

Blue Star Donuts

Decadent sweet treats with unique flavors, such as Mexican hot chocolate.

3753 N Mississippi Av
bluestardonuts.com

St. Honoré Bakery

Enjoy a croissant or a slice of quiche at this French bakery.

2335 NW Thurman St
sainthonore bakery.com

Salt & Straw

Unusual but delicious ice-cream flavors, like pear and blue cheese, are on offer at this branch.

3345 SE Division St
saltandstraw.com

DRINK

Hopworks Urban Brewery
This microbrewery is one of the best places for sampling delicious, powerful local brews.
2944 SE Powell Blvd
hopworksbeer.com

Doug Fir Lounge
Open 365 days a year, this is the perfect place for a Sunday brunch with cocktails or their draft beers. There's also live music every night downstairs.
830 E Burnside St
dougfirlounge.com

The Lamp
Try to catch a show at this former vaudeville theater followed by a drink in its bar, which also has sidewalk tables.
Aladdin Theater, 3017 SE Milwaukie Av
lamppdx.com

McMenamins Bagdad Theater & Pub
Head to this bar for a wide range of local beers and ciders, and flights from local distilleries, before taking in a movie in the ornate theater.
3702 SE Hawthorne Blvd mcmenamins.com/bagdad-theater-pub

Stumptown Coffee Roasters
No trip to Portland is complete without trying a delicious Stumptown brew at their original location.
4525 SE Division St
stumptowncoffee.com

8

Sellwood District

SE 13th to SE 17th avs, from SE Tacoma St to SE Bybee Blvd

Sellwood, a quiet residential neighborhood on a bluff above the Willamette River in the southeast corner of the city, has become the antiques center of Portland. Long gone are the days when Sellwood was a bargain-hunter's paradise, but shoppers continue to descend upon Sellwood's 30 or so antique shops – many of which occupy old Victorian houses along Southeast 13th Avenue, known as Antique Row. You can then enjoy a meal in one of the area's many restaurants or in the adjoining Westmoreland neighborhood.

The riverbank just below the Sellwood bluff is made festive by the presence of the Ferris wheel, roller coaster, roller-skating rink, and other attractions of Oaks Park, a shady amusement park that opened during the 1905 Lewis and Clark Exposition*(p82)*.

HIDDEN GEM
Oregon Rail Heritage Center
This museum *(2250 SE Water Av)* is only an 8-minute walk from Southeast Division Street and has three steam locomotives, two of them working, and other cool railway items on display.

9

Southeast Division Street

SE Division St corridor, from SE 19th St to SE 45th St

Not long ago, Southeast Division Street was a thoroughfare known for hardware shops, auto-body repair and seedy bars. However, a series of high-profile restaurants have opened, making this stretch the hottest area on the Portland dining scene. It began in 2005 with

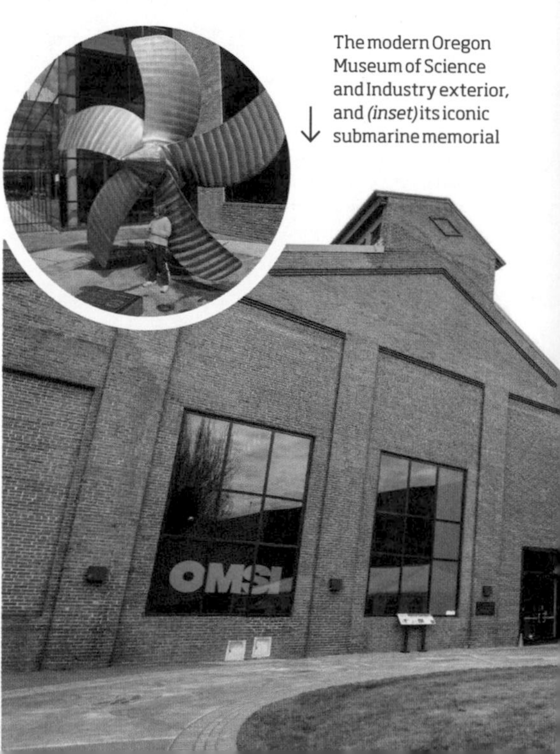

The modern Oregon Museum of Science and Industry exterior, and *(inset)* its iconic submarine memorial

Andy Ricker's wildly popular Thai cocktail and snack shack, Pok Pok, which has since inspired a bestselling cookbook. The culinary streak has intensified with exciting, quirky farm-to-table concept restaurants and cafes springing up one after another. From old-world Italian at Ava Gene's to small-batch ice cream in experimental, savory flavors at Salt & Straw, restaurant-hop your way down this street full of "it" eats.

Oregon Museum of Science and Industry

1945 SE Water Av
OMSI/SE Water Av
A Loop Jun-Aug: 9:30am-7pm daily; Sep-May: 9:30am-5:30pm Tue-Sun Major hols
omsi.edu

Commonly referred to as OMSI, the Oregon Museum of Science and Industry is one of the top science museums in the US. The multiple exhibition halls and science labs of this world-class tourist attraction house hundreds of interactive exhibits. You can enjoy hands-on experiences in subjects such as physics, space exploration, computers, chemistry, and mathematics. A favorite is the earthquake simulator, in which visitors are shaken and rattled while learning about the tectonic plates that continue to shift beneath Portland.

The Kendall Planetarium, a state-of-the-art facility, places OMSI at the forefront of astronomical education. For kids under nine, the Science Playground is a wonderland with interactive zones. The Empirical Theater, four stories tall, is the largest screen in Portland and shows various science-themed documentaries and feature films.

Moored alongside the museum is the USS *Blueback*, first launched in 1959 and the last diesel submarine to be used by the US Navy. Guided tours provide a chance to look at downtown through a periscope and to experience the claustrophobic conditions in which 85 submariners lived.

Hawthorne District

NE Hawthorne Blvd, from SE 17th to SE 39th sts

An east-side residential and business area somewhat reminiscent of parts of Berkeley, California, the Hawthorne District is bustling with young people, many of whom attend nearby Reed College *(p104)*. Hawthorne Boulevard is lined with coffeehouses, clothing boutiques, bookstores, bakeries, delis, and restaurants serving a range of cuisines, including Vietnamese, East Indian, Lebanese, and Ethiopian. Buskers add their sounds to the area's vibrant street scene.

↑ Hawthorne Boulevard in Portland's vibrant Hawthorne District

The district's surrounding residential neighborhoods, dating from the early 20th century, were among Portland's first so-called "streetcar suburbs." Of these, Ladd's Addition is one of the oldest planned communities in the western US. Built in a circular grid of streets that surround five rose gardens, the plan was considered radical when it was laid out in 1939. Today, the area features many styles of 20th-century architecture: Bungalow, Craftsman, Mission, Colonial Revival, and Tudor.

To the east, Hawthorne Boulevard ascends the slopes of Mount Tabor, an extinct volcano whose crater is now surrounded by a forested park, popular with picnickers. Walking trails can be found throughout the park.

A covered wagon at the End of the Oregon Trail Interpretive Center

12 

End of the Oregon Trail Interpretive Center

1726 Washington St, Oregon City 9:30am-5pm daily (from 10:30am Sun; last entry 1 hour before closing) Jan 1, Thanksgiving, Dec 25 historicoregoncity.org

Although many of the pioneers who crossed the country on the Oregon Trail went their separate ways once they reached eastern Oregon, for those who continued west across the Cascade Mountains, Abernethy Green near Oregon City was the end of the trail. Here they stocked up on provisions and set up farmsteads in the fertile Willamette Valley.

The End of the Oregon Trail Interpretive Center tells the story of life on the trail. Exhibits of heirlooms, the *Bound for Oregon* feature film, as well as hands-on experiences and pioneer crafts, such as packing a wagon and candle dipping, bring past hardships to life. You can also take a guided walk of one-thousandth of the trail.

NORTHWEST MODERN

During the mid-20th century the US was having an architectural revolution. Portland was fortunate enough to have several visionary architects who designed not only public buildings but private homes too. The use of lots of wood and floor-to-ceiling glass windows became known as Northwest Modern. Many examples remain, and others have been restored, especially in some of the neighborhoods around Reed.

13

Reed College

3203 SE Woodstock Blvd  **Dawn-dusk daily reed.edu**

Founded in 1908 with a bequest from Oregon pioneers Simeon and Amanda Reed, Reed College occupies a wooded campus at the edge of Eastmoreland, one of Portland's most beautiful residential neighborhoods. Reed College's brick Tudor Gothic buildings, along with others designed in traditional Northwest timber style, are set amid rolling lawns. These lawns surround the "canyon," a wooded wetland; shade is provided by 125 species of maples, cedars, and other trees.

Reed College occupies a wooded campus at the edge of Eastmoreland, one of Portland's most beautiful residential neighborhoods.

14

Oregon City

 **1726 Washington St, Oregon City; (503) 657-9336**

Terminus of the Oregon Trail and capital of the Oregon Territory from 1849 to 1852, Oregon City's past prominence is largely due to its location beside the 40-ft (12-m) Willamette Falls, which powered flour and paper mills. The mills brought prosperity to the city, which was the site of the first meeting of the territory's provisional legislature, in 1843. The **Museum of the Oregon Territory** traces the history from the days when John

McLoughlin, an Englishman sympathetic to the cause of bringing Oregon into the US, settled the town in 1829. In 1846, the "Father of Oregon" built the then-grandest home in Oregon, now the **McLoughlin House**, a unit of Fort Vancouver National Historic Site.

Museum of the Oregon Territory
211 Tumwater Dr 10:30am–4:30pm Wed-Sat Major hols clackamas history.org

McLoughlin House
713 Center St 10am-4pm Fri & Sat Mid-Dec-Jan & major hols mcloughlin house.org

Aurora

Old Aurora Colony Museum; (503) 678-5754

The town of Aurora traces its roots to the Aurora Colony, a Utopian community founded by Prussian immigrant William Keil in 1852. Similar to Shaker communities in the east, it was a collective society based on the principles of Christian fundamentalism and shared property. The colony thrived for more than a decade, until it was decimated by a smallpox epidemic. Exhibits tracing the colony's history fill the **Old Aurora Colony Museum**'s handsome white-frame buildings. Many of Aurora's other historic buildings now house antique shops.

Nearby **Champoeg State Heritage Area** is the site of an 1843 convention at which settlers voted to break from Britain and establish a provisional American government in Oregon. By that time, Champoeg was a thriving trading post on the banks of the Willamette River, having been established by the Hudson's Bay Company in 1813. The town that grew up around the trading post was abandoned as a result of devastating floods in 1861 and 1890; the park now comprises of meadows and stately stands of oaks and evergreens.

Displays in the visitor center pay tribute to the Kalapuya American Indians, who once lived here on the banks of the river, and to the traders and pioneers who came in the wake of the Hudson's Bay settlement. Its historic buildings include a jail, a schoolhouse, a barn, and some early dwellings.

Old Aurora Colony Museum
15018 2nd St NE Feb-Dec: 11am-4pm Tue-Sat, noon-4pm Sun Jan, major hols aurora colony.org

Champoeg State Heritage Area
Rte 99 W, 12 miles (7.5 km) W of Aurora (503) 678-1251 Dawn-dusk daily

SHOP

Aurora Mills Architectural Salvage
Seek out vintage paintings, lighting equipment, antique and reclaimed furniture, and industrial items in this 19th-century mill complex.
14971 1st St NE, Aurora (503) 678-6083 Mon

You Can Leave Your Hat On
You can find unique hats for men and women at this friendly and upbeat shop. It also stocks beautiful scarves, handbags, fans, and other items.
212 7th St, Oregon City mercantile portland.com

→ Perusing the items on sale at one of Aurora's stores

OREGON

The home of American Indians, such as the Chinook, Bannock, Klamath, Nez Perce, and Killamuk, Oregon was contested territory well into the 1800s. The Americans pressed their claim to what was now being called Oregon Territory (the origin of the name remains a mystery), after the expedition of Lewis and Clark in 1805. Great Britain and the US initially shared control, but the large numbers of American settlers arriving from the 1830s made Britain's claims unrealistic, and in 1846 the country gave up its claim. Oregon became a state in 1859 and began its economic ascent in the 1880s when the transcontinental railroad reached Portland.

Despite its sometimes harsh climate, people were drawn to Oregon's rugged grandeur and fertile land. This growth in population resulted in a growth in industry, which continued during World War II, when Oregon was a base for wartime shipbuilding. In recent years the state has become known for its libertarian values, being among the first in the US to legalize gay marriage, assisted suicide, and the recreational use of marijuana.

The wilderness of the Wallowa Mountains reflected in Sunshine Lake

OREGON

Must Sees

1. Salem
2. Eugene
3. Bend
4. Crater Lake National Park
5. Columbia River Gorge
6. Mount Hood

Experience More

7. Astoria
8. Cannon Beach
9. Steens Mountain
10. Newport
11. Yachats
12. McMinnville
13. Florence
14. Lincoln City
15. Oregon Dunes National Recreation Area
16. Tillamook
17. Three Capes Scenic Route
18. Smith Rock State Park
19. Cape Perpetua Scenic Area
20. Silverton
21. Oregon Caves National Monument & Preserve
22. Bandon
23. Sisters
24. Pendleton
25. Newberry National Volcanic Monument
26. Jordan Valley
27. Madras and Warm Springs
28. Ashland
29. Joseph
30. Wallowa Lake
31. John Day Fossil Beds National Monument
32. Jacksonville
33. Malheur National Wildlife Refuge

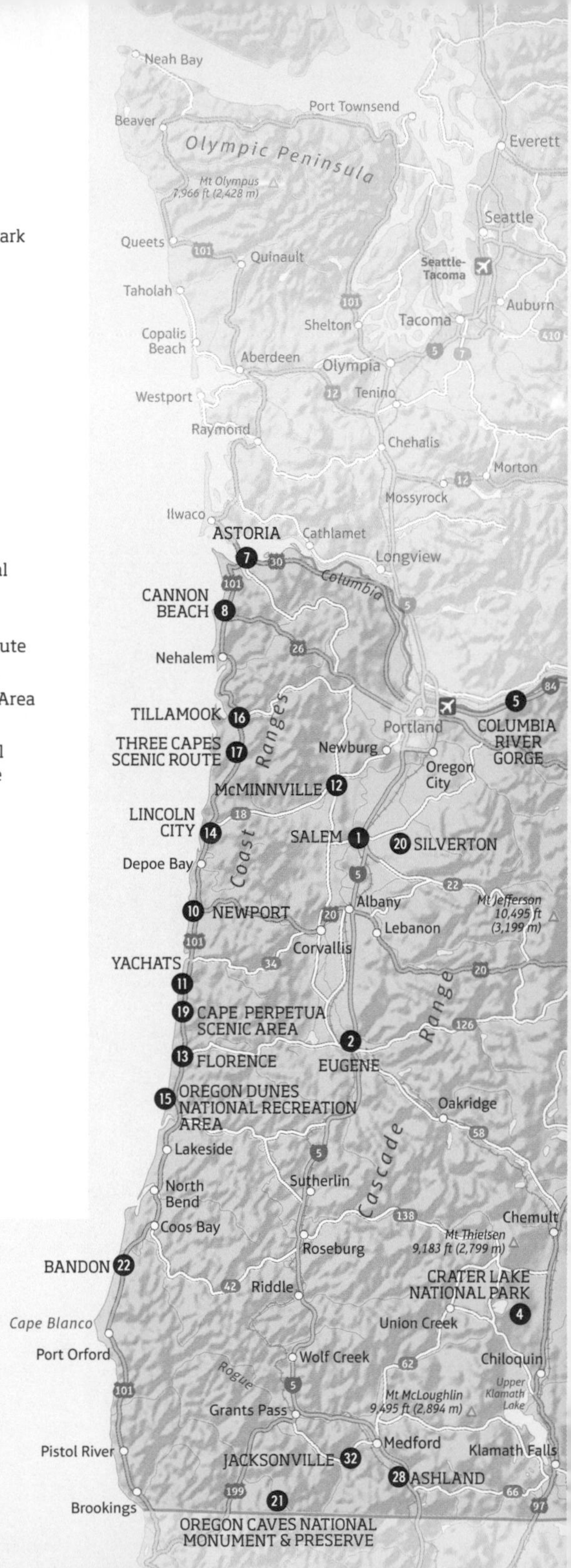

0 kilometers 60

0 miles 60

N

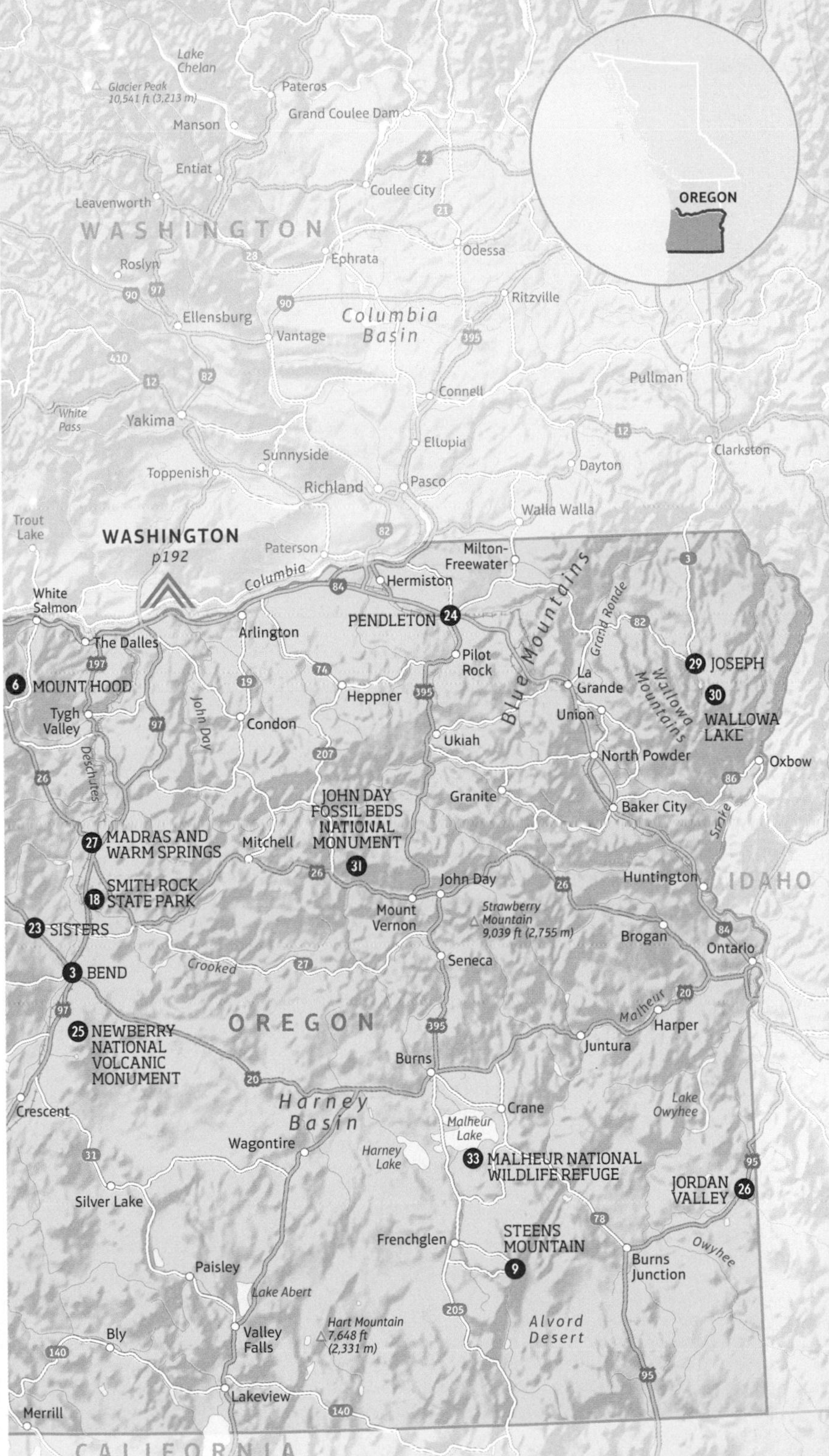
OREGON
WASHINGTON
Lake Chelan
Glacier Peak 10,541 ft (3,213 m)
Pateros
Grand Coulee Dam
Manson
Entiat
Coulee City
Leavenworth
Ephrata
Odessa
Roslyn
Ritzville
Ellensburg
Columbia Basin
Vantage
Pullman
Yakima
White Pass
Connell
Ellopia
Clarkston
Sunnyside
Dayton
Toppenish
Richland
Pasco
Walla Walla
Trout Lake
WASHINGTON p192
Paterson
Milton-Freewater
Columbia
Hermiston
White Salmon
PENDLETON
Blue Mountains
Grand Ronde
Arlington
The Dalles
Pilot Rock
JOSEPH
MOUNT HOOD
Heppner
La Grande
Wallowa Mountains
WALLOWA LAKE
Tygh Valley
John Day
Condon
Union
Ukiah
North Powder
Oxbow
Deschutes
JOHN DAY FOSSIL BEDS NATIONAL MONUMENT
Granite
Baker City
Snake
MADRAS AND WARM SPRINGS
Mitchell
Huntington
IDAHO
SMITH ROCK STATE PARK
John Day
Mount Vernon
Strawberry Mountain 9,039 ft (2,755 m)
SISTERS
Brogan
Ontario
BEND
Crooked
Seneca
Malheur
Harper
NEWBERRY NATIONAL VOLCANIC MONUMENT
OREGON
Juntura
Burns
Crescent
Harney Basin
Crane
Lake Owyhee
Malheur Lake
Wagontire
Harney Lake
MALHEUR NATIONAL WILDLIFE REFUGE
JORDAN VALLEY
Silver Lake
Frenchglen
STEENS MOUNTAIN
Owyhee
Paisley
Burns Junction
Lake Abert
Alvord Desert
Bly
Valley Falls
Hart Mountain 7,648 ft (2,331 m)
Lakeview
Merrill
CALIFORNIA

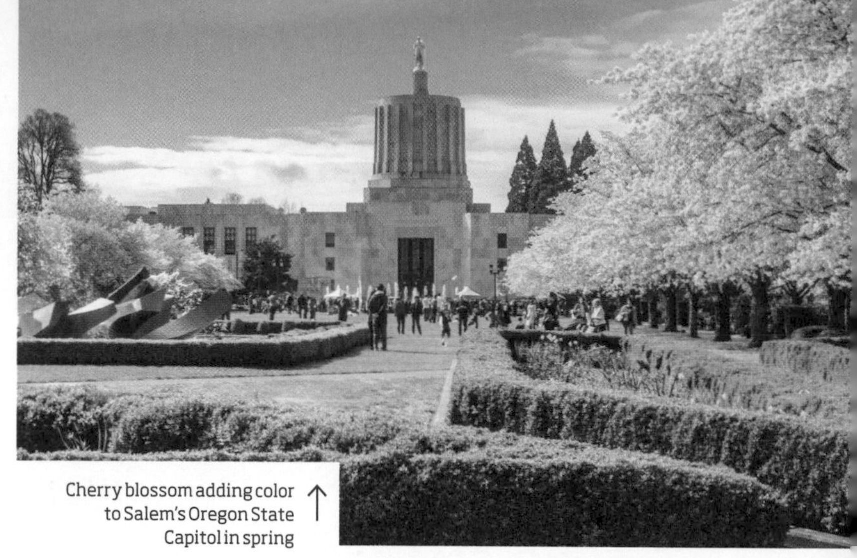

Cherry blossom adding color to Salem's Oregon State Capitol in spring

SALEM

A4 388 State St; www.travelsalem.com

Salem may not be as well known to visitors as Portland but, thanks in part to its location on the Willamette River which runs through the city, it has a lot going for it. Oregon's second city and state capital since 1851, Salem's fascinating history can be explored in its illuminating museums, grand estates, and historic homes. Home also to Willamette University, the student population here provides a contemporary balance and a lively, thriving social scene.

Riverfront Park

200 Water St NE Dawn-dusk daily cityofsalem.net

This 23-acre (9-ha) park alongside the Willamette River is a popular place with locals, offering beautiful river views and an amphitheater that hosts regular concerts. A big attraction for children is the Riverfront Carousel, which has 42 hand-carved wooden horses, as well as a children's museum. Look out for the *Eco-Earth Globe* sculpture, created by local artists using a former acid storage ball.

Bush House Museum

600 Mission St SE For tours: Apr-Sep 1-4pm Thu-Sun bushhousemuseum.org

Located in Bush's Pasture Park, this house was built for newspaper magnate Asahel Bush, who lived there from 1878 till his death in 1913. It opened as a museum in 1953 and retains many original features and furniture, giving an intriguing look at the life of a wealthy local family. Also on the grounds is a conservatory, and the park includes a rose garden and playgrounds.

Oregon State Capitol

900 Court St NE 8am-5pm Mon-Fri oregonlegislature.gov

Oregon's third state capitol was completed in 1938, after the first two were destroyed by fire. A gilded pioneer stands atop the rotunda of the building and marble sculptures of Lewis and Clark and a covered wagon with a map of the Oregon Trail on it flank the entrance. Whether touring the interior yourself or joining one of the regular guided tours, you'll be rewarded with stunning murals that depict Captain Robert Gray's discovery of the Columbia River in 1792, as well as other historic paintings and sculptures.

HIDDEN GEM

Enchanted Forest

This charming family-owned theme park has attractions like a western town where you can pan for gold and regular live shows. Visit www.enchantedforest.com for more details.

Waller Hall

950 State St 8am-5pm Mon-Fri willamette.edu

On the Willamette University campus is Waller Hall, the oldest college building in Oregon, completed in 1867. This grand building, home to the university's administrative office, is designed in the shape of a Greek cross, which makes it symmetrical from whichever way you look at it. It has been on the National Register of Historic Places since 1975.

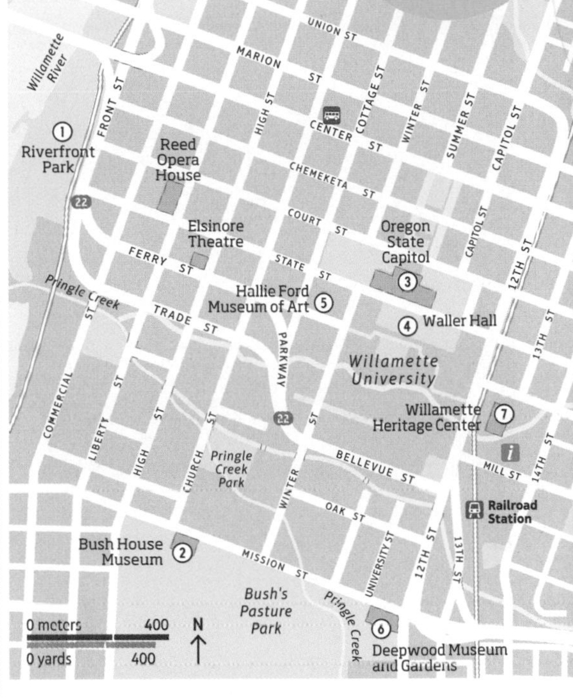

5   

Hallie Ford Museum of Art

700 State St 10am-5pm Tue-Sat, 1-5pm Sun Major hols willamette.edu

The third-largest art museum in the state, the Hallie Ford Museum of Art houses an outstanding collection of 20th-century American Indian basketry. There's also an impressive number of Oregon-related historical items and pieces of art from around the world in its permanent collection. Its six galleries also showcase work from regional artists.

Deepwood Museum and Gardens

1116 Mission St SE For tours: 9am-noon Wed-Sat deepwoodmuseum.org

Built in 1894 by Dr Luke A. Port, this was one of the most impressive houses in Salem at the time, though Port and his family would only live there for 16 months. He sold the house to the Bingham family, who lived in it until 1924, followed by the Brown-Powell family who lived there until 1968. The house was then put up for sale and the citizens of Salem came together to save the house for the city, turning it into a history museum and community asset. The grounds cover 5 acres (2 ha) and have both formal gardens and a nature area with a nature trail.

Willamette Heritage Center

1313 Mill St SE 10am-5pm Mon-Sat willamette heritage.org

This 5-acre (2-ha) site preserves some of the state's earliest structures: the 1841 home of Jason Lee, who helped found Salem; the 1847 home of state treasurer John Boon; and the Kay Woolen Mill, where waterwheels from the 1890s remain intact. There are 14 historic structures on the site, including a railway *caboose* (a carriage at the back of a train for crew accommodations) from 1909, so allow plenty of time for a visit. There's also a library, both permanent and temporary exhibitions, shops, art galleries, artists' studios, and a textile learning center.

TOP 3 FARMERS' MARKETS

Salem Saturday Market
865 Marion St NE Daily
Over 150 stalls, held near the State Capitol.

Monday Hospital Market
880 Oak St SE May-Sep: 9:30am-1:30pm Mon
Browse crafts and fresh local produce.

West Salem Farmers' Market
1260 Edgewater St NW May-Sep: 9:30am-1:30pm Thu
Vendors include several farms and bakeries.

↑ The colorful city of Eugene surrounded by dense forest

2

EUGENE

A5 754 Olive St; www.eugenecascadescoast.org

Beautifully located where the Willamette and McKenzie rivers meet, Eugene was founded in the mid-19th century when a settler, Eugene Franklin Skinner, built a log cabin on what is now Skinner Butte Park. Today, Eugene is Oregon's third-largest city and lives up to its reputation as a great city for the arts and outdoors. It has an alternative vibe to it, with unique museums, cultural events throughout the year, and gorgeous woodlands inviting scenic strolls.

TOP 3 FESTIVALS IN EUGENE

Oregon Truffle Festival
Go truffle-hunting (and enjoy eating your finds) in late January.

Oregon Asian Celebration
A weekend celebration of the arts, culture, food, and drink of the Asian nations in mid-February.

Oregon Bach Festival
Celebrate Bach's musical legacy with lectures and concerts in June and July.

1

Hult Center for the Performing Arts

1 Eugene Center hult center.org

This peak-roofed, glass-and-timber center, designed by the New York firm Hardy Holzman Pfeiffer Associates and completed in 1982, is considered to be one of the best-designed performing arts complexes in the world. It has a large concert hall and a smaller venue, and is home to Eugene's ballet, choir, opera, and other musical groups. There are also art exhibitions, drama, and touring shows.

2 

Cascades Raptor Center

32275 Fox Hollow Rd 10am-4pm Tue-Sun cascadesraptorcenter.org

This excellent place is well worth a visit to both see and support the work they are doing. It's also a rehabilitation center and a wildlife hospital. Injured birds are looked after and restored to health, and helped to return to the wild. There are also about 50 birds that have been unable to survive in the wild and these are kept in large aviaries where they can fly free.

3   

5th Street Public Market

High and 5th sts 10am-7pm Mon-Sat, 11am-5pm Sun 5stmarket.com

This collection of shops and restaurants in a converted feed mill features a charming courtyard with seating and a fountain. Dining options include Greek and Thai, while upscale shops sell toys, jewelry, and more.

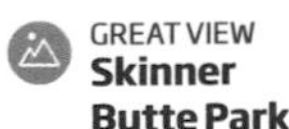

GREAT VIEW
Skinner Butte Park

Named for Eugene's founder, Eugene Skinner, this park is not only a lovely place to relax and wander, it also provides panoramic views over the city and to the mountains inland.

University of Oregon Museum of Natural and Cultural History

1680 E 15th Av 11am-5pm Tue-Sun (to 8pm Thu) mnch.uoregon.edu

The University of Oregon Museum of Natural and Cultural History, commonly referred to as the Natural History Museum, has origins that date back to 1876 when the university was founded. Its collections, built up over the years, are now housed in a building in the style of a Pacific Northwest traditional longhouse, and range from geology to zoology. Among its holdings are the world's oldest shoes – a pair of sandals dating from 9500 BC.

Jordan Schnitzer Museum of Art

1430 Johnson Lane Wed 11am-8pm, Thu-Sun 11am-5pm jsma.uoregon.edu

Based on the campus of the University of Oregon, this art museum opened in 1933. The collection was based around a donation by the first director, Gertrude Bass Warner, of 3,700 items from her collection of Oriental art. Today, the collection includes work from Japan, China, and Korea, as well as Europe, and, naturally, the Pacific Northwest.

Shelton McMurphey Johnson House

303 Willamette St Tue-Fri 10am-1pm, Sat-Sun 1pm-4pm smjhouse.org

This bright- turquoise house, known as The Castle on the Hill, was built in 1887. Its triple-barreled name reflects the three owners it has had since this time. Tours of the remarkable house show how it has changed over the years.

Saturday Market

8th Av and Oak St Apr-Nov: 10am-5pm Sat eugenesaturdaymarket.org

One of the best markets in the region, Eugene's Saturday Market has almost 300 vendors. It's primarily a crafts and produce market and has an International Food Court where you can feast on various cuisines, as well as live music.

↑ Picking up fresh vegetables at a farmers' market downtown

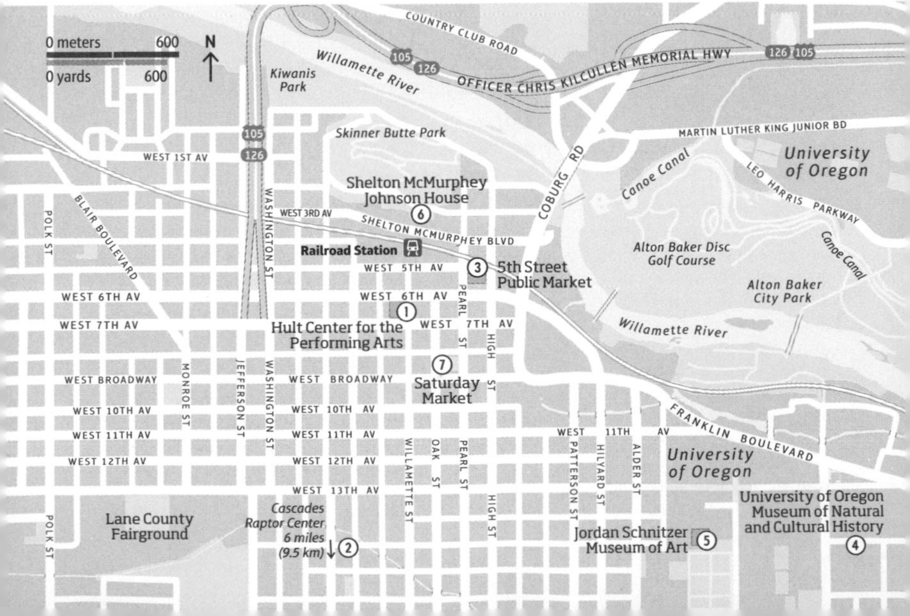

0 meters 600
0 yards 600
N
Country Club Road
Willamette River
Kiwanis Park
Officer Chris Kilcullen Memorial Hwy
Skinner Butte Park
Martin Luther King Junior BD
University of Oregon
West 1st Av
Shelton McMurphey Johnson House ⑥
Coburg Rd
Canoe Canal
Leo Harris Parkway
West 3rd Av
Shelton McMurphey Blvd
Railroad Station
Polk St
Blair Boulevard
Washington St
West 5th Av
③ 5th Street Public Market
Alton Baker Disc Golf Course
Alton Baker City Park
West 6th Av
West 7th Av
① Hult Center for the Performing Arts
Pearl St
High St
Willamette River
⑦ Saturday Market
West Broadway
Monroe St
Jefferson St
West 10th Av
West 11th Av
West 12th Av
West 13th Av
Franklin Boulevard
University of Oregon
Willamette St
Oak St
Patterson St
Hilyard St
Alder St
Lane County Fairground
Cascades Raptor Center 6 miles (9.5 km) ↓ ②
Jordan Schnitzer Museum of Art ⑤
University of Oregon Museum of Natural and Cultural History ④

3 BEND

A B5 i 750 NW Lava Rd, Suite 160; www.visitbend.com

Busy Bend, once a sleepy lumber town, is alluringly close to lakes, streams, and many other natural attractions. The nearby Cascade mountain range brings skiing within easy reach in winter, while endless river-side trails make summer hiking a past time. The city itself is also home to superlative museums and historic landmarks, but its claim to fame is down to having the most breweries per capita in the Pacific Northwest.

1 High Desert Museum

59800 S Hwy 97 Nov-Mar: 10am-4pm daily; Apr-Oct: 9am-5pm daily W highdesertmuseum.org

The High Desert Museum celebrates life in the rugged, arid High Desert terrain that covers much of central and eastern Oregon. Walk-through dioramas use dramatic lighting and sound effects in many authentic re-creations of American Indian dwellings and other scenes of desert settlement. Outdoors are replicas of a settler's cabin and a sawmill, and natural habitats, including an otter pond.

2 Deschutes Historical Museum

129 NW Idaho Av 10am-4:30pm Tue-Sat W deschuteshistory.org

Housed in the 1914 Reid School building, this local history museum was opened in 1980 after the school had closed and the building was given to Deschutes County. A re-creation of one of the original classrooms gives a fascinating insight into what life was like in the school in 1914. There are also displays on pioneers, the local timber trade, and the history of Bend.

3 Tower Theatre

835 NW Wall St Box office: 10am-5pm Mon-Fri W towertheatre.org

The historic Tower Theatre is as busy now as when it opened in 1940. It closed briefly in 1993, and again in 1996, until it was bought by the city of Bend, renovated with modern equipment, and reopened in 2004. Today it's a hub of the local community and hosts drama productions, comedy shows, movies, music concerts, and lectures.

DESCHUTES RIVER TRAIL

The scenic, popular 8.5-mile (14-km) Deschutes River Trail is actually a network of trails that can be done in various combinations, ranging from easy to challenging. The trailhead is in Farewell Bend Park *(1000 SW Reed Market Rd)* from where you can go east or west, crossing the river several times before looping back to the start.

↑ The pristine wilderness surrounding Bend and the Deschutes River

④

Drake Park

⌂777 NW Riverside Blvd
◷5am-10pm daily Ⓦbendparksandrec.org

The lovely Drake Park covers 13 acres (5 ha) and is part of the Drake Park Historic Neighborhood. A popular park feature is Mirror Pond, which is part of the Deschutes River and provides plenty of riverfront walkways. A trip to the park is best combined with a stroll around the area to see the grand homes that were built in the early 20th century.

---

⑤

Deschutes Brewery

⌂1044 NW Bond St
◷11am-10pm daily (to 11pm Fri & Sat)
Ⓦdeschutesbrewery.com

This brewery began life in 1988 as a brewpub but has since expanded with pubs in Portland. There are four daily brewery tours on the hour from 1pm to 4pm, or you can visit their original pub at the same location. This has 19 beers on tap, and serves food sourced locally with some recipes using spent grain left over from the brewing process.

EAT

900 Wall

Classy menu combining North American cuisine with French and Italian influences, including stone-oven pizzas.

⌂900 NW Wall St
Ⓦ900wall.com

$$$

Spork

This place has received high praise for its mix of Mexican and Asian dishes. They may sound simple, but one mouthful of their *pozole rojo* and you know this is the real deal.

⌂937 NW Newport Av
Ⓦsporkbend.com

$$$

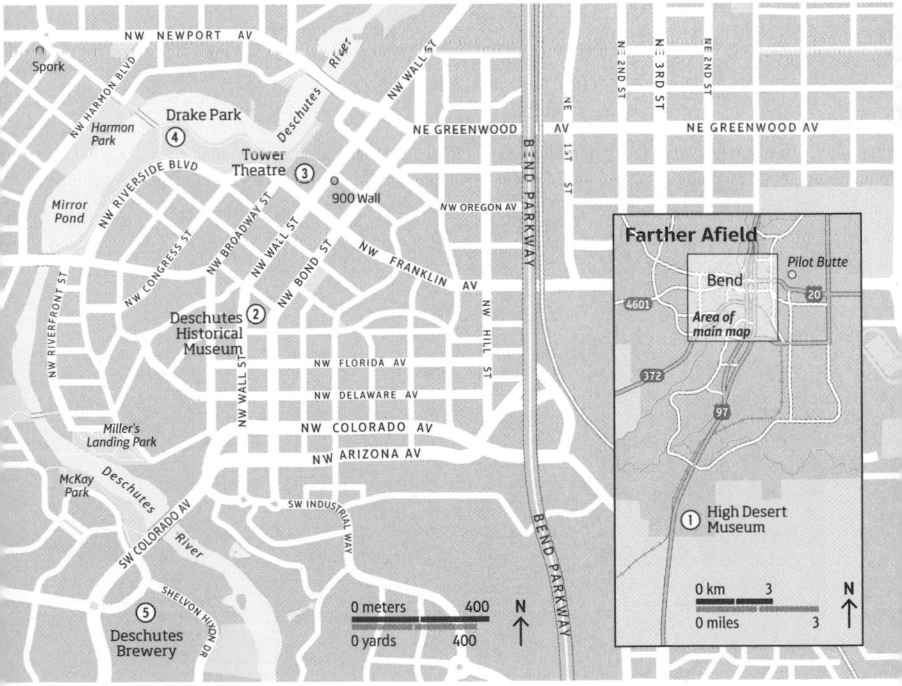

NW NEWPORT AV
Spork
NW HARMON BLVD
Harmon Park
Drake Park ④
Deschutes River
NW WALL ST
NE GREENWOOD AV
NE 2ND ST
NE 3RD ST
NE 1ST ST
Tower Theatre ③
NW RIVERSIDE BLVD
900 Wall
Mirror Pond
NW OREGON AV
BEND PARKWAY
NW CONGRESS ST
NW BROADWAY ST
NW BOND ST
NW FRANKLIN AV
NW RIVERFRONT ST
Deschutes Historical Museum ②
NW HILL ST
NW FLORIDA AV
NW DELAWARE AV
NW COLORADO AV
NW ARIZONA AV
Miller's Landing Park
McKay Park
SW COLORADO AV
SW INDUSTRIAL WAY
SHELVON HIXON DR
⑤ Deschutes Brewery
0 meters 400
0 yards 400
N

Farther Afield
Bend
Pilot Butte
4601
20
Area of main map
372
97
① High Desert Museum
0 km 3
0 miles 3
N

4

CRATER LAKE NATIONAL PARK

B5/6 Crater Lake-Klamath Klamath Falls then Amtrak shuttle bus (Jun-Oct) Daily (subject to weather) Rim Village Visitor Center, Rim Drive; www.nps.gov/crla

Oregon's only national park surrounds a lake that, at 1,949 ft (594 m), is the deepest in the US and the ninth-deepest in the world. Beyond the lake's vivid blue depths, the park is shrouded in old-growth forests that provide sanctuary to an array of flora and fauna, inviting thrilling hiking adventures and a wildlife-watching haven.

The creation of Crater Lake began about 7,700 years ago when Mount Mazama erupted and then collapsed, forming the caldera in which the lake now sits. The crater rim rises an average of 1,000 ft (300 m) above the lake. The breathtaking lake is unusual in having no water running into or out of it; its intense blue water is maintained solely by rain and snowfall, balanced by gradual evaporation over the year to maintain its consistent depth. The surface of the lake is measured at 6,178 ft (1,883 m), while the surrounding caldera varies from about 7,000 to 8,000 ft (2,134 to 2,438 m).

INSIDER TIP
Trolley Tour

Reduce your carbon footprint by taking a Crater Lake Trolley around the lake from July through fall. They stop several times and have a National Park Ranger onboard to provide information.

Hikers following a trail toward the summit of Crater Lake National Park on a clear, sunny day

Activities For All Seasons

With more than 90 miles (144 km) of hiking trails, Crater Lake National Park is a hiker's paradise. Many of the trails lie around the Rim Village area, with a fairly easy (and therefore popular) one being to the Wizard Island Overlook, a 5-mile (8-km) round-trip that affords breathtaking lake views. As the air is thinner at the park's elevations, you may feel yourself getting out of breath easily, so it's advisable to have a comfortable level of fitness before setting off on any hike. Winters are also long and can be harsh here, and sometimes access roads are closed as early as October as a result. Nonetheless, this also means that Crater Lake offers some of the best winter sports and cross-country skiing in the US, with options to suit all abilities.

WILDLIFE TO SPOT

Black Bears
The largest creatures here can be seen from spring through fall.

Coyotes
According to legend, the lake was formed by the tears of a coyote. Spot them year-round.

Elk
Roosevelt elks prevail in summer and winter.

Bull Trout
The only fish native to the lake is sadly a threatened species.

Mazama Newt
Unique to the lake but also under threat.

Snow blanketing the landscape surrounding Crater Lake in winter, and *(inset)* a ground squirrel

A DRIVING TOUR
CRATER LAKE

Length 33 miles (53 km) **Stopping-off points** Meals are offered at Crater Lake Lodge; snacks are sold in Rim Village. Two-hour boat trips (Jun–Sep) depart from Cleetwood Cove.

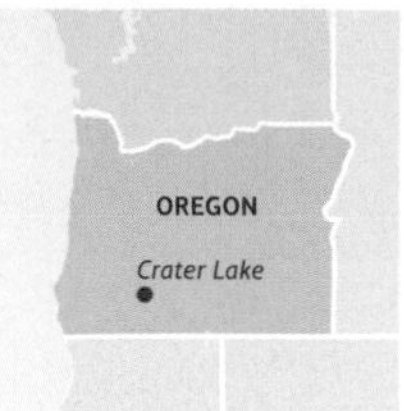

Locator Map

The 33-mile (53-km) Rim Drive that circles the lake offers spectacular vistas of the waters, the islands, and the surrounding mountains at every turn. The drive is open from the end of June to the middle of October, subject to weather conditions. It offers numerous stopping points with access to 90 miles (144 km) of hiking trails and a beautiful lodge that offer magnificent views. The Rim Visitor Center or the Steel Visitor Center on Rim Drive are great sources of information before setting off.

Named for its historic fire tower, **the Watchman** *can be reached after a moderate climb. It is the nearest lookout to Wizard Island.*

Merriam Point *is a great spot from which to admire the west side of the lake, with the cone-shaped Wizard Island.*

Spectacular views of the lake, the islands, and the surrounding mountains unfold at every turn of the 33-mile (53-km) **Rim Drive**.

The strenuous 1-mile (1.6-km) **Cleetwood Trail** *drops a steep 700 ft (210 m) and is the only access to the lake. In summer, a boat tour departs from the dock at the base.*

Weather permitting, views from **Mount Scott** *extend as far as California's Mount Shasta.*

A 300-ft- (90-m-) wide crater sits at the summit of the small volcanic **Wizard Island**, *which juts 764 ft (233 m) above the surface of the lake.*

Perched on top of the caldera rim, the rustic **Crater Lake Lodge** *has been welcoming guests since 1915. Magnificent views can be enjoyed from this lodge.*

Beautiful views reward the traveler who attempts the short descent to **Sinnott Memorial Overlook** *just below the caldera rim. Park rangers give geology talks here.*

Pumice spires, or fossil fumaroles, rise from the caldera's eastern base and form the eerie **Pinnacles** *landscape.*

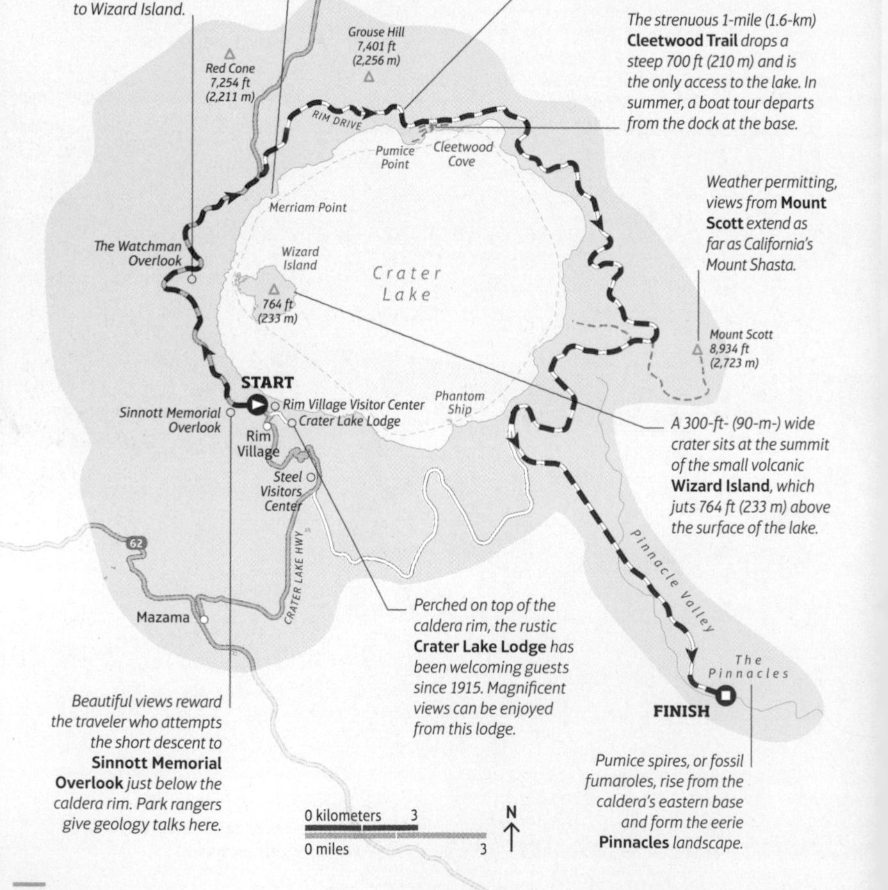

Red Cone 7,254 ft (2,211 m)
Grouse Hill 7,401 ft (2,256 m)
RIM DRIVE
Pumice Point
Cleetwood Cove
Merriam Point
The Watchman Overlook
Wizard Island
764 ft (233 m)
Crater Lake
Mount Scott 8,934 ft (2,723 m)
START
Sinnott Memorial Overlook
Rim Village Visitor Center
Crater Lake Lodge
Phantom Ship
Rim Village
Steel Visitors Center
62
CRATER LAKE HWY
Mazama
Pinnacle Valley
The Pinnacles
FINISH

0 kilometers 3
0 miles 3
N

↑ Cross-country skiing amid the magnificent scenery of the expansive Crater Lake

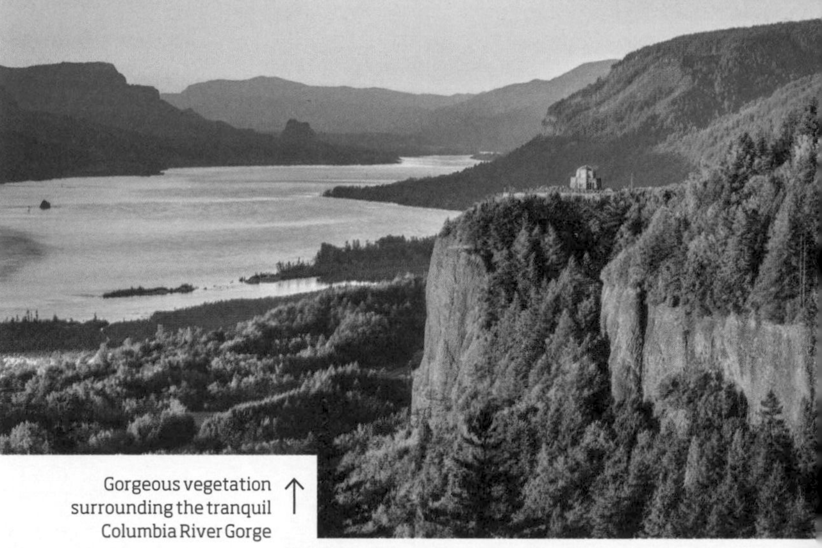

Gorgeous vegetation surrounding the tranquil Columbia River Gorge ↑

COLUMBIA RIVER GORGE

B4 402 W 2nd St, The Dalles; www.crgva.org

This 80-mile (130-km) river corridor is one of the most spectacular and scenic stretches in Oregon. Created by the same Ice Age floods that carved the Willamette Valley, the Gorge cuts through the volcanic rock of the Cascade Mountains. Gushing waterfalls, hiking trails past moss-covered boulders, and plateaus carpeted with wildflowers all await the intrepid traveler here.

Bonneville Lock and Dam

Star Route, Cascade Locks 9am-5pm daily nwp.usace.army.mil/bonneville

The Bonneville Lock and Dam was built in the 1930s and is managed by the US Army Corps of Engineers. The two main visitor centers, one on the Oregon side and the other on the Washington side, offer free ranger tours of the large, still-functioning hydroelectric powerhouses. There's also a fish hatchery and California sea lions can often be seen around the dam during the spawning season in September. Recreational areas around the dam have picnic sites, nature trails, and shoreline access.

Hood River

720 E Port Marina Dr; www.visithoodriver.com

Known as the windsurfing capital of the world, the city of Hood River is located right at the dramatic crossroads of the Gorge and the Cascade Mountains. Both beginner and expert windsurfers will appreciate the wind conditions and balmy temperatures, and there are plenty of outfitters for gear and lessons. While both windsurfing and kiteboarding are hugely popular in Hood River, another thrilling watersport, flyboarding, is also getting a lot of traction, where willing participants stand on a small board and are propelled through the water and into the air by water

DRIVING TOUR OF THE RIVER

The best way to explore the area is to take the Historic Columbia River Highway. Blasted out of narrow cliffs, this road was designed to maximize viewing pleasure while minimizing environmental damage as much as possible. Starting from I-84 in Portland, this driving route encompasses a diverse sampling of Oregon scenery, including the banks of the Columbia River. The most scenic place to stop off is at the historic lodge at Multnomah Falls. You can also take a detour to the spectacular summit of Mount Hood *(p122)*.

The number of wildflower species that can only be found in the Gorge.

jet streams. Give it a try yourself with Gorge Flyboard *(www.gorgeflyboard.com)*.

Mosier Plateau Trail

Hwy 30, Mosier

Part of a large network of the Gorge Towns to Trails project, this 3.5-mile (5.6-km) moderate trail begins by crossing the century-old Mosier Creek Bridge and past the historic Mosier Pioneer Cemetery from the 1870s. Hikers are then treated to the refreshing Mosier Creek Falls, where you can take a dip in the water during the hot summer months. A series of mild switchbacks follow through meadows that are in full bloom in spring. The final stretch ends on a stunning plateau with views of the Gorge and Mosier Valley, and where bald eagles often soar.

Columbia River Gorge Discovery Center

5000 Discovery Dr, The Dalles 9am-5pm daily gorgediscovery.org

Located at the east end of the Gorge, in The Dalles region, this center offers intriguing exhibits on the Lewis and Clark Expedition, the geology of the Gorge, local flora and fauna, and Indigenous Peoples culture. You can also get up close to various live raptors, including bald eagles, hawks, and owls. Ask the center for a free map of the interpretive nature trails that surround the area, which pass by ponds, wetlands, and many scenic viewpoints.

Multnomah Falls

53000 E Historic Columbia River Hwy; www.multnomahfallslodge.com

Just off Interstate 84, this spectacular waterfall, the fourth-highest in the US tumbles 620 ft (188 m) in two picturesque cascades. Various hiking trails lead up to the falls, including one up to the picturesque Benson Bridge built by Italian stonemasons in 1914. The falls are best viewed early in the morning to avoid the hordes of crowds, and if you come during the winter time the freezing temperatures will have partially encased the falls in magical ice formations. Skip any car parking hassles and take the inexpensive Columbia Gorge Express shuttle bus instead.

↑ Water flowing from the spectacular Multnomah Falls on a fall afternoon

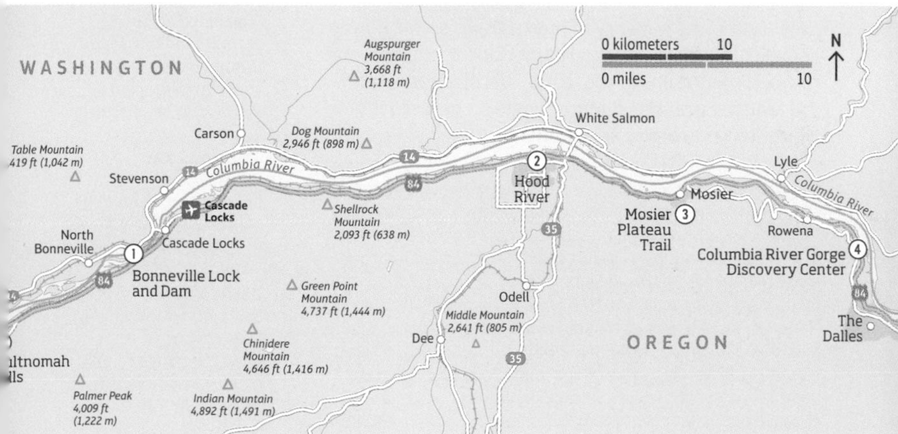

Mount Hood reflected in the shimmering blue waters of the picturesque Trillium Lake

6

MOUNT HOOD

B4 Mount Hood Cultural Center & Museum, 88900 E Government Camp Loop; www.mthoodmuseum.org

An outstanding network of hiking trails, scenic byways, and glistening lakes makes Mount Hood one of the most climbed mountains in the world. Wildflowers carpet the landscape in the summer, while its perpetually white slopes promise scenic adventures all year.

Mount Hood is most famous for being one of the only year-round ski resorts on the continent, with six separate ski areas to enjoy. Timberline Lodge *(www.timberlinelodge.com)* offers fantastic ski and snowboard camps, as well as river rafting, windsurfing, and mountain biking. Mt. Hood Skibowl *(www.skibowl.com)* is famed for its night-skiing runs, while the Snow Bunny area in Mount Hood National Forest is perfect for kids, with tobogganing and tubing hills. If you're after a slower pace, drive the 105-mile (169-km) Mount Hood Scenic Byway, which follows the slopes through pastoral valley landscapes. Another wonderful way to tour Mount Hood is with the Mount Hood Railroad *(www.mthoodrr.com)*, which departs several days a week from Hood River.

MOUNT HOOD HIKING TRAILS

Ramona Falls Trail
This 7-mile (11.3-km) round trip is a popular day hike that includes a thrilling river crossing.

Timberline National Historic Trail
An epic trail skirting around Mount Hood that can be started at various access points.

Trillium Lake Loop Trail
Family-friendly, barrier free loop with good bird-watching spots.

Glade Trail
Starting at Timberline Lodge, you can snow-shoe this gentle 6-mile (9.7-km) trail in winter or hike it in the summer.

STAY

Hood River Hotel
A vintage hotel dating from 1912 with modern rooms and a Scandinavian cafe.

102 Oak St, Hood River
hoodriverhotel.com

$$

Timberline Lodge
A beautiful 1930s ski lodge with cosy rooms, fireside lounges, and an outdoor pool that's heated all year round.

27500 E Timberline Rd, Government Camp
timberlinelodge.com

$$$

1 Mount Hood is home to nearly a dozen glaciers that beckon activity.

2 Artisans crafted every detail of the Timberline Lodge, from the door handles to its massive wood beams.

3 Trillium Lake in Mount Hood National Forest provides ideal kayaking and fishing conditions.

EXPERIENCE MORE

Astoria

A3/4 111 W Marine Dr; www.travelastoria.com

Throughout the damp winter of 1805–1806, explorers Lewis and Clark *(p58)* passed the time recording in their journals accounts of bear attacks and the almost continual rain at a crude stockade near Astoria. This enclosure at **Lewis and Clark National Historical Park – Fort Clatsop Unit** was rebuilt after the first replica was destroyed by fire in 2005. In 1811, John Jacob Astor sent fur traders around Cape Horn to establish a trading post in this location at the mouth of the Columbia River, making Astoria the oldest American settlement west of the Rocky Mountains.

These days, the town is a major port for fishing fleets and commercial vessels; its Victorian homes climb a hillside above the river. One such home, the stately **Captain George Flavel House Museum**, retains the cupola from which the captain and his wife once observed river traffic. A better view can be enjoyed from atop the 164-step spiral staircase of the **Astoria Column**, encircled with bas relief friezes paying homage to the region's past.

The town honors its seagoing past at the **Columbia River Maritime Museum**. The lightship *Columbia*, berthed in front, once guided ships across the mouth of the river.

The restored 1913 **Astoria Riverfront Trolley** runs on original railroad tracks from East End Mooring Basin to West End Mooring Basin. This 3-mile (5-km) route provides great views, and covers docks, piers, shops, and restaurants along the historic waterfront.

The lively **Astoria Sunday Market,** held in downtown Astoria, features up to 200 local farmers, craftspeople, and artisans, as well as live music and a food court. Art walks take place every second Saturday evening in downtown Astoria. Venues, highlighted with colorful pinwheels, exhibit original works of art, while many businesses stay open late to provide food and entertainment.

→ The Astoria Column, with a scenic lookout over the port at its top

PICTURE PERFECT
Shipwreck

It's not often you get to see a shipwreck up-close so take your camera to Astoria's Fort Stevens State Park. The *Peter Iredale* was abandoned here in 1906 and its skeletal remains make for terrific photos.

The **Oregon Film Museum** in the former County Jail celebrates movies that have been made in the state, such as *The Goonies* (1985), and teaches visitors interesting movie-making skills.

Some 10 miles (16 km) west of Astoria, **Fort Stevens State Park** dates back to the Civil War, when it guarded the Columbia River from Confederate incursions.

Lewis and Clark National Historical Park - Fort Clatsop Unit
6 miles (10 km) southwest of Astoria, off Hwy 101 (503) 861-4414 Times vary, call ahead

Captain George Flavel House Museum
441 8th St (503) 325-2203 10am–5pm daily (Oct–Apr: from 11am) Jan 1, Thanksgiving, Dec 24 & 25

Astoria Column
Atop Coxcomb Hill, off 16th St Dawn–dusk daily astoriacolumn.org

Columbia River Maritime Museum
1792 Marine Dr 9:30am–5pm daily Thanksgiving, Dec 25 crmm.org

Astoria Riverfront Trolley
480 Industry St Times vary, check website old300.org

Astoria Sunday Market
Commercial St & 12th St
May-Oct: 10am-3pm Sun
astoriasundaymarket.com

Oregon Film Museum
732 Duane St Times vary, check website
oregonfilmmuseum.org

Fort Stevens State Park
Off Hwy 101
Dawn-dusk daily Dec 25
visitftstevens.com

Cannon Beach

A4 207 N Spruce St; www.cannonbeach.org

Despite its status as Oregon's favorite beach town, Cannon Beach retains a great deal of quiet charm. The surrounding forests grow almost up to Hemlock Street, where buildings clad with weathered cedar shingles house art galleries. Haystack Rock, one of the tallest coastal monoliths in the world, towers 235 ft (72 m) above a long beach and tidal pools teeming with life.

Ecola State Park, at the beach's north end, carpets Tillamook Head, a 1,100-ft (335-m) basalt headland, with forests accessible via Tillamook Head Trail. Viewpoints look across raging surf to Tillamook Rock Lighthouse, built in 1880 and known as "Terrible Tillie," as waves, logs, and rocks continually washed through the structure. Decommissioned in 1957, the lighthouse served as a private mortuary and is currently closed to the public.

Ecola State Park
2 miles (3 km) N of Cannon Beach, off Hwy 101
(503) 436-2844 Dawn-dusk daily

Steens Mountain

D6 Off Hwy 205

Scenery does not get much more rugged and grand than it does here on this 9,700-ft (2,960-m) mountain. Steens Mountain is a fault-block, formed when land on two sides of a geological fault rose and fell to different levels. As a result, the west slope of this mountain rises gradually from sagebrush country through stands of aspen, juniper, and mountain mahogany, while the east face drops precipitously for more than a mile (1.5 km). Pronghorn, bighorn sheep, and wild horses roam gorges and alpine tundra carpeted with wildflowers, and eagles and falcons soar overhead. The Steens Mountain National Back Country Byway traverses this remarkable landscape.

↑ Cannon Beach overlooked by Haystack Rock

STAY

The Ocean Lodge
A pet-friendly hotel that sits right on the beach, close to Haystack Rock.
A4 2864 S Pacific St, Cannon Beach
theoceanlodge.com
$$$

Surfsand Resort
This beachfront resort offers great views and nightly beach bonfires.
A4 148 W Gower Av, Cannon Beach surfsand.com
$$$

Cannon Beach Hotel
This New-England style boutique hotel is full of historic charm.
A4 1116 S Hemlock St, Cannon Beach
cannonbeachhotel lodgings.com
$$$

Newport

A4 555 SW Coast Hwy; www.discovernewport.com

This salty old port on Yaquina Bay is home to the largest commercial fishing fleet on the Oregon coast and supports many oystering operations. The town is well accustomed to tourists, too. Shingled resort cottages in the Nye Beach neighborhood date from the 1880s, and in the late 1990s travelers came from around the world to visit Keiko, an orca whale that resided in the internationally renowned **Oregon Coast Aquarium** and gained stardom in the *Free Willy* films. Keiko left the aquarium in 1998. The place is still popular, however, with plenty to see and experience. Surfperch, Pacific cod, and flounders swim around pier pilings in the Sandy Shores exhibit, jellyfish float through the Coastal Waters exhibit, and Wolf Eels peek out of crevices along the Rocky Shores gallery. In Passages of the Deep, sharks and rays swim in an 800,000-gallon (3-million-liter) tank over, and alongside glass viewing tunnels. Outdoors, tufted puffins and murres fly through the aviary, and sea otters, sea lions, and seals frolic in saltwater pools. At the **Hatfield Marine Science Center**, headquarters of Oregon State University's marine research programs, thoughtful exhibits encourage you to explore oceanic science in fascinating ways, from viewing plankton through a microscope to spotting patterns of sand build-up in time-lapse photography.

Yaquina Head Outstanding Natural Area, a narrow finger of lava that juts into the Pacific Ocean on the north end of town, makes it easy to watch marine animals in their natural habitats. Platforms at the base of the restored Yaquina Head Lighthouse are within close sight of rocks where seabirds nest. Pathways lead to the edge of tidal pools occupied by kelp crabs, sea anemones, and more. The interpretive center looks at human and nonhuman inhabitants of the headland; shell debris attests to the presence of the former more than 4,000 years ago.

Newport's waterfront stretches along the north side of Yaquina Bay. The masts of the fishing schooners tower over shops and restaurants, and crab pots and pesky sea lions trying to steal bait are as much of an attraction as underwater shows and waxwork replicas of sea animals.

ORCAS

The largest members of the dolphin family, orcas are found throughout the world's oceans. Along the coast of the Pacific Northwest, transient orcas roam the ocean from California to Alaska in groups of up to 60. Resident orcas, on the other hand, remain faithful to a location. Although you can sometimes see orcas from the shoreline, take a whale-watching tour to dramatically increase your chances.

Oregon Coast Aquarium

2820 SE Ferry Slip Rd Times vary, check website aquarium.org

Hatfield Marine Science Center

2030 SE Marine Science Dr Times vary, check website seagrant.oregonstate.edu

Yaquina Head Outstanding Natural Area

3 miles (5 km) N of Newport, off Hwy 101 (541) 574-3100 Dawn-dusk daily

Yachats

A5 241 Hwy 101; www.yachats.org

The town of Yachats (pronounced "ya-hots"), once home to the Alsea people who gave Yachats its name, is the sort of place a shore-lover dreams about: small, unspoiled, and surrounded by forested mountainsides and rocky headlands. In the center of town, the Yachats River meets the sea in a little estuary shadowed by fir trees and laced with tidal pools. A stunning sunset can be admired from the **Yachats Ocean Road State Natural Site**, a paved seaside loop on the south side of town.

Yachats Ocean Road State Natural Site

South of Yachats River, west of Hwy 100 (800) 551-6949 Dawn-dusk daily

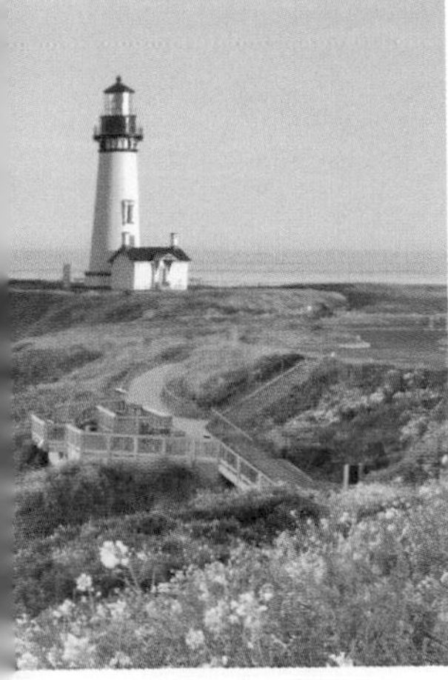

↑ Yaquina Head Lighthouse watching over the Pacific Ocean

↑ Howard Hughes' "Spruce Goose" at the Evergreen Aviation & Space Museum

McMinnville

A4 417 NW Adams; www.visitmcminnville.com

In this prosperous town surrounded by the Willamette Valley vineyards, the Downtown Historic District is graced by the old Oregon Hotel, McMinnville Bank, and many other late 19th- and early 20th-century buildings. The excellent reputation of ivy-clad Linfield College, chartered in 1858, has long put McMinnville on the map, but these days the university shares the honor with the "Spruce Goose." This wooden flying boat, built in the 1940s, is housed in the **Evergreen Aviation & Space Museum**, where its 320-ft (97.5-m) wingspan spreads above early passenger planes, World War II fighters, and other vintage civilian and military aircraft. The nearby indoor Wings & Waves Waterpark, once part of this museum, is an excellent stop for families and offers waterslides and a wave pool.

Evergreen Aviation & Space Museum

500 NE Capt Michael King Smith Way 9am-5pm daily Major hols evergreenmuseum.org

EAT

Local Ocean Seafoods

Casual restaurant on the marina, serving freshly caught fish.

A4 213 SE Bay Blvd, Newport localocean.net

$$$

Clearwater Restaurant

This place throws in fishy surprises alongside the usual suspects.

A4 325 SW Bay Blvd, Newport clearwater restaurant.com

$$$

Ocean Bleu Seafoods at Gino's

A lively fish market and cafe with fish as fresh as anywhere in Newport.

A4 808 SW Bay Blvd, Newport oceanbleu seafoods.com

$$$

13

Florence

A5 290 Hwy 101; www.florencechamber.com

It is easy to speed through Florence en route to the nearby sand dunes but the historic old town, tucked away along the banks of the Siuslaw River, warrants a stop. Many of its early 20th-century buildings house art galleries, and a sizable commercial fishing fleet docks alongside them, adding color and providing bounty for the riverside fish markets and restaurants.

At nearby **Darlingtonia State Natural Site**, a short trail loops through a bog where Darlingtonia, also known as cobra lily, thrive. These rare, tall, carnivorous plants are reminiscent of the human-eaters of horror films.

Darlingtonia State Natural Site

5 miles (8 km) N of Florence, off Hwy 101 (800) 551-6949 Dawn-dusk daily

Lincoln City

A4 540 NE Hwy 101; www.oregoncoast.org

In 1965, five individual communities united to form one town called Lincoln City.

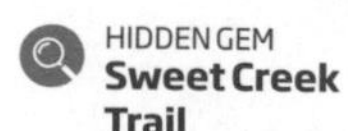

HIDDEN GEM
Sweet Creek Trail

Just outside Florence, you'll find Sweet Creek Road, just 5 miles (8 km) along the river, where you can enjoy a hike along the Sweet Creek Trail, which takes you past several beautiful waterfalls.

Situated along Highway 101, the long city is home to several natural attractions. Formerly called Devil's River, the D River flows only 120 ft (36 m) – from Devil's Lake to the Pacific Ocean – making it one of the world's shortest rivers. The 7.5-mile- (12-km-) long beach, littered with driftwood and agates, is popular with kite enthusiasts, who enjoy the strong winds off the sea.

To the north, the steep cliffs of **Cascade Head Preserve** rise out of the surf, then give way to mossy rainforests of Sitka spruce and hemlock and a maritime grassland prairie. Many rare plants and animals thrive in the preserve, which can be explored on steep but well-maintained trails.

At Depoe Bay, a little fishing port 12 miles (19 km) south of Lincoln City, rough seas blast through narrow channels in the basalt rock, creating geyser-like plumes that shoot as high as 60 ft (18 m).

The Otter Crest State Scenic Viewpoint atop Cape Foulweather, so named by Captain James Cook in 1778 because of the high winds that regularly buffet it, provides an excellent view of the adjacent **Devil's Punchbowl State Natural Area**, where the sea thunders into rocky hollows formed by the collapse of sea caves. The park is a popular whale-watching site.

Cascade Head Preserve

2 miles (3 km) N of Lincoln City, off Hwy 101 (503) 230-1221 Lower trail: dawn-dusk daily; upper trail: mid-Jul-Dec

Devil's Punchbowl State Natural Area

15 miles (24 km) S of Lincoln City, off Hwy 101 (800) 551-6949 Dawn-dusk daily

Oregon Dunes National Recreation Area

A5 855 Highway 101 S, Reedsport; www.fs.usda.gov/siuslaw

Massive sand dunes stretch south from Florence for 40 miles (64 km). The desert-like landscape has been created over thousands of years, as winds, tides, and ocean currents force sand as far as 2.5 miles (4 km) inland and sculpt it into towering formations that reach heights of as much as 300 ft (90 m). Not only sand, but streams, lakes, grasslands, and isolated beaches attract a wide variety of recreation enthusiasts.

Boardwalks make it easy to enjoy stunning vistas from Oregon Dunes Day Use site, about 20 miles (32 km) south of Florence, and the 2.7-mile- (4.3-km-) John Dellenback Dunes Trail, 35 miles (56 km) south of Florence, leads to a beach over large dunes.

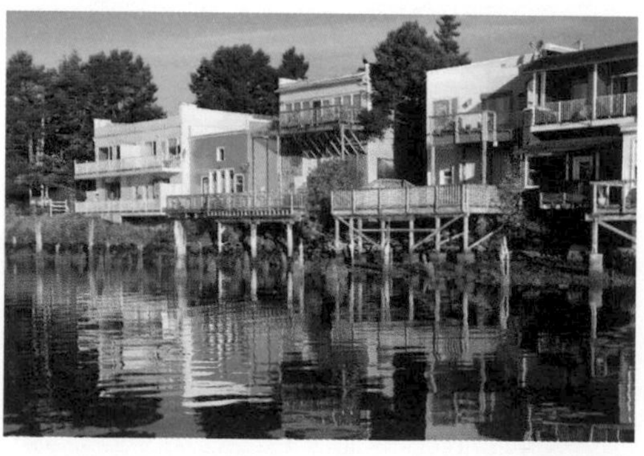

↑ Houses lining the waterfront of Siuslaw Bay in the town of Florence

Impressive sandstone cliffs at Cape Kiwanda State Natural Area

Tillamook

A4 3705 Hwy 101 N; www.gotillamook.com

Tillamook sits about 10 miles (16 km) inland from the sea in rich bottomland fed by five rivers that empty into Tillamook Bay. Green pastures, nurtured by more than 70 inches (178 cm) of rain a year, sustain 40,000 cows that supply milk for the historic **Tillamook County Creamery Association**, commonly known as "The Cheese Factory." Here, visitors can view the facilities and sample its output of 78 million lb (35 million kg) of cheese per year, including smoked cheddar and pepper jack.

During World War II, Tillamook was the base for giant blimps that patrolled the coast for Japanese submarines. One of the hangars at 1,100 ft (335 m) long and 15 stories tall the largest wood structure in the world – houses the **Tillamook Air Museum**, which displays a fine collection of flying boats, early helicopters, and some 30 other restored vintage aircraft.

Tillamook County Creamery Association

4175 Hwy 101 N
Mid-Jun-Labor Day: 8am-8pm daily; Labor Day-mid-Jun: 8am-6pm daily
Thanksgiving, Dec 25
tillamook.com

Tillamook Air Museum

6030 Hangar Rd
10am-5pm daily
Thanksgiving, Dec 25
tillamookair.com

TOP 3 OREGON DUNES BUGGY TOURS AND RENTALS

Spinreel Dune Buggy
67045 Spinreel Rd, Tenmile
ridetheoregondunes.com
A family-run company renting dune buggies and ATVs all year round.

Sand Dunes Frontier
83960 US-101, Florence
sanddunesfrontier.com
Stay in the campsite nearby and drive straight out onto the dunes, or book a tour with an expert driver.

Sandland Adventures
85366 US-101, Florence
sandland.com
As well as sand dune tours, this company has a mini theme park for the family to enjoy.

Three Capes Scenic Route

A4 Oregon State Parks Association; www.oregonstateparks.org

Nature is the main attraction along this 35-mile (56-km) loop that follows the marshy shores of Tillamook Bay.

The rocks below Cape Meares State Scenic Viewpoint and Cape Meares Lighthouse are home to one of the largest colonies of nesting seabirds in North America. In Cape Lookout State Park, trails pass through old-growth forests to clifftop viewpoints – good places to spot migrating gray whales – and to a sand spit between the ocean and Netarts Bay. This is also a popular camping area, with campsites, cabins, and yurts. In the Cape Kiwanda State Natural Area, waves crash into huge sandstone cliffs and offshore rock formations. The beach along the cape draws surfers as well as fishermen. Pacific City, at the route's south end, is home to a fleet of fishing dories that daringly ply the surf on their way out to sea.

The Oregon State Parks Association provides detailed information about the sights along this stunning route.

Smith Rock State Park

B5 Dawn-dusk daily oregonstateparks.org

At Smith Rock, the Crooked River flows beneath towering rock faces of welded tuff – volcanic ash that has been compressed under intense heat and pressure. These unusually shaped peaks and pinnacles – with compelling names like Morning Glory Wall and Pleasure Palace – are a lure for risk-taking rock climbers, who can choose from over 1,300 climbing routes, some of which lead up sheer faces that exceed 550 ft (168 m). The less intrepid can enjoy the spectacle and take incredible photographs from roadside viewpoints or from one of the many hiking trails that follow the base of the cliffs.

Cape Perpetua Scenic Area

A5 Dawn-dusk daily Christmas, New Year's Day 2400 Hwy 101; (541) 547-3289

Part of the Siuslaw National Forest, Cape Perpetua is the highest – albeit often cloud-shrouded – viewpoint on the coast. A road ascends to the top at 800 ft (245 m), but those with time and stamina may prefer to make the climb on trails that wind through the old-growth rainforests from the interpretive center.

From Cape Perpetua, Highway 101 descends into **Heceta Head State Park**, where trails offer spectacular ocean views. Birds nest on the rocks and sea lions and gray whales swim offshore.

A herd of Steller sea lions inhabits the **Sea Lion Caves**, the only rookery for wild sea lions found on the North American mainland. An elevator descends 208 ft (63.5 m) from the clifftop to platforms near the floor of the 12-story cavern. Some 200 animals live in the cave during fall and winter.

Just 3 miles (5 km) south of Yachats, Thor's Well is one of several natural openings along the coast that turn into beautiful spouting fountains when the tide comes in. They are best seen just before or after high tide.

Heceta Head State Park

Hwy 101, 19 miles (30.5 km) south of Yachats (541) 547-3416 Times vary, call ahead

Sea Lion Caves

91560 Hwy 101 N, 11 miles (17.5 km) north of Florence 9am-7pm daily Thanksgiving, Dec 25 sealioncaves.com

Silverton

B4 426 S Water St; www.silvertonchamber.org

This pleasant old farming town in the foothills of the Cascade Mountains is the entryway to **Silver Falls State Park**, the largest state park in Oregon.

Photographing the river of Smith Rock State Park, and *(inset)* a brave climber taking on a sheer rock face

The Trail of Ten Falls follows Silver Creek through a temperate rainforest of Douglas firs to the trail's cataracts.

At the southern edge of Silverton is **The Oregon Garden**. Rising high above the landscape is a magnificent stand of 100-year-old oaks.

Silver Falls State Park
Hwy 214, 10 miles (16 km) E of Salem Dawn-dusk daily oregonstateparks.org

The Oregon Garden
879 W Main St Times vary, check website oregongarden.org

Oregon Caves National Monument & Preserve

A6 Late Apr-early Nov; for tours only 19000 Caves Hwy; www.nps.gov/orca

Visitors on the compulsory 70-minute guided tours of these vast underground caverns follow lighted trails past strange formations, cross underground rivers, squeeze through giant ribs of marble, and clamber into enormous chambers hung with stalactites. Discovered in 1874, the caves have been formed by the steady trickling of water over the past hundreds of thousands of years. Above ground, three trails cross a remnant old-growth coniferous forest.

Bandon

A5 300 2nd St; www.bandon.com

The small town of Bandon, near the mouth of the Coquille River, is most famous for its tasty cranberries, which are harvested in bogs north of the town. In the south, craggy, wind-sculpted rock formations rise from the sea just off Bandon's beach. A wilder landscape of dunes and sea grass prevails at **Bullards Beach State Park**, which lies across the marshy, bird-filled Coquille Estuary from Bandon.

In the early 1900s, lumber baron Louis J. Simpson built Shore Acres, an estate atop oceanside bluffs outside the town of Coos Bay, 25 miles (40 km) north of Bandon. It is now the site of **Shore Acres State Park**. An enclosed observatory offers a stunning view of the ocean, while interpretive panels educate you about the history of the site. Although the mansion is long gone, the gardens continue to thrive next to **Cape Arago State Park**, where seals and sea lions bask in the sun on offshore rocks.

Cape Blanco State Park, 27 miles (43 km) south of Bandon, is the westernmost point in the 48 contiguous states and one of the windiest spots on earth, with winter gusts exceeding 180 mph (290 km/h). The park's lighthouse, first lit in 1870, is the oldest on the Oregon coast.

ELKHORN DRIVE NATIONAL SCENIC BYWAY TOUR

This 83-mile (134-km) mountain drive from Baker City takes in some of the finest scenery in eastern Oregon, especially in summer and fall. To the west, the route climbs across the Elkhorn Range of the Blue Mountains, where dense pine forests give way to historic gold-mining towns. To the east rise the snowcapped summits of the spectacular Wallowa mountain range.

Highway 101 nears the California border in a stretch of dense forests, towering cliffs, and offshore rock formations. Some of the most spectacular scenery is within the **Samuel H. Boardman State Scenic Corridor**, 4 miles (6.5 km) north of Brookings.

Bullards Beach State Park
2 miles (3 km) N of Bandon, off Hwy 101 (541) 347-2209 Dawn-dusk daily

Shore Acres State Park
Cape Arago Hwy, 13 miles (21 km) SW of Coos Bay (541) 888-3732 8am-dusk daily

Cape Arago State Park
End of Cape Arago Hwy, 15 miles (24 km) SW of Coos Bay (800) 551-6949 Dawn-dusk daily

Cape Blanco State Park
9 miles (14.5 km) north of Port Orford, off Hwy 101 (800) 551-6949 Dawn-dusk daily; Lighthouse: Apr-Oct: 10am-3:30pm daily

Samuel H. Boardman State Scenic Corridor
Hwy 101, 4 miles (6.5 km) N of Brookings (800) 551-6949 Dawn-dusk daily

Admiring quilts displayed in the charming Sisters Outdoor Quilt Show

Sisters

B5 291 E Main Av; www.sisterscountry.com

Sisters is a ranching town that cashes in on its cowboy history with Old West-style storefronts and wooden sidewalks. The setting, though, is incredibly authentic – the peaks of the Three Sisters, each exceeding 10,000 ft (3,000 m), tower majestically above the town and the surrounding pine forests, alpine meadows, and rushing streams.

The McKenzie Pass climbs from Sisters to a 1-mile (1.6-km) summit amid a massive lava flow. The **Dee Wright Observatory**, built from lava rock, provides panoramic views of more than a dozen Cascades peaks and buttes and of the sweeping lava fields, which can be examined at close range on the half-mile (0.8-km) Lava River Interpretive Trail.

Dee Wright Observatory

Hwy 242, 15 miles (24 km) west of Sisters (541) 822-3381 Mid-Jun-Oct: dawn-dusk daily Nov-mid-Jun, depending on snow conditions

SHOP

Montana Peaks Hat Company

Pick up some fine felt cowboy hats - some of which have featured in iconic movies.

C4 24 SW Court Av, Pendleton montanapeaks.net

Pendleton Woolen Mills

Since 1863, this wool mill has woven colorful geometric blankets in tribal and southwestern patterns. It also sells factory scraps.

C4 1307 SE Court Pl, Pendleton pendleton-usa.com

Pendleton

C4 501 S Main St; www.travelpendleton.com

Pendleton's reputation for raucous cowboys and lawless cattle rustlers is matched by the fact that it is eastern Oregon's largest town. While these colorful days belong to the past, cowboy lore comes alive during the Pendleton Round-Up each September, when rodeo performers and some 50,000 spectators crowd into town. Previous rodeos are honored in the memorabilia at the **Pendleton Round-Up and Happy Canyon Hall of Fame Museum**.

Pendleton Underground Tours reveal much about the town's notoriety. The tours begin in an underground labyrinth of opium dens, gaming rooms, and Prohibition-era drinking establishments.

Another chapter of local history is commemorated at the **Tamástslikt Cultural Institute**, where exhibits depict the horse culture, seasonal migrations, forced resettlements, and current success of the Cayuse, Umatilla, and Walla Walla peoples, who have lived on the Columbia River plateau for more than 10,000 years.

The town of La Grande, 52 miles (84 km) southeast of Pendleton, is best known as the jumping-off point for trips into the scenic wilds of the Blue and Wallowa Mountains and Hells Canyon.

Pendleton Round-Up and Happy Canyon Hall of Fame Museum

1114 SW Court Av 10am-4pm Mon-Sat Major hols pendletonroundup.com

Pendleton Underground Tours

37 SW Emigrant Av 10am-4pm Mon & Wed-Sat Major hols pendletonundergroundtours.org

Tamástslikt Cultural Institute

47106 Wildhorse Blvd Times vary, check website tamastslikt.org

Hiking the cliffs that rise above the Deschutes River, near Madras

Newberry National Volcanic Monument encompasses eerie landscapes of black lava, sparkling mountain lakes, waterfalls, hemlock forests, and snowcapped peaks.

Newberry National Volcanic Monument

B5 Apr–Oct: dawn-dusk daily fs.usda.gov

Newberry National Volcanic Monument encompasses eerie landscapes of black lava, sparkling mountain lakes, waterfalls, hemlock forests, and snowcapped peaks. Exhibits at the **Lava Lands Visitor Center** explain how Newberry Volcano has been built by thousands of eruptions that, seismic activity suggests, may begin again. Other exhibits highlight central Oregon's cultural history.

Well-marked roads and interpretive trails lead to major sites within the monument. In addition to magnificent scenery, the monument provides opportunities for hiking, fishing, boating, camping, and winter recreation.

Lava Lands Visitor Center
58201 Hwy 97 Times vary, check website fs.usda.gov

Jordan Valley

D5 cityofjordanvalley.com

This scruffy desert settlement, peppered with cattle ranches and surrounded by snow-capped mountains, is one of only a few towns in sparsely populated Malheur County. A cemetery 17 miles (27 km) south of town on Highway 95 is the final resting place of Jean Baptiste Charbonneau, son of the American Indian guide Sacagawea.

Madras and Warm Springs

B4 Madras: 274 SW 4th St; www.madraschamber.com; Warm Springs: 1233 Veterans St; www.warmsprings-nsn.gov

Madras is a desert ranching town surrounded by rimrock and vast tracts of wilderness recreation lands. **Crooked River National Grassland** provides endless vistas, and fishing and rafting on two US National Wild and Scenic Rivers – the Deschutes and the Crooked. **Cove Palisades State Park** surrounds Lake Billy Chinook, where deep waters reflecting surrounding cliffs are popular with boaters.

The Treaty of 1855 between the US government and the Wasco, Walla Walla, and Paiute peoples established lands for the peoples on the 1,000-sq-miles (2,590-sq-km) Warm Springs Reservation, located on the High Desert plateaus and forested Cascade slopes of central Oregon. These Confederated Tribes preserve their heritage at the **Museum at Warm Springs** with a stunning collection of basketry and beadwork, historic photographs, and videotapes of traditional ceremonies.

Crooked River National Grassland
10 miles (16 km) S of Madras, off Hwy 26 Dawn-dusk daily 274 SW 4th St, Madras; www.fs.usda.gov

Cove Palisades State Park
15 miles (24 km) SW of Madras, off Hwy 97 Dawn-dusk daily oregonstateparks.org

Museum at Warm Springs
2189 Hwy 26, Warm Springs Times vary, check website museumatwarmsprings.org

→ The magnificent Painted Hills at John Day Fossil Beds National Monument

Ashland

B6 110 E Main St; www.ashlandchamber.com

Amiable Ashland promises fine dining, craft beer, and walkable shopping but the town is most famous for the **Oregon Shakespeare Festival**, which welcomes 400,000 theatergoers every year. The schedule includes plays by Shakespeare as well as by classical and contemporary playwrights. Theater buffs can also view props and costumes and take tours of the festival's three venues.

Many commercial outfitters launch raft and jet-boat trips from Grants Pass, 40 miles (64 km) north of Ashland on I-5. The Rogue River rushes 215 twisting miles (346 km) through Siskiyou National Forest before reaching the Pacific Ocean. Elk, mountain lions, bears, and bald eagles can often be seen on the way.

↑ Musicians performing at the renowned Oregon Shakespeare Festival

Oregon Shakespeare Festival

15 S Pioneer St osfashland.org

Joseph

D4 201 E 2nd St; (541) 426-5546

This city is named for Chief Joseph, leader of the Nez Perce people. In 1877, he led his people on a 1,800-mile (2,880-km) flight to resist resettlement from their lands in the Wallowas; they were apprehended near the Canadian border and relocated to Washington State.

The brick storefronts, snow-capped Wallowa Mountains, and outlying grasslands still lend Joseph a frontier-town air. Housed in a former newspaper office, hospital, and bank built in 1888 is the **Wallowa County Museum**, devoted to Chief Joseph's famous retreat. Chief Joseph Days, held in July, feature a rodeo. Other festivals include the Annual Arts Festival and the Wallowa Mountain Quilt Show, in June.

Wallowa County Museum

110 S Main St Memorial Day–3rd weekend Sep: 10am–4pm daily co.wallowa.or.us

Wallowa Lake

D4 4 miles (6 km) S of Joseph

The crystal-clear waters of this long glacial lake sparkle at the foot of the Wallowa Mountains, which form a 10,000-ft- (3,050-m-) high, 40-mile- (64-km-) long wall of granite. Much of the shoreline falls within the boundaries of national forest lands and **Wallowa Lake State Park**.

The popular **Wallowa Lake Tramway** whisks riders up 3,700 ft (1,100 m) to the summit of Mount Howard, where there are views of the lake below and the Wallowa Mountains. Deep wilderness is only a short hike away from the lake in the Eagle Cap Wilderness.

Wallowa Lake State Park

6 miles (10 km) S of Joseph off Hwy 82 Dawn–dusk daily oregonstateparks.org

Wallowa Lake Tramway

59919 Wallowa Lake Hwy, Joseph Mid-May–Sep wallowalaketramway.com

John Day Fossil Beds National Monument

C4 Dawn-dusk daily 32651 Hwy 19; www.nps.gov/joda

Prehistoric fossil beds litter the John Day Fossil Beds National Monument, where sedimentary rocks preserve the plants and animals that flourished in jungles and savannas for 40 million years, between the extinction of the dinosaurs and the beginning of the most recent ice age. The monument comprises three units with trails that allow for close-up observation. Painted Hills presents volcanic rock formations in vivid hues of red, pink, tan, bronze, and black. Clarno contains the oldest formations, dating back 54 million years, including some of the finest fossil plant remains on earth. At Sheep Rock, the visitors' center displays important finds from the beds.

Jacksonville

A6 185 Oregon St; www.jacksonvilleoregon.com

Once a Gold Rush boomtown, Jacksonville is now the heart of the burgeoning southern Oregon wine region. With more than 80 brick and wood-frame 19th-century buildings, the city has been designated a National Historic Landmark. The **Beekman House** is a museum offering a glimpse of how the town's prosperous burghers once lived.

Visit in the summer for the annual **Britt Festivals**, the Pacific Northwest's premier outdoor performing arts summer festival, where internationally famous artists represent various music genres.

Beekman House
470 E California St (541) 245-3650 By appointment

Britt Festivals
216 W Main St, Medford brittfest.org

Malheur National Wildlife Refuge

D4 Dawn-dusk daily 36391 Sodhouse Ln, Princeton; www.fws.gov/malheur

One of the nation's largest wildlife refuges, Malheur spreads across 292 sq miles (756 sq km) of the Blitzen Valley floor. More than 320 species of birds and 58 species of mammals inhabit the wetlands, meadows, and uplands, ensuring prime wildlife viewing.

Spring and fall are the best times to view birds, which alight in the refuge on their annual migrations. A small museum houses specimens of birds commonly seen in the refuge. Starting at the visitor center, the Central Patrol Road traverses the 40-mile (64-km) length of the refuge and gives access to prime viewing spots.

From the refuge, the 69-mile (111-km) **Diamond Loop National Back Country Byway** heads into sage-covered hills and red rimrock canyons. Along the route are Diamond Craters, a volcanic landscape formed between 17,000 and 25,000 years ago; and Diamond, a small ranch town.

Diamond Loop National Back Country Byway
28910 Hwy 20 W, Hines; www.blm.gov/or

INSIDER TIP

Dig For Fossils

The only place you can legally dig for fossils in Oregon is the town of Fossil, 100 miles (160 km) northwest of John Day. The fossil field is behind Wheeler High School, and there's a small entrance fee.

A DRIVING TOUR

WINE COUNTRY OF THE NORTH WILLAMETTE VALLEY

Length 35 miles (56 km) **Starting point** On Hwy 99 W a few miles east of Newberg, 38 miles (58 km) west of Portland **Stopping-off points** Dundee, Newberg, and McMinnville are home to many well-known restaurants.

The rich, wet, temperate valley that surrounds the Willamette River as it flows north from Eugene to join the Columbia River has yielded a bounty of fruits and vegetables ever since Oregon Trail pioneers began farming the land in the mid-19th century. In the 1960s, the valley's soil was also found to be ideal for growing grapes, especially the Pinot Noir, Pinot Gris, and Chardonnay varietals. Today, vineyards carpet the rolling hillsides, especially in Yamhill County. It is easy to conduct a taste test since dozens of wineries are conveniently located just off Highway 99 W between McMinnville and Newberg. So bring a designated driver and unwind in the valley's beautiful surroundings.

The views of the Willamette Valley are one attraction of the hilltop **Anne Amie Vineyards**; *fine white wines are another.*

Finish your tour at **EIEIO & Company**, *where the wines of many small producers – whose wineries are not open to the public – are available for tasting and purchase.*

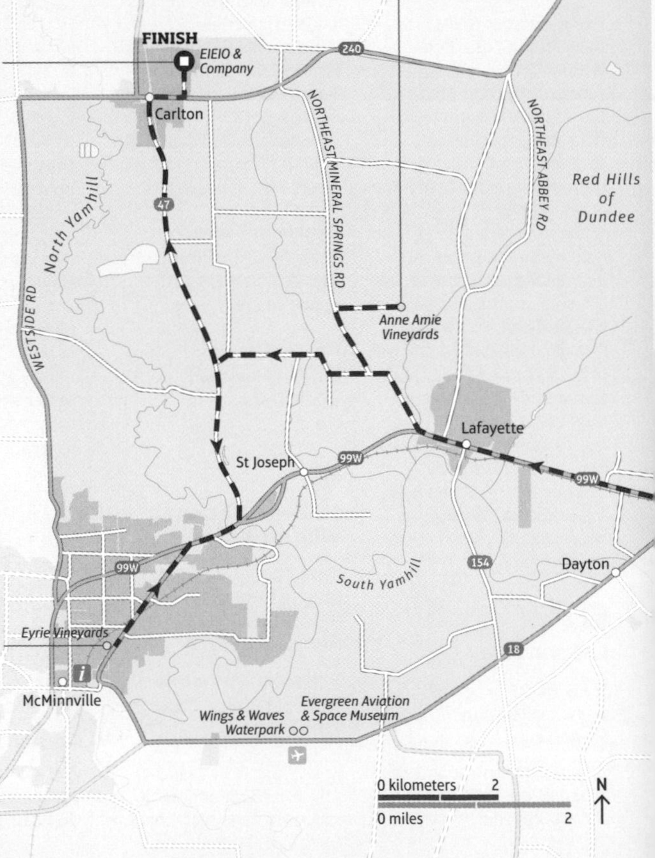

The pioneering **Eyrie Vineyards** *winery, established in 1966, produced the Willamette Valley's first Pinot Noir and Chardonnay and the USA's first Pinot Gris.*

↑ Fog rising over the Maresh Red Barn Vineyard, with Douglas firs in the distance

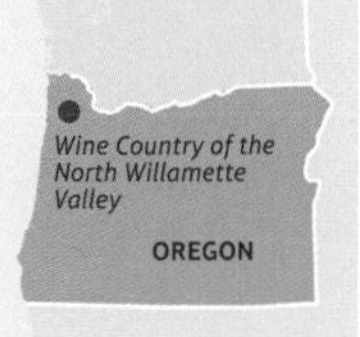

Locator Map

Shady hillside gardens and an antiques-filled tasting room, warmed by a fire, are lovely spots to taste the award-winning Pinot Noirs at **Rex Hill Vineyards**.

Wines from Maresh vineyard grapes, custom-made by three Oregon wineries, are on offer at the **Maresh Red Barn Vineyard**.

240

Rex Hill Vineyards

START

99W

Sunnycrest

Newberg

219

74

99W

18

Torii Mor

Dundee

Maresh Red Barn Vineyard

Argyle Winery

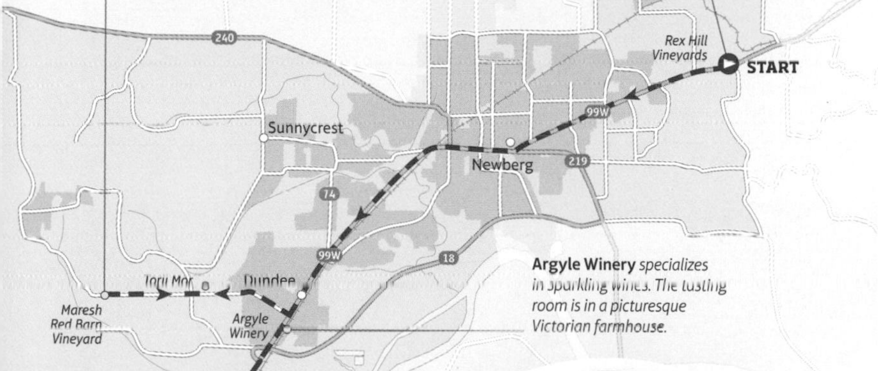

Argyle Winery *specializes in sparkling wines. The tasting room is in a picturesque Victorian farmhouse.*

Sokol Blosser Winery

99W

Willamette

Yamhill

At **Sokol Blosser Winery**, *one of the region's oldest and largest wineries, visitors are offered a self-guided tour of the vineyards and a glass of dry white wine.*

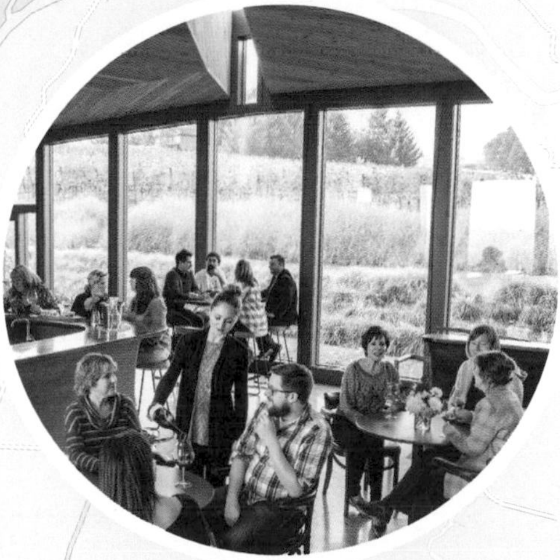

↑ Indulging in white wine tastings at the renowned Sokol Blosser Winery

A DRIVING TOUR

CASCADE LAKES NATIONAL SCENIC BYWAY

Cascade Lakes National Scenic Byway
OREGON

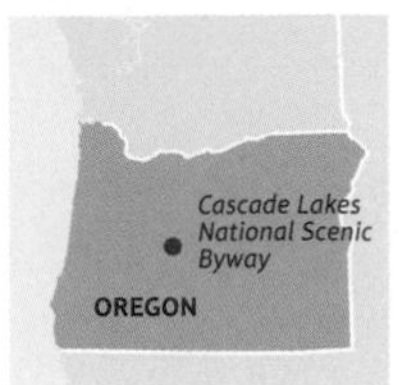

Locator Map

Length 95 miles (153 km) **Starting points** Hwy 372 or Hwy 97 out of Bend **Stopping-off points** Elk Lake has good restaurants and grocery stores

This loop, best experienced from June to mid-October, is often called Century Drive because the circuit is just under 100 miles (160 km) long. A stunning display of forest and mountain scenery unfolds in this relatively short distance. Trails into the deep wilderness, idyllic picnic and camping spots, lakes and streams brimming with trout and salmon, and ski slopes and rustic resorts are likely to tempt even the most time-pressed traveler to linger on this scenic byway for as long as possible.

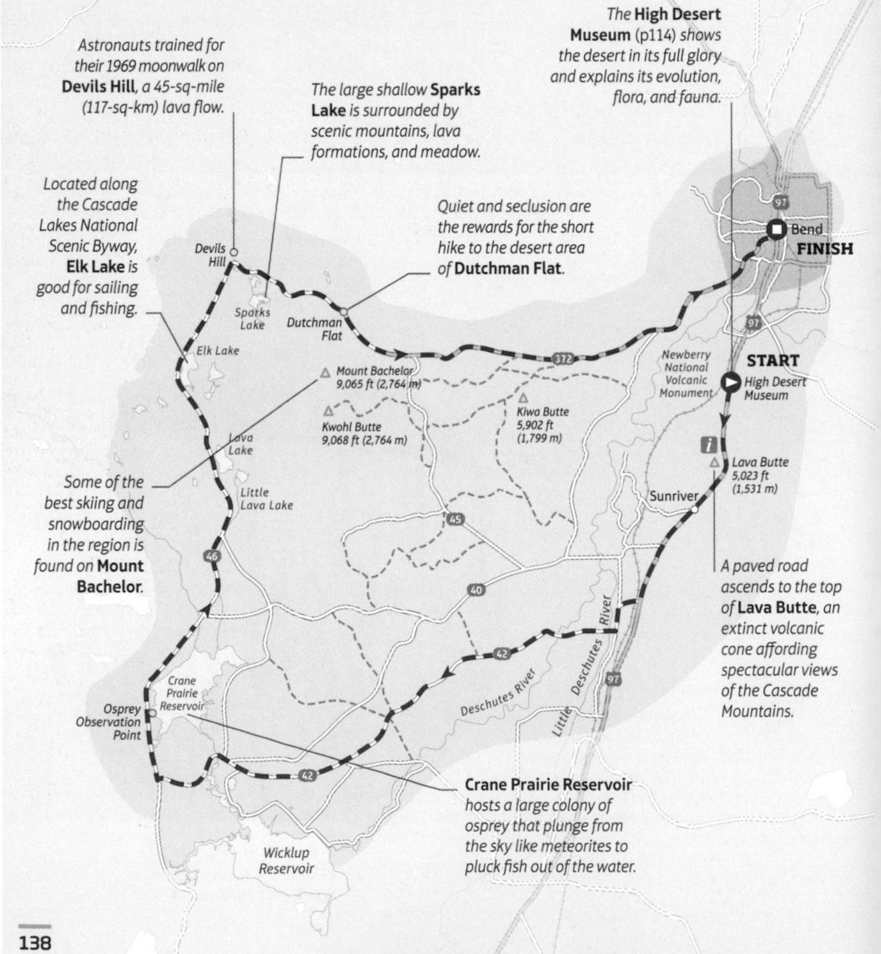

0 km 8
0 miles 8
N
The High Desert Museum (p114) shows the desert in its full glory and explains its evolution, flora, and fauna.
Astronauts trained for their 1969 moonwalk on Devils Hill, a 45-sq-mile (117-sq-km) lava flow.
The large shallow Sparks Lake is surrounded by scenic mountains, lava formations, and meadow.
Located along the Cascade Lakes National Scenic Byway, Elk Lake is good for sailing and fishing.
Quiet and seclusion are the rewards for the short hike to the desert area of Dutchman Flat.
Devils Hill
Sparks Lake
Dutchman Flat
Elk Lake
Bend
FINISH
START
High Desert Museum
Newberry National Volcanic Monument
Mount Bachelor 9,065 ft (2,764 m)
Kwohl Butte 9,068 ft (2,764 m)
Kiwa Butte 5,902 ft (1,799 m)
Lava Butte 5,023 ft (1,531 m)
Lava Lake
Little Lava Lake
Sunriver
372
97
45
46
40
42
Some of the best skiing and snowboarding in the region is found on Mount Bachelor.
A paved road ascends to the top of Lava Butte, an extinct volcanic cone affording spectacular views of the Cascade Mountains.
Crane Prairie Reservoir
Osprey Observation Point
Deschutes River
Little Deschutes River
Crane Prairie Reservoir hosts a large colony of osprey that plunge from the sky like meteorites to pluck fish out of the water.
Wicklup Reservoir

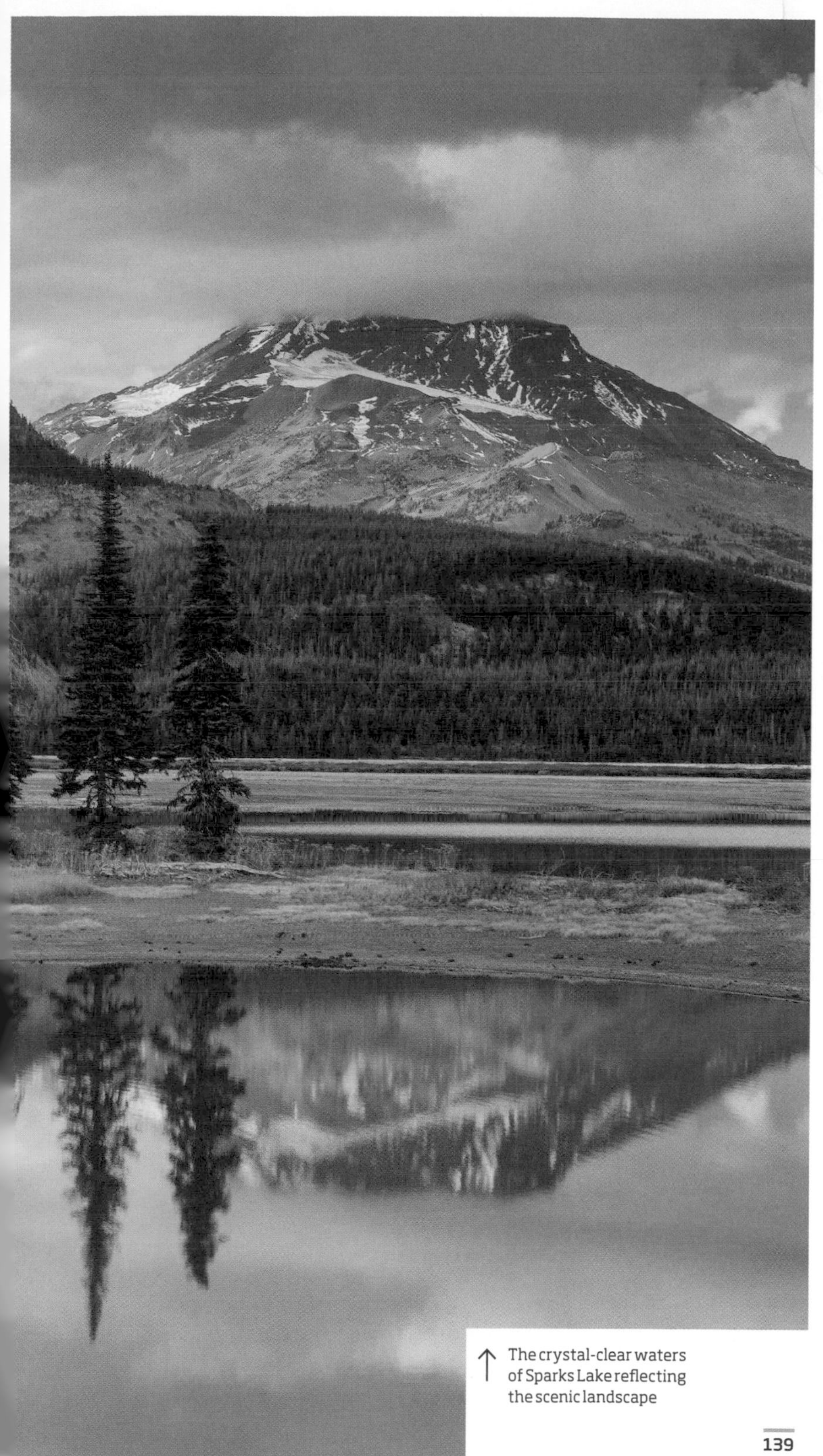

↑ The crystal-clear waters of Sparks Lake reflecting the scenic landscape

A DRIVING TOUR

HELLS CANYON NATIONAL RECREATION AREA

Length 214 miles (345 km) **Starting point** Oregon SR 350, 8 miles (13 km) E of Joseph **Stopping-off points** Imnaha offers good food and lodging

Some of the wildest terrain in North America clings to the sides of craggy, 9,400-ft (2,865-m) peaks at Hells Canyon and plunges to the famed basin far below, where the Snake River rushes through North America's deepest river-carved gorge. A drive through this area – only available to traverse in the summer months – is one of the best ways to delight in the massive canyon walls rising 7,993 ft (2,436 m), and the dense upland pine forests and delicate flower-covered alpine meadows. Much of the terrain is too rugged to cross, even on foot, making sections of the Snake River accessible only by boat.

*One of many overlooks in the Hells Canyon area, the remote **Buckhorn Overlook** offers superb views of the Imnaha River canyon.*

FINISH

Buckhorn Lookout

Nee-Me-Poo Trail

*Hikers on the **Nee-Me-Poo Trail** follow in the footsteps of Chief Joseph and Nez Perce American Indians who, in 1877, embarked on a trek toward freedom in Canada.*

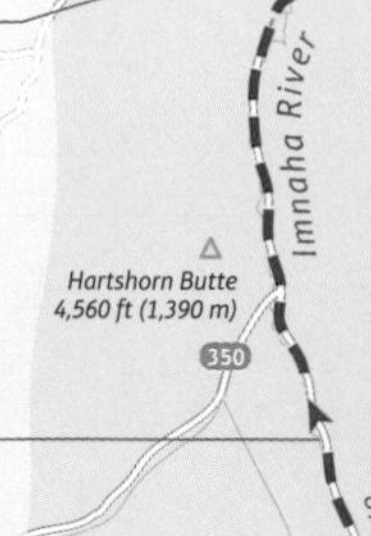

*A road from the town of Imnaha follows the frothy **Imnaha River** through a pine-scented valley, passing isolated ranches and a fish weir.*

UPPER IMNAHA ROAD

Big Sheep Creek

Harl Butte
6,056 ft (1,846 m)

Grouse Creek

39

← Dramatic mountainous landscape seen from the Buckhorn Overlook

Hells Canyon Reservoir

*Formed by Oxbow Dam to the south and Hells Canyon Dam to the north, the 25-mile- (40-km-) long **Hells Canyon Reservoir** is part of a huge power-generating complex on the Snake River.*

39

START

Oxbow Dam

86

Pine Creek

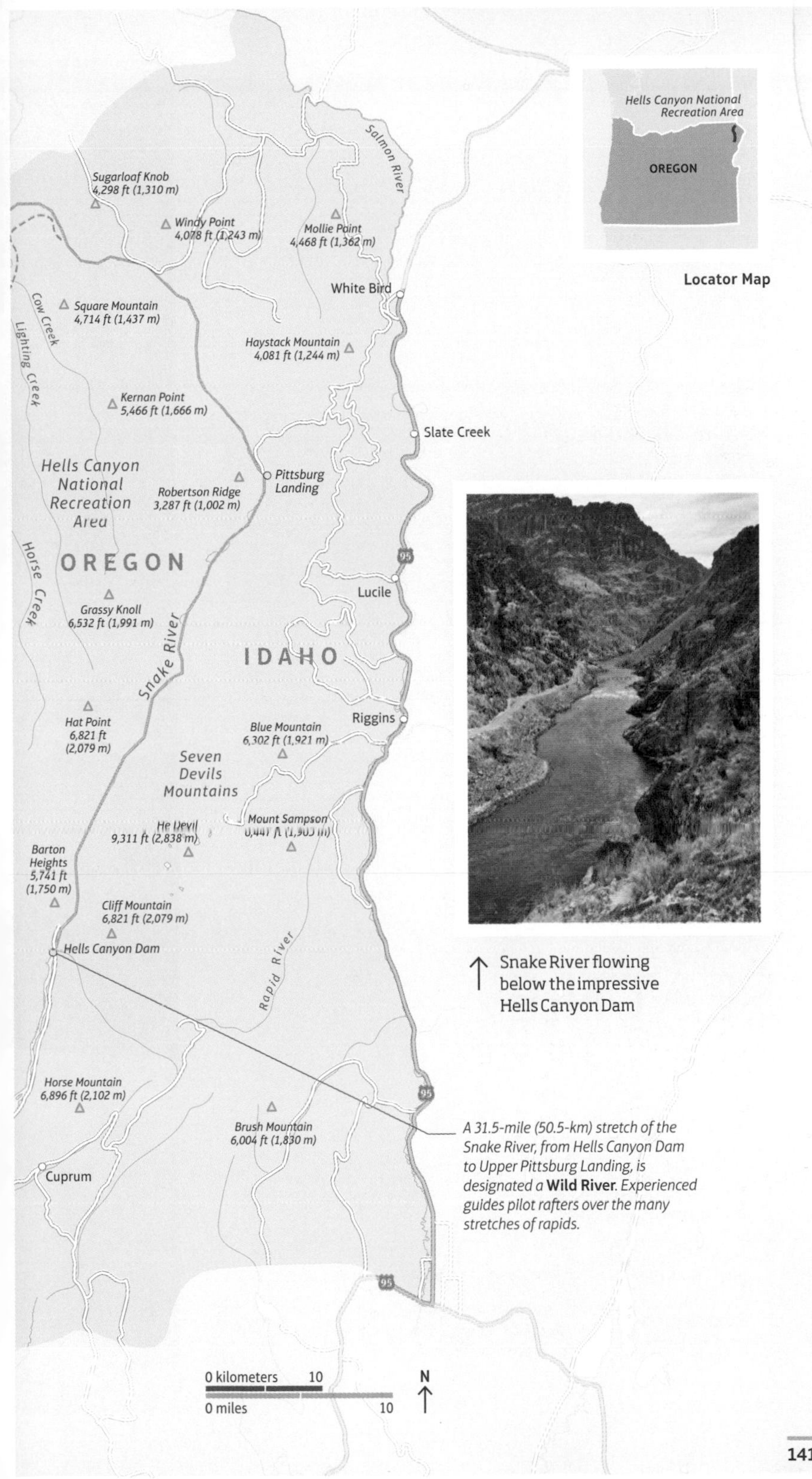

↑ Snake River flowing below the impressive Hells Canyon Dam

A 31.5-mile (50.5-km) stretch of the Snake River, from Hells Canyon Dam to Upper Pittsburg Landing, is designated a ***Wild River****. Experienced guides pilot rafters over the many stretches of rapids.*

SEATTLE

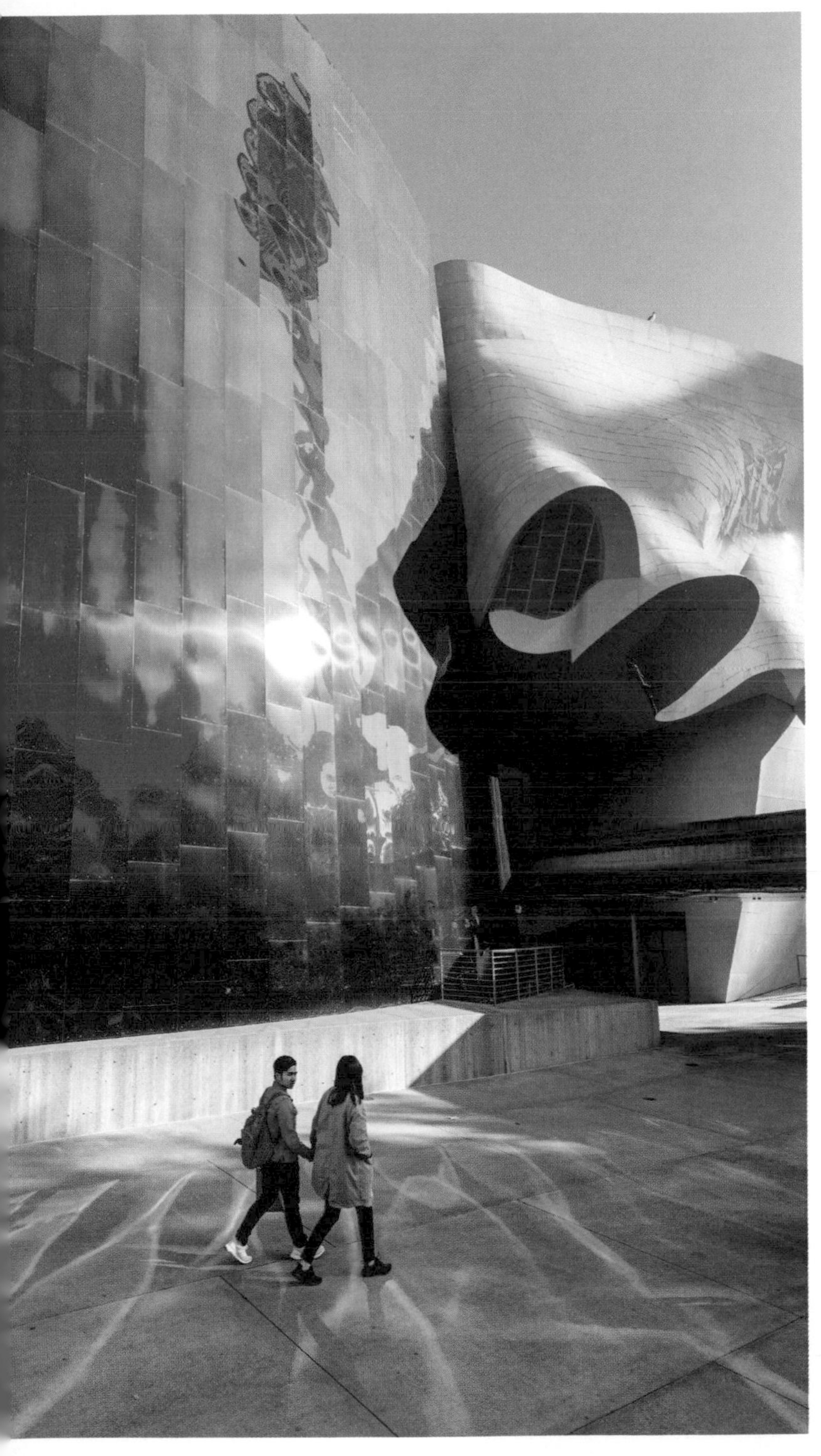

The funky, modern facade of the Museum of Pop Culture

EXPLORE SEATTLE

This guide divides Seattle into four sightseeing areas: the three on this map and a chapter for sights beyond the city center. Find out more about each area on the following pages.

NORTH AMERICA
CANADA
PACIFIC NORTHWEST
Seattle
UNITED STATES OF AMERICA
Pacific Ocean
Atlantic Ocean
MEXICO
CUBA
Lake Union
Museum of History and Industry
Center for Wooden Boats
SEATTLE CENTER AND BELLTOWN
p172
Bill and Melinda Gates Foundation
Amazon Spheres
BELLTOWN
PACIFIC PLACE
Pacific Place
Westlake Center
Macy's
Paramount Theatre
Washington State Convention Center
CAPITOL HILL
Broadway Performance Hall
Egyptian Theatre
Seattle University
FIRST HILL
DOWNTOWN
Benaroya Hall
Seattle Tower
Seattle Art Museum
Central Library
Columbia Center
Pike Place Market
Seattle Aquarium
Seattle Great Wheel
PIKE PLACE MARKET AND THE WATERFRONT
p162
PIONEER SQUARE
Pioneer Building
PIONEER SQUARE AND DOWNTOWN
p150
Klondike Gold Rush National Historic Park
Wing Luke Museum
Union Station
Pinball Museum
INTERNATIONAL DISTRICT
YESLER TERRACE
CenturyLink Field
0 meters 500
0 yards 500
N

GETTING TO KNOW SEATTLE

Though a hilly city, Seattle is easy to navigate on foot. Downtown is the perfect base from which to explore the city, surrounded as it is by a patchwork of seven different neighborhoods, each with its own distinct character, cultural offerings, and vibrant residents.

PAGE 150

PIONEER SQUARE AND DOWNTOWN

The area to the south of central Seattle marries the birthplace of the modern city with the business district of downtown. Pioneer Square is a revitalized historic neighborhood, home to a thriving arts scene and an entrepreneurial spirit. A short walk north leads to downtown, where upscale shops, luxury hotels, and gourmet restaurants welcome indulgence. Lending cultural panache is the boldly designed Seattle Art Museum and the state-of-the-art Benaroya Hall.

Best for
Historical sites, multicultural dining, and fine art

Home to
Seattle Art Museum

Experience
Taking an entertaining and informative underground tour of Seattle, revealing its riotous past

PAGE 162

PIKE PLACE MARKET AND THE WATERFRONT

Situated above the shores of Elliott Bay, this historic district is the heart of the city. Exuberant and engaging, it is known as much for its colorful personalities as it is for its abundance of local produce. Here, Seattleites spend weekends browsing the underground arcade at Pike Place Market, a veritable feast for the senses, and departing on adventures from the waterfront on its array of ferries, cruise ships, and harbor tour boats. Pike Street Hillclimb connects the market to Seattle's bustling waterfront, with its briny scents, squawking seagulls, fish-and-chip joints, and fine seafood restaurants. Once night hits, there's no better place from which to witness the bustle and bright lights of the wider city than from the Seattle Great Wheel on Pier 57.

Best for

Market shopping, seafood dining, and nightlife

Home to

Pike Place Market

Experience

A tasting tour of Pike Place Market, sampling sweet and savory treats and witnessing a fish throwing show

→

PAGE 172

SEATTLE CENTER AND BELLTOWN

Located north of downtown, Seattle Center is the site of lavish presentations of art, theater, dance, and music all year long. Best known as the home of the iconic Space Needle, the center also offers numerous cultural venues and excellent museums, including the innovative Museum of Pop Culture (MoPOP). Just to the south lies trendy Belltown, its hub stretching from Virginia to Vine streets along 1st Avenue. Here, among the pricey condominiums, you'll find upscale clothing boutiques, antique shops, home accessories stores, great bars, and a fashionable crowd to match.

Best for
Family-friendly museums, city vistas, and shopping

Home to
Museum of Pop Culture (MoPOP), Space Needle

Experience
Seeing Seattle and beyond from the Space Needle at sunset

PAGE 184

BEYOND THE CENTER

Seattle's outlying areas offer plenty of opportunities for exploration and recreation. To the south sit two spectacular professional sports stadiums – the pride and joy of baseball and soccer fans. The east side opens into two of Seattle's prominent hills, First and Capitol, which offer notable museums, grand cathedrals, and an eclectic assortment of shops and bars. For active outdoor pursuits, head to Green Lake, Discovery Park, and Alki Beach for strolling, jogging, biking, and hiking paths. Other Seattle neighborhoods, such as Ballard, Fremont, and Madison Park, are ideal destinations for a day trip.

Best for

Spectator sports, city parks, and beaches

Home to

Capitol Hill, Ballard, Fremont

Experience

Watching the Seattle Mariners play a baseball game at T-Mobile Park

TICKETING
MUSEUM
GALLERIES
SAM GALLERY
AND SHOP

John Grade's *Middle Fork* installation in the Seattle Art Museum

PIONEER SQUARE AND DOWNTOWN

The birthplace of Seattle, Pioneer Square was the city's original downtown, established in 1852 when Arthur and David Denny arrived with a handful of fellow pioneers. Emerging from the ashes of the Great Fire of 1889, the rebuilt commercial area prospered as the 19th century drew to a close. Many of the buildings in this area were constructed between the Great Fire and the Klondike Gold Rush of 1897–98, two pivotal events in the city's history. By the time the much-touted Smith Tower opened in 1914, however, the city core had begun spreading north and Pioneer Square was less and less a prestigious business address. Following the stock market crash in 1929, it eventually became the city's Skid Row, and in the 1960s many of its buildings were threatened with demolition. However, in 1969 it was designated as a National Historic District and therefore protected.

The city's growth since the Klondike Gold Rush of 1897–98 has been vigorous. Another boom in construction soared in the area in the 1980s, and today, the revitalized Pioneer Square is a thriving arts center. A short walk leads to downtown – home to the city's modern skyscrapers, upscale shops, and luxury hotels, as well as green spaces.

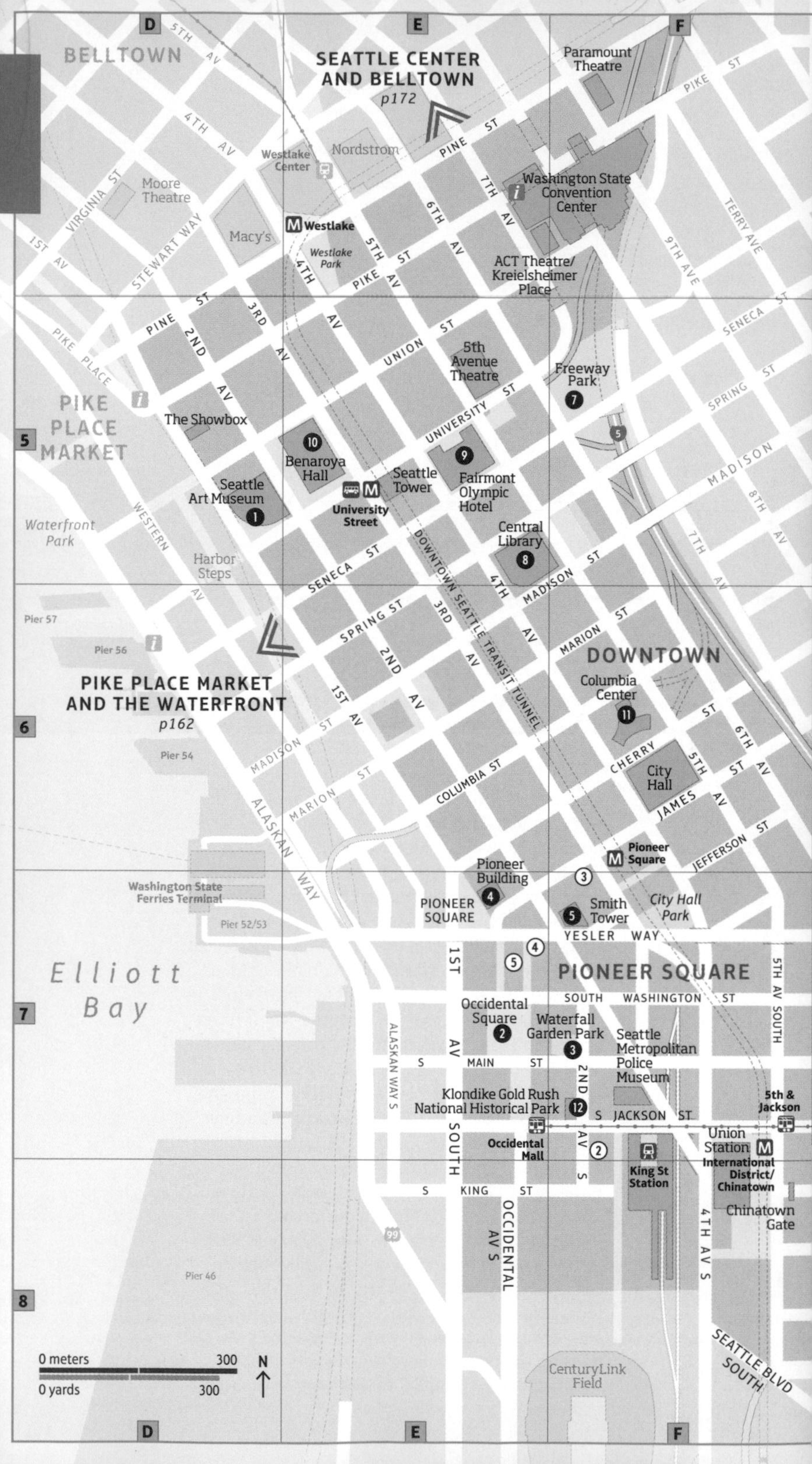

D
E
F
BELLTOWN
SEATTLE CENTER AND BELLTOWN
p172
Paramount Theatre
Westlake Center
Nordstrom
Moore Theatre
Macy's
Westlake
Westlake Park
Washington State Convention Center
ACT Theatre/ Kreielsheimer Place
5th Avenue Theatre
Freeway Park
PIKE PLACE MARKET
The Showbox
Benaroya Hall
Seattle Tower
Fairmont Olympic Hotel
Seattle Art Museum
University Street
Central Library
Waterfront Park
Harbor Steps
Pier 57
Pier 56
PIKE PLACE MARKET AND THE WATERFRONT
p162
DOWNTOWN
Columbia Center
Pier 54
City Hall
Pioneer Square
Pioneer Building
Washington State Ferries Terminal
PIONEER SQUARE
Smith Tower
City Hall Park
Pier 52/53
YESLER WAY
Elliott Bay
PIONEER SQUARE
Occidental Square
Waterfall Garden Park
Seattle Metropolitan Police Museum
Klondike Gold Rush National Historical Park
5th & Jackson
Occidental Mall
Union Station
King St Station
International District/ Chinatown
Chinatown Gate
Pier 46
CenturyLink Field
0 meters 300
0 yards 300
N
5
6
7
8

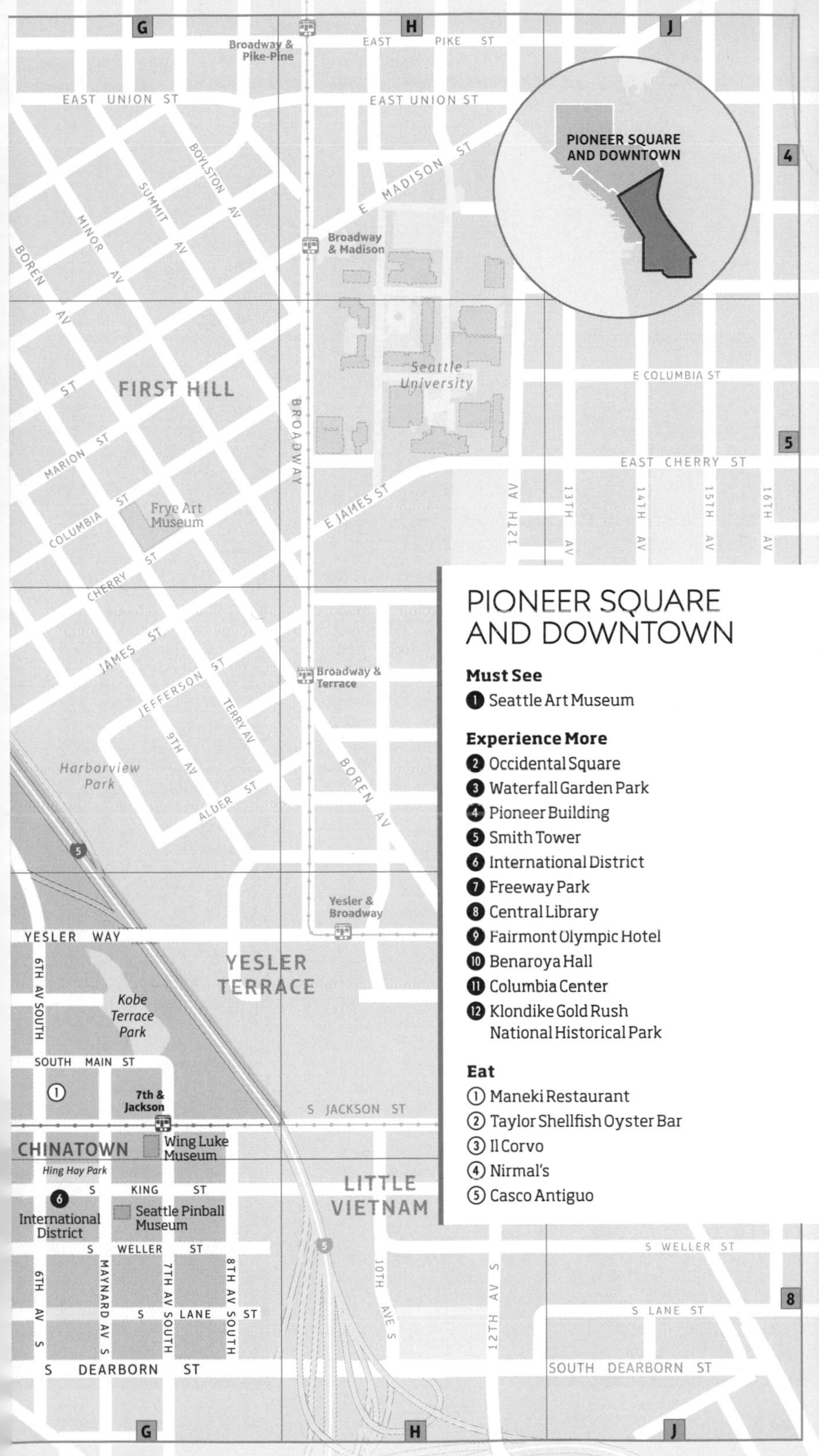
PIONEER SQUARE AND DOWNTOWN
Must See
1 Seattle Art Museum
Experience More
2 Occidental Square
3 Waterfall Garden Park
4 Pioneer Building
5 Smith Tower
6 International District
7 Freeway Park
8 Central Library
9 Fairmont Olympic Hotel
10 Benaroya Hall
11 Columbia Center
12 Klondike Gold Rush National Historical Park
Eat
① Maneki Restaurant
② Taylor Shellfish Oyster Bar
③ Il Corvo
④ Nirmal's
⑤ Casco Antiguo
G
H
J
4
5
8
Broadway & Pike-Pine
EAST PIKE ST
EAST UNION ST
EAST UNION ST
E MADISON ST
BOYLSTON AV
SUMMIT AV
MINOR AV
BOREN AV
Broadway & Madison
FIRST HILL
Seattle University
E COLUMBIA ST
BROADWAY
MARION ST
ST
EAST CHERRY ST
COLUMBIA ST
Frye Art Museum
E JAMES ST
12TH AV
13TH AV
14TH AV
15TH AV
16TH AV
CHERRY ST
JAMES ST
Broadway & Terrace
JEFFERSON ST
TERRY AV
9TH AV
Harborview Park
ALDER ST
BOREN AV
5
Yesler & Broadway
YESLER WAY
YESLER TERRACE
6TH AV SOUTH
Kobe Terrace Park
SOUTH MAIN ST
①
7th & Jackson
S JACKSON ST
CHINATOWN
Wing Luke Museum
Hing Hay Park
S KING ST
6
International District
Seattle Pinball Museum
LITTLE VIETNAM
S WELLER ST
S WELLER ST
5
MAYNARD AV S
7TH AV SOUTH
8TH AV SOUTH
10TH AVE S
12TH AV S
6TH AV S
S LANE ST
S LANE ST
S DEARBORN ST
SOUTH DEARBORN ST

→

The striking, modern facade of the SAM as night falls on the city, and *(inset)* the *Hammering Man* working away during the day outside the south entrance

SEATTLE ART MUSEUM

D5 1300 1st Av 10am-5pm Wed-Mon (to 9pm Thu) Major hols seattleartmuseum.org

Lending cultural panache to the city's downtown core is the boldly designed Seattle Art Museum (SAM). With a collection of over 25,000 items, it's no wonder this is one of the premier art museums in the Pacific Northwest.

Designed by the Philadelphia firm Venturi Scott Brown and Associates, the original bold limestone and sandstone building was completed in 1991. It now connects seamlessly to the spacious 2007 expansion, designed by American architect Brad Cloepfil. At the museum's south entrance is one of the most iconic works of art here, the giant *Hammering Man*. A tribute to workers, Jonathan Borofsky's 48-ft (15-m) animated steel sculpture "hammers" silently and continuously from 7am to 10pm daily, resting only on Labor Day.

Gallery Guide

The museum's permanent collection ranges from ancient Egyptian relief sculpture and wooden African statuary to Old Master paintings and contemporary American art. Traveling exhibits are featured on the fourth floor, as are the permanent collections of African and European art. Northwest Coast American Indian art figures on the third floor. The third floor also houses American art, ancient Mediterranean and Islamic art, and modern and contemporary art, including works by contemporary Pacific Northwest artists.

Also in this museum family is the Asian Art Museum, in Volunteer Park *(p187)*, and the Olympic Sculpture Park *(p181)*.

Strolling past treasures in the museum's light-filled galleries

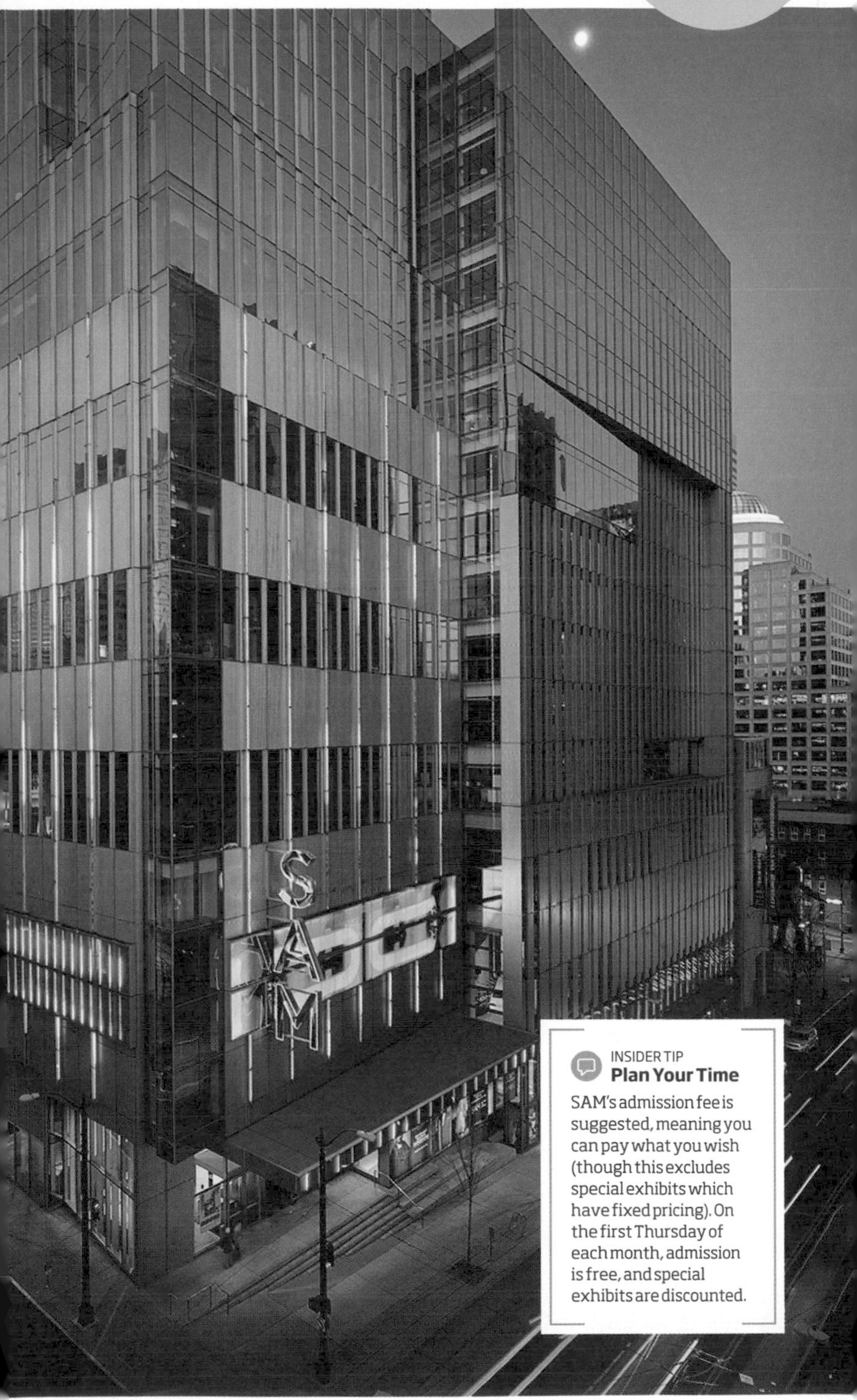

INSIDER TIP
Plan Your Time

SAM's admission fee is suggested, meaning you can pay what you wish (though this excludes special exhibits which have fixed pricing). On the first Thursday of each month, admission is free, and special exhibits are discounted.

EXPERIENCE MORE

2

Occidental Square

E7 Occidental Av between S Main & S Jackson sts

The brick-paved plaza known as Occidental Square offers relief from the busy traffic of Pioneer Square. The tree-lined pedestrian walk is flanked by upscale shops, galleries, and coffeehouses, many housed in attractive Victorian buildings.

Across South Main Street is Occidental Park, where the ambience changes because of the local contingent of homeless people and panhandlers. Of special note here are four cedar totem poles carved by Northwest artist Duane Pasco and the Fallen Firefighters' Memorial, a tribute to the 34 Seattle firefighters who have died in the line of duty since the Seattle Fire Department was founded in 1889.

↑ Occidental Square's Fallen Firefighters' Memorial by Hai Ying Wu

3

Waterfall Garden Park

F7 219 2nd Av S
8am-3:45pm daily
pioneersquare.org

A peaceful, secluded oasis in the middle of busy Pioneer Square, this little park is the perfect place to relax and enjoy a picnic. The sounds of the man-made waterfall cascading over huge rocks soften any street noise.

The park was designed by Masao Kinoshita and built in 1977 by the Annie E. Casey Foundation to honor the workers of the United Parcel Service (UPS). Jim Casey of Seattle was one of the founders of UPS, which was originally formed as the American Messenger Service in a saloon at this site in 1907.

4   

Pioneer Building

E7 600 1st Av
For tours only underground tour.com

Completed in 1892, the Pioneer Building was voted the "finest building west of Chicago" by the American Institute of Architects. It is one of more than 50 buildings designed by the architect Elmer Fisher following the devastating fire of 1889. The brick building houses offices and Doc Maynard's Public House, starting point of Bill Speidel's Underground Tour. This 75-minute walk offers a lively look at Seattle's colorful past and the original streets beneath the modern city, including the 1890s stores abandoned in the 1900s when streets were raised. Beware: the subterranean portion is dusty. While the Pioneer Building itself does not offer tours, you can see the first floor via the bar and the Underground Tour.

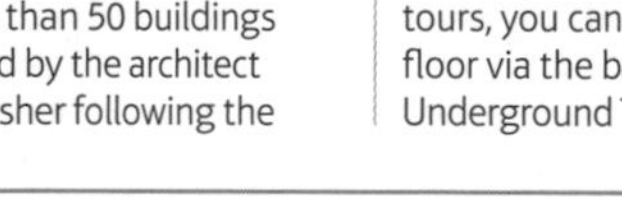

THE GREAT SEATTLE FIRE

On June 6, 1889, in a cabinet shop near Pioneer Square, a pot of flaming glue overturned, igniting wood shavings. The tide, which the city's water system depended on, was low at the time, and as numerous hoses were connected to hydrants, the water supply eventually gave out. The fire spread rapidly, engulfing 60 city blocks before burning itself out. Miraculously, no one died in the blaze. Sturdy brick and stone buildings were erected where flimsy wood structures once stood; streets were widened and raised; and the sewer system was overhauled. From the ashes of disaster rose a city primed for prominence as the 20th century approached.

The stately Smith Tower, defining Seattle's downtown skyline

5 

Smith Tower

F7 506 2nd Av Observation deck: times vary, check website smithtower.com

When it opened in 1914, the 42-story Smith Tower was heralded as the tallest office building in the world outside New York City and for nearly a half century it reigned as the tallest building west of Chicago.

Commissioned by rifle and typewriter tycoon Lyman Cornelius Smith, Seattle's first skyscraper is clad in white terra-cotta. While its height of 489 ft (149 m) is no longer its claim to fame, the city's landmark is home to the last manually operated elevator of its kind on the West Coast. For a fee, you can ride one of the gleaming brass-cage originals to the 35th-floor Observatory. The deck here offers panoramic views of Mount Rainier, the Olympic and Cascade mountain ranges, and Elliott Bay.

6 

International District

G8 East of 6th Av S, S of Yesler Way

Settled by Asian-Americans in the late 19th century, this bustling area still serves as the cultural hub for the city's Chinese, Japanese, Filipino, Vietnamese, Korean, and Laotian residents.

In addition to its numerous restaurants, the area is home to Uwajimaya *(600 5th Avenue South)*, the largest Asian market in the Pacific Northwest. The **Wing Luke Museum of the Asian Pacific American Experience**, a Smithsonian affiliate, is named after the first Asian Pacific American elected to office in the Pacific Northwest. It highlights the history, culture, and art of Asian Pacific Americans.

Wing Luke Museum of the Asian Pacific American Experience

 719 S King St 10am–5pm Tue–Sun Major hols wingluke.org

HIDDEN GEM

Seattle Pinball Museum

Pay the modest entry fee to this museum and entertainment center in the International District *(508 Maynard Av S)* and you can play on pinball machines dating back to the 1930s for as long as you like.

7

Freeway Park

F5 Seneca St & 6th Av 6am–10pm daily seattle.gov/parks

Tucked into the heart of Seattle's bustling commercial district, and adjoining the Washington State Convention and Trade Center, Freeway Park straddles the I-5 freeway. Inside the park, thundering waterfalls drown out the traffic roar, and shady footpaths invite leisurely strolling. Outdoor concerts are held here in summer.

Central Library

E5 1000 4th Av
10am-8pm Mon-Thu, 10am-6pm Fri & Sat, noon-6pm Sun Major hols
spl.org

This striking glass-and-steel structure, completed in 2004, was designed by the award-winning Dutch architect Rem Koolhaas as a replacement for the city's 1960 Central Library. The unusual shape of the building was once a source of controversy, but the Central Library is now regarded as one of Seattle's architectural highlights. The 11-floor library includes works of art and an innovative "Books Spiral," allowing visitors maximum access to the collection, which includes 2 million items. Other facilities include Wi-Fi, computers for public use, and separate centers for children, teenagers, and adult readers.

Fairmont Olympic Hotel

E5 411 University St
fairmont.com

When it debuted in 1924, the Olympic Hotel was *the* place to see and be seen – not surprising since the bondholders who funded the construction were among the city's most socially prominent citizens. Designed by the New York firm of George B. Post and Sons, the Italian Renaissance-style building features high, arched Palladian windows, gleaming oak-paneled walls, and terrazzo floors laid by Italian workmen who were sent to Seattle for the task. Elegant furnishings include antique mirrors, Italian oil jars, and bronze statuary. A glamorous venue for parties, weddings, and debutante balls, it reigned as the grande dame of Seattle hotels for half a century. In 1979, it was listed on the US National Register of Historic Places.

TOP 3 DOWNTOWN MUSIC VENUES

The Showbox
1426 1st Av
showboxpresents.com
Opened in 1939, this Art Deco venue is now devoted to rock music.

Paramount Theatre
911 Pine St
stgpresents.org
A leading performing arts venue featuring music, drama, dance, and comedy acts.

The Triple Door
216 Union St
thetripledoor.com
This intimate music venue plays host to a diverse range of music.

Benaroya Hall

E5 200 University St
seattlesymphony.org

Home of the fantastic Seattle Symphony, the Benaroya Hall contains two performing halls, including the S. Mark Taper Foundation Auditorium, acclaimed for its superior acoustics. The multi-level Grand Lobby, dramatic at night when lit, offers stunning views of the city skyline.

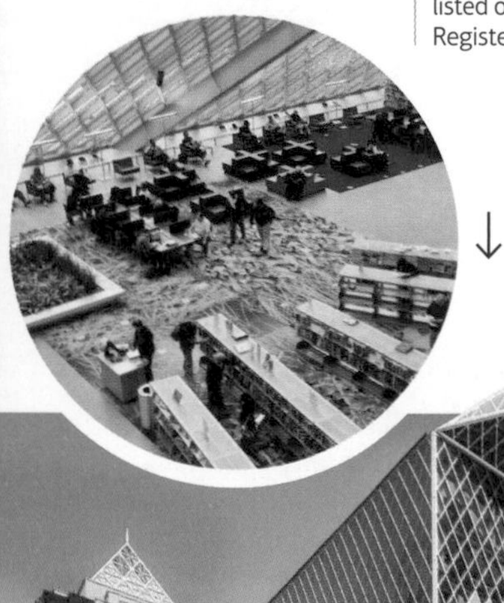

Seattle's striking, modern Central Library, and (*inset*) visitors enjoying its spacious interior

↑ An audience taking in a performance by the Seattle Symphony at Benaroya Hall

Even if time doesn't permit attending a performance, you can gain an appreciation of this magnificent facility by joining one of the excellent tours offered.

Within the outdoor space along 2nd Avenue is the Garden of Remembrance, which honors more than 8,000 Washington citizens who have given their lives in the service of their country since 1941.

Columbia Center

F6 701 5th Av

Columbia Center is the tallest building in the city, rising 1,049 ft (320 m) above sea level. The 76-story skyscraper was completed in 1985 and today is a prestigious business address for more than 5,000 Seattle-area workers. It also attracts visitors to its 73rd-floor observation deck, the **Sky View Observatory**, which offers spectacular vistas of the Cascade and Olympic mountain ranges, Mount Rainier, and Puget Sound. The four-level retail atrium houses shops, food vendors, and the Columbia City Gallery.

Sky View Observatory

May-Aug: 10am-10pm daily; Sep-Apr: 10am-8pm daily Major hols skyviewobservatory.com

Klondike Gold Rush National Historical Park

F7 319 2nd Av S 9am-5pm daily Jan 1, Thanksgiving, Dec 25 nps.gov

The Gold Rush (*p32*) triggered a frenzied stampede of gold-seekers to the Klondike. The largest and closest US city to the gold fields, Seattle became the primary outfitting and embarkation point. While few Klondikers struck it rich, Seattle merchants made a fortune and established the city's reputation as the premier commercial center of the Pacific Northwest.

Established by Congress in 1976, Klondike Gold Rush National Historical Park comprises five units, one of which is in Seattle's Pioneer Square Historic District. The Seattle visitors' center celebrates the city's role in North America's last great Gold Rush. On display here are evocative black-and-white photographs and simulations of the "ton of provisions" that Canadian law required each prospector to bring with him.

The park offers an expanded program in the summer, including ranger-led walking tours of Pioneer Square, gold-panning demonstrations, and scheduled screenings of Gold Rush-themed films.

EAT

Maneki Restaurant

Japanese place with a relaxed elegance. Seafood is a specialty.

G7 304 6th Av S Mon maneki restaurant.com

Taylor Shellfish Oyster Bar

This small upscale chain of oyster bars operates its own shellfish farms.

F7 410 Occidental Av S taylor shellfishfarms.com

Il Corvo

Chef Mike Easton fell in love with fresh pasta in Italy and now serves it in his unpretentious restaurant.

F7 217 James St Dinner, Sat, Sun ilcorvopasta.com

Nirmal's

Lovers of Indian cuisine should head here, where food zings with flavor. There's also a wide choice of vegan dishes.

E7 106 Occidental Av S Times vary, check website nirmal seattle.com

Casco Antiguo

This casual Mexican cantina is famous for the tasty *carne asada* - tender, grilled meat.

E7 115 Occidental Av S cascoantiguo restaurants.com

A SHORT WALK

PIONEER SQUARE

Distance 0.6 miles (1 km) **Time** 15 minutes
Nearest bus stop 2nd Av Ext & S Jackson St

Pioneer Square, Seattle's first downtown and later a decrepit skid row, is today a revitalized business neighborhood and National Historic District. The tall totem poles gracing the square are reminders of the Coast Salish American Indian village that originally occupied this spot. The grand Victorian architecture, social service missions, and upscale shops that you will encounter as you walk through the area are further reminders of the area's checkered past and redevelopment since the 1960s. Many of the buildings standing today were constructed in the years between the Great Fire of 1889 *(p156)* and the Klondike Gold Rush of 1897–98 *(p59)*, both pivotal events in Seattle's history. Lose yourself in art galleries, boutiques, and antique shops that now reside here as you walk through the bustling streets and the pretty cobblestone plazas.

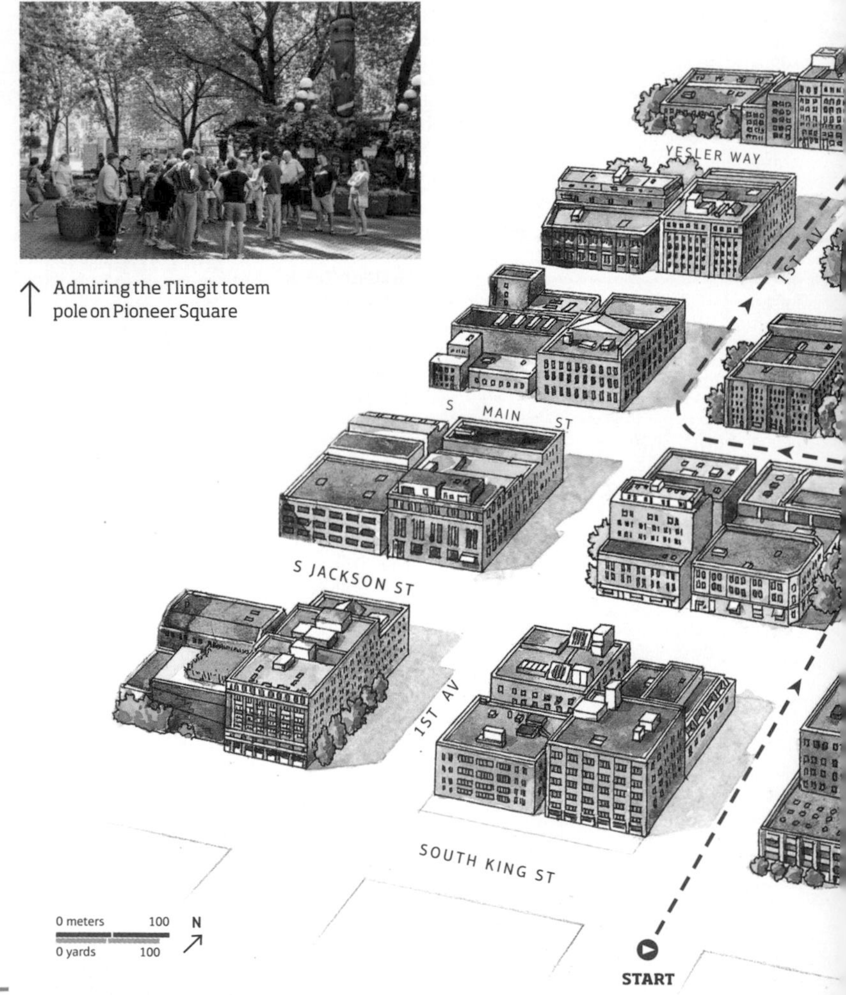

↑ Admiring the Tlingit totem pole on Pioneer Square

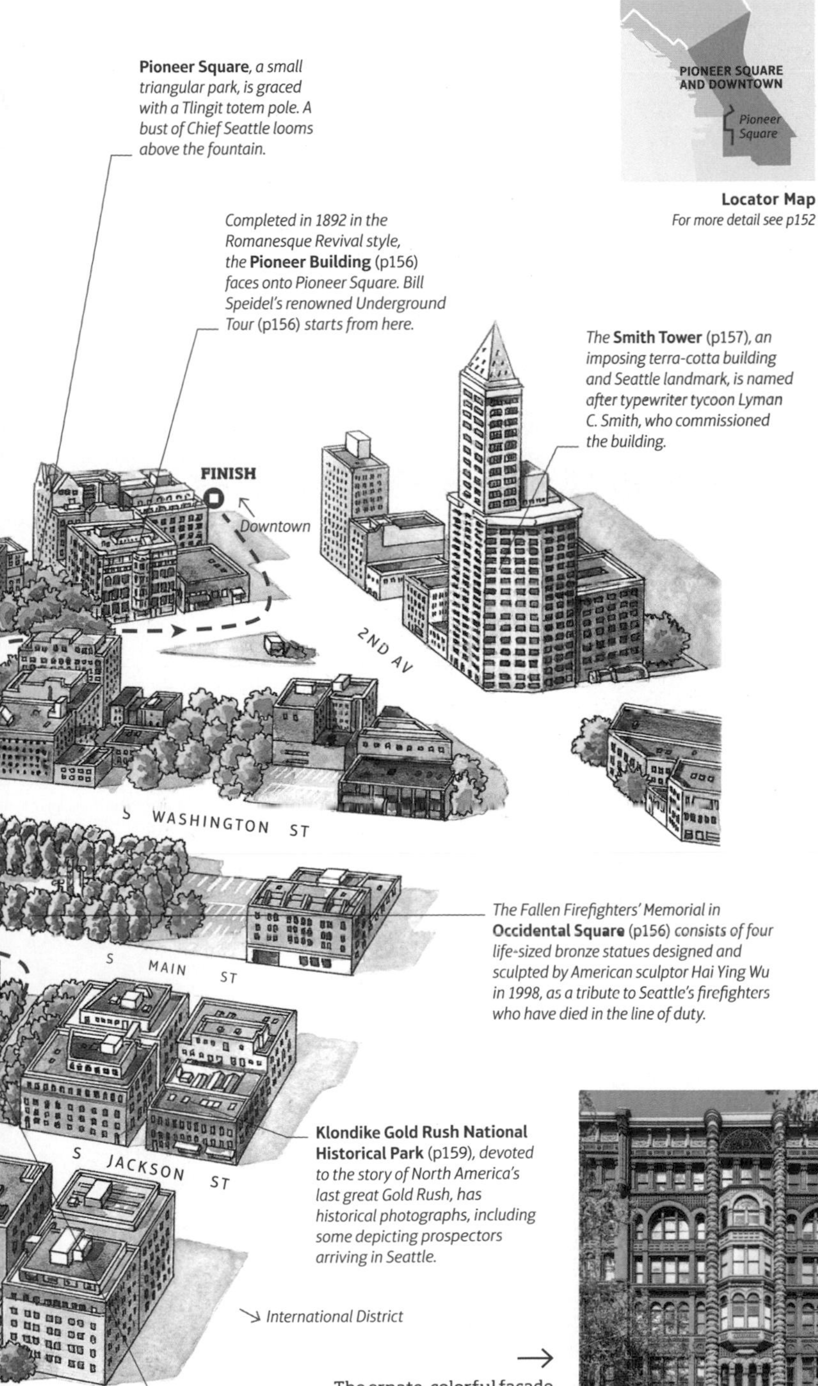

Locator Map
For more detail see p152

Pioneer Square, *a small triangular park, is graced with a Tlingit totem pole. A bust of Chief Seattle looms above the fountain.*

Completed in 1892 in the Romanesque Revival style, the **Pioneer Building** (p156) *faces onto Pioneer Square. Bill Speidel's renowned Underground* Tour (p156) *starts from here.*

The **Smith Tower** (p157), *an imposing terra-cotta building and Seattle landmark, is named after typewriter tycoon Lyman C. Smith, who commissioned the building.*

The Fallen Firefighters' Memorial in **Occidental Square** (p156) *consists of four life-sized bronze statues designed and sculpted by American sculptor Hai Ying Wu in 1998, as a tribute to Seattle's firefighters who have died in the line of duty.*

Klondike Gold Rush National Historical Park (p159), *devoted to the story of North America's last great Gold Rush, has historical photographs, including some depicting prospectors arriving in Seattle.*

Occidental Walk

→ The ornate, colorful facade of the Pioneer Building in the heart of Seattle

COCKTAILS
SEAFOOD

Ambling through the bustling Pike Place Market

PIKE PLACE MARKET AND THE WATERFRONT

It's hard to believe it today as you make your way through the area's busy crowds, but Seattle's Central Waterfront district was once home to small settlements of the Indigenous Duwamish Peoples. It remained that way until the late 18th century when the first Europeans arrived and were greeted by American Indians living, fishing, and hunting here. By the mid-19th century this idyllic existence began to change when settlers built a wharf and a sawmill, creating the roots of what was to become Seattle. With the Klondike Gold Rush of 1897-98, the city became the gateway for sailing to Alaska, creating more development along the waterfront. After a lull during the Depression, the expansion of the waterfront continued, bringing huge container ships.

Pike Place Market was established in 1907 by the city council, who wanted to allow farmers to sell their produce directly to citizens without middlemen. Despite a decrease in visitors and sales after World War II due to the opening of supermarkets, the market returned to its former glory in the 1970s. Still in operation today, Pike Place Market is a historic district that bustles with stalls and street performers.

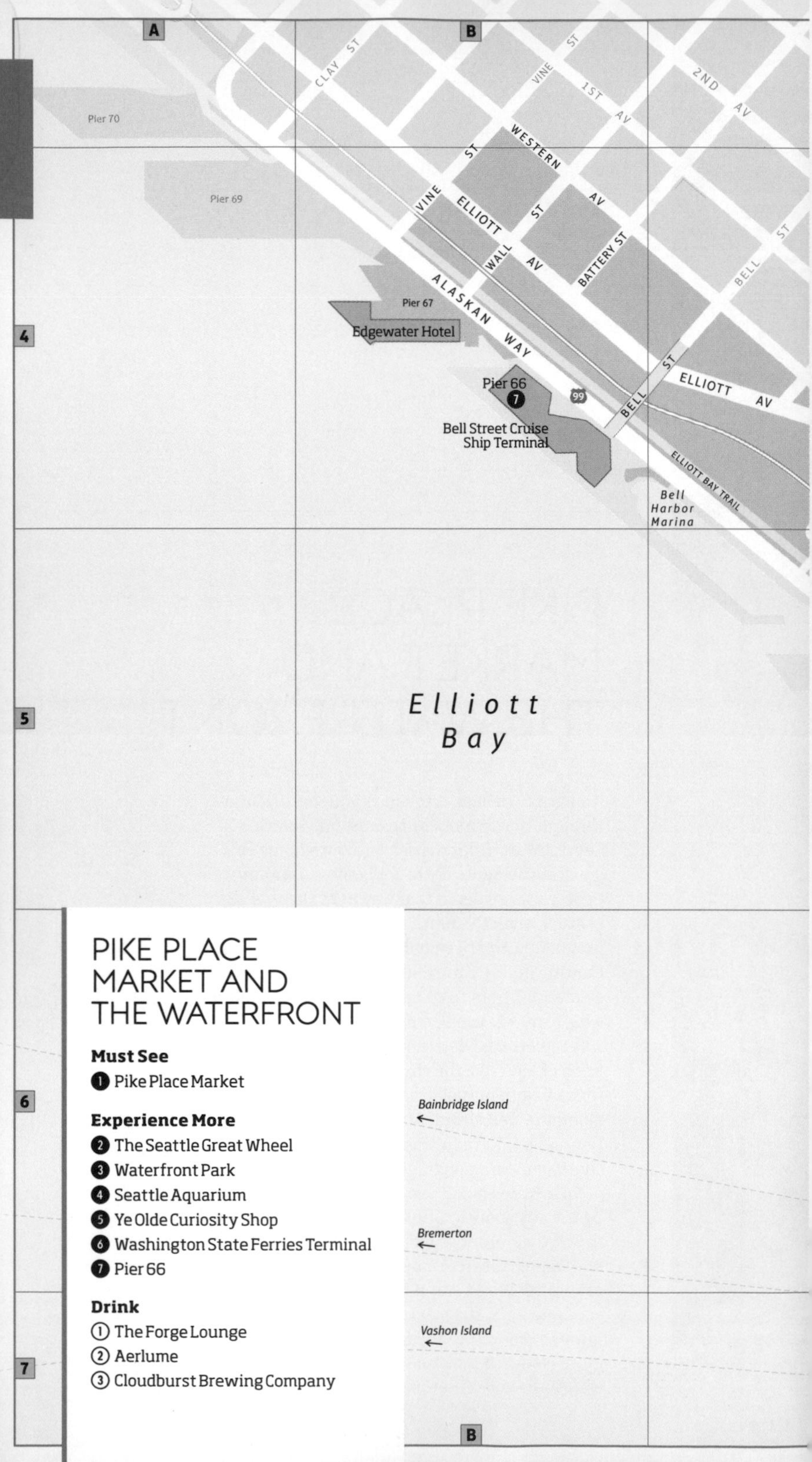

PIKE PLACE MARKET AND THE WATERFRONT

Must See

1. Pike Place Market

Experience More

2. The Seattle Great Wheel
3. Waterfront Park
4. Seattle Aquarium
5. Ye Olde Curiosity Shop
6. Washington State Ferries Terminal
7. Pier 66

Drink

① The Forge Lounge
② Aerlume
③ Cloudburst Brewing Company

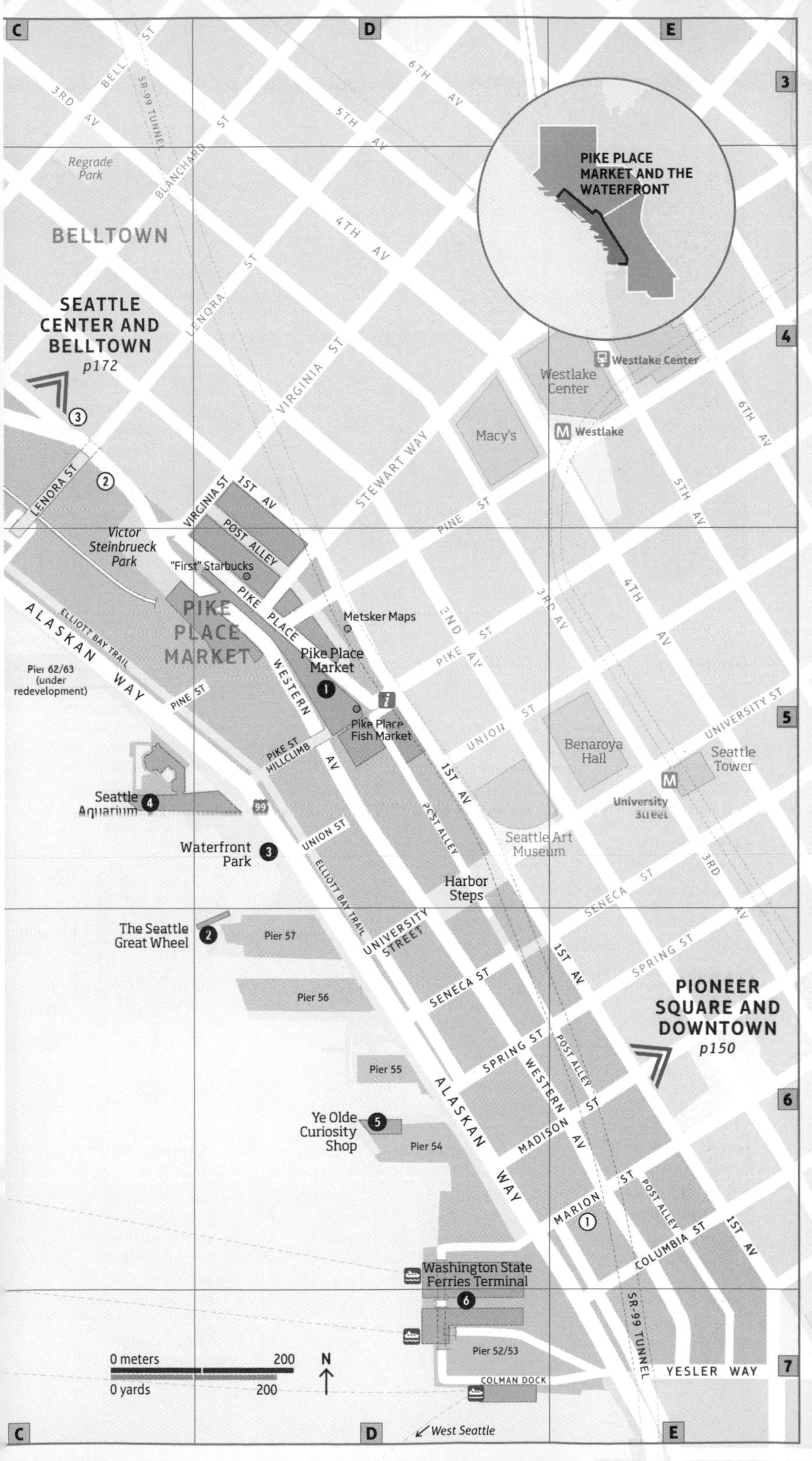

PIKE PLACE MARKET AND THE WATERFRONT
SEATTLE CENTER AND BELLTOWN
p172
PIONEER SQUARE AND DOWNTOWN
p150
BELLTOWN
Regrade Park
Victor Steinbrueck Park
PIKE PLACE MARKET
"First" Starbucks
Metsker Maps
Pike Place Market
Pike Place Fish Market
Westlake Center
Westlake
Macy's
Benaroya Hall
Seattle Tower
University Street
Seattle Art Museum
Harbor Steps
Pier 62/63 (under redevelopment)
Seattle Aquarium
Waterfront Park
The Seattle Great Wheel
Pier 57
Pier 56
Pier 55
Ye Olde Curiosity Shop
Pier 54
Washington State Ferries Terminal
Pier 52/53
COLMAN DOCK
West Seattle
ALASKAN WAY
ELLIOTT BAY TRAIL
WESTERN AV
1ST AV
2ND AV
3RD AV
4TH AV
5TH AV
6TH AV
POST ALLEY
PIKE PLACE
PIKE ST HILLCLIMB
PIKE ST
PINE ST
UNION ST
UNIVERSITY ST
UNIVERSITY STREET
SENECA ST
SPRING ST
MADISON ST
MARION ST
COLUMBIA ST
YESLER WAY
STEWART WAY
VIRGINIA ST
LENORA ST
BLANCHARD ST
BELL ST
SR-99 TUNNEL
0 meters 200
0 yards 200
N

1

PIKE PLACE MARKET

D5 Bounded by Pike & Virginia sts, from 1st to Western avs Daily; times vary, check website Thanksgiving, Dec 25 pikeplacemarket.org

An integral part of the Seattle experience, America's oldest farmers' market is famous for its fresh seafood, local produce, and multicultural cuisine. Stretching for several blocks high above Elliott Bay, this district offers more than just a traditional market, though, with other treasures ***(p168)*** **all built around an arcade.**

Pike Place Starbucks®, a former feed store, is the site of the first Starbucks® coffee shop, which moved here from its original Western Avenue location in 1976. The Starbucks® sign in the window sports the chain's original logo.

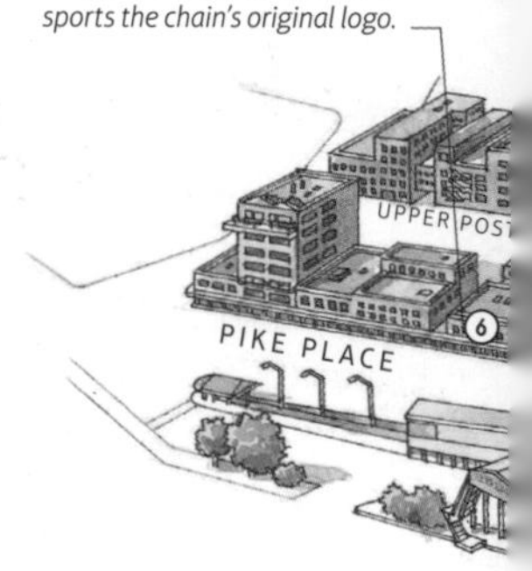

Established in 1907, Pike Place Market is said to be the soul of Seattle. Over the years, the market has mirrored national waves of immigration, with new arrivals from countries including Mexico, Laos, and the Philippines flocking here to set up businesses. Bustling with some 100 farmers, 200 craftspeople, and engaging street performers, the area contains galleries, specialty groceries, bistros, and an eclectic mix of shops. The heart of Pike Place Market is the Main Arcade and the adjacent North Arcade, where low metal-topped counters display seasonal fruit, vegetables, herbs, and flowers. Shoppers at these low stalls get to "meet the producer," and each morning, the Market Master does roll call, assigning stalls to farmers and artists based on seniority. This often results in vendors selling their wares from a different stall each day. High stalls leased by commercial greengrocers on a permanent basis are also found in the Main Arcade.

HIDDEN GEM

Rooftop Retreat

A little rooftop garden with pretty views, the Urban Garden *(81 Pike St)* offers a quiet spot away from the busy market below. The produce grown in the raised beds is donated to the local senior center and food bank.

THE HISTORY OF PIKE PLACE MARKET

Hungry for fresh produce and fair prices, Seattleites mobbed Pike Place Market when it opened on August 17, 1907, in effort by the city council to eliminate "greedy middlemen" and allow farmers to sell directly to the public. Sensing opportunity, local developer Frank Goodwin used his Klondike gold to build permanent arcades. At its height in the 1930s, hundreds of farmers sold their produce here, but by the late 1960s, developers were lobbying to tear it down. Seattleites rebelled, however, voting in 1971 to make the market a historic district.

↑ The iconic public market sign at the entrance to Pike Place Market, a hub of activity

Upper Post Alley, a pedestrian walkway, is lined with specialty shops, restaurants, and pubs. Its sister, Lower Post Alley, is home to similar businesses.

The historic Athenian Inn restaurant is renowned for its succulent seafood offerings and diner-style sandwiches, which can be enjoyed while sitting at a booth overlooking Elliott Bay.

There are several newsstands in and around Pike Place Market, offering a wide range of US and international publications.

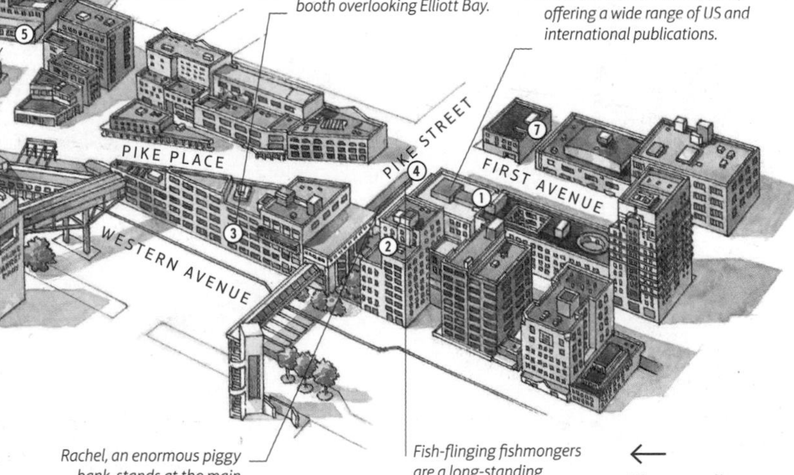

Rachel, an enormous piggy bank, stands at the main entrance to Pike Place Market. Sculpted by Pacific Northwest artist Georgia Gerber, it collects funds for low-income families.

Fish-flinging fishmongers are a long-standing tradition at the Pike Place Fish store.

← The sprawling Pike Place Market and its excellent multi-level arcade

Underground Mezzanines

The market's five lower levels are often overlooked but are full of surprises. Bookstores, candy shops, artists' studios, and curio shops are just some of the treasures to be found down below. Put some quarters in the Market Magic Shop's fortune teller for an entertaining future prediction, commission a portrait, or check out the test kitchen of ChefSteps *(www.chefsteps.com)* and join one of their classes.

Hmong Flower Stalls

Over 45 vendors contribute to the market's incredible array of fresh and dried flowers that fill the air with a tropical fragrance throughout the year. Many of these vendors are Hmong farmers who originally came to Seattle from the mountainous regions of Southeast Asia as refugees in the 1970s and 1980s. Now their farms, which are mostly in the Snoqualmie Valley just outside of the city, grow and produce the marvelous bouquets. Walk by, meet the friendly florists, and pick some vibrant flowers.

Athenian Inn

1517 Pike Pl (Main Arcade) 8am-9pm Mon-Sat, 9am-4pm Sun athenianseattle.com

The Athenian Inn has been in operation nearly as long as the market itself. Opened by three brothers in 1909, it evolved from a bakery and luncheonette to a tavern and, later, a restaurant. It was, in 1933, one of the first restaurants in Seattle to get a liquor license. Neither flashy nor fancy, this diner serves old-time favorites like corned beef hash. However, the best reason to visit is not for the food but for the view of Elliott Bay. Nab one of the wooden booths at the back to see the Duwamish waterway and ferries across the bay.

Did You Know?

If Athenian Inn seems familiar, that may be because of its role in the 1993 movie *Sleepless in Seattle.*

Pike Place Fish

86 Pike Pl pikeplacefish.com

Pike Place Fish, located in the Main Arcade, is not Pike Place Market's only seafood vendor. It is, however, certainly the best known. Situated beneath the market's landmark clock, this busy stall always draws a crowd, thanks to the loud, lively banter and high-spirited antics of its fishmongers, who are amazingly adept at tossing fish over the heads of cheering spectators to co-workers behind the shop's counter. The repartee is as fresh as the seafood, which ranges from wild king salmon and Dungeness crab to rainbow trout and live clams. Should you care to buy, Pike Place Fish will even ship your seafood home.

↑ Dining and socializing along Post Alley, just behind Pike Place Market

Post Alley

Stewart to Virginia sts between Pike Pl & 1st Av

Along this brick-paved passageway are two of the city's favorite haunts. The Pink Door *(1919 Post Alley)* is an Italian trattoria identified only by an unmarked pink door with a lovely terrace, while Kell's Irish Restaurant and Pub *(1916 Post Alley)* pours Guinness and offers live Celtic music. One of the more unusual sights here is the Gum Wall, dotted with thousands of colorful pieces of gum. Snap a quirky photo or leave your own mark.

Starbucks® Pike Place

1912 Pike Pl 6am-9pm daily starbucks.com

Seattle is said to be the most caffeinated city in the US, a distinction Seattleites don't refute. To see where the coffee craze started, visit Starbucks® Pike Place, the first shop in the omnipresent chain. Opened in 1971, at 2000 Western Avenue, Starbucks® Coffee, Tea and Spices moved to its Pike Place location in 1976. Named after the first mate in Herman Melville's *Moby Dick*, the company's first logo – a voluptuous two-tailed mermaid encircled by the original name – still greets visitors at this small store.

If you're after more coffee delights, head to the fascinating (and first) **Starbucks Reserve® Roastery & Tasting Room**. This 15,600-sq-ft (1,449-sq-m) vast expanse includes roasting facilities, coffee bars, shops, a great restaurant, and a library, spread over two floors.

Starbucks Reserve® Roastery & Tasting Room

1124 Pike St 7am-11pm daily starbucksreserve.com

Rows of crab and other tempting seafood at the renowned Pike Place Fish

First and Pike News

93 Pike St 8am-8pm daily

A classic market shop with rows of national and international newspapers and magazines, this newsstand is a rarity in today's digital world. It's been around since 1979 and also sells souvenirs, postcards, and gum for the nearby Gum Wall.

EAT

Matt's in the Market

Reserve a window seat at this relaxed spot that uses fresh ingredients sourced straight from the market right below.

94 Pike St mattsinthemarket.com

$$$

Sushi Kashiba

The city's top spot for sushi, with master Chef Shiro Kashiba at the helm. Try the *Omakase* ("chef's choice") for a memorable meal.

86 Pine St Dinner sushikashiba.com

$$$

Daily Dozen Doughnut Company

This tempting spot serves hot and fresh mini cinnamon and sugar doughnuts.

93 Pike St (206) 467-7769

$$$

Joe Chocolate Co.

An espresso bar and chocolate factory in one. Try the dark chocolate bar, loaded with salted caramel and roasted coffee beans.

1606 Pike Pl joechocolateco.com

$$$

Cantina de San Patricio

Sit outside under the colorful umbrellas and enjoy tasty tacos.

1914 Post Alley cantinadesanpatricio.com

$$$

EXPERIENCE MORE

The Seattle Great Wheel

D6 Pier 57, 1301 Alaskan Way Times vary, check website seattlegreatwheel.com

The Seattle Great Wheel, perched over Elliott Bay, offers spectacular views of the city skyline and the Olympic Mountains. Standing 175-ft (53-m) tall, The Seattle Great Wheel is the largest observation wheel on the West Coast. You can get a ride lasting up to 20 minutes in 41 fully enclosed, climate-controlled gondolas. There is a special VIP gondola as well, with leather bucket seats, a stereo system, and a glass-bottom floor, that can seat up to four people. Each ride is accompanied by a narration of Seattle's waterfront history.

It is worth visiting the Ferris wheel when it is lit up each night with white lights. For certain events, such as Seattle Seahawks home football matches, and on holidays, a special light show is held on the wheel.

IVAR'S ACRES OF CLAMS

A waterfront landmark since 1938, the seafood restaurant Ivar's Acres of Clams on Pier 54 was founded by Seattle-born Ivar Haglund (1905–85), a radio and television personality and self-promoter. Eighteen years before opening his restaurant, Haglund established Seattle's first aquarium. Wearing his trademark captain's hat, he entertained visitors by singing songs he had written about his favorite sea critters. Haglund's food enterprise began with a fish-and-chips counter and grew to include three restaurants, nearly 30 fish bars throughout the Pacific Northwest, and Ivar's own brand of clam chowder.

Waterfront Park

D5 Pier 57-59, 1401 Alaskan Way 6am-10pm daily seattle.gov/parks

The Waterfront Park comprises the area between Pier 57 and Pier 59. The park offers excellent views of the Seattle skyline and the waterfront, and visitors have even been known to spot a seal. The park is dotted with interesting sculptures, including one of Christopher Columbus at the south end, as well as coin-operated telescopes, picnic tables, and benches.

The Waterfront Streetcar, officially known as the George Benson Waterfront Streetcar Line, began in 1982 and was the first streetcar to run in Seattle since 1941. It used to be a great way to see Seattle's best attractions but was suspended in 2005. The track and eight stations remain, but it is unclear whether it will ever be operational again.

The Seattle Great Wheel on Seattle's busy waterfront

Seattle Aquarium

C5 Pier 59, 1483 Alaskan Way 9:30am-5pm daily (to 3pm some major hols) First Fri in Jun, Dec 25 seattleaquarium.org

One of the top aquariums in the country, the Seattle Aquarium offers a fascinating window into Pacific Northwest marine life, showcasing more than 400 different species of fish, plants, and mammals indigenous to the area. Take the opportunity to learn about the aquarium's ecological and conservation work with the local environment, and even meet the wildlife in one of the brilliant interactive exhibits.

Ye Olde Curiosity Shop

D6 Pier 54, 1001 Alaskan Way 9am-9:30pm daily Major hols yeoldecuriosityshop.com

This Seattle institution has been a fixture of the city's waterfront since 1899, when Joseph Edward Standley of Ohio started this family-run shop. Among the legendary curiosities are a "freak pig" with two tails, two faces, three eyes, and eight legs, and a walrus skull with three tusks.

But there is more to this store than quirky curios and unusual souvenirs. From its first days of business, this waterfront shop has been an American Indian trading post. Today, the arts and crafts of the region's American Indians are sold through the store.

Washington State Ferries Terminal

D7 Pier 52, 801 Alaskan Way wsdot.wa.gov/ferries

Washington State ferries transport 23 million residents and travelers a year. Seattle's main terminal is Colman Dock, located on the waterfront at the foot of Columbia Street. The dock will be undergoing a restoration and redevelopment project until 2023.

A popular tourist activity is the 35-minute ferry ride to Winslow on Bainbridge Island *(p202)*, where galleries, shops, restaurants, and a waterfront park are all within walking distance of the ferry dock, making for a pleasant day trip.

Pier 66

B4 Bell St Pier Cruise Terminal, Pier 66, Alaskan Way portseattle.org

One of the liveliest parts of the waterfront is the Port of Seattle's Pier 66, also known as Bell Street Pier Cruise Terminal. It is home to a thriving luxury cruise ship terminal, a pleasure craft marina, a conference center, and a handful of restaurants.

There is a constant hub of activity, with Bell Street Pier Cruise Terminal and Smith Cove Terminal (at Pier 91, north of downtown) together greeting more than 200 cruise ships every year, most of which are bound for Alaska's stunning Inside Passage.

Pier 66 is also home to the Bell Harbor Marina, a small in-city marina for pleasure boats. For spectacular views of the moored boats here, you can gaze out from Bell Street Pier Cruise Terminal's rooftop plaza.

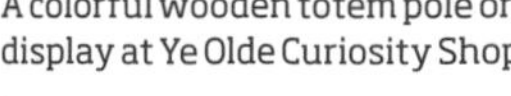

A colorful wooden totem pole on display at Ye Olde Curiosity Shop

DRINK

The Forge Lounge

If you're a spirits aficionado, you'll want to check out this relaxed bar, with a cocktail list that features locally distilled spirits.

E6 65 Marion St theforgelounge.com

Aerlume

A bar/restaurant with draft beer, an extensive wine list, and unique cocktails to accompany stunning views of the Puget Sound.

C4 2003 Western Av Suite C aerlumeseattle.com

Cloudburst Brewing Company

This friendly brewery has a tiny taproom where they serve their impressive array of beers.

C4 2116 Western Av Times vary, check website cloudburstbrew.com

The imposing Space Needle alongside MoPOP

SEATTLE CENTER AND BELLTOWN

Located north of downtown, Seattle Center is the proud legacy of the city's 1962 World's Fair. This exposition saw various ambitious buildings constructed, including the iconic Space Needle, and the area became a popular spot for locals and visitors to gather. Just to the south of Seattle Center, Belltown was originally home to a very steep slope. It took on a new identity between 1905 and 1930, when Denny Hill was regraded and washed into Elliott Bay. Over 50 city blocks were lowered by up to 100 ft (30 m), turning Denny Hill into the Denny Regrade, an unremarkable area of labor union halls, car lots, inexpensive apartments, and sailors' taverns. This began to change in the 1970s when artists were attracted here by cheap rents and abundant studio space. At that time, a neighborhood association renamed the area Belltown, after William M. Bell, one of the area's pioneers. By the 1980s, as Seattleites and suburbanites began taking an interest in cosmopolitan urban living, condominiums began appearing on Belltown's periphery. Fueled by the software boom of the 1990s, the area experienced a huge building boom, attracting well-paid high-tech types to its amenity-rich towers.

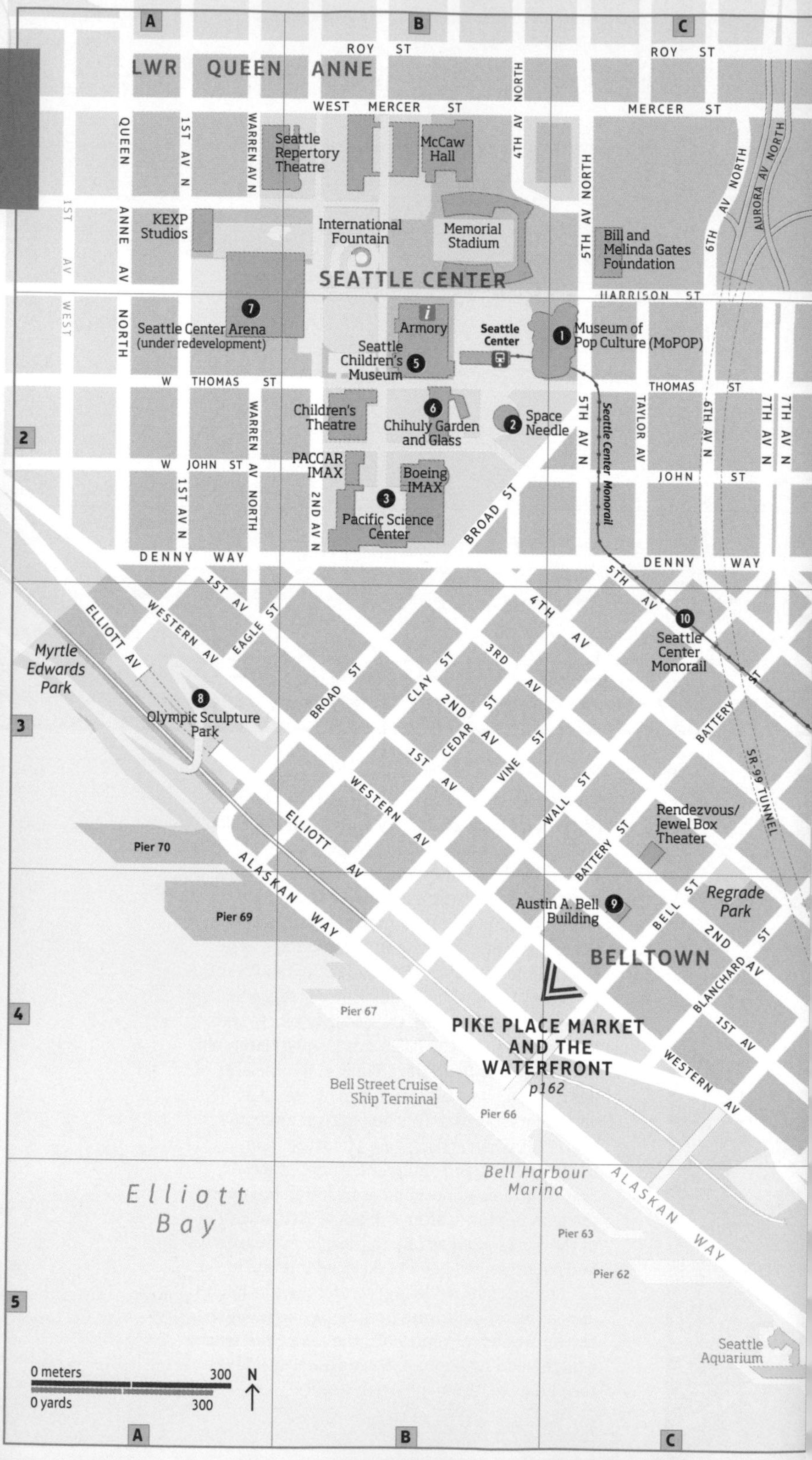

LWR QUEEN ANNE
SEATTLE CENTER
BELLTOWN
Seattle Repertory Theatre
McCaw Hall
KEXP Studios
International Fountain
Memorial Stadium
Bill and Melinda Gates Foundation
Seattle Center Arena (under redevelopment)
Armory
Seattle Center
Museum of Pop Culture (MoPOP)
Seattle Children's Museum
Children's Theatre
Chihuly Garden and Glass
Space Needle
PACCAR IMAX
Boeing IMAX
Pacific Science Center
Seattle Center Monorail
Myrtle Edwards Park
Olympic Sculpture Park
Rendezvous/ Jewel Box Theater
Austin A. Bell Building
Regrade Park
PIKE PLACE MARKET AND THE WATERFRONT p162
Pier 70
Pier 69
Pier 67
Pier 66
Pier 63
Pier 62
Bell Street Cruise Ship Terminal
Bell Harbour Marina
Elliott Bay
Seattle Aquarium
ROY ST
WEST MERCER ST
MERCER ST
HARRISON ST
W THOMAS ST
THOMAS ST
W JOHN ST
JOHN ST
DENNY WAY
QUEEN ANNE AV NORTH
1ST AV N
1ST AV WEST
WARREN AV N
4TH AV NORTH
5TH AV NORTH
6TH AV NORTH
AURORA AV NORTH
5TH AV N
TAYLOR AV
6TH AV N
7TH AV N
2ND AV N
BROAD ST
5TH AV
4TH AV
3RD AV
2ND AV
1ST AV
WESTERN AV
ELLIOTT AV
ALASKAN WAY
EAGLE ST
CLAY ST
CEDAR ST
VINE ST
WALL ST
BATTERY ST
BELL ST
BLANCHARD ST
SR-99 TUNNEL
0 meters 300
0 yards 300
N

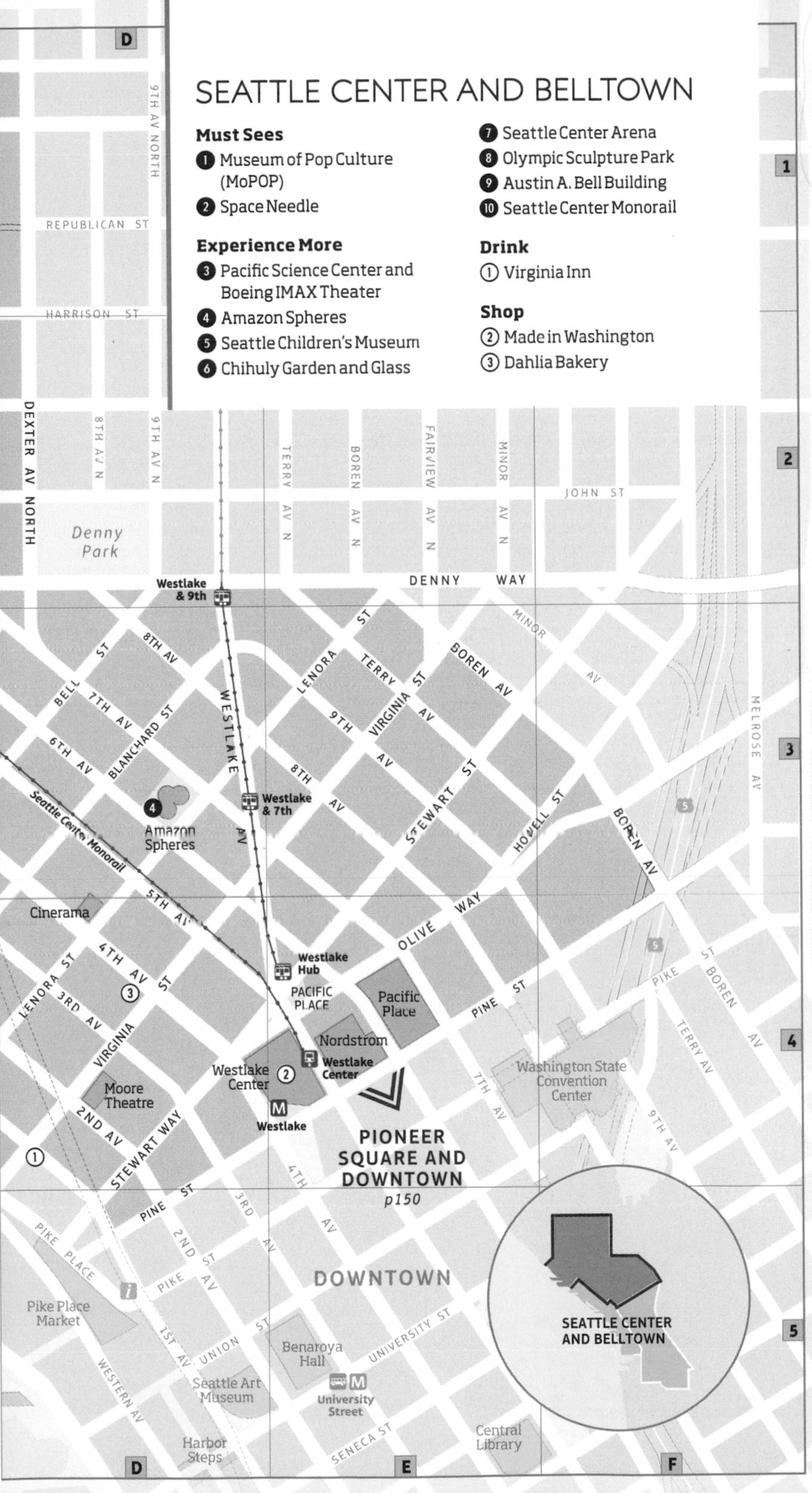
SEATTLE CENTER AND BELLTOWN
Must Sees
1 Museum of Pop Culture (MoPOP)
2 Space Needle
Experience More
3 Pacific Science Center and Boeing IMAX Theater
4 Amazon Spheres
5 Seattle Children's Museum
6 Chihuly Garden and Glass
7 Seattle Center Arena
8 Olympic Sculpture Park
9 Austin A. Bell Building
10 Seattle Center Monorail
Drink
① Virginia Inn
Shop
② Made in Washington
③ Dahlia Bakery
D
E
F
1
2
3
4
5
9TH AV NORTH
REPUBLICAN ST
HARRISON ST
DEXTER AV NORTH
8TH AV N
9TH AV N
TERRY AV N
BOREN AV N
FAIRVIEW AV N
MINOR AV N
JOHN ST
Denny Park
DENNY WAY
Westlake & 9th
MINOR AV
BELL ST
8TH AV
7TH AV
BLANCHARD ST
6TH AV
LENORA ST
TERRY AV
VIRGINIA ST
BOREN AV
9TH AV
WESTLAKE AV
8TH AV
STEWART ST
HOWELL ST
MELROSE AV
Westlake & 7th
Amazon Spheres
Seattle Center Monorail
5TH AV
Cinerama
OLIVE WAY
Westlake Hub
4TH AV
3RD AV
PACIFIC PLACE
Pacific Place
PINE ST
PIKE ST
BOREN AV
TERRY AV
Nordstrom
Westlake Center
Westlake Center
Westlake
VIRGINIA ST
Moore Theatre
2ND AV
STEWART WAY
7TH AV
Washington State Convention Center
9TH AV
PIONEER SQUARE AND DOWNTOWN
p150
PINE ST
3RD AV
4TH AV
PIKE PLACE
2ND AV
PIKE ST
DOWNTOWN
Pike Place Market
1ST AV
UNION ST
UNIVERSITY ST
WESTERN AV
Benaroya Hall
Seattle Art Museum
University Street
SENECA ST
Harbor Steps
Central Library
SEATTLE CENTER AND BELLTOWN

MUSEUM OF POP CULTURE (MOPOP)

C2 325 5th Av N Seattle Center 10am-6pm daily (Labor Day-Memorial Day: to 5pm daily) Thanksgiving, Dec 25 mopop.org

Seattle's iconic Museum of Pop Culture (MoPOP) celebrates American popular music and culture, with rare memorabilia, interactive exhibitions, and a live performance space – all housed in an exuberant structure that swoops and swirls at the base of the Space Needle.

Formerly known as the EMP Museum, MoPOP was launched by Microsoft co-founder Paul Allen *(p61)* in 2000. Designed by Frank Gehry, an architect with a penchant for atypical shapes and angles, innovative building materials, and bold colors, the building is said to resemble a smashed electric guitar. MoPOP houses fantastic science fiction, horror, fantasy, and independent video games galleries and exhibitions.

The museum has three exciting levels. The main galleries and exhibitions are on Levels Two and Three, while the lower level offers a theater for lectures, films, and classes; the Learning Labs; and a restaurant that serves regional American cuisine. Exhibitions, such as Infinite Worlds of Science Fiction, Fantasy, and Scared to Death take you through fantastical worlds of pop culture. Through films like Bram Stoker's *Dracula* and *Back to the Future*, the exhibitions explore the implications of new technology.

PICTURE PERFECT
Abstract Architecture

The colors of MoPOP's cool exterior fluctuate depending on the light and angle, so to avoid reflective glare, shoot in the early morning.

↑ Seattle Monorail speeding through MoPOP, with the Space Needle behind

3,000

stainless steel and aluminum panels were used to create the museum's facade.

↑ Relaxing on the steps next to MoPOP's vibrant exterior, which changes color depending on the angle and light

Museum Highlights

Nirvana: Taking Punk to the Masses

▶ This exhibit features an extensive collection of rare memorabilia from Seattle's iconic grunge band. Gems on display include photographs, a guitar smashed by lead singer Kurt Cobain, the sweater he wore in the music video for "Smells Like Teen Spirit," and the band's first demo recording tape.

Sky Church

▼ The "heart and soul" of MoPOP, this great hall is used as a performance space, which includes a large video screen. To this end, it hosts Campout Cinema - movie screenings that invite you to bring sleeping bags and cushions to accompany tasty food and drink. The name of the hall pays homage to a concept thought up by Jimi Hendrix of a space where people from different backgrounds could experience music together.

Guitar Gallery

In this gallery, nearly 20 famous guitars are on display, including one that belonged to Eddie van Halen. Informative timelines also trace the evolution of the guitar in American music.

Sound Lab

Sound Lab encourages visitor interaction and experimentation with music. Record your own song in the Jam Studio, learn how DJs work their trade, and delve into the recording process.

If VI Was IX: Roots and Branches

▶ A perfect photo opportunity, this sculpture by Gerhard Trimpin consists of more than 500 instruments and computers. It offers a dynamic, interactive, and historical journey into the origins and evolution of American popular music. An audiovisual tour also explores American musical roots and influences.

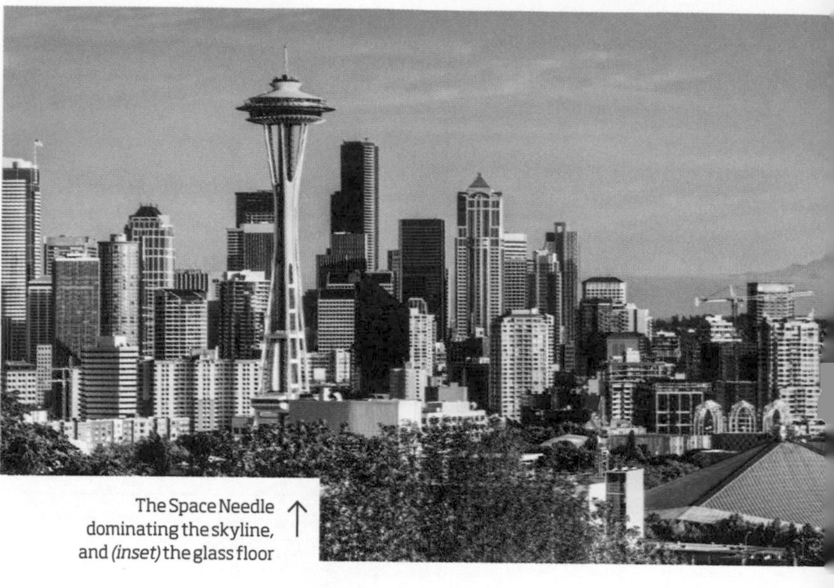

The Space Needle dominating the skyline, and *(inset)* the glass floor

2

SPACE NEEDLE

B2 400 Broad St Seattle Center 8am-midnight daily
spaceneedle.com

What started as a rough sketch on the back of a paper placemat has become Seattle's internationally recognized landmark and top tourist attraction. Weather permitting, you can enjoy panoramic views of downtown Seattle and the Olympic and Cascade mountain ranges.

Built for the 1962 World's Fair, the 605-ft (184-m) Space Needle was the brainchild of Edward Carlson, the fair's chairman, who was inspired by Germany's Stuttgart Tower. The final design by John Graham and Company, architects of the first shopping mall in the US, was approved just 18 months before the fair's opening date. At the time, it was the tallest building west of the Mississippi River.

The glass-enclosed tophouse offers a viewing deck and, below it, a revolving restaurant – the second in the world. The underground foundation, buried 30 ft (9 m) deep, took 467 cement trucks to fill. The tower is attached to the foundation with 72 30-ft- (9-m-) long bolts.

Solidly constructed, the Space Needle has weathered several earthquakes and has closed fewer than ten times because of high winds. During the Seattle World's Fair, nearly 20,000 people a day rode the high-speed elevators to the top, enduring waits of up to 3 hours for the 43-second ride. Thankfully, the wait is much shorter today, and the view just as spectacular.

Observation deck with three viewing areas

Revolving restaurant

Supported by three curved steel legs

Outside elevators

The futuristic design of the Space Needle, a Seattle landmark

EXPERIENCE MORE

3   

Pacific Science Center and Boeing IMAX Theater

B2 200 2nd Av N Seattle Center Times vary, check website pacificsciencecenter.org

The Pacific Science Center features four exhibit halls and two IMAX theaters surrounding five arches that rise over reflecting pools and fountains. While enjoyed by all ages, the exhibits are especially appealing to kids. Dinosaurs: A Journey Through Time takes you back to the Mesozoic Era to meet lifelike dinosaurs, while the Tropical Butterfly House is filled with free-flying butterflies. In Body Works you can pedal on the Calorie Bicycle to see how much energy you produce, and in Tech Zone you can challenge an industrial robot to games.

The Center also houses a planetarium, laser theater, the PACCAR IMAX Theater, and the futuristic Boeing IMAX Theater. The latter has laser projectors and a cutting-edge sound system, and shows documentaries and a variety of children's films.

4 

Amazon Spheres

D3 2111 7th Av Virginia St & 6th Av 10am-8pm Mon-Sat, 11am-7pm Sun seattlespheres.com

The three domes that make up the Amazon Spheres, or Seattle Spheres, cover half a city block on the Amazon campus and provide meeting and office spaces for Amazon employees. The Spheres have 2,600 panes of glass and house 40,000 plants from over 30 countries to surround workers with nature. There's an exhibition space open to the public, and tours of The Spheres and other parts of the Amazon HQ can be booked in advance.

HIDDEN GEM

Be Inspired

The free Bill and Melinda Gates Foundation Discovery Center *(www.discovergates.org)*, an 8-minute walk from the Pacific Science Center, invites you to explore inspiring challenges and ideas, Seattle-style.

SEATTLE WORLD'S FAIR

Officially known as the Century 21 Exposition, Seattle's second World's Fair was conceived to commemorate the 50th anniversary of the Alaska-Yukon-Pacific Exposition held here in 1909. Billed "America's Space Age World's Fair," the new exposition was dedicated to science and life in the 21st century. Big plans pushed the original opening date back a few years, from 1959 to 1962. Among the fair's most ambitious buildings and lasting legacies is the Space Needle. Designed to appear futuristic, to fit with the Century 21 theme, it now has a rather retro appeal.

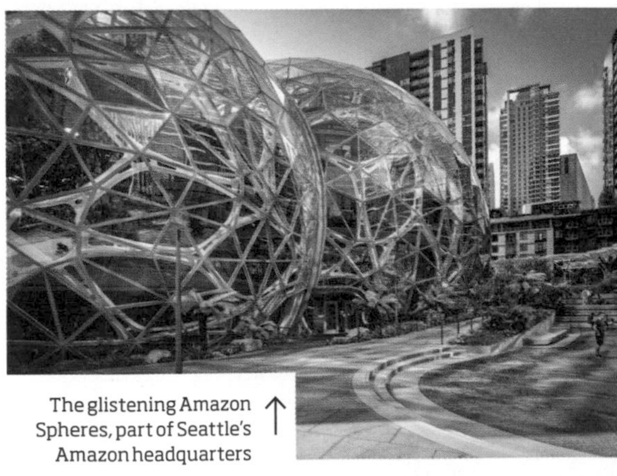

The glistening Amazon Spheres, part of Seattle's Amazon headquarters ↑

One of Dale Chihuly's vibrant sculptures hanging at Chihuly Garden and Glass

SHOP

Made in Washington
One of five branches, this shop sells locally produced food, drink, arts, and crafts. You can even purchase gift baskets loaded with goodies.

E4 400 Pine St madeinwashington.com

Dahlia Bakery
An outstanding bakery serving fresh bread, cakes, and pastries to eat in or take away. Don't miss their triple coconut cream pies.

D4 2001 4th Av dahliabakery.com

DRINK

Virginia Inn
This brick-and-tile place was established in 1903. It now hosts art exhibitions and has a broad range of beers on tap, cocktails, and wines.

D4 1937 1st Av virginiainnseattle.com

5 

Seattle Children's Museum

B2 305 Harrison St Seattle Center 10am-5pm Tue-Sun Jan 1, Labor Day weekend, Thanksgiving, Dec 24 & Dec 25 thechildrensmuseum.org

While most of Seattle Center is a delight for kids, the Seattle Children's Museum, located on the first level of the Seattle Center's Center House, is very popular with youngsters.

Permanent exhibits include Global Village, where young visitors are introduced to the cultures and lifestyles of their contemporaries around the world. Children can visit a tailor shop in Ghana and taste sushi in Japan. In the Mountain Forest exhibit, kids learn about Washington's natural environment as they hike through a re-creation of a Pacific Northwest forest, complete with a bat-inhabited cave, a waterfall, and flowing lava. Interactive elements include sliding down a glacier. There is also an interactive exhibit designed for toddlers.

Three to four changing exhibitions throughout the year guarantee that there is always something new to see. The museum also features an artist-in-residence and a drop-in arts studio for kids – the first of its kind in the region.

6   

Chihuly Garden and Glass

B2 305 Harrison St Seattle Center 8:30am-8:30pm daily (to 9:30pm Fri & Sat; last entry 1 hr before closing) chihulygardenandglass.com

Chihuly Garden and Glass showcases the life and career of American glass sculpture artist Dale Chihuly (b. 1941). The highlight is one of Chihuly's largest suspended sculptures, a mesmerizing 100-ft- (30-m-) long work in shades of red, orange, and yellow. Several of his other works, including intricate chandeliers, are displayed in the eight galleries, and highlight the artist's glassblowing expertise and his creative use of shapes and colors. The complex also includes a garden with sculptures surrounded by trees, plants, and flowers.

7

Seattle Center Arena

A2 305 Harrison St Seattle Center  For renovations until 2021 keyarena.com

In its first life, Seattle Center Arena, formerly known as KeyArena, was the Washington State Coliseum, offering Seattle World's Fair visitors a glimpse into the 21st century. Hailed as an architectural masterpiece in 1962 for its shape (a hyperbolic paraboloid) and lack of interior roof supports, this structure was designed by Paul Thiry (1904–93) to last well into the 21st century as a sports and convention facility.

After the fair, the futuristic building was converted into a sports arena and has become one of the top big-ticket concert venues on the West Coast. The arena is currently undergoing reconstruction.

Part of the Seattle Art Museum, the Olympic Sculpture Park is a unique green space for public recreation and outdoor art.

Olympic Sculpture Park

A3 2901 Western Av Seattle Center Dawn-dusk daily seattleartmuseum.org

Opened to the public in January 2007 as part of the Seattle Art Museum *(p154)*, the Olympic Sculpture Park is a unique green space for public recreation and outdoor art.

The park is made up of three areas linked by a 2,200-ft (670-m) Z-shaped path. Over 20 modern sculptures are scattered throughout a variety of typical Pacific Northwest landscapes, such as The Shore, which features a beach and a naturally developing tidal garden. The PACCAR Pavilion is the park headquarters and houses a car park and a cafe where you can buy food for picnics. Guided tours of the park are also available starting from the Pavilion.

Austin A. Bell Building

C4 2326 1st Av To the public

The Austin A. Bell Building was designed by Elmer Fisher, Seattle's foremost commercial architect at the end of the 19th century. Combining Richardsonian, Gothic, and Italianate design elements, the handsome four-story brick structure was commissioned in 1888 by Austin Americus Bell, the wealthy son of Seattle pioneer William M. Bell, for whom Belltown is named. It was to be an apartment building and the young Bell's first major building project in the city, but as he died before the building was finished, his wife oversaw its completion. Listed on the National Register of Historic Places, the Austin A. Bell Building now houses pricey condominiums on its upper three floors and a coffee shop at street level.

Seattle Center Monorail

C3 Westlake Center, Seattle Center Times vary, check website seattlemonorail.com

Built in only 10 months for Seattle's second World's Fair, Seattle's Alweg monorail provided a link between the fairgrounds (now the Seattle Center) and downtown Seattle. At the time, it was described as a preview of the mass transit system of the future. The fastest full-sized monorail system in the US, the Seattle Center Monorail covers 1-mile (1.6-km) in 2 minutes, at a speed of up to 60 mph (97 km/h), zipping through the Museum of Pop Culture *(p176)*, which was built around and over the Monorail's tracks.

Seattle's super-sleek and reliably fast monorail ↑

A SHORT WALK
SEATTLE CENTER

Distance 1 mile (2 km) **Time** 30 minutes
Nearest rail station Seattle Center

The Seattle Center grounds have long been a lively gathering spot. In 1962, the site was transformed into a fairground for the World's Fair – Century 21 Exposition *(p179)*. Today, the site is one of the most visited urban parks in the US. Strolling the pedestrian boulevards, you'll see several legacies of the World's Fair. Among the most notable and noticeable is the Space Needle, which now shares the spotlight with such innovative structures as the Museum of Pop Culture (MoPOP). Performing arts companies, sports teams, and a children's museum all call Seattle Center home.

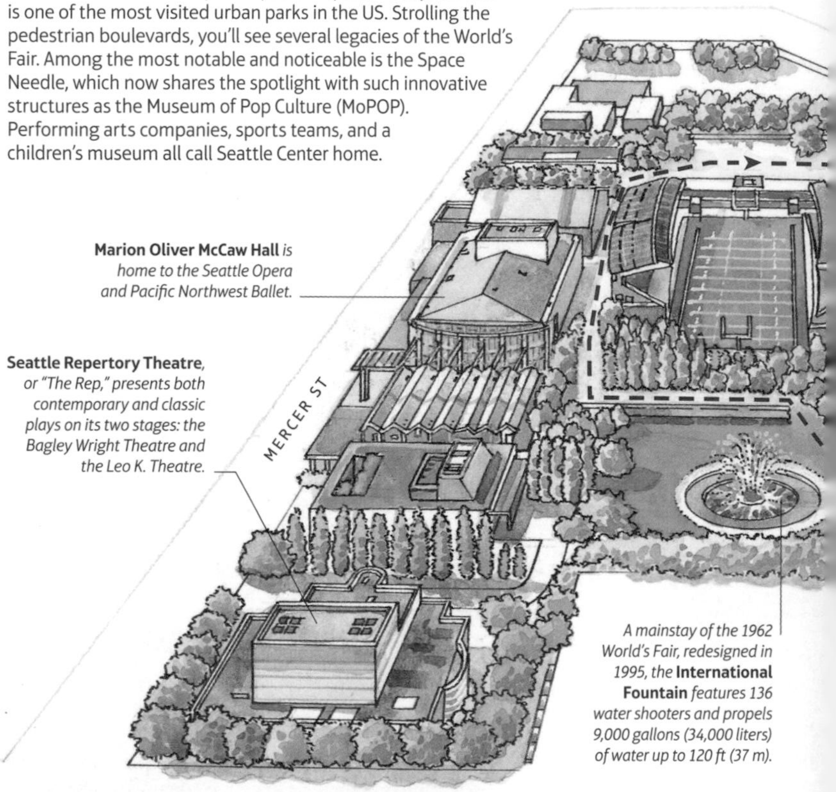

Marion Oliver McCaw Hall *is home to the Seattle Opera and Pacific Northwest Ballet.*

Seattle Repertory Theatre, *or "The Rep," presents both contemporary and classic plays on its two stages: the Bagley Wright Theatre and the Leo K. Theatre.*

MERCER ST

A mainstay of the 1962 World's Fair, redesigned in 1995, the **International Fountain** *features 136 water shooters and propels 9,000 gallons (34,000 liters) of water up to 120 ft (37 m).*

0 meters 50
0 yards 50
N ←

Playing under the spraying International Fountain, with the Space Needle behind

SEATTLE CENTER AND BELLTOWN

Seattle Center

Locator Map

For more detail see p174

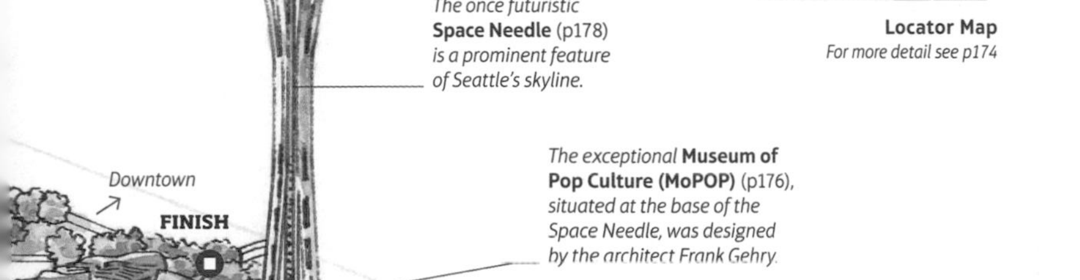

The once futuristic **Space Needle** (p178) *is a prominent feature of Seattle's skyline.*

Downtown

FINISH

The exceptional **Museum of Pop Culture (MoPOP)** (p176), *situated at the base of the Space Needle, was designed by the architect Frank Gehry.*

BROAD ST

Chihuly Garden and Glass (p180) *exhibits Dale Chihuly's stunning, colorful glassworks.*

DENNY WAY

START

The **Seattle Center Monorail** (p181) *travels directly through the MoPOP before it enters the Seattle Center Station. Each train has traveled over one million miles (1.6 million km) since 1962.*

Fisher Pavilion, *facing the South Fountain Lawn, is a popular venue for trade shows and festivals.*

Interactive exhibits devoted to science; two IMAX theaters; and a planetarium are housed in the **Pacific Science Center** (p179).

Did You Know?

In 1978, the city of Fife, in Washington, attempted to buy the Space Needle for $1 million.

→ The diverse interactive exhibits engaging families at the Pacific Science Center

Sifting through vinyls in a record store

BEYOND THE CENTER

A community of students, artists, and other bohemians have left their mark on Seattle's outyling areas over the last two centuries. To the east, Capitol Hill has been a prominent LGBT+ neighborhood since the 1970s, when a varied assortment of shops and restaurants introduced a vibrant culture. The city has also been home to the eclectic University of Washington, the heart of the University District, since the late-19th century. The neighborhood of Freemont fittingly became a student enclave in the 1960s, attracting a non-conforming community with its low rents.

Experience

1. First Hill
2. T-Mobile Park
3. CenturyLink Field
4. Volunteer Park
5. Woodland Park Zoo
6. University District
7. Museum of History & Industry
8. Madison Park
9. Capitol Hill
10. Burke-Gilman Trail
11. Gas Works Park
12. Ballard
13. Fremont
14. Green Lake
15. Museum of Flight
16. Discovery Park
17. Alki Beach

First Hill's Frye Art Museum displaying a wide range of 19th- and 20th-century art

EXPERIENCE

First Hill

Bounded by E Pike St, E Yesler Way, 12th Av E & I-5

Nicknamed Pill Hill for its several hospitals and numerous doctors' offices, First Hill lies just east of downtown. A pedestrian-friendly district (more than 40 percent of its residents walk to work), First Hill was Seattle's first neighborhood, home to the city's pioneer families. It still has a number of the original mansions from Seattle's early days.

First Hill's most recognizable landmark, St. James Cathedral *(804 9th Avenue)*, is a parish church and the cathedral of the Catholic Archdiocese of Seattle. Designed by the New York firm Heins and LaFarge, the Italian Renaissance structure dating to 1907 features two tall spires.

One block southeast of St. James Cathedral, the **Frye Art Museum** showcases the extensive art collection of Seattle pioneers Charles and Emma Frye, which features 19th- and 20th-century French, German, and American paintings. Temporary exhibitions are held throughout the year.

Frye Art Museum
704 Terry Av
11am–5pm Tue–Sun (to 7pm Thu) fryemuseum.org

HIDDEN GEM
Tech-Savvy

The Living Computers: Museum + Labs *(www.livingcomputers.org)*, an 11-minute walk south of T-Mobile Park, explores technology with fun immersive exhibits and hands-on experiences.

T-Mobile Park

1250 1st Av S For tours: times vary, check website mlb.com

T-Mobile Park's size is very impressive, seating over 47,000 baseball fans, who enter the stadium through the curved entranceway, behind the field's home plate. The stadium's state-of-the-art retractable roof contains enough steel to build a skyscraper 55 stories tall and cost an unprecedented $516 million. Designed by the Seattle firm NBBJ and completed in 1999, T-Mobile Park became the nation's most expensive stadium ever built.

With its sweeping views of the Seattle skyline, $1.3 million in public art, and such amenities as a children's playfield and picnic patio, T-Mobile Park provides an excellent atmosphere in which to watch the Seattle Mariners play a Major League ball game. While many games are sold out, you may visit the stadium by taking one of the regularly scheduled tours or visiting the Mariners Hall of Fame.

CenturyLink Field

800 Occidental Av S Times vary, check website centurylinkfield.com

The designers of CenturyLink Field, which opened in 2002, were intent on factoring the city's often inclement winter weather into its design. So, despite the harsh winds and rains associated with winter in

Seattle, the stadium was left roofless. The end result is a spacious, open-air stadium with unobstructed views of the Seattle skyline. With two massive 760-ft (232-m) eaves, most of the seats are shielded from falling rain. The stadium is home to the NFL's Seattle Seahawks, the MLS team, Seattle Sounders FC, and the Seattle Dragons (XFL).

Just as the stadium design by Minneapolis-based Ellerbe Becket is unconventional, so, too, is the mix of art scattered within it, which draws visitors from around the world.

Volunteer Park

1247 15th Av E
6am-10pm daily
seattle.gov/parks

This elegant park was designed in 1904–9 by the Olmsted Brothers, the USA's famous landscape-architecture firm. It is named for the Seattle men who enlisted to fight in the Spanish-American War of 1898.

The Olmsteds' design called for an observation tower. The city obliged by building a 75-ft (23-m) brick water tower with an observation deck. A steep climb up the 107-step spiral staircase rewards you with spectacular views of the Space Needle, Puget Sound, and the Olympic mountain range.

↑ Potted plants outside the Volunteer Park Conservatory

A children's playground, wading pool, tennis courts, and bandstand make the park a favorite outing for families.

Volunteer Park is the site of the **Asian Art Museum**, located in an Art Deco building which formerly housed the Seattle Art Museum *(p154)*. The museum's collection includes works from Japan, Korea, China, and Southeast Asia.

Across from the museum is the **Volunteer Park Conservatory**, a botanical garden also home to plants confiscated by US Customs. The seasonal display house includes lilies, poinsettias, azaleas, and a jade plant more than 95 years old that blooms November to January.

Asian Art Museum
1400 E Prospect St
Times vary, check website
seattleartmuseum.org

Volunteer Park Conservatory
1400 E Galer St
10am-4pm Tue-Sun
seattle.gov/parks

Woodland Park Zoo

N 55th St & Phinney Av N or N 50th St & Fremont Av N 9:30am-6pm daily (Oct-Apr: to 4pm daily)
zoo.org

Purchased by the City of Seattle in 1899, Woodland Park Zoo is one of the oldest zoos on the West Coast. Of the nearly 300 animal species that reside at Woodland Park, most live in environments that closely resemble their native habitats. Unlike typical zoo models where animals are grouped by species, Woodland Park's animals are grouped in bioclimatic zones. Seven of the zoo's naturalistic exhibits have won top honors. One of these, the Trail of Vines, includes the first open-forested canopy for orangutans to be created at a zoo.

EAT

Dick's Drive-In

This Seattle-based fast-food chain is a local favorite. Fans claim it serves the best burgers and fries in town.

115 Broadway E
ddir.com

Melrose Market

Various restaurants and food-and-drink stalls - all offering local produce - are housed in an industrial-style building.

1531 Melrose Av
melrosemarketseattle.com

Macrina Bakery and Cafe

There are five of these bakeries around Seattle selling award-winning baked goods.

746 19th Av E
macrinabakery.com

Tacos Chukis

Get an authentic taste of Mexico at this simple place started up by a homesick Mexican.

219 Broadway E
(206) 328-4447

Mountaineering Club

A popular and cosy rooftop lounge with panoramic views that gives simple dishes a sophisticated edge.

4507 Brooklyn Av NE
graduatehotels.com

TOP 3 LGBT+ CLUBS IN THE AREA

The Cuff Complex
1533 13th Av
cuffcomplex.com
DJs, country dancing, and pool tournaments.

Queer/Bar
1518 11th Av
thequeerbar.com
Hosts a queer variety show every Friday, and Sunday brunch shows.

Crescent Lounge
1413 E Olive Way
(206) 659-4476
Loved by regulars, this grungy dive bar specializes in karaoke.

University District

Bounded by NE 55th St, Portage Bay, Montlake Blvd NE & I-5 UW Visitors Center: ground floor, Odegaard Undergraduate Library, near 15th Av NE and NE 41 St

Eclectic and energetic thanks to the vibrant youth culture surrounding the University of Washington campus, this district is worth a visit. Just inside the main campus entrance is the **Burke Museum of Natural History and Culture**, featuring dinosaur fossils and a notable collection of Northwest American Indian art. On the western edge of the campus sits the **Henry Art Gallery**, the first public art museum in Washington. The museum has a special focus on photography.

The university's main avenue is University Way Northeast, known to locals as "The Av." Located west of campus, it is lined with bookstores, pubs, inexpensive restaurants, and shops. University Village, located east of the campus, offers upscale shopping and dining.

A must-see, especially spring through autumn, is the **Washington Park Arboretum**, a garden and living plant museum. The arboretum also features a Japanese garden.

Burke Museum of Natural History and Culture
4300 15th Av NE
Times vary, check website
burkemuseum.org

Henry Art Gallery
NE 41st St & 15th Av NE 11am-4pm Wed-Sun (to 9pm Thu)
henryart.org

Washington Park Arboretum
2300 Arboretum Dr E Dawn-dusk
botanicgardens.uw.edu

Museum of History and Industry

860 Terry Av N South Lake Union Streetcar and Terry Av N 10am-5pm daily
mohai.org

Also known as MOHAI, the Museum of History and Industry has around 4 million items in its collections. The museum dates back to the start of the 20th century, although a suitable permanent home was only found when this purpose-built venue opened in 1952. Permanent exhibits include True Northwest, a multimedia account of how Seattle developed from the 1790s onward; The Bezos Center for Innovation, named for Amazon founder Jeff Bezos; and for younger children, the Kid-Struction Zone. There are also changing exhibits, interesting daytime and evening events, and an excellent gift shop.

Fossil exhibits at the Burke Museum in the University District ↓

→ Walking alongside Lake Union on the picturesque Burke-Gilman Trail at sunset

Madison Park

Bounded by E Madison St, Lake Washington Blvd & Lake Washington
Park: 4am-11:30pm daily
seattle.gov/parks

Seattle's lakeside community of Madison Park is one of the city's most affluent, with tree-shaded streets lined with charming older homes, most built between 1910 and 1930.

The area was established in the early 1860s, when Judge John J. McGilvra purchased a section of land, cutting a road through the forest from downtown Seattle to his property, which was later named Madison Street after former US president James Madison (1751–1836). McGilvra set aside an area for public use, now known as Madison Park. By the end of the 19th century, this park had become the most popular beach in the city, with a boathouse, bathhouse, piers and floating bandstands.

Today the friendly neighborhood offers popular restaurants, upscale boutiques, and home accessories shops.

Capitol Hill

Bounded by Montlake Blvds E & NE, E Pike & E Madison Sts, 23rd Av E & I-5

Northeast of downtown, lively Capitol Hill is a colorful and diverse urban neighborhood, and the center of the city's LGBT+ community. The district's commercial hub is Broadway (East Roy to East Pike streets), which offers shopping (from books to home accessories to vintage clothing), a number of ethnic restaurants, and bronze footsteps embedded in the sidewalk to teach passersby the tango and foxtrot.

Capitol Hill's vintage single-screen movie house, the SIFF Cinema Egyptian *(805 East Pine Street, 206/324-9996)*, specializes in independent and foreign films and restored classics. The internationally acclaimed Cornish College of the Arts *(710 East Roy Street)* features a full roster of student exhibits and performances.

Burke-Gilman Trail

Numerous access points; main access point at Gas Works Park
4am-11:30pm daily
seattle.gov/parks

When the sun comes out in Seattle, cyclists, walkers, and joggers flock to the scenic Burke-Gilman Trail, a 27-mile (43-km) paved trail built on an old railway bed.

The popular trail officially begins at Gas Works Park, at the north end of Lake Union. From there, it follows Lake Washington from the University of Washington to Kenmore, where it connects with the Sammamish River Trail.

A warning to pedestrians: cyclists comprise roughly 80 percent of all trail users, so attentiveness and keeping to the right-hand side is a must.

PICTURE PERFECT
Step To It

Try your hand at the foxtrot or tango on Broadway in Capitol Hill. Numbered bronze footsteps sunk into the sidewalk indicate a sequence of steps for the dances, making for a unique social media shot or video.

Gas Works Park

2101 N Northlake Way
6am-10pm daily
seattle.gov/parks

Huge rusty pipes and pieces of decrepit machinery are not typically found in a park. But Gas Works Park on Lake Union is anything but typical. Established in 1906 as a gasification plant, Gas Works was once a primary source of power for Seattle. Shut down in 1956, the plant's machinery and towers stood dormant until 1975, when the site was renovated into an award-winning park under the direction of landscape architect Richard Haag. Today, Gas Works Park is a scenic haven for kite flying, kayaking, picnicking, and viewing the 4 July fireworks.

DRINK

The Walrus and the Carpenter

This oyster bar is a small family business serving clever cocktails, local draft beers, and wines from around the world.

4743 Ballard Av NW
thewalrusbar.com

Percy's and Co.

Cocktails here include fruit and herbs from the rooftop garden or family farm. They range from classics to one-off creations by bartenders.

5233 Ballard Av NW
Times vary, check website **percysseattle.com**

Tractor Tavern

Music acts for every taste - from gentle folk to hard rock - play tunes most nights at this cool bar.

5213 Ballard Av NW
Times vary, check website **tractortavern.com**

Fremont Brewing Company

This vast beer hall serves seasonal ales and encourages friendliness with its long shared tables, inside and out.

1050 N 34th St
fremontbrewing.com

WILDROSE

One of the first lesbian bars on the West Coast, WILDROSE has events most nights and serves excellent cocktails.

1021 E Pike St
Times vary, check website **thewildrosebar.com**

12

Ballard

Bounded by Salmon Bay, Shilshole Bay & Phinney Ridge

Settled by Scandinavian fishermen and loggers in 1853, Ballard was a mill town at the turn of the 19th century. Ballard Avenue was the commercial center of this then-booming area.

The area's Scandinavian heritage is celebrated at the annual Norwegian Constitution Day Parade every May 17, at the excellent National Nordic Museum *(2655 NW Market Street)*, and at the Bergen Place mural in Bergen Place Park. The **Hiram M. Chittenden Locks**, located at the west end of Ballard, allow container ships, tugboats, fishing boats, and pleasure craft to travel between saltwater Puget Sound and freshwater Lake Union and Lake Washington. The best times to observe migrating salmon on the fish ladder are June through October. The locks' grounds include botanical gardens.

Hiram M. Chittenden Locks

3015 NW 54th St
Times vary, check website
ballardlocks.org

Fremont

Bounded by N 50th St, Lake Washington Ship Canal, Stone Way Av N & 8th Av NW

In the 1960s, when it was a community of students, artists, and bohemians attracted by low rents, Fremont declared itself an "artists' republic." By the late 1990s, the neighborhood's character began to shift, after a high-tech firm settled its Seattle office here. However, Fremont has managed to hold on to cherished traditions, such as the Summer Solstice Parade, and today it is still one of Seattle's funkiest districts.

Public art is a fixture of Fremont. A 13.5-ft- (4-m-) tall statue of Lenin towers above pedestrians at Fremont Place, and on 34th Street, sculptor Richard Beyer's *People Waiting for the Interurban* is regularly clothed by locals.

Green Lake

7201 E Green Lake Dr N
seattle.gov/parks

On any given day Green Lake hosts a spirited parade of people, from joggers, walkers, cyclists, and skaters to bird-watchers and dog walkers.

While kayaking, windsurfing, and paddleboating are popular pursuits during the warmer months, and boats can be rented at the lake, swimming may be restricted due to algae blooms and other problems caused by water stagnation.

Likened to New York's Central Park, the park offers an indoor public pool, tennis courts, a soccer field, basketball court, baseball diamond, and pitch-and-putt golf course.

→ A bronze statue of Lenin by Emil Venkov in the Fremont district

↑ Historic airplanes hanging above visitors at the Museum of Flight

Museum of Flight

9404 E Marginal Way S
10am–5pm daily
museumofflight.org

The West Coast's largest air and space museum, the Museum of Flight takes you on a fascinating journey from the earliest days of aviation to the Space Age. It features 39 historic airplanes, of which more than half are suspended from the ceiling of the six-story Great Gallery. You can sit in the cockpit of an SR-71 Blackbird or F/A-18 Hornet, and board the first Air Force One, the US presidential jet.

The restored Red Barn, Boeing's original 1910 airplane factory and a National Historic Site, is part of the museum. Its exhibits include the world's first fighter plane. The Personal Courage Wing houses the Champlin Fighter collection containing 28 aircraft, mainly from World Wars I and II.

Especially popular are the simulators, including the challenging space-docking simulators in which participants try to link up with the Hubble space telescope.

Discovery Park

3801 Discovery Park Blvd
4am–11:30pm daily
Major hols **seattle.gov/parks**

Located on Magnolia Bluff, Discovery Park is Seattle's largest park. It occupies most of the former Fort Lawton site, a defensive base for soldiers during World Wars I and II and the Korean War. Built at the turn of the 20th century, the still-occupied Officers' Quarters are listed on the National Register of Historic Places. A visitors' center at the east entrance offers trail maps.

Home to over 250 species of birds and other wildlife, the park offers more than 7 miles (11 km) of hiking trails, including the 2.8-mile (4.5-km) Loop Trail, which circles the park and passes through forests, meadows, and dunes. Discovery Park is also home to the **Daybreak Star Cultural Center**. Operated by the United Indians of All Tribes Foundation, this cultural and educational center houses American Indian art.

Did You Know?

The Museum of Flight's Vietnam Veterans' Memorial Park features a restored B-52 bomber.

Daybreak Star Cultural Center

Near north parking lot of Discovery Park **(206) 285-4425** **9am–5pm Mon–Fri, weekend by appt only**

Alki Beach

1702 Alki Av SW
(206) 684-4075

When the first European settlers landed on Alki Beach on a stormy November day in 1851, they were welcomed by Chief Seattle and his Duwamish people. Today, this lively beach is the coolest place in town to be on a warm day. It offers spectacular views of Puget Sound, the Olympic Mountains, and the Seattle skyline.

WASHINGTON

The oldest known human skeleton in the US, Kennewick Man, was found in Washington in 1996, indicating that humans were living here some 9,000 years ago. The area's only inhabitants were American Indians until Spanish explorers arrived in the 1770s, and though Europeans had been charting the Pacific Northwest coast since the 18th century, the Lewis and Clark *(p58)* expedition only arrived as US emissaries in 1805. The region was disputed territory with British Canada until 1846. Following the Walla Walla Treaty of 1855, the US bought land from Indigenous Peoples, but these agreements were soon voided by the flood of settlers coming in, prompting a series of wars through the 1870s. In 1872 the border with Canada was fixed, and in 1889 Washington became the 42nd state in the Union: the only state named for a president of the US. Washington continued to grow economically thanks to its vast supplies of timber and its plentiful agricultural land. Industry also arrived, with the forming of Boeing in 1916, a trend that continued over the decades and on into the software boom of the 1970s.

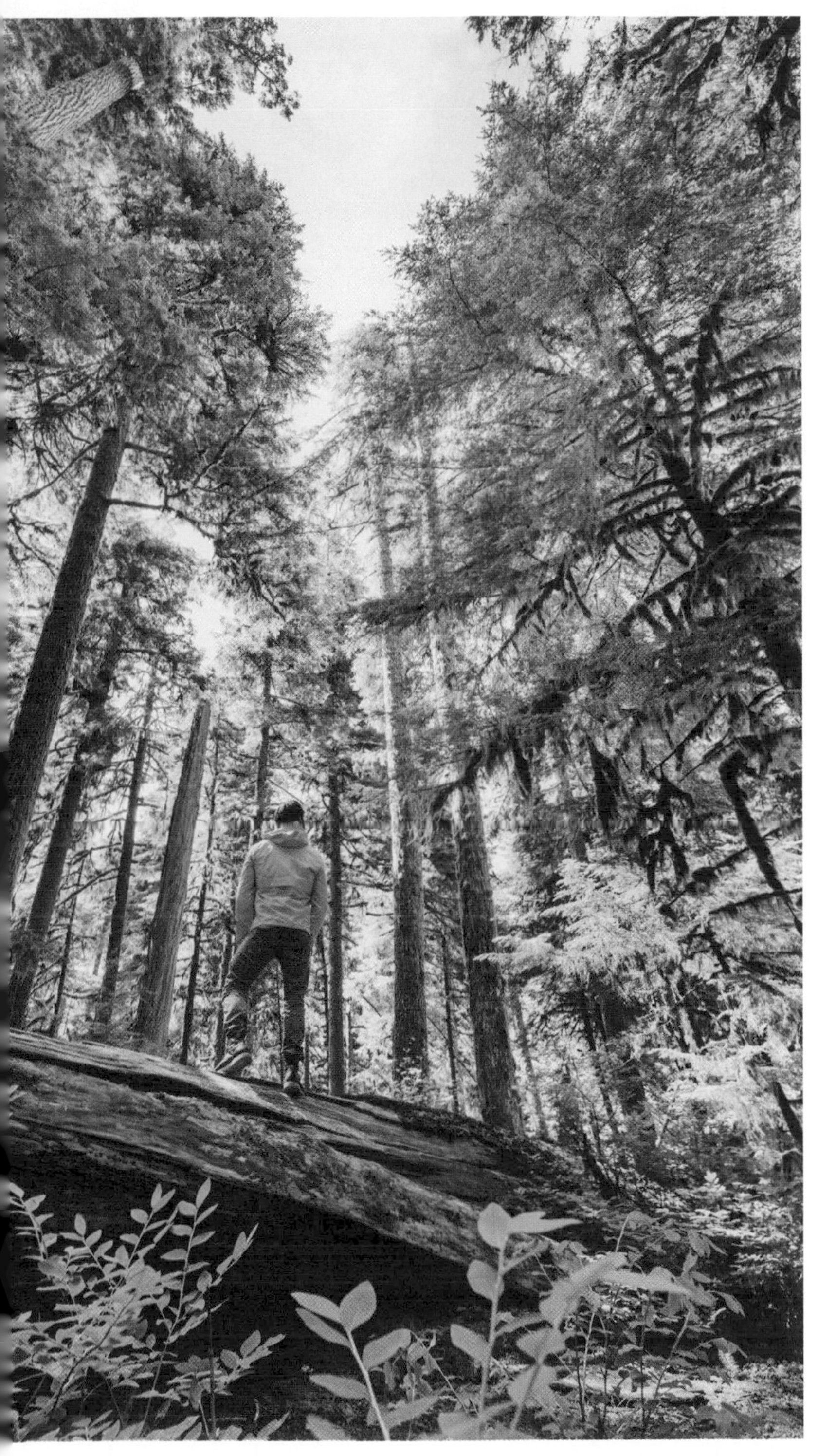

Admiring the beauty of Olympic National Park

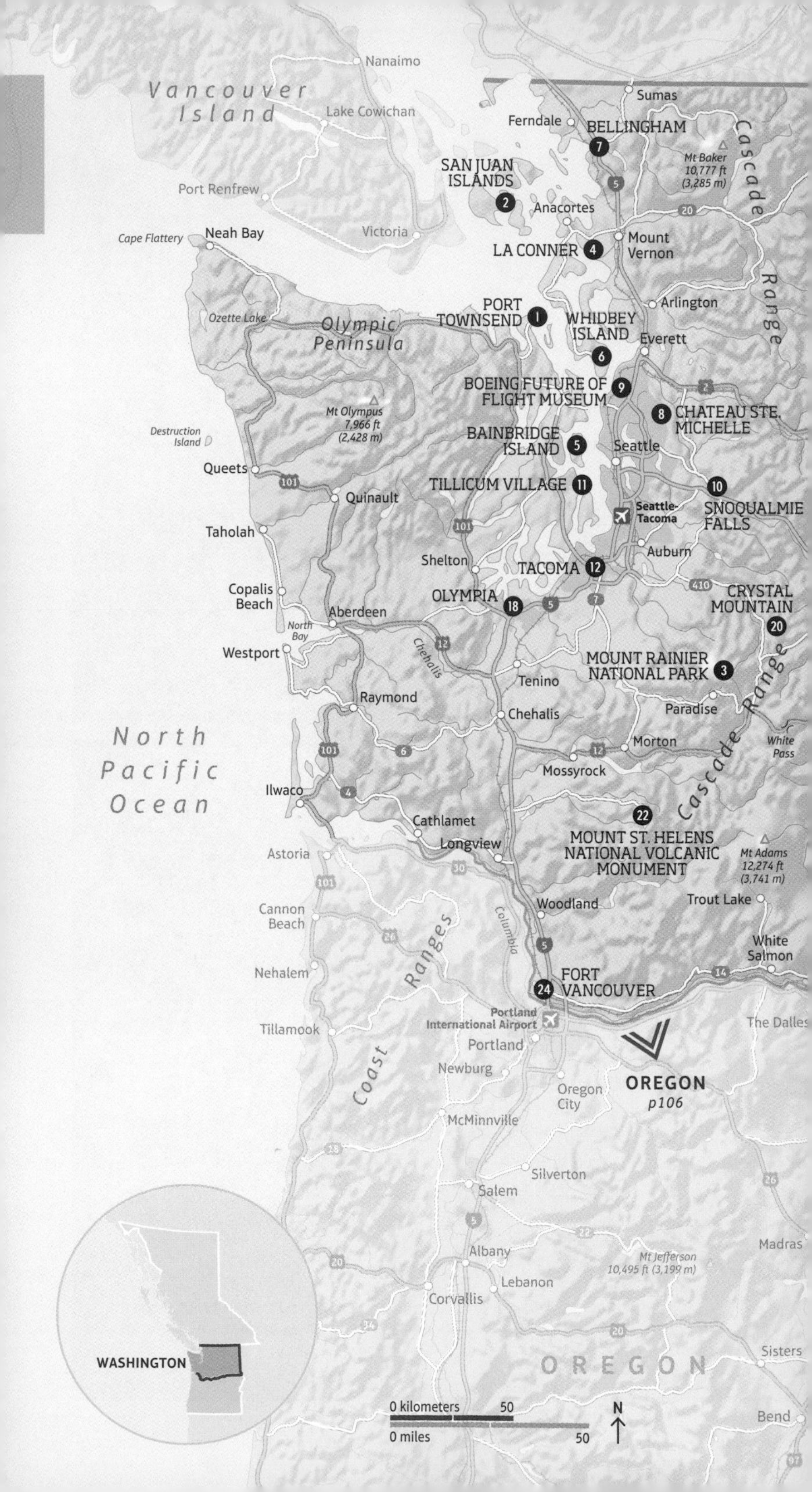

Vancouver Island
Nanaimo
Lake Cowichan
Port Renfrew
Victoria
Sumas
Ferndale
BELLINGHAM 7
Cascade Range
Mt Baker 10,777 ft (3,285 m)
SAN JUAN ISLANDS 2
Anacortes
Cape Flattery
Neah Bay
LA CONNER 4
Mount Vernon
Arlington
Ozette Lake
Olympic Peninsula
PORT TOWNSEND 1
WHIDBEY ISLAND 6
Everett
BOEING FUTURE OF FLIGHT MUSEUM 9
8 CHATEAU STE. MICHELLE
Mt Olympus 7,966 ft (2,428 m)
Destruction Island
BAINBRIDGE ISLAND 5
Seattle
Queets
TILLICUM VILLAGE 11
10 SNOQUALMIE FALLS
Quinault
Seattle-Tacoma
Taholah
Auburn
Shelton
TACOMA 12
Copalis Beach
OLYMPIA 18
CRYSTAL MOUNTAIN 20
Aberdeen
North Bay
Chehalis
Westport
MOUNT RAINIER NATIONAL PARK 3
Tenino
Raymond
Paradise
Chehalis
Cascade Range
North Pacific Ocean
Morton
White Pass
Mossyrock
Ilwaco
22
Cathlamet
MOUNT ST. HELENS NATIONAL VOLCANIC MONUMENT
Longview
Astoria
Mt Adams 12,274 ft (3,741 m)
Cannon Beach
Columbia
Woodland
Trout Lake
Coast Ranges
White Salmon
Nehalem
24 FORT VANCOUVER
Portland International Airport
Tillamook
The Dalles
Portland
Newburg
Oregon City
OREGON p106
McMinnville
Silverton
Salem
Albany
Madras
Mt Jefferson 10,495 ft (3,199 m)
Lebanon
Corvallis
WASHINGTON
OREGON
Sisters
0 kilometers 50
0 miles 50
N
Bend

BRITISH COLUMBIA
p264
CANADA
North Cascades National Park
Tiffany Mountain 8,241 ft (2,512 m)
Oroville
Orient
Northport
Metaline Falls
Mazama
Tonasket
Republic
Colville
Jared
Mt Logan 9,088 ft (2,770 m)
13 WINTHROP
Franklin D. Roosevelt Lake
Chewelah
16 STEHEKIN
Newport
Hunters
Glacier Peak 10,541 ft (3,213m)
Lake Chelan
Columbia
Pateros
14 GRAND COULEE DAM
Deer Park
Manson
17 LAKE CHELAN
Grand Coulee
Wilbur
Spokane
SPOKANE 15
Stevens Pass
Entiat
Davenport
Coulee City
19 LEAVENWORTH
Cheney
WASHINGTON
Odessa
Ephrata
Sprague
Roslyn
Columbia Basin
Tekoa
Quincy
Ritzville
Moses Lake
Ellensburg
Vantage
Colfax
Othello
Pullman
Connell
Yakima
Clarkston
Snake
YAKIMA VALLEY 21
Yakima
Eltopia
Sunnyside
Dayton
Richland
Toppenish
Pasco
Kennewick
Prosser
25 WALLA WALLA
Goldendale Observatory State Park
Paterson
Milton-Freewater
OREGON
p106
Columbia
MARYHILL
23
WASHINGTON
Must Sees
1 Port Townsend
2 San Juan Islands
3 Mount Rainier National Park
Experience More
4 La Conner
5 Bainbridge Island
6 Whidbey Island
7 Bellingham
8 Chateau Ste. Michelle
9 Boeing Future of Flight Museum
10 Snoqualmie Falls
11 Tillicum Village
12 Tacoma
13 Winthrop
14 Grand Coulee Dam
15 Spokane
16 Stehekin
17 Lake Chelan
18 Olympia
19 Leavenworth
20 Crystal Mountain
21 Yakima Valley
22 Mount St. Helens National Volcanic Monument
23 Maryhill
24 Fort Vancouver
25 Walla Walla

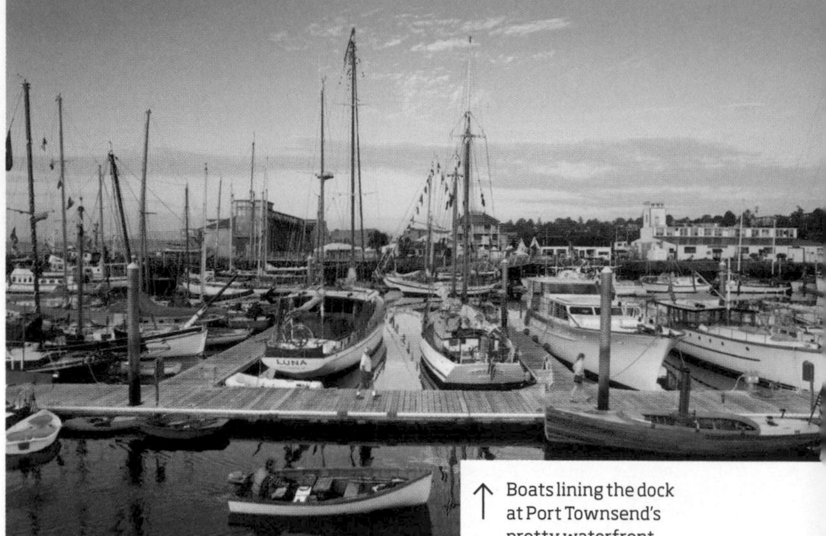

Boats lining the dock at Port Townsend's pretty waterfront

PORT TOWNSEND

A2 · 2409 Jefferson St; www.enjoypt.com

This seaport, a National Historic Landmark, is one of only three seaports on the National Registry. A building boom in the late 1800s left the town with several grand Victorian mansions, which now form the cornerstone of its thriving tourism industry. Aside from offering art galleries and upscale shops, this town is also a great base from which to make kayaking or cycling day trips.

Jefferson County Courthouse

1820 Jefferson St
8:30am-4:30pm Mon-Fri Major hols
co.jefferson.wa.us

The jewel of Port Townsend's Victorian architecture, this Neo-Romanesque building was designed in 1892 by architect Willis A. Ritchie, who ordered its bricks to be hauled west from St. Louis, rather than using the soft, local ones. The building's 124-ft- (38-m-) tall clock tower has long been a landmark for sailors.

Fort Worden State Park

200 Battery Way
parks.state.wa.us

This former military base is now a state park. You can explore the fort's bunkers, attend arts and cultural events, and tour the **Commanding Officer's Quarters** (1904). A museum refurbished in late Victorian style, it offers a glimpse into the lives of the officers in the early 20th century. The **Puget Sound Coast Artillery Museum** is devoted to harbor-defense operations from the late 19th century through World War II. On the east side of the park is the **Port Townsend Marine Science Center**, a mix of museum and aquarium with displays about the area's marine life.

Commanding Officer's Quarters
(360) 385-1003
May-Sep: 11am-4pm Wed-Mon

Puget Sound Coast Artillery Museum
11am-4pm daily
Major hols coastartillery.org

Port Townsend Marine Science Center
532 Battery Way Noon-5pm Fri-Sun (summer: 11am-5pm Wed-Mon) ptmsc.org

INSIDER TIP
Port Townsend Farmers' Market

During the summer months, a true Farmers' Market is set up at Jefferson Transit Haines Place Park-and-Ride on Wednesday between 11am and 3pm. Head here for local produce.

Rothschild House

Franklin & Taylor sts (360) 379-8076 11am-4pm Wed-Mon

A departure from the city's more elaborate homes, this estate reflects the simplicity of the New England-style design that predated Victorian architecture. Built in 1868 for David C. H. Rothschild, it was donated to the Washington State Parks and Recreation Commission in 1959. Restored and listed on the National Register of Historic Places, it contains original furnishings.

St. Paul's Episcopal Church

1020 Jefferson St 9am-noon Mon-Thu stpaulspt.org

The oldest surviving church in Port Townsend, the Gothic Revival-style St. Paul's was built in 1865. Originally located below the bluff, it was placed on logs and rolled to its present location in 1883.

Jefferson Museum of Art and History

540 Water St 11am-4pm daily Major hols jchsmuseum.org

Occupying the old City Hall, this building once housed the town's fire station, jail, courtroom, and city offices. Today it is home to the city council, as well as an excellent museum that showcases the county's heritage through artifacts, archives, and photographs.

Ann Starrett Mansion

744 Clay St To hotel guests only starretthouse.com

Built in 1889 by contractor George Starrett as a wedding gift for his bride, Ann, this grand Queen Anne-style mansion has received national recognition for its architecture, frescoed ceilings, and three-tiered spiral staircase. A National Historic Landmark, it is now privately owned and rents out rooms.

STAY

Ravenscroft Inn

This upscale B&B is in a quiet neighborhood a few blocks walk from downtown. The Colonial-style house offers rooms with views over the bay or as far as Mount Rainier.

533 Quincy St
ravenscroftinn.com

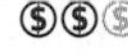

Bishop Victorian Hotel

Dating from 1890, this 16-suite hotel perfectly blends a Victorian look and feel with modern comforts like flat-screen TVs and free Wi-Fi. There are also extensive gardens, dotted with benches.

714 Washington St
bishopvictorian.com

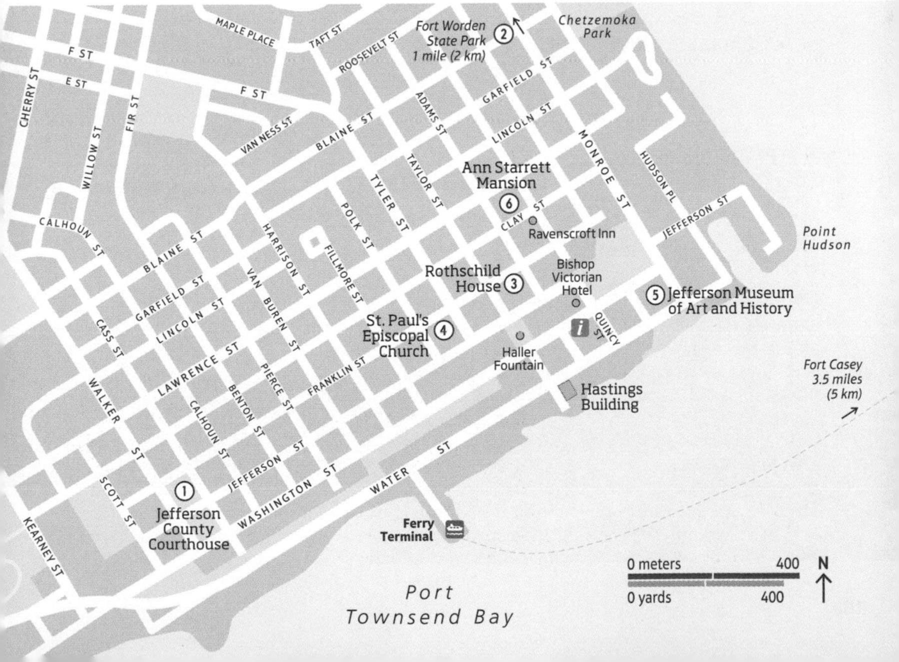

2

SAN JUAN ISLANDS

A/B2 From Anacortes or Sidney, BC, to the San Juan Islands visitsanjuans.com

Unspoiled and remote, this is the arcadian San Juan archipelago. Scattered between the Washington mainland and Vancouver Island, the San Juan archipelago consists of more than 700 islands, just 176 of them named. The San Juan Islands make for a wonderful expedition after visiting one of Washington's cities, with each island having its own distinct character.

Friday Harbor

fridayharbor.com

The largest town in the San Juans, Friday Harbor offers a number of restaurants, inns, galleries, and shops – all within easy walking distance of the ferry dock. It's linked to Anacortes on the Washington mainland year-round by several ferries a day, and from May to October by additional services to Bellingham, Port Townsend, and Seattle, and to Sidney in BC. You can rent cars, jeeps, and bicycles here.

Roche Harbor

10 miles (16 km) NW of Friday Harbor

A charming seaside village, Roche Harbor has a marina, Victorian gardens, a chapel, and the historic Hotel de Haro, built in 1886 and named after the Spanish explorer Gonzalo López de Haro. Though only a small place, Roche Harbor packs a lot in. You can book kayak tours and whale-watching trips, wander round the charming boutiques that sell local arts and crafts, or relax in one of the lovely waterfront restaurants.

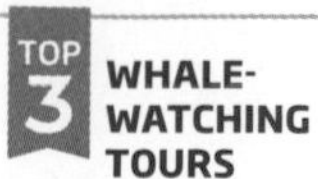

TOP 3 WHALE-WATCHING TOURS

Western Prince
Friday Harbor
orcawhalewatch.com
Half-day tours or private charters.

Discovery Sea Kayaks
Friday Harbor
discoveryseakayak.com
Half-day or full-day kayak tours in groups.

Outer Island Excursions
Lopez outerislandx.com
Daily afternoon trips from May to September.

↑ Kayaking on the calm waters of Friday Harbor on a clear day

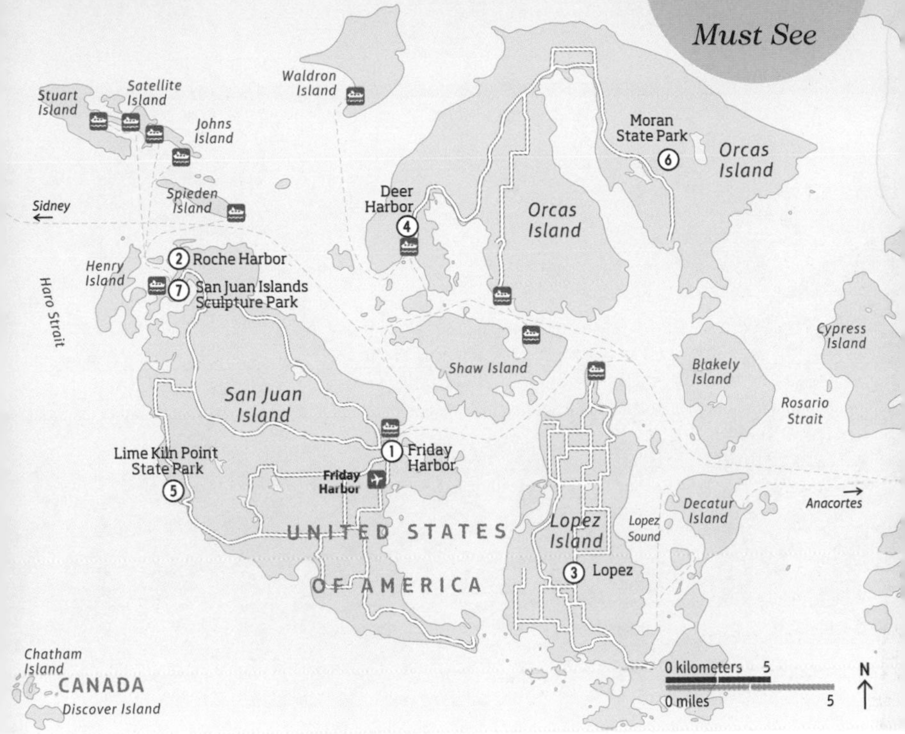

Stuart Island
Satellite Island
Johns Island
Waldron Island
Spieden Island
Sidney
Henry Island
Haro Strait
2 Roche Harbor
7 San Juan Islands Sculpture Park
Deer Harbor 4
Orcas Island
Moran State Park 6
Orcas Island
Shaw Island
San Juan Island
Lime Kiln Point State Park 5
1 Friday Harbor
Friday Harbor
UNITED STATES OF AMERICA
Lopez Island
Lopez Sound
3 Lopez
Blakely Island
Cypress Island
Rosario Strait
Decatur Island
Anacortes
Chatham Island
CANADA
Discover Island
0 kilometers 5
0 miles 5
N

Lopez

15 miles (24 km) SE of Friday Harbor lopez island.com

Despite its gently rolling hills, Lopez is the flattest of the San Juan Islands, making it a popular destination for recreational cyclists. There are beaches and hiking trails too, and sea-based activities include kayaking and fishing.

Deer Harbor

15 miles (24 km) N of Friday Harbor deerharbor.org

Deer Harbor on Orcas Island is especially good for kayaking but also for hiking and whale-watching trips. Centrally located, it's a good place from which to explore the area by boat. Though small, there are several places to stay and eat.

Lime Kiln Point State Park

1567 West Side Rd, Friday Harbor parks.state.wa. us/540/Lime-Kiln-Point

Named for the lime kilns that used to stand here, this state park is considered one of the best places in the world to view orca whales from land. There's also a picturesque 1919 lighthouse that's worth a visit.

Moran State Park

3572 Olga Rd, Olga 6:30am-10pm (Oct-Mar: from 8am) moranstate park.com

This park has 38 miles (61 km) of trails for hiking and biking, as well as 151 camping sites. You can also drive to the top of Mount Constitution (2,399 ft/ 731 m) for marvelous views over the San Juan Islands.

San Juan Islands Sculpture Park

9083 Roche Harbor Rd Dawn-dusk daily sji sculpturepark.com

The San Juan Islands Sculpture Park near Roche Harbor has over 150 sculptures from artists all over the world. The works, which can be purchased, change regularly, and range from the dramatic to the amusing. There are five trails to guide you round the park, which is a haven for wildlife.

PICTURE PERFECT

Lovely Lavender

The free Pelindaba Lavender Farm *(45 Hawthorne Ln, Friday Harbor)* is best visited in July or August, when the lavender is in full bloom. Arrive just before the sunset for a magical, vibrant shot.

MOUNT RAINIER NATIONAL PARK

B3 Hwy 706 near Ashford Jackson Visitor Center, Paradise; www.visitrainier.com

Mount Rainier is the seventh-highest mountain in the US, an active volcano, and an icon of Washington state. Set in its own national park, the mountain is decked in snow and ice for much of the year, with animals and flowers appearing on its slopes in the short summer months. Whatever the time of year, outdoor activities and stunning views await.

Established in 1899, Mount Rainier National Park encompasses 369 sq miles (956 sq km), of which 97 percent is designated wilderness. Its centerpiece is Mount Rainier, an active volcano towering 14,410 ft (4,392 m) above sea level. Surrounded by old-growth forest and wildflower meadows, Mount Rainier was named in 1792 by Captain George Vancouver for fellow British naval officer Peter Rainier. Designated a National Historic Landmark District in 1997, the park, which features 1920s and 1930s National Park Service rustic architecture, attracts two million visitors a year. The summer draws hikers, mountain climbers, and campers; the winter lures snowshoers and cross-country skiers. Note that the national park has several entrances, with the Nisqually Entrance open year-round. For all other entrances, it's worth checking in advance as these tend to be open seasonally. For a nearby stopping-off point, try the inn in Longmire, just 6 miles (4 km) southwest of Mount Rainier.

INSIDER TIP
Be Road Safe

You'll need a car to visit Mount Rainier. Carry chains in the trunk in winter. Some roads are steep and winding, so drive carefully and always check the status of the roads before setting out, as conditions can change quickly and closures may be made at short notice.

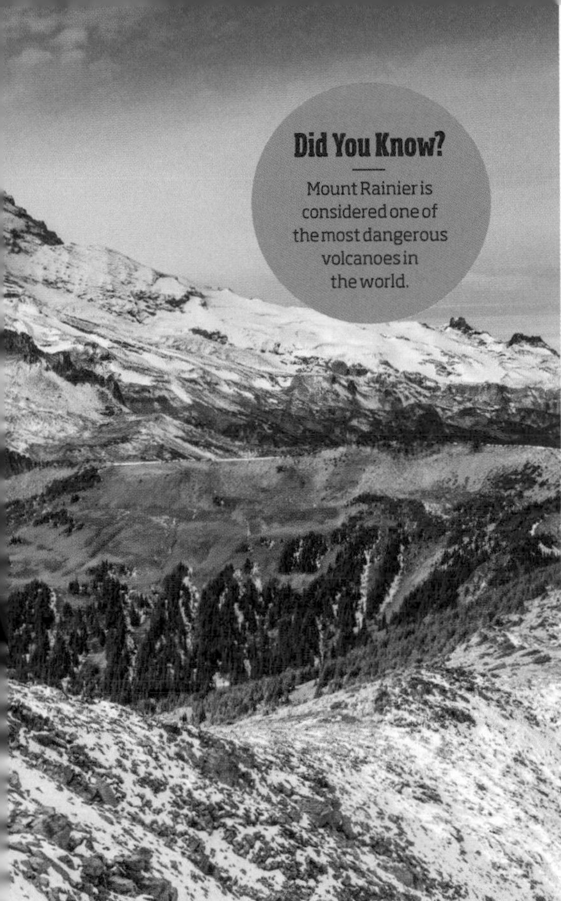

Did You Know?

Mount Rainier is considered one of the most dangerous volcanoes in the world.

Hiking the Mount Fremont Lookout Trail, Mount Rainier National Park

TOP 3 MOUNT RAINIER HIKES

Mount Fremont Lookout Trail
This day-long, 6-mile (10-km) trail starts at the Sunrise visitor center. It's best enjoyed in Jun-Sep when you can view the park's pretty wildflowers.

Northern Loop Trail
Lasting for 40 miles (64 km), this trail takes in the park's pristine wilderness, including forests, meadows, and mountain lakes.

Wonderland Trail
This is the most difficult of the trails, circumnavigating Mount Rainier. Traveling for 93 miles (150 km), it takes 10 to 12 days to complete.

1 Narada Falls, along Paradise River, is a short, steep hike from Highway 706. The falls plummet 168 ft (51 m).

2 A small and cosy inn, located in Longmire, makes for a lovely spot from which to enjoy stunning views of Mount Rainier.

3 Paradise, on the south slope of Mount Rainier, has marked trails and bursts with wildflowers in summer.

EXPERIENCE MORE

4 La Conner

B2 413 Morris St; www.lovelaconner.com

Long associated in the minds of Washingtonians with tulips, the town of La Conner draws thousands to the Skagit Valley Tulip Festival. There is, however, more to La Conner than flowers. A magnet for artists since the 1940s, this tiny town is a thriving arts community. The highly respected **Museum of Northwest Art** showcases works by Mark Tobey, Guy Anderson, Morris Graves, and Kenneth Callahan, as well as Dale Chihuly and other prominent Pacific Northwest artists.

Listed on the National Register of Historic Places, La Conner was founded in the early 1860s. The area's first residents were the Swinomish American Indians. In 1869, merchant John Conner renamed the town after his wife, Louisa Ann, combining her first two initials and her married name. She was the town's first non-American Indian woman. For a glimpse into the lives of early settlers, visit the **Skagit County Historical Museum**.

Museum of Northwest Art
121 S 1st St Noon-5pm Sun & Mon, 10am-5pm Tue-Sat Major hols monamuseum.org

Skagit County Historical Museum
501 S 4th St (360) 466-3365 11am-5pm Tue-Sun

EAT

Inn at Langley
Delicious local produce served on a fixed-price multi-course menu.
B2 400 1st St, Langley innatlangley.com
$$$

Boomer's Drive-In
This burger joint also has an indoor area for those without cars. Try the Boomer Burger.
B2 310 N Samish Way, Bellingham boomersdrivein.com

$$$

Temple Bar
A simple bar with both little and large plates. Prides itself on using local produce.
B2 306 W Champion St, Bellingham templebarbellingham.com

$$$

5 Bainbridge Island

B3 395 Winslow Way E; www.visitbainbridge.com

A 35-minute ferry ride from Seattle, this island makes for a pleasant outing. Near the ferry terminal, a path leads through Waterfront Park to downtown Winslow's galleries, shops, and cafes. The island's charming inns make it a popular stop for travelers to the Kitsap and Olympic peninsulas. **Bloedel Reserve**, with its Japanese garden, English landscape, and bird refuge, is worth a visit.

HIDDEN GEM
Blue Fox Drive-In
There aren't all that many drive-in movie theaters left, so don't miss this American classic in Whidbey Island's Oak Harbor. Visit www.bluefoxdrivein.com for more details.

Bloedel Reserve
7571 NE Dolphin Dr 10am-4pm Tue-Sun (Jun-Aug: to 6pm) Dec 25 bloedelreserve.org

6 Whidbey Island

B2 905 NW Alexander St, Coupeville; www.whidbeycamanoislands.com

Whidbey Island is home to seven state parks and two charming seaside villages. Coupeville has Victorian homes, old barns, and a quaint waterfront. Nearby, Ebey's Landing National Historical Reserve includes the historic army post, **Fort Casey State Park**. At the island's south, the community of Langley has historic

→ Fort Casey State Park, the army post, near Coupeville on Whidbey Island

buildings, upscale shops, art galleries, and friendly bed-and-breakfasts.

Fort Casey State Park
1280 Engle Rd 8am-dusk parks.state.wa.us

Bellingham

B2 Bellingham Airport 904 Potter St, www.bellingham.org

Overlooking Bellingham Bay and many of the San Juan Islands, this town consists of four original towns – Whatcom, Sehome, Bellingham, and Fairhaven – consolidated into a single entity in 1904. The town's historic architecture includes the Old City Hall, built in 1892, which is now the **Whatcom Museum**. It Includes a great children's museum and exhibits on the Indigenous Peoples of the Northwest Coast.

South of downtown, the historic Fairhaven district is an artsy enclave of galleries, restaurants, and bookstores.

Not far from downtown sits the campus of Western Washington University. It has a collection of outdoor sculptures by artists including Mark di Suvero and Richard Serra.

↑ Relaxing in the sun on the pretty lawn at the Chateau Ste. Michelle winery

South of town, Chuckanut Drive (Highway 11) is a scenic 21-mile (34-km) loop with outlooks to Puget Sound and the San Juan Islands. Just 55 miles (88.5 km) east of Bellingham is Mount Baker, where the ski season runs from November through April.

Whatcom Museum
Old City Hall, 121 Prospect St Times vary, check website Major hols whatcom museum.org

Western Washington University
S College Dr & College Way; www.wwu.edu

Chateau Ste. Michelle

B3 14111 NE 145th St, Woodinville 10am-5pm daily Major hols ste-michelle.com

Washington's founding winery, Chateau Ste. Michelle is located on a wooded estate in Woodinville, 20 miles (32 km) north of Seattle. All Chateau Ste. Michelle's acclaimed white wines are produced here. Complimentary tours and tastings are offered daily. The winery's summer concerts draw top blues, jazz, classical, and contemporary talents to its outdoor amphitheater.

Boeing Future of Flight Museum

B2 8415 Paine Field Blvd, Mukilteo 8:30am-5:30pm daily futureofflight.org

This is the only place in the world where you can take a factory tour and see modern jet aircraft being assembled, including 787 Dreamliners. There's more here than just the 90-minute assembly line tour, though, with displays in the museum section, a cockpit you can sit in, and a chance to design your own plane. Children must be at least 4 ft (122 cm) tall to join the tours, and it's best to visit Monday to Friday as only routine maintenance work takes place on weekends.

Martin Blank's *Fluent Steps* (2009) at Tacoma's Museum of Glass

Snoqualmie Falls

B3 6501 Railroad Av SE Dawn-dusk daily snoqualmiefalls.com

The most famous waterfall in the state, Snoqualmie Falls is Washington's second-most-visited tourist attraction after Mount Rainier. This 268-ft (82-m) picturesque waterfall on the Snoqualmie River draws one and a half million visitors each year. Long regarded as a sacred site by the Snoqualmie American Indians and other local Indigenous peoples, the cascade also fascinated the naturalist John Muir, who, in 1889, described it as the most interesting he had ever seen.

An observation deck 300 ft (91 m) above the river provides an excellent view of the thundering water. For a closer look, you can follow a steep half-mile (0.8-km) trail down to the river.

Water gushing from the beautiful Snoqualmie Falls

11   

Tillicum Village

B3 Blake Island State Park Apr-Sep: two trips per day, 11:30am-3:30pm, 4:30-8:30pm argosy cruises.com

Tillicum Village, located in Blake Island State Park, offers visitors a fascinating cultural and culinary experience. Guests are taken on a 4-hour tour of the village which starts with a cruise from Pier 55 on Seattle's waterfront. Once at the village, you can observe whole Chinook salmon being prepared and cooked around alder wood fires, in the traditional style of the Northwest Coast American Indians. A buffet-style meal is served, followed by a performance of the "Dance on the Wind" stage show, a combination of traditional songs, dances, and stories about the Northwest Coast Indigenous culture. Also held here are demonstrations of the traditional carving techniques and the creation of local artwork.

Blake Island State Park is named after Captain George Blake, commander of the US Coast Survey vessel in 1837. The park is the ancestral campground of the Squamish and Duwamish peoples and offers unspoiled scenery. The island is an excellent example of Pacific Northwest lowland forest and is home to numerous native trees and shrubs as well as deer, otter, squirrels, mink, and many varieties of bird. The island's large number of walking trails and a 5-mile (8-km) saltwater beach make it an excellent destination for hikers.

Tacoma

B3 Seattle-Tacoma International Airport 1516 Commerce St; www.traveltacoma.com

Washington's third-largest city, Tacoma was founded as a sawmill town in the 1860s. It prospered in the late 1880s, becoming a shipping port.

The undisputed star of the city's revitalized waterfront is the striking **Museum of Glass**. This landmark building was designed to showcase contemporary art, with a focus on glass. The museum includes a glassblowing studio housed within a dramatic 90-ft (37-m) metal-encased cone.

The stunning Chihuly Bridge of Glass serves as a pedestrian walkway linking the museum to downtown Tacoma and the unique **Washington State History Museum**. Tales of the state's past are related using interactive exhibits and theatrical storytelling by characters in period costume.

The spectacular home of the **Tacoma Art Museum** was designed to be a showpiece for the city. The 50,000 sq ft (4,645-sq-m), stainless-steel-wrapped museum showcases works from the 18th century to today, including local art, European Impressionist pieces, Japanese woodblock prints, and American graphic art.

Tacoma's most popular attraction is Point Defiance Park, ranked among the 20 largest urban parks in the US. Its grounds include Fort Nisqually, the first European settlement on Puget Sound; specialty gardens; a scenic drive; hiking and biking trails; and beaches.

Highlighting a Pacific Rim theme, the world-class **Point Defiance Zoo and Aquarium** is home to over 9,000 animals.

Did You Know?

The popular teen movie *Ten Things I Hate About You* (1999) was filmed in Tacoma.

Museum of Glass
1801 E Dock St
10am-5pm Mon-Sat, noon-5pm Sun Major hols
museumofglass.org

Washington State History Museum
1911 Pacific Av
10am-5pm Tue-Sun
Major hols wshs.org

Tacoma Art Museum
1701 Pacific Av
10am-5pm Tue-Sun
Major hols tacomaartmuseum.org

Point Defiance Zoo and Aquarium
5400 N Pearl St
9:30am-4pm daily
Some hols pdza.org

STAY

Salish Lodge & Spa

Above the Snoqualmie Falls, this luxury lodge has hot tubs, a cookery school, and a spa.

B3 6501 Railroad Av, Snoqualmie salishlodge.com

$$$

Campbell's Resort

A prime beachfront location promises luxury at this resort, which offers a spa, outdoor heated pool, and a bar.

C2 104 W Woodin Av, Chelan campbellsresort.com

$$$

Hotel Murano

This hip downtown spot showcases sculptures and art in public spaces. Modern rooms are met with an excellent upscale restaurant and relaxing spa services.

B3 1320 Broadway, Tacoma hotelmuranotacoma.com

$$$

13

Winthrop

C2 202 Hwy 20; www.winthropwashington.org

The Wild West lives on in Winthrop. In the spring or fall, more than one astonished traveler has witnessed a genuine cattle drive – right down the main street.

The town was founded in 1891 by Guy Waring, a Boston-bred businessman whose Winthrop enterprises included the Duck Brand Saloon. The saloon, now home to the Winthrop Town Hall, is still standing, as is Waring's pioneer log house, which sits on the grounds of the **Shafer Museum**, along with other relics from the past.

DRINK

Peacock Room Lounge

The Davenport Hotel's classy bar has a beautiful stained-glass ceiling and serves stylish cocktails.

D3 10 S Post St, Spokane davenporthotelcollection.com

Method Juice Cafe

This organic, plant-based cafe serves delicious smoothies and juices.

D3 718 W Riverside Av Ste 101, Spokane methodjuicecafe.com

No-Li Brewhouse

Pub and microbrewery overlooking the river. Choose from a good selection of beer.

D3 1003 E Trent Av Ste 170, Spokane nolibrewhouse.com

↑ The interior of a typical American pioneer log house at the Shafer Museum, Winthrop

By the 1960s, Winthrop resembled any other small, non-descript town in the American West before it was "renovated" to give it an Old West ambience. A popular overnight and vacation spot for tourists exploring the North Cascades, the Winthrop area offers a wealth of outdoor recreation possibilities.

Shafer Museum

285 Castle Av May-Sep: 10am-5pm daily shafermuseum.org

14

Grand Coulee Dam

C2 66 miles (106 km) E of Chelan (509) 633-9265 From 9am daily; closing times vary, call ahead

Considered one of the modern engineering wonders of the world, Grand Coulee Dam is one of the largest concrete structures ever built, the largest hydroelectric dam in North America, and one of the largest producers of electricity in the world. Spanning the mighty Columbia River, it generates more power than a million locomotives, supplying electricity to 11 western states. Construction of the dam began in 1933 and took over nine years. The dam was built primarily to supply irrigation water to eastern Washington, where inadequate rainfall threatened the livelihood of the region's farmers.

In summer evenings there is a laser light show. It lasts 30 minutes and is free of charge.

Spokane

D3 Spokane International Airport Riverfront Park, 620 Spokane Falls Blvd; www.visitspokane.com

Washington's largest inland city, Spokane is the commerce and culture center for the Inland Northwest. Founded in 1873, the city suffered a disastrous fire in 1889. It responded by rebuilding in brick and terra-cotta. Many handsome reminders of the building boom remain. Regional history is showcased at the **Northwest Museum of Arts and Culture**. Nearby Campbell House (1898) is an interactive museum.

The smallest city ever to host a world's fair (Expo '74), Spokane's fair site is now Riverfront Park, a nice, large expanse in the heart of the city that offers views of dramatic Spokane Falls.

Scrambling across the rocky shore of Lake Chelan

Other attractions are an IMAX theater and a 1909 carousel. The 37-mile (59-km) Centennial Trail starts at **Riverside State Park** and extends to the Washington-Idaho border. The park, just 6 miles (10 km) northwest of Spokane, offers plenty of freshwater shoreline.

Northwest Museum of Arts and Culture

2316 W 1st Av 10am-5pm Tue-Sun Major hols northwestmuseum.org

Riverside State Park

9711 W Charles St, Nine Mile Falls (509) 465-5064 Dawn-dusk

16 Stehekin

C2 Golden West Visitor Center; www.stehekin.com

At the northernmost tip of Lake Chelan, nestled at the base of the North Cascade Mountains, rustic Stehekin invites travelers to slow down and savor life without the distractions of TV or cell phones. You won't find one single ATM in this tiny community, but you will see some of the most beautiful scenery in the state – accessible only by foot, horse, plane, or boat.

The Lady of the Lake boat service ferries passengers from Chelan to Stehekin. This ride takes 4 hours; a faster option is the Lady Express with a 2.5-hour ride.

Bird-watching, biking, hiking, horseback riding, fishing, and rafting are all popular summer activities in the Stehekin Valley; cross-country skiing and snow-shoeing are popular in winter.

17 Lake Chelan

C2 216 E Woodin Av, Chelan; www.lakechelan.com

Chelan, a resort town on the southeast end of Lake Chelan, has been a popular summer vacation spot for generations of western Washingtonians seeking the sunny, dry weather on the eastern side of the state.

The third-deepest lake in the country, Lake Chelan reaches 1,500 ft (457 m) at its deepest point. Fed by 27 glaciers and 59 streams, the lake, which is less than 2 miles (3 km) wide, stretches for 50.5 miles (81 km). During the summer months, Lake Chelan buzzes with activity: water-skiing, boating, snorkeling, fishing, and windsurfing.

In Chelan town, you can admire the vintage Ruby Theatre *(135 East Woodin Avenue)*. Listed on the National Register of Historic Places, it is one of the oldest continuously running movie theaters in the Northwest US. The 15 murals painted on various buildings are another highlight of the town. They depict the agricultural, recreational, cultural, and ecological history of the Lake Chelan Valley.

INSIDER TIP

Rainbow Falls

Just 3 miles (5 km) south of Stehekin, these impressive falls tumble 392 ft (119.5 m) in two stages. In summer the National Parks Service provides a shuttle to the falls departing from the docks at Stehekin.

During the summer months, Lake Chelan buzzes with activity: water-skiing, boating, snorkeling, fishing, and windsurfing.

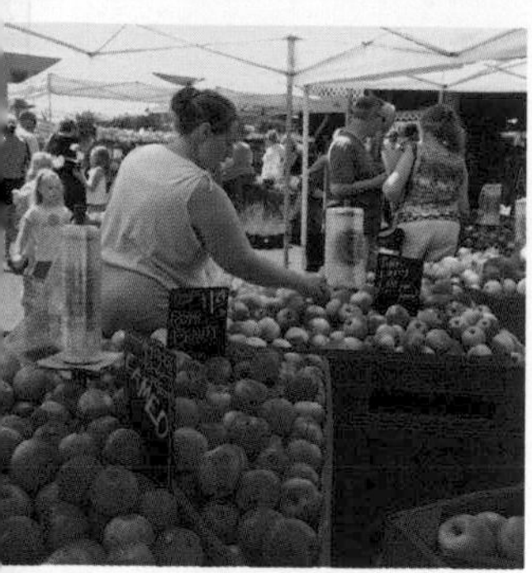

↑ Fruit stalls at the bustling Olympia Farmers' Market

18

Olympia

A3 103 Sid Snyder Av SW; www.experience olympia.com

Washington's state capital since 1853, Olympia was named for its magnificent view of the Olympic Mountains. Located 60 miles (97 km) south of Seattle at the southern tip of Puget Sound, the city is known for its lovely **State Capitol Campus**, one of the most beautiful in the nation. It is dominated by the 28-story domed Legislative Building, and has stunning buildings, landscaped grounds, and numerous fountains and monuments. The Legislative Building (the Capitol) has a 287-ft (87-m) sandstone dome, one of the tallest masonry domes in the world.

The **State Archives** stores Washington's historical records and artifacts. You can view such treasures as documents from the Canwell Committee, which blacklisted suspected Communists in the 1950s.

Tree-lined streets, old homes, a picturesque waterfront, and a thriving cultural community all contribute to Olympia's charm. Tucked among the historic buildings are restaurants, galleries, and shops. Within walking distance are attractions such as the **Olympia Farmers' Market**, offering local produce, seafood, baked goods, and crafts.

Percival Landing *(4th Avenue between Sylvester and Water streets)*, a 1.5-mile (2.5-km) boardwalk, offers views of the Olympic Mountains, Capitol Dome, and Puget Sound.

INDIE ROCK IN OLYMPIA

A musical powerhouse, Olympia is the birthplace of the underground feminist punk genre known as riot-grrrl, as well as being a hotbed for indie and grunge. Thanks to Evergreen College and record labels such as K Records, Olympia's live music scene is brimming with punk hipsters and indie rockers. K Records famously put out records by Moldy Peaches, Built To Spill, and Modest Mouse.

State Capitol Campus

Times vary, check website Major hols 416 Sid Snyder Av SW; www.ga.wa.gov/visitor

State Archives

1129 Washington St SE 8:30am-4:30pm Mon-Fri des.wa.gov

Olympia Farmers' Market

700 Capitol Way N Jan-Mar: 10am-3pm Sat; Apr-Oct: 10am-3pm Thu-Sun; Nov-Dec: 10am-3pm Sat & Sun olympiafarmers market.com

19

Leavenworth

B3 940 Highway 2; www.leavenworth.org

Crossing over the Cascade Mountains from the western part of the state, first-time visitors to Leavenworth never fail to be surprised to see an enchanting Bavarian-style village seemingly straight out of a fairy tale. But this small town was not always so charming. In the early 1960s it was a dying logging town, with plenty of drive-through traffic but no real business to sustain it. Inspired by the town's spectacular mountain backdrop, a Bavarian village theme was developed to revitalize the town. Buildings were remodeled to echo Bavarian architecture and, today, every commercial building in town looks as though it belongs in the Alps.

Leavenworth now bustles with festivals, art shows, and summer theater productions. Among its most popular festivals are Maifest, with its 16th-century costumes, maypole dances, Tyrolean Haflinger horses, and jousting; the Leavenworth International Accordion Celebration, in June, with competitions and concerts; Oktoberfest, the traditional celebration of German beer, food, and music; and Christkindlmarkt, an open-air Christmas market. In addition to its many shops and restaurants featuring Bavarian specialties, the **Leavenworth Nutcracker Museum** showcases 7,000 nutcrackers from 38 countries, some dating back 1,800 years.

Leavenworth Nutcracker Museum

735 Front St May-Oct: 1-5pm daily; Nov-Apr: 2-5pm Sat & Sun nutcracker museum.com

→ A wooden statue at the Leavenworth Nutcracker Museum

Skiing on the sparkling snow-covered slopes of Crystal Mountain ↑

HIDDEN GEM

Leavenworth Reindeer Farm

Reindeer are not just for Christmas; in fact, their calves are born April to June. The Leavenworth Reindeer Farm *(10395 Chumstick Highway, Leavenworth)* is worth a visit any time of year.

20   

Crystal Mountain

A B3 ⌂ 33914 Crystal Mountain Blvd, Enumclaw W crystalmountain resort.com

Located near the northeast corner of Mount Rainier National Park and rising above the town of the same name, Crystal Mountain is Washington's largest ski resort. The town's recreational attributes were discovered in 1949, when attempts to put a chairlift on Mount Rainier failed, and a group of avid Puget Sound skiers began looking for another spot to develop as a ski area. Crystal Mountain opened for business in 1962, receiving national attention three years later when it hosted the National Alpine Championships, an event that attracted skiing legends such as Jimmie Heuga, Billy Kidd, and Jean-Claude Killy.

The ski area, with over 57 named runs, encompasses 3.5 lift-serviced sq miles (9 sq km) plus a large area of back-country terrain. Eleven lifts, including two high-speed, six-passenger chairs, transport more than 19,000 skiers per hour. There is also a large network of trails for downhill skiers. Lessons and equipment hire cater to all ages.

Snowshoe tours are also a popular option. They allow people who don't ski, or want to take a break to get out into the forests and see their natural beauty. You take a chairlift up and then wend your way back down, following knowledgeable guides and spotting some wildlife.

During summer, mountain biking, hiking, and scenic gondola rides are Crystal Mountain's main attractions. On weekends, high-speed lifts whisk passengers to the 6,872-ft (2,095-m) summit and its panoramic views of the Olympic and Cascade mountains, with Mount Rainier dominating the western horizon. Herds of elk and black-tailed deer grazing the grassy slopes are often spotted.

Yakima Valley

A C3 i 10 N 8th St, Yakima; www.visityakima.com

Boasting rich volcanic soil, an abundance of irrigation water, and 300 days of sunshine per year, the Yakima Valley is one of the largest producers of fruits and vegetables in the US, and home to over 100 wineries.

For a taste of the valley's award-winning wines, drive 10 minutes south of Yakima on I-82. Begin the wine tour at Exit 40 (Treveri Cellars), then continue on the Yakima Valley Highway. Columbia Crest and Frichette Winery have some of the best tours.

The outstanding weather and beautiful landscape lend themselves to outdoor activities. The two mountain passes, White Pass and Chinook Pass, offer great hiking, mountain biking, and skiing in the winter; streams encourage fishing; and boating is available on lakes. The area is also rich in wildlife, including bald eagles.

Mount St. Helens National Volcanic Monument

B3 3029 Spirit Lake Hwy, Castle Rock fs.usda.gov

On the morning of May 18, 1980, Mount St. Helens exploded. Triggered by a powerful earthquake, the conical peak erupted, spewing a cubic mile (4.17 cubic km) of rock into the air and causing the largest avalanche in recorded history. In the blink of an eye, the mountain lost 1,314 ft (400 m), and 234 sq miles (606 sq km) of forest-land were destroyed. The eruption also claimed 57 human lives and those of millions of animals and fish.

The 170-sq-mile (445-sq-km) monument was created in 1982 to allow the environment to recover naturally and to encourage research, recreation, and education. NASA scientists have placed high-tech devices inside the volcanic crater to detect an impending eruption.

Roads and trails allow visitors to explore this fascinating region by car and on foot. On the mountain's west side, Highway 504 leads to three visitor centers. The first is the Mount St. Helens National Volcanic Monument Visitor Center, at exit 49 from Interstate 5, featuring interpretive exhibits of the mountain's history. The Forest Learning Center, at milepost 37, open in the summer only, teaches about reforestation efforts. Johnston Ridge Visitor Center, at milepost 52, offers a close-up view of the crater and lava dome.

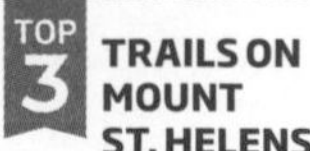

TOP 3 TRAILS ON MOUNT ST. HELENS

Coldwater Lake Trail
A fairly easy 9.5-mile (15-km) hike along the north side of the lake.

Hummocks Trail
Easy 2.5-mile (4-km) round-trip through hills formed by the volcano.

Meta Lake Trail
Short, 0.6-mile (1-km) kid-friendly walk to the lake and back.

Maryhill

B4 Klickitat County Visitor Center; (509) 773-4395

A remote sagebrush bluff overlooking the Columbia River is where entrepreneur Sam Hill chose to build his palatial residence. In 1907, he purchased 7,000 acres

↓ Wildflowers surrounding Mount St. Helens, and *(inset)* the visitor center

(2,800 ha), with the vision of creating a utopian colony for Quaker farmers. He called the community Maryhill, in honor of his daughter, Mary. Utopia never materialized, however. No one wanted to live in such a desolate place, and Hill was persuaded to turn his unfinished mansion into a museum. The **Maryhill Museum of Art** houses the throne and gold coronation gown of his friend Queen Marie of Romania, 87 sculptures and drawings by sculptor Auguste Rodin, and an impressive collection of American Indian art.

At the original Maryhill town site, 2.5 miles (4 km) east of the museum, is a replica Stonehenge built by Hill to honor locals killed in World War I.

Maryhill Museum of Art
 35 Maryhill Museum Dr, Goldendale Mid-Mar-mid-Nov: 10am-5pm daily maryhill museum.org

24 Fort Vancouver

B4 1501 E Evergreen Blvd Mid-Mar-Oct: 9am-5pm Tue-Sat; Nov-mid-Mar: 9am-4pm Tue-Sat Major hols nps.gov/fova

Between 1825 and 1849, this was a major trading outpost for British-based Hudson's Bay Company, the giant fur-trading organization *(p58)*. Located close to major tributaries and natural resources, it was the center of political and commercial activities in the Pacific Northwest during these years. In the 1830s and 1840s, the fort also provided essential supplies to settlers. A National Historic Site, Fort Vancouver features accurate reconstructions of nine of the original buildings, including the jail, fur store, and wash house, all on their original sites. Guided tours and re-enactments offer a window into the fort's past.

↑ The Hot Air Balloon Stampede, held in Walla Walla every October

25 Walla Walla

D4 26 E Main St; www.wallawalla.org

Located in the southeast corner of the state, Walla Walla is a green oasis in the midst of an arid landscape. The town features a large number of National Register buildings, lovely parks, and a wealth of public art. Whitman College, one of the nation's top-rated liberal arts colleges, is just three blocks from downtown. The attractive campus is a delight to stroll, as are the surrounding streets.

A popular destination for wine connoisseurs, the Walla Walla area has won national and international recognition for its wines and is especially known for its reds. Among the town's other claims to fame are its delicious sweet onions and its annual Hot Air Balloon Stampede, a rally of some 45 pilots, held in October.

GREAT VIEW
Goldendale Observatory State Park

Perched atop a 2,100-ft (640-m) hill, the Goldendale Observatory, 14 miles (23 km) north of Maryhill, has more than a dozen telescopes to observe the countryside and the night sky.

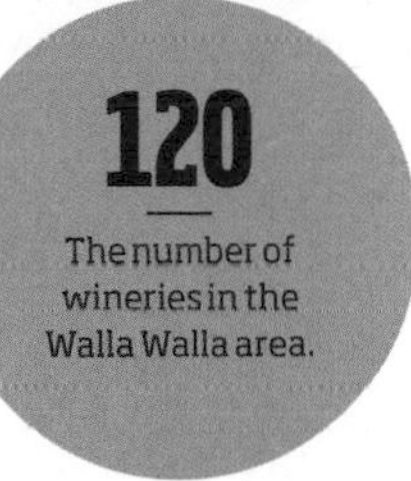

For a historical perspective on the area, visit **Fort Walla Walla Museum**, a pioneer village with 17 original and replica buildings, as well as the **Whitman Mission National Historic Site**. Here, you can discover the story of pioneer missionaries Marcus and Narcissa Whitman and their subsequent massacre by the Cayuse people. On weekends, the Living History Company performs with music and dance.

Fort Walla Walla Museum
755 Myra Rd 10am-5pm daily (Nov-Feb: to 4pm) Jan 1, Thanksgiving, Dec 25 fwwm.org

Whitman Mission National Historic Site
328 Whitman Mission Rd Dawn-dusk Jan 1, Thanksgiving, Dec 25 nps.gov/whmi

A DRIVING TOUR
OLYMPIC PENINSULA

Length 272 miles (438 km) **Starting point** Port Gamble on Hwy 104 **Stopping-off points** Numerous campgrounds and lodges are situated in or near Olympic National Park

The Olympic Peninsula, in the far northwestern corner of Washington, offers many opportunities for spectacular sightseeing. The centerpiece of the peninsula is Olympic National Park, a UNESCO biosphere reserve and World Heritage Site. Encompassing 1,442 sq miles (3,735 sq km), the park contains mountains with snowcapped peaks, as well as pretty lakes, waterfalls, rivers, and rainforests. Opportunities for outdoor activities abound in the peninsula, so leave the car and give deep-sea fishing and fly-fishing, kayaking, white-water rafting, mountain biking, and bird-watching a go.

Ancient trees tower to nearly 300 ft (91 m) in the old-growth ***Hoh Rain Forest****, which receives 14 ft (4 m) of rainfall a year.*

The former logging town of ***Forks*** *shot to fame in 2005 as the setting for Stephenie Meyer's bestselling vampire novels, the* Twilight *series.*

The long ***Rialto Beach*** *offers terrific views of the Pacific coast, with its tide pools, sea stacks, rocky islands, and the Hole in the Wall.*

Snowcapped mountains encircle ***Lake Quinault*** *and the accompanying Lake Quinault Lodge.*

↑ Prominent, accessible sea stacks on the rugged shores of Rialto Beach

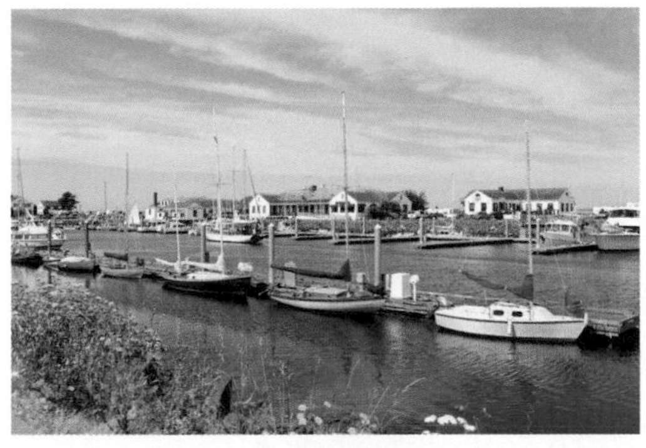

Boats lined up in the marina of the seaport town of Port Townsend

Olympic Peninsula Tour
WASHINGTON

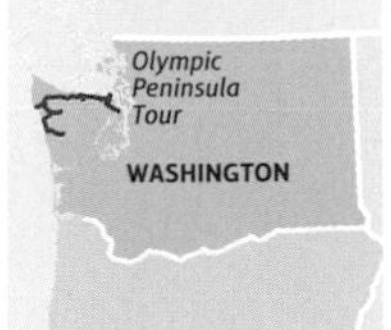

Locator Map

Sitting in the rain shadow of the Olympic Mountains, **Sequim** *features an elk-viewing site and the Olympic Game Farm, home to endangered wild animals.*

Port Townsend (p196), *a National Historic Landmark, is known for its Victorian architecture and vibrant arts community. The town is also an excellent base for kayaking, whale-watching, and cycling trips.*

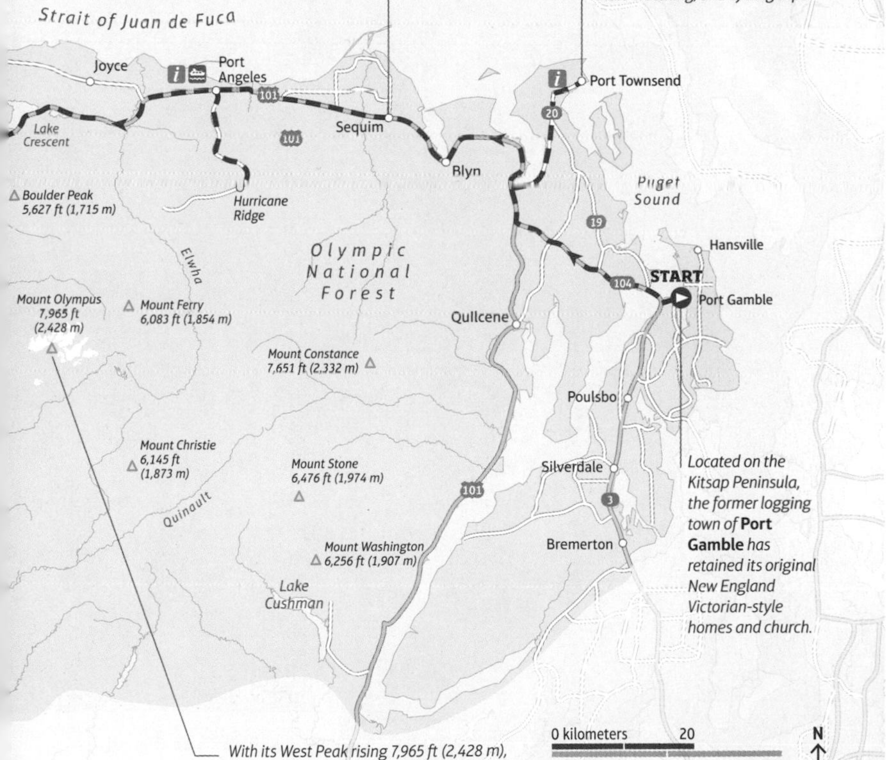

Strait of Juan de Fuca
Joyce
Port Angeles
101
Lake Crescent
101
Sequim
Blyn
Port Townsend
20
Puget Sound
19
Hansville
START
104
Port Gamble
Boulder Peak 5,627 ft (1,715 m)
Hurricane Ridge
Elwha
Olympic National Forest
Quilcene
Mount Olympus 7,965 ft (2,428 m)
Mount Ferry 6,083 ft (1,854 m)
Mount Constance 7,651 ft (2,332 m)
Poulsbo
Mount Christie 6,145 ft (1,873 m)
Mount Stone 6,476 ft (1,974 m)
Silverdale
Quinault
101
3
Bremerton
Mount Washington 6,256 ft (1,907 m)
Lake Cushman
0 kilometers 20
0 miles 20
N

Located on the Kitsap Peninsula, the former logging town of **Port Gamble** *has retained its original New England Victorian-style homes and church.*

With its West Peak rising 7,965 ft (2,428 m), the three-peaked, glacier-clad **Mount Olympus** *is the highest in Washington state's Olympic range.*

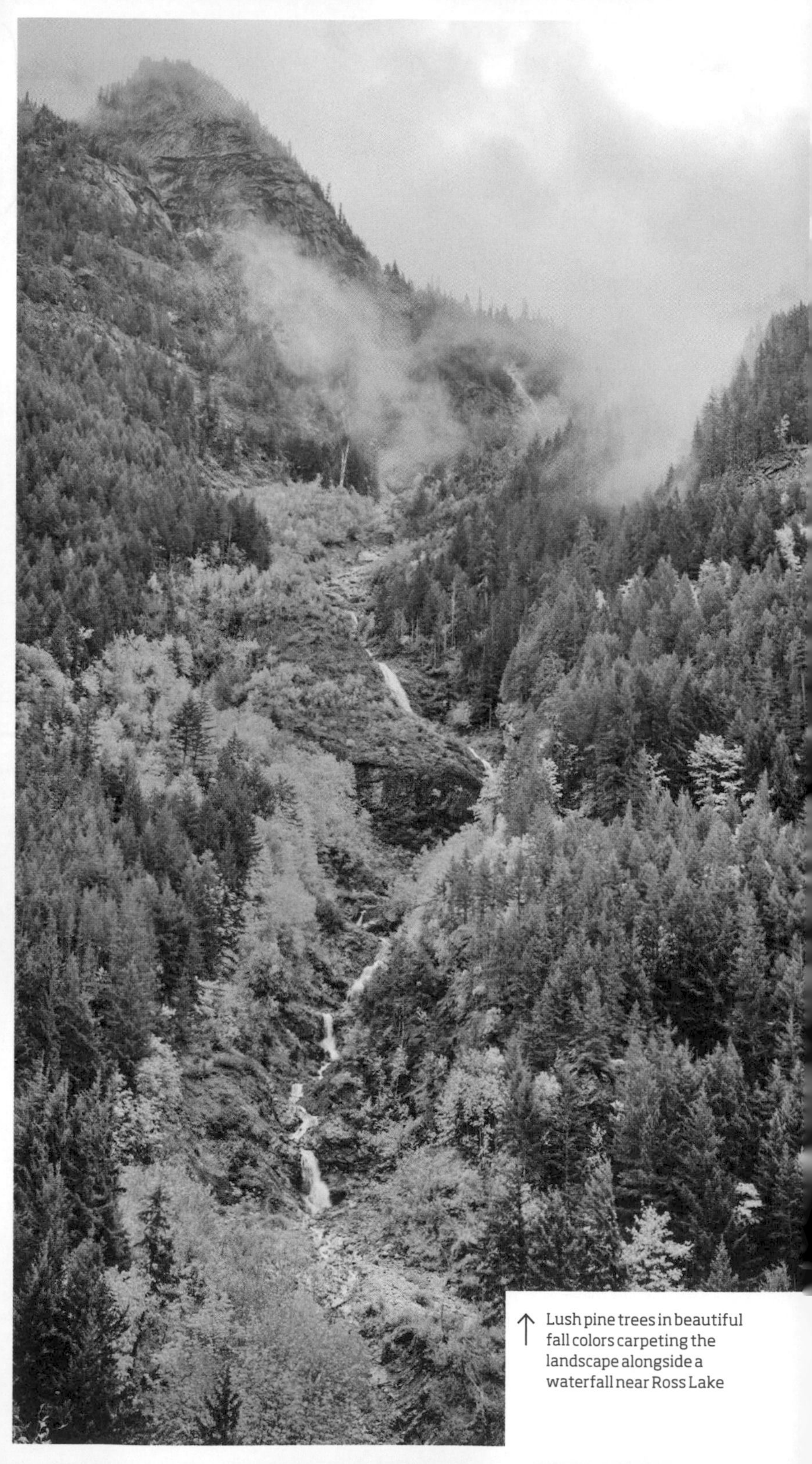

↑ Lush pine trees in beautiful fall colors carpeting the landscape alongside a waterfall near Ross Lake

A DRIVING TOUR

NORTH CASCADES NATIONAL PARK

Length 56 miles (90 km) **Starting point** State Route 20 (North Cascades Hwy) at the entrance to Ross Lake National Recreation Area, 5 miles (8 km) N of Marblemount **Stopping-off points** The park only has picnic facilities

The North Cascades National Park is a beautiful ecosystem of jagged snowcapped peaks, forested valleys, and cascading waterfalls. Its many wonders can be accessed from the scenic North Cascades Highway, which bisects the park. With more than 300 glaciers, the park is the most heavily glaciated region in the lower 48 states. The North Cascades Highway and the Lake Chelan National Recreation Area are linked by hiking trails to the town of Stehekin on Lake Chelan, which is serviced by a ferry from Chelan *(p207)*. This tour is best driven from mid-April to mid-October, when all of Route 20 is open. Stock up on groceries before you set off to make the most of the picnic facilities inside the park.

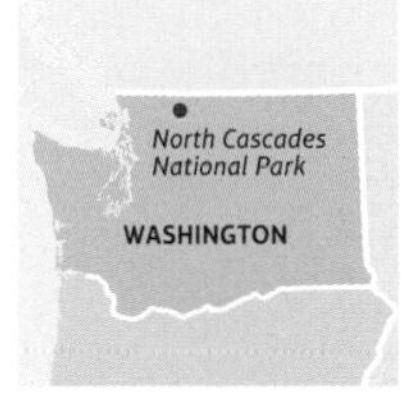

Locator Map

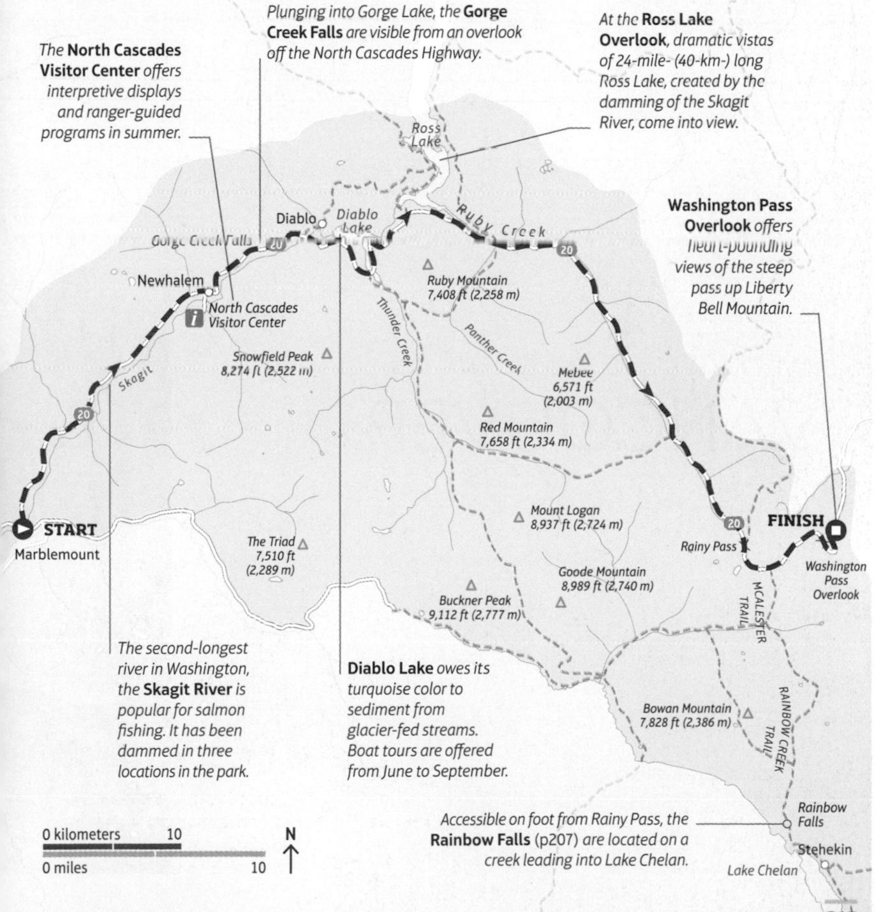

The ***North Cascades Visitor Center*** *offers interpretive displays and ranger-guided programs in summer.*

Plunging into Gorge Lake, the ***Gorge Creek Falls*** *are visible from an overlook off the North Cascades Highway.*

At the ***Ross Lake Overlook****, dramatic vistas of 24-mile- (40-km-) long Ross Lake, created by the damming of the Skagit River, come into view.*

Washington Pass Overlook *offers heart-pounding views of the steep pass up Liberty Bell Mountain.*

The second-longest river in Washington, the ***Skagit River*** *is popular for salmon fishing. It has been dammed in three locations in the park.*

Diablo Lake *owes its turquoise color to sediment from glacier-fed streams. Boat tours are offered from June to September.*

Accessible on foot from Rainy Pass, the ***Rainbow Falls*** *(p207) are located on a creek leading into Lake Chelan.*

START Marblemount

FINISH Washington Pass Overlook

Ross Lake, Diablo, Diablo Lake, Gorge Creek Falls, Newhalem, North Cascades Visitor Center, Ruby Creek, Thunder Creek, Panther Creek, Skagit, Rainy Pass, McAlester Trail, Rainbow Creek Trail, Rainbow Falls, Stehekin, Lake Chelan

Ruby Mountain 7,408 ft (2,258 m)
Snowfield Peak 8,274 ft (2,522 m)
Mebee 6,571 ft (2,003 m)
Red Mountain 7,658 ft (2,334 m)
Mount Logan 8,937 ft (2,724 m)
The Triad 7,510 ft (2,289 m)
Goode Mountain 8,989 ft (2,740 m)
Buckner Peak 9,112 ft (2,777 m)
Bowan Mountain 7,828 ft (2,386 m)

0 kilometers 10
0 miles 10
N

VANCOUVER

The magical steam clock on Water Street, Gastown

EXPLORE VANCOUVER

This guide divides Vancouver into four sightseeing areas: the three on this map and one for sights beyond the city center. Find out more about each area on the following pages.

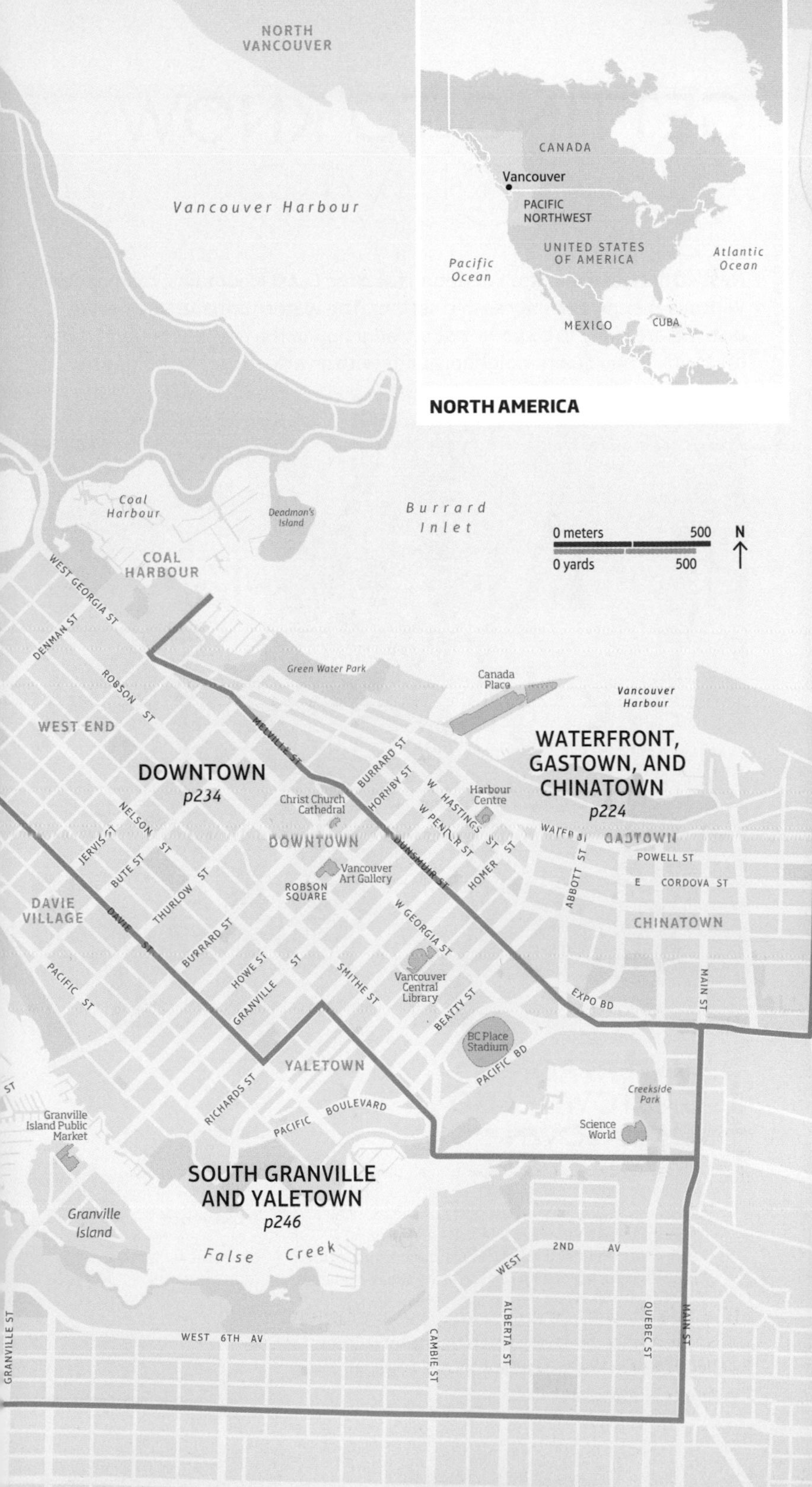
NORTH VANCOUVER
Vancouver Harbour
CANADA
Vancouver
PACIFIC NORTHWEST
UNITED STATES OF AMERICA
Pacific Ocean
Atlantic Ocean
MEXICO
CUBA
NORTH AMERICA
Coal Harbour
Deadman's Island
Burrard Inlet
0 meters 500
0 yards 500
N
COAL HARBOUR
WEST GEORGIA ST
DENMAN ST
ROBSON ST
Green Water Park
Canada Place
Vancouver Harbour
WEST END
MELVILLE ST
WATERFRONT, GASTOWN, AND CHINATOWN
p224
DOWNTOWN
p234
BURRARD ST
HORNBY ST
W HASTINGS ST
Harbour Centre
Christ Church Cathedral
NELSON ST
W PENDER ST
HOMER ST
WATER ST
GASTOWN
DOWNTOWN
DUNSMUIR ST
POWELL ST
JERVIS ST
BUTE ST
Vancouver Art Gallery
ABBOTT ST
E CORDOVA ST
THURLOW ST
ROBSON SQUARE
DAVIE VILLAGE
DAVIE ST
BURRARD ST
W GEORGIA ST
CHINATOWN
HOWE ST
GRANVILLE ST
SMITHE ST
Vancouver Central Library
MAIN ST
PACIFIC ST
EXPO BD
BEATTY ST
BC Place Stadium
YALETOWN
PACIFIC BD
RICHARDS ST
Creekside Park
Granville Island Public Market
PACIFIC BOULEVARD
Science World
SOUTH GRANVILLE AND YALETOWN
p246
Granville Island
False Creek
2ND AV
WEST
WEST 6TH AV
GRANVILLE ST
CAMBIE ST
ALBERTA ST
QUEBEC ST
MAIN ST

GETTING TO KNOW VANCOUVER

Nestled between the Strait of Georgia and the Coast Mountains, cosmopolitan Vancouver enjoys an impressive setting. The Waterfront and Downtown districts are likely to be your first introduction to the city, but beyond these areas you'll find quaint neighborhoods with an eclectic sense of identity.

PAGE 224

WATERFRONT, GASTOWN, AND CHINATOWN

The area to the east of central Vancouver pulses with activity. Vancouver's waterfront, the city's birthplace, is one of the largest and busiest ports on the continent. If the bustle of boats wasn't enough, art galleries, sushi restaurants, and luxury hotels stand shoulder to shoulder here. A block away is Gastown, where home decor showrooms and tempting eateries have taken up space in the area's most historic buildings. Next door, colorful Chinatown attracts throngs of shoppers looking for authentic Chinese food and souvenirs.

Best for
Eating out, cocktail lounges, and souvenir shopping

Home to
Dr. Sun Yat-Sen Classical Chinese Garden, Harbour Centre and Vancouver Lookout

Experience
Authentic dim sum in Chinatown, followed by a cocktail at the Keefer Bar

PAGE 234

DOWNTOWN

Vancouver's Downtown core is a sophisticated urban landscape, its wide streets lined with grand landmark buildings, vintage theaters, and fine art galleries. Cutting through it all is is Robson Street, known for its excellent shopping and people-watching opportunities. This area is also where you'll find one of the city's most famous landmarks: the historic Fairmont Hotel Vancouver, which still hosts royalty and other celebrities from around the world. Downtown is always alive with a frenetic pace of activity, with the fashionable locals rushing about to finish their day with a cocktail at one of the happening neighborhood lounges.

Best for
Shopping, dining, and fine art

Home to
Stanley Park

Experience
A quiet moment on top of the Vancouver Central Library's rooftop garden

→

PAGE 246

SOUTH GRANVILLE AND YALETOWN

The neighborhoods of South Granville and Yaletown are separated by False Creek, a short inlet in the center of Vancouver. On the south shore, South Granville is home to the busy Granville Island, as well as a pleasant mix of cafes and restaurants, upscale shops, and numerous commercial art galleries that justify the local moniker "gallery row." Yaletown, on the north shore of False Creek, is a magnet for Downtown dwellers. Once an underused warehouse district, it's now full of terrace cafes, designer outlets, and interior design stores that draw visitors in the day, and nightclubs and brewpubs that attract revelers come evening.

Best for
Breweries, museums, and green spaces

Home to
Vanier Park, Granville Island

Experience
A mini-cruise on the Aquabus to Granville Island and strolling through the public market

PAGE 256

BEYOND THE CENTER

Just a short distance from Vancouver's Downtown district, a mind-blowing array of outdoor pursuits and cultural excursions awaits. A lovely mix of old and modern architecture can be found at the University of British Columbia, as well as the splendid Museum of Anthropology and the UBC Botanical Garden with its suspended walkways. Other intriguing sights are located in outer cities, easily reached by car or public transit. The iconic Lions Gate Bridge leads to West Vancouver, featuring miles of scenic shoreline, as well as North Vancouver, which offers the physical wonders of Capilano Canyon and Grouse Mountain. By the coast, the city of Richmond reflects Greater Vancouver's multicultural character and is making waves as a foodie destination with its Asian malls and markets.

Best for

Indigenous culture, hiking, and international cuisine

Home to

Museum of Anthropology at UBC, Stanley Park

Experience

Hiking up the strenuous Grouse Grind and riding the scenic gondola back down

CITY OF VANCOUVER
1886 1986
JACK CHOW INSURANCE
周永職燕梳
Autoplan

Walking past colorful business fronts in Chinatown

WATERFRONT, GASTOWN, AND CHINATOWN

The history of Vancouver, as with many coastal towns and cities in the Pacific Northwest, begins with its waterfront. This is where the earliest American Indians settled, living off freshly caught fish. In this regard Vancouver is particularly blessed, with numerous rivers and bays.

Nearby Gastown began as a haven for gold-seekers, loggers, and a host of ruffians. This changed when, in 1885, Canadian Pacific Railway (CPR) chose the town as its western terminus. After the Great Vancouver Fire of 1886, the newly renamed Vancouver – a CPR marketing decision – settled into respectability. Boutiques and restaurants now occupy the area's historic buildings, and its bustling sidewalks and markets highlight an enduring presence.

At the same time, neighboring Chinatown was born when Chinese workers came to the city, many to work in the new sawmills. By 1911 there were over 3,500 Chinese residents, with their own grocery stores, bars, tailors, a benevolent society, and a theater. It was – and still is – the largest Chinese community in Canada.

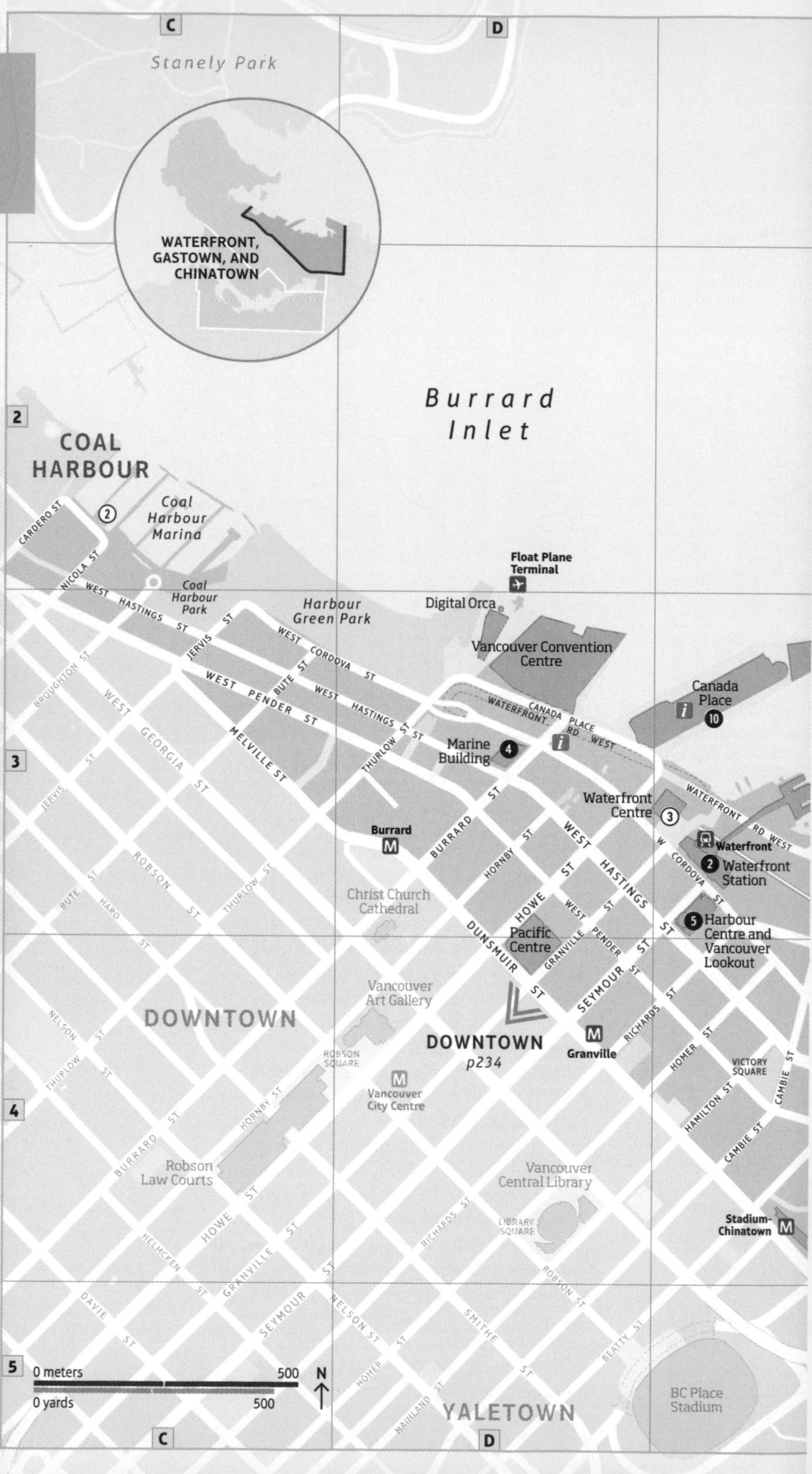

C
D
Stanely Park
WATERFRONT, GASTOWN, AND CHINATOWN
Burrard Inlet
2
COAL HARBOUR
Coal Harbour Marina
CARDERO ST
NICOLA ST
WEST HASTINGS ST
Coal Harbour Park
Harbour Green Park
Float Plane Terminal
Digital Orca
Vancouver Convention Centre
Canada Place
JERVIS ST
WEST CORDOVA ST
BUTE ST
WEST PENDER ST
WEST HASTINGS ST
WATERFRONT
CANADA PLACE RD WEST
BROUGHTON ST
WEST GEORGIA ST
MELVILLE ST
THURLOW ST
Marine Building
3
Waterfront Centre
WATERFRONT RD WEST
Burrard
BURRARD ST
HORNBY ST
WEST HASTINGS ST
W CORDOVA ST
Waterfront
Waterfront Station
JERVIS ST
ROBSON ST
BUTE ST
HARO ST
THURLOW ST
Christ Church Cathedral
HOWE ST
WEST PENDER ST
Harbour Centre and Vancouver Lookout
DUNSMUIR ST
Pacific Centre
GRANVILLE ST
SEYMOUR ST
RICHARDS ST
Vancouver Art Gallery
DOWNTOWN
NELSON ST
THURLOW ST
ROBSON SQUARE
DOWNTOWN p234
Granville
HOMER ST
VICTORY SQUARE
CAMBIE ST
Vancouver City Centre
4
HORNBY ST
BURRARD ST
HAMILTON ST
CAMBIE ST
Robson Law Courts
Vancouver Central Library
HOWE ST
LIBRARY SQUARE
Stadium-Chinatown
HELMCKEN ST
GRANVILLE ST
RICHARDS ST
ROBSON ST
DAVIE ST
SEYMOUR ST
NELSON ST
SMITHE ST
BEATTY ST
5
0 meters
500
0 yards
500
N
HOMER ST
MAINLAND ST
YALETOWN
BC Place Stadium
C
D

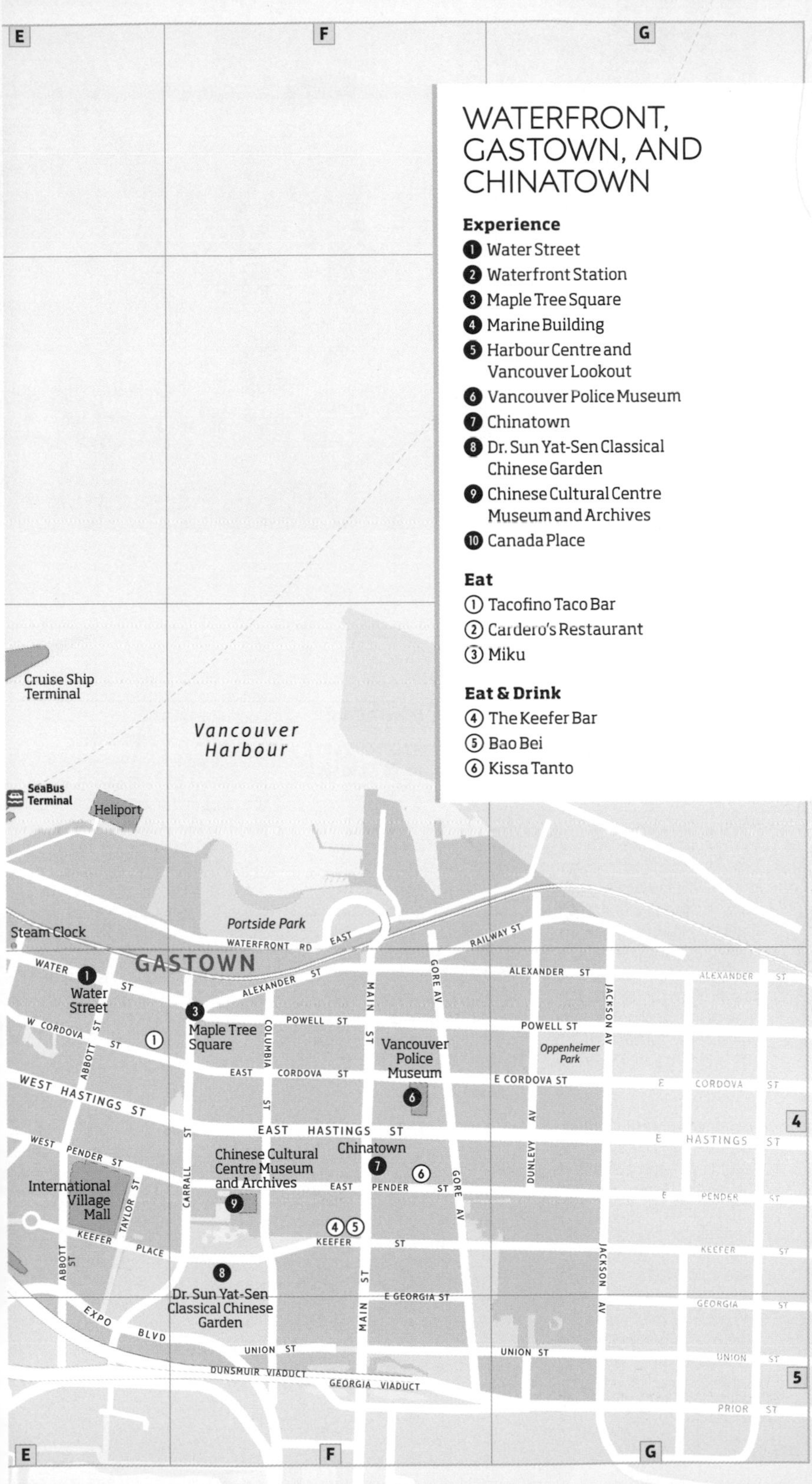
E
F
G
WATERFRONT, GASTOWN, AND CHINATOWN
Experience
1 Water Street
2 Waterfront Station
3 Maple Tree Square
4 Marine Building
5 Harbour Centre and Vancouver Lookout
6 Vancouver Police Museum
7 Chinatown
8 Dr. Sun Yat-Sen Classical Chinese Garden
9 Chinese Cultural Centre Museum and Archives
10 Canada Place
Eat
① Tacofino Taco Bar
② Cardero's Restaurant
③ Miku
Eat & Drink
④ The Keefer Bar
⑤ Bao Bei
⑥ Kissa Tanto
Cruise Ship Terminal
Vancouver Harbour
SeaBus Terminal
Heliport
Portside Park
Steam Clock
GASTOWN
Water Street
Maple Tree Square
Vancouver Police Museum
Oppenheimer Park
Chinese Cultural Centre Museum and Archives
Chinatown
International Village Mall
Dr. Sun Yat-Sen Classical Chinese Garden
WATERFRONT RD
RAILWAY ST
ALEXANDER ST
POWELL ST
EAST CORDOVA ST
E CORDOVA ST
WEST HASTINGS ST
EAST HASTINGS ST
E HASTINGS ST
WEST PENDER ST
EAST PENDER ST
E PENDER ST
KEEFER ST
KEEFER PLACE
E GEORGIA ST
GEORGIA ST
UNION ST
PRIOR ST
EXPO BLVD
DUNSMUIR VIADUCT
GEORGIA VIADUCT
WATER ST
W CORDOVA ST
ABBOTT ST
TAYLOR ST
CARRALL ST
COLUMBIA ST
MAIN ST
GORE AV
DUNLEVY AV
JACKSON AV
4
5

Water Street in Gastown, with Vancouver Lookout in the background

EXPERIENCE

Water Street

E4 From Richards to Carrall sts Waterfront SeaBus: Waterfront

Water Street is Gastown's main thoroughfare and popular with tourists. Its turn-of-the-19th-century buildings house a mix of restaurants, nightclubs, shops, rug merchants, and art galleries.

Water Street was not always so well liked, though. Having slipped into decline after World War I, it wasn't until the 1960s that the area's potential was recognized and a wave of restoration began. By 1971, the street was designated a historic area. Old-fashioned street lamps and mews enhance its historic flavor.

The world's first steam-operated clock stands 16 ft (5 m) tall at the corner of Water and Cambie streets. It strikes its chimes on the hour and every 15 minutes emits a blast of steam. Other notable sights include the 1899 Dominion Hotel, and the historically seedy Blood Alley.

Waterfront Station

E3 601 W Cordova St Waterfront SeaBus: Waterfront

A busy transportation hub, Waterfront Station is the convergence point of the SeaBus, SkyTrain, and West Coast Express trains. Built by Canadian Pacific Railway, the current Waterfront Station is the third passenger train station built on the site. The first cross-Canada passenger train pulled into the original timber station on May 23, 1887. The second station here was a chateau-style structure built in 1898–99.

The present-day building was completed in 1914 and restored in 1976–77 to make the most of its expansive waiting area, arches, and columns. Murals circling the upper walls portray romantic versions of Canadian landscapes. Excellent shops and cafes now occupy the former waiting room.

Outside the station is *Wounded Soldier*, a sculpture by Charles Marega (1871–1939), Vancouver's premier artist of his day.

THE GREAT VANCOUVER FIRE OF 1886

On June 13, 1886, the lethal combination of a powerful westerly wind and sparks from a Canadian Pacific Railway brush fire near Drake and Homer streets, in what is now Yaletown *(p255)*, burned through Vancouver's motley assortment of 1,000 wooden buildings. In 20 minutes, the city was devastated, barely two months after its incorporation. The raging fire - so hot it not only burned nearby St. James' Anglican Church but also melted its bell - killed at least 21 people; the exact number is unknown. Within 12 hours, rebuilding had begun. The Burns Block in Maple Tree Square was built that same year and still exists.

On the facade of the Marine Building, terra-cotta marine fauna frolic amid frothy waves. The main entrance features bronze grilles and brass bas-relief castings of starfish, crabs, and seashells.

3

Maple Tree Square

F4 Water St at Carrall St

Search as you might, you will not find a maple tree in Gastown's Maple Tree Square. The famous tree, destroyed in the Great Vancouver Fire of 1886, was a popular meeting spot for residents.

Standing in the square is Okanagan artist Vern Simpson's 6-ft- (1.8-m-) copper statue of John "Gassy Jack" Deighton, for whom Gastown is named. Built in 1970, the statue notes this voluble, or "gassy," entrepreneur's place in history.

In 1867, Deighton built, near Maple Tree Square, the first watering hole on Burrard Inlet. He persuaded local millworkers to build the Globe Saloon in just 24 hours. He died on May 29, 1875, aged 44, and was buried in an unmarked grave in New Westminster, 13 miles (20 km) from Gastown.

4

Marine Building

D3 355 Burrard St Waterfront SeaBus: Waterfront

Architects McCarter and Nairne described the Marine Building as "a great crag rising from the sea." Their design, built in 1929 in an extravagant Art Deco style near the waterfront, cost its Toronto developers $2.35 million before they went broke.

Now an office building, it has been massively restored since the mid-1980s. It is the most impressive of all Vancouver's historic buildings. On the facade of the Marine Building, terra-cotta marine fauna frolic amid frothy waves. The main entrance features bronze grilles and brass bas-relief castings of starfish, crabs, and seashells. A 40-ft- (12-m-) high arch shows a jutting ship's prow and Canada geese.

The lobby is a dramatic step back in time, with aqua-green and blue tiles and carved maritime-inspired friezes.

5   

Harbour Centre and Vancouver Lookout

E3 555 W Hastings St Waterfront SeaBus: Waterfront Times vary, check websites vancouverlookout.com; harbourcentre.com

Glass elevators glide 553 ft (169 m) up the tower of Harbour Centre to Vancouver Lookout, an enclosed observation deck with a superb 360-degree view of Vancouver and informative plaques to help visitors identify the sights below. These interpretive panels locate, among other sights, the distinctive retractable roof of BC Place Stadium, Stanley Park, and Mount Baker in Washington.

When it opened on August 13, 1977, Harbour Centre was the tallest building in British Columbia. Among the guests at the grand opening was the first man on the moon, Neil Armstrong, who left his footprint in cement as an official memento of the opening. A ticket to the observation deck is valid all day, so return to watch the sun set over Vancouver Island. Also at the top of the tower is a revolving restaurant, providing fabulous views.

The copper statue of "Gassy Jack" Deighton in Maple Tree Square, Gastown

EAT

Tacofino Taco Bar

Stylish eatery with superb Mexican tacos.

E4 15 W Cordova St tacofino.com

Cardero's Restaurant

Fine local seafood and wine is served here.

C2 1583 Coal Harbour Quay vancouverdine.com

$$$

Miku

Classic Japanese dishes in a sophisticated waterfront setting.

E3 Suite 70-200 Granville St miku restaurant.com

$$$

6 

Vancouver Police Museum

F4 240 E Cordova St 9am-5pm Tue-Sat Major hols vancouverpolicemuseum.ca

Opened in 1986 to mark the centennial of the Vancouver police force and housed in the former Coroner's Court Building, this museum includes the city's original morgue. Step into the autopsy laboratory to view the forensic table where actor Errol Flynn was declared dead on October 14, 1959. Scenes for the popular TV series *Da Vinci's Inquest* have been filmed here. A large mural depicts the colorful history of the police department. Street weaponry, prohibited weapons, and antique firearms are on display in the Sins gallery. In the True Crime gallery, you can see real evidence from some of Vancouver's unsolved historical crimes. There is also an area where children can dress up in real police uniforms.

EAT & DRINK

The Keefer Bar

This snug bar concocts inventive cocktails to pair with small plates.

F4 135 Keefer St thekeeferbar.com

$$$

Bao Bei

Chinese brasserie serving dumplings and steamed buns alongside creative cocktails.

F4 163 Keefer St bao-bei.ca

$$$

Kissa Tanto

Italian-Japanese fusion cuisine and cocktails in a chic setting. Try the octopus salad.

F4 263 E Pender St Sun & Mon kissatanto.com

$$$

Relaxing in the peaceful Dr. Sun Yat-Sen Classical Chinese Garden

7 

Chinatown

F4 E Hastings to Union sts, from Carrall to Gore sts Stadium-Chinatown vancouver-chinatown.com

Vancouver's Chinatown is older than the city itself. Pender Street, the main byway, is straddled near Taylor Street by Millennium Gate, a good spot from which to view the area's restored buildings. The 1907 Chinese Freemasons Building *(5 W Pender Street)* was once home to Dr. Sun Yat-Sen. The 1913 Sam Kee Building *(8 W Pender Street)* is the result of government expropriation of property in order to widen the street. In defiance, the owner built what was once the world's thinnest commercial building on the 5-ft- (1.5-m-) wide plot that was left. The 1889 Wing Sang Building *(51 E Pender Street)*, the oldest in Chinatown, has now been turned into an exhibition space for the Rennie Museum.

Known for traditional shops, Chinese herbs, housewares, and tearooms, Chinatown is largely a daytime place.

8 

Dr. Sun Yat-Sen Classical Chinese Garden

F4 578 Carrall St Stadium Times vary, check website vancouverchinesegarden.com

Modeled after private gardens in the city of Suzhou during the Ming Dynasty, this is the first complete Classical Chinese garden created outside China. A team of experts from Suzhou spent an entire year constructing the garden, building with materials shipped from China. No nails, screws, or power tools were used during construction.

At first, the garden, named in honor of the founder of the Republic of China, seems a maze of walls within walls. Designed to appear larger than it really is, the garden

→ Canada Place, with its distinctive fabric "sails," at Vancouver Harbour

is sprinkled with windows and moon gates – large circular openings in walls – that allow inviting glimpses of tiny courtyards wrapped around still smaller courtyards, miniature pavilions, intricate mosaic pathways, bridges, and galleries.

Chinese Cultural Centre Museum and Archives

F4 555 Columbia St Stadium, Main St-Science World 11am-5pm Tue-Sun Jan 1, Dec 25 & 26 (except to gallery) cccvan.com

The three-story Chinese Cultural Centre Museum and Archives building, styled after the architecture of the Ming Dynasty (1368–1644), is an impressive sight. At the edge of its curving tiled roof stand a superb pair of ornamental dragons, protecting the building from harm.

The museum and archives opened in 1998 as part of the Chinese Cultural Centre complex *(50 E Pender Street)*. On the first floor of the museum is the To-Yick Wong Gallery, with exhibits of both established and up-and-coming artists.

On the second floor are permanent exhibits of artifacts and photos that portray the history of BC's Chinese population from the Gold Rush of 1858 to the present. The Chinese Canadian Military Museum here recounts the lives of Chinese–Canadian veterans of World War II.

On the third floor, the S. K. Lee Academy hosts seminars and symposiums to promote cross-cultural understanding.

VANCOUVER'S CHINESE COMMUNITY

Vancouver's Chinatown is home to tens of thousands of people of Chinese descent. The success of the community, which sprang up as a shanty town in the 1880s after immigration to the city to build the cross-Canada railway, did not come easily. Chinatown's growth was seen as a threat to non-Asian seasonal workers. In 1885, a closed-door immigration policy became law. Racial tensions culminated in two major riots in Vancouver, in 1887 and 1907. But by the 1940s, Chinatown was drawing tourists, prompting the government to grant Chinese Canadians citizenship and reopen immigration in 1947.

Did You Know?

Vancouver is home to a second Chinatown, located in Richmond, just beyond the city center.

Canada Place

E3 999 Canada Pl Waterfront SeaBus: Waterfront Daily canadaplace.ca

Originally built for Expo '86, today, Canada Place is home to a cruise ship terminal, the Vancouver Convention Centre, Vancouver's World Trade Centre, and an upscale hotel.

The structure's five white Teflon-coated fabric "sails" make possible a huge interior area free of support structures. On the west side of the complex, a fountain, shady trees, and ample outdoor seating provide an oasis in the heart of the bustling city.

The three-block, open-air Canada Place Promenade juts into Vancouver Harbour and offers a panorama of busy sea and air traffic. Every year on July 1 Canada Place hosts a spectacular celebratory fireworks display over the harbor.

A SHORT WALK
WATERFRONT AND GASTOWN

Distance 0.6 miles (1 km) **Time** 15 minutes
Nearest station Waterfront

One of Vancouver's oldest areas, Gastown, which faces the waters of Burrard Inlet, is bounded by Columbia Street to the east and Burrard Street to the west. Gastown is a charming mix of cobblestone streets and restored 19th-century public buildings and storefronts. Browse the chic boutiques and galleries that line Water Street, dip into the delightful restaurants and cafes that fill the mews, courtyards, and passages, and watch the steam rise from the steam clock every 15 minutes as you walk through the area.

Canada Place (p231) *is a waterside architectural marvel of white sails and glass that houses a hotel, two convention centers, a flight simulation ride, and a cruise-ship terminal.*

The **SeaBus** *ferries passengers across Burrard Inlet between the central Waterfront Station and Lonsdale Quay in North Vancouver. The ride offers stunning views of the harbor.*

Waterfront Station (p228) *occupies the imposing 19th-century Canadian Pacific Railway building.*

Harbour Centre (p229) *is a high-rise building best known for* **Vancouver Lookout**, *a viewing deck 553 ft (169 m) above the city. On a clear day it is possible to see as far as Vancouver Island.*

Five sails adorning the roof of Canada Place, echoing Canada's nautical past

↑ The famed steam clock on the cobblestones of Water Street

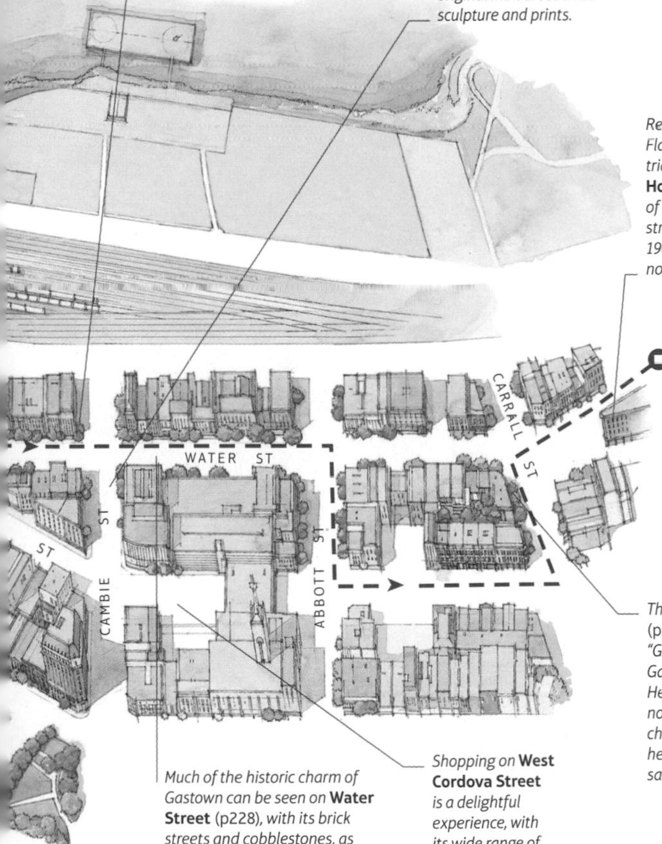

Waterfront and Gastown

WATERFRONT, GASTOWN, AND CHINATOWN

Locator Map

For more detail see p226

0 meters 100 N
0 yards 100

The **steam clock** *is said to be one of the world's few steam-powered clocks. It chimes every hour, on the hour.*

The **Inuit Gallery of Vancouver** *displays original Inuit art such as sculpture and prints.*

Reminiscent of New York's Flatiron Building, the triangular structure of **Hotel Europe***, at the corner of Powell and Alexander streets, was built between 1908 and 1909 as a hotel. It now houses apartments.*

FINISH

CARRALL ST

WATER ST

CAMBIE ST

ABBOTT ST

The **"Gassy Jack" Statue** (p229) *commemorates "Gassy Jack" Deighton, who Gastown was named after. He was an English sailor noted both for his endless chatter and for the saloon he opened here for local sawmill workers in 1867.*

Much of the historic charm of Gastown can be seen on **Water Street** (p228)*, with its brick streets and cobblestones, as well as shops, cafes, and the famous steam clock.*

Shopping on **West Cordova Street** *is a delightful experience, with its wide range of small galleries and trendy boutiques.*

Cyclists and joggers on the Seawall in Stanley Park

DOWNTOWN

Originally a logging settlement surrounded by swamps, mills, and a few taverns, Vancouver's Downtown core has transformed and emerged as a sophisticated urban landscape lined with landmark buildings. When the Canadian Pacific Railway (CPR) decided to build its new train terminus in Gastown in 1885, speculators began buying up property there and further south in what is now Downtown, knowing it could only increase in value. The CPR had promised to build a hotel and an opera house, but protests erupted when they built a new post office that was virtually on the edge of the forest.

By 1891 the area had grown so much that a tram-based public transportation system was introduced, and in 1895 Christ Church Cathedral was built, adding some grandeur to the fast-developing town. In 1939 one of Downtown's major landmarks, the 17-story Fairmont Hotel Vancouver, opened at a cost of $12 million. It still hosts royalty, politicians, and other celebrities, and Downtown remains the vibrant hub of Vancouver life.

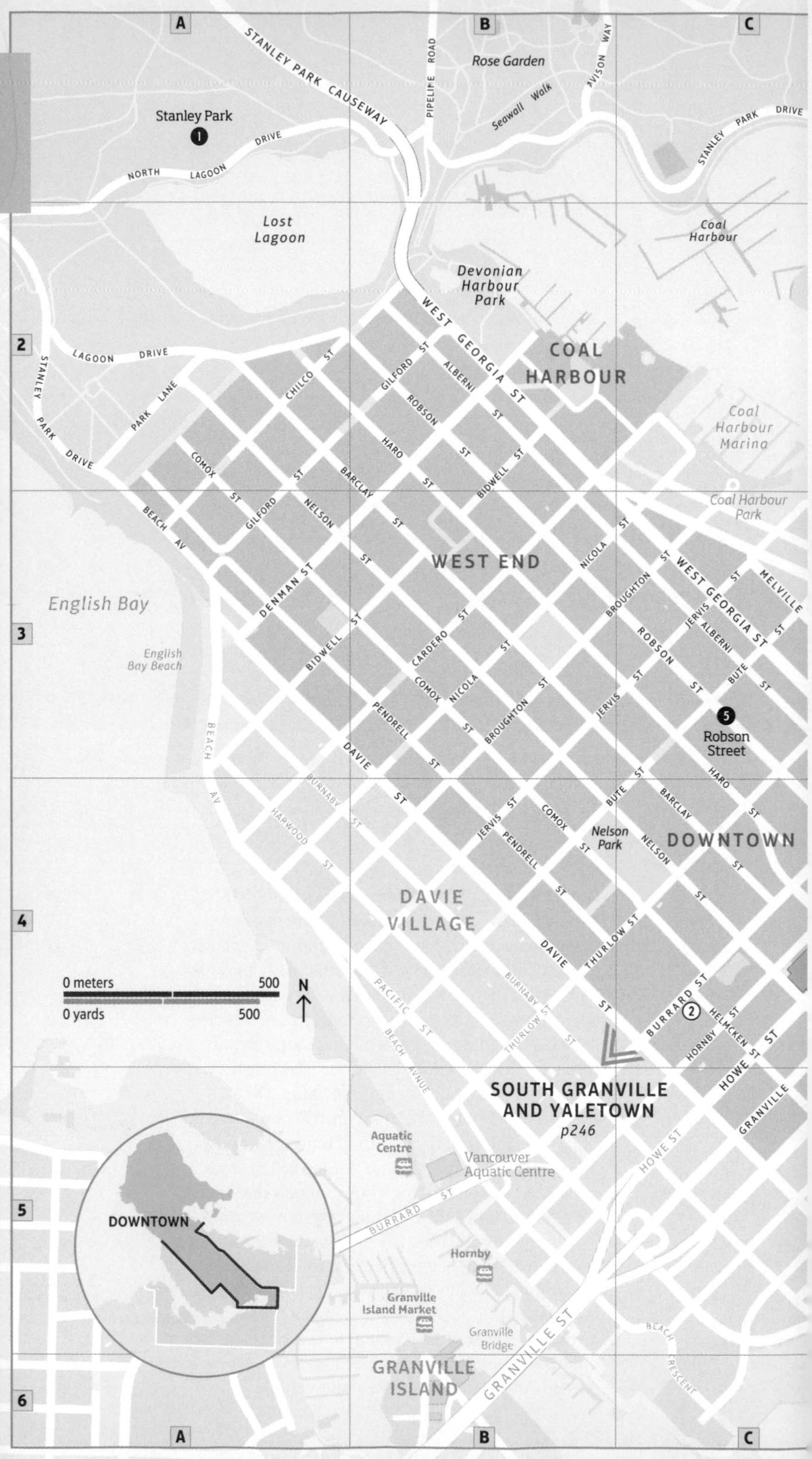

A
B
C
Stanley Park
Rose Garden
Seawall Walk
Stanley Park Causeway
Pipeline Road
Avison Way
Stanley Park Drive
North Lagoon Drive
Lost Lagoon
Coal Harbour
Devonian Harbour Park
COAL HARBOUR
Coal Harbour Marina
Coal Harbour Park
Lagoon Drive
West Georgia St
WEST END
English Bay
English Bay Beach
Robson Street
Nelson Park
DOWNTOWN
DAVIE VILLAGE
0 meters
500
0 yards
500
N
SOUTH GRANVILLE AND YALETOWN
p246
Aquatic Centre
Vancouver Aquatic Centre
Hornby
Granville Island Market
Granville Bridge
GRANVILLE ISLAND
Granville St
DOWNTOWN
2
3
4
5
6

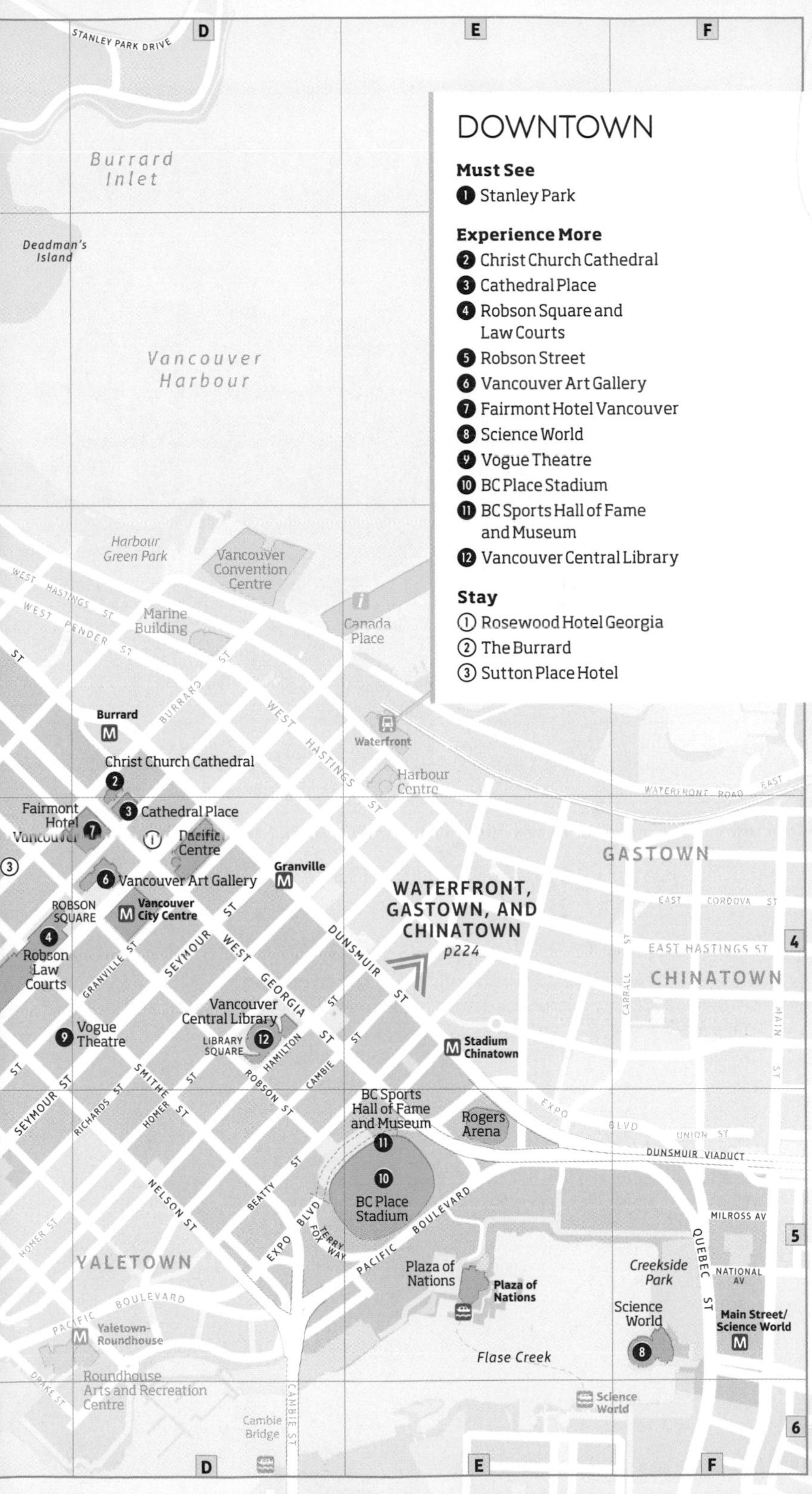
DOWNTOWN
Must See
1 Stanley Park
Experience More
2 Christ Church Cathedral
3 Cathedral Place
4 Robson Square and Law Courts
5 Robson Street
6 Vancouver Art Gallery
7 Fairmont Hotel Vancouver
8 Science World
9 Vogue Theatre
10 BC Place Stadium
11 BC Sports Hall of Fame and Museum
12 Vancouver Central Library
Stay
① Rosewood Hotel Georgia
② The Burrard
③ Sutton Place Hotel
D
E
F
4
5
6
Stanley Park Drive
Burrard Inlet
Deadman's Island
Vancouver Harbour
Harbour Green Park
Vancouver Convention Centre
Canada Place
Marine Building
West Hastings St
West Pender St
Burrard St
Burrard
Waterfront
Harbour Centre
Waterfront Road East
Christ Church Cathedral
Cathedral Place
Fairmont Hotel Vancouver
Pacific Centre
Vancouver Art Gallery
Granville
Robson Square
Vancouver City Centre
Robson Law Courts
Granville St
Seymour St
West Georgia St
Dunsmuir St
WATERFRONT, GASTOWN, AND CHINATOWN
p224
GASTOWN
East Cordova St
East Hastings St
CHINATOWN
Carrall St
Main St
Vancouver Central Library
Library Square
Vogue Theatre
Hamilton
Cambie
Stadium Chinatown
Smithe St
Homer St
Richards St
Robson St
Expo Blvd
Union St
Dunsmuir Viaduct
BC Sports Hall of Fame and Museum
Rogers Arena
BC Place Stadium
Beatty St
Nelson St
Terry Fox Way
Pacific Boulevard
Milross Av
Quebec St
National Av
Creekside Park
Science World
Main Street/ Science World
Plaza of Nations
Flase Creek
YALETOWN
Yaletown-Roundhouse
Roundhouse Arts and Recreation Centre
Drake St
Cambie Bridge
Cambie St

Did You Know?

At 9pm every night, a cannon is fired at Hallelujah Point, on the southeastern tip of the park.

→ The Lost Lagoon, Coal Harbour, and Vancouver's skyline, and *(inset)* exploring the Seawall

STANLEY PARK

A1 2099 Beach Av Burrard 24 hrs daily vancouver.ca

This beloved green oasis in the middle of the city offers a vast area of natural West Coast rainforest to explore. Discover hiking and biking trails among majestic cedar trees, gaze up at colorful totem poles, and enjoy scenic views of the ocean from the Seawall.

Stanley Park is a magnificent 1,000-acre (405-ha) area of tamed wilderness. The land here was originally home to the Musqueam and Squamish Indigenous Peoples, but was used by the colonialists as a military reserve because of its strategic position. In 1888 it was established as a city park, dedicated to Governor General Stanley.

Today, the park is filled with natural, cultural, and historical landmarks, sandy beaches, rocky coves, and beautiful picnic areas. Local wildlife, ever-blooming gardens, and the meandering

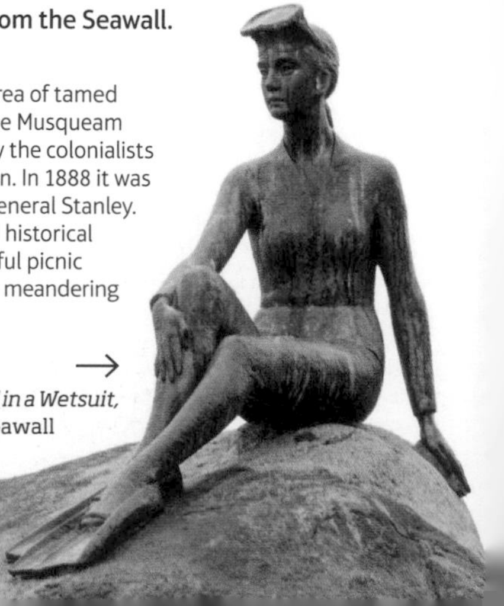

→ Elek Imredy's *The Girl in a Wetsuit*, on an offshore rock by the Seawall

Seawall – a 5.5-mile (9-km) perimeter trail that can be walked, jogged, or biked – are all part of this amazing urban escape.

The park is also home to the Vancouver Aquarium, where visitors can get up close to various species of marine and jungle life, including sea lions, sharks, penguins, fish, birds, monkeys, and reptiles.

For spectacular views, head to Prospect Point. Set on the northernmost tip of the peninsula, this is the park's highest point, with panoramas stretching across the waters of Burrard Inlet to the Coast Mountains.

INSIDER TIP
Getting Around

Bikes can be rented from shops just outside the southern entrance to the park. Horse-drawn carriage and historic trolley tours are also available, with pick-ups near the visitor information booth.

Looking out from the Seawall over Coal Harbour and Vancouver in the fall

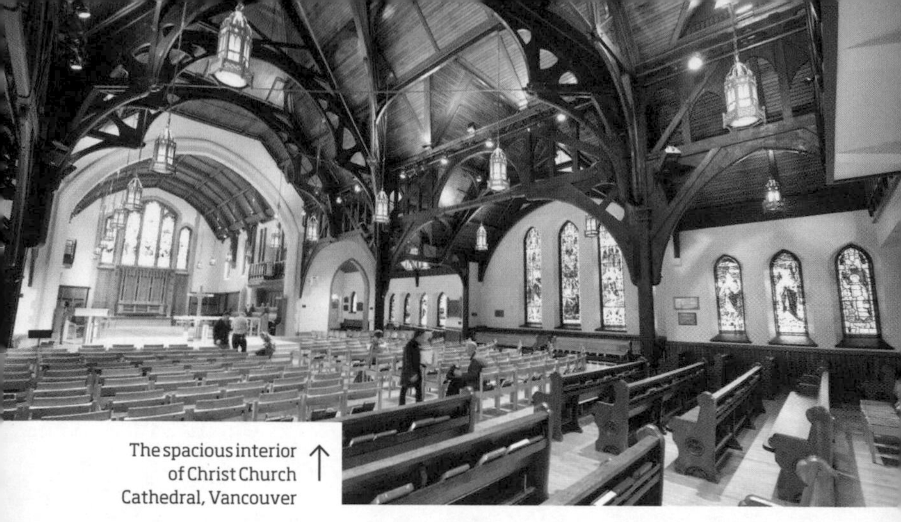

The spacious interior of Christ Church Cathedral, Vancouver

EXPERIENCE MORE

Christ Church Cathedral

D3 690 Burrard St Burrard 10am-4pm Mon-Fri & Sun for services Non-religious hols thecathedral.ca

Originally known as "the light on the hill," Christ Church Cathedral was once a beacon for mariners entering Vancouver's harbor. After undergoing several expansions since its consecration in 1895, the oldest surviving church in Vancouver now sits in the midst of the downtown business center. Modeled after a Gothic parish church by its designer, Winnipeg architect C. O. Wickenden, the interior features arched ceiling beams of Douglas fir.

In 1929, the church became a cathedral and, in 1930, the spacious chancel was added. The overhead lanterns were installed in 1937. Thirty-nine impressive British- and Canadian-made stained-glass windows feature pivotal scenes from Old and New Testament stories. Several unique windows include images of Vancouver people and places. Three William Morris windows, on permanent loan from the Vancouver Museum, are set in the office vestibule. To see them, use the Burrard Street entrance.

After a major renovation in 2004, a new Kenneth Jones organ was installed in the cathedral. In 2016, the slate roof was replaced with a zinc roof and a bell tower made of stained glass was added. The sandstone cathedral remains to this day a quiet sanctuary.

Cathedral Place

D4 925 W Georgia St Burrard 7am-6pm Mon-Fri, 10am-5pm Sat Major hols 925westgeorgia.com

Cathedral Place is a high-rise makeover of the 1929 Art Deco Georgia Medical Dental Building that once stood here. The 23-story tower was designed by Paul Merrick Architects and built in 1990–91.

The building preserves the stylistic ambience of its predecessor. Sculpted figures on the 11th-story parapet are copies of the three famous terra-cotta nurses dressed in World War I uniforms that graced the Medical Dental Building and were demolished along with it. Lions that adorned the third-story parapet are now at home at each of the entrances to Cathedral Place. Eight gargoyles on the 16th-story parapet echo those of the Fairmont Hotel Vancouver. The fine exterior is a collection of 20,000 pieces of Kansas limestone, polished, cut to shape, numbered, and then hoisted by crane.

The Art Deco-inspired lobby is dominated by the glass-and-steel sculpture *Navigation Device: Origin Unknown*, by Robert Studer. Some 17,000 pieces of Spanish granite are set geometrically into the floor. Behind the lobby is an outdoor grassy courtyard offering benches and serenity.

Did You Know?

Christ Church Cathedral prides itself on being a church of inclusion for the LGBT+ community.

Robson Square and Law Courts

C4 800 Hornby St Vancouver City Centre 9am-4pm Mon-Fri Major hols robson square.ubc.ca

Designed by BC architect Arthur Erickson, the four-level Robson Square stretches several blocks. On Robson Street's south side, trees and a waterfall provide a shaded background to Alan Chung Hung's red steel sculpture, *Spring*. Steps to the right of the waterfall lead to a pool and parkette; from here, a walkway leads to the law courts. Jack Harman's statue *Themis Goddess of Justice* overlooks the Great Hall.

For the holiday season, from early December till the end of February, the Robson Square Ice Rink is set up, offering free ice skating. Skate and helmet rentals are available for a small fee. In the evenings music, from live jazz to DJs, adds to the atmosphere.

Robson Street

C3 Vancouver City Centre robson street.ca

Once known as Robsonstrasse due to a multitude of German businesses, Robson Street, named after former BC premier John Robson (in office 1889–92), today offers restaurants from almost every continent. Local chic celebrities and tourists alike flock here, making people-watching from outdoor cafes a popular pastime.

Shopping is the street's main attraction. Soaps, accessories, chocolates, lingerie, men's wear, and souvenirs are sold in stylish shops stretching along Robson Street from Granville to Denman streets. A women's lingerie megastore at the corner of Robson and Burrard streets is located in the old Vancouver Public Library building, constructed in 1957.

Vancouver Art Gallery

D4 750 Hornby St Burrard 10am-5pm daily (to 9pm Tue) van artgallery.bc.ca

What was once British Columbia's imposing provincial courthouse now houses the Vancouver Art Gallery. The building was completed in 1906 by Francis Rattenbury.

Among an impressive range of Canadian art, including works by the Group of Seven, the gallery houses the world's largest collection of paintings by one of Canada's best-loved artists, Emily Carr. Born in Victoria in 1871, Carr studied local Indigenous Peoples cultures, capturing their way of life and the scenery of the western coastline. She often depicted Haida artifacts such as totem poles in her pictures. Her palette is dominated by the blues, greens, and grays of the stormy West Coast.

THE IRON ROAD

In 1887, construction of the Canadian Pacific Railway (CPR) to unite the new Dominion of Canada was completed. The Iron Road linked eastern financial centers and Vancouver. Progress came at the price of the lives of many Chinese laborers, many of whom did the most dangerous of jobs. Hotels were built along the route to accommodate travelers, including Hotel Vancouver, part of the Fairmont chain.

Fairmont Hotel Vancouver

D4 900 W Georgia St Burrard fairmont. com

The first Hotel Vancouver was built by the Canadian Pacific Railway (CPR) in 1887. Construction of the current hotel was completed in 1939.

The buildings distinctive peaked green copper roof is a Vancouver landmark that has set the style for many downtown office towers. Craftsmen worked for a year to carve the exterior stonework, which shows boats, griffins, and rams.

→ The facade of Vancouver Art Gallery in the Downtown district

Heading toward the striking, futuristic dome of Science World

STAY

Rosewood Hotel Georgia

An elegant, luxurious hotel from the 1920s, home to a spa, restaurant, and bar.

D4 801 W Georgia St rosewoodhotels.com

$$$

The Burrard

This converted motor inn from the 1950s offers guests a retro vibe, a lively courtyard, and free bicycle rentals.

C4 1100 Burrard St theburrard.com

Sutton Place Hotel

A lavishly appointed property decked out with plush rooms, a spa, and health center.

C4 845 Burrard St suttonplace.com

$$$

Science World

F5 1455 Quebec St Main Times vary; check website Dec 25 scienceworld.ca

Overlooking the waters of False Creek, the 155-ft- (47-m-) tall steel geodesic dome built for Expo '86 now houses Science World, Vancouver's interactive science museum. The dome was designed by inventor Richard Buckminster Fuller (1895–1983), and it is one of the city's most striking landmarks.

Science World hosts both traveling and permanent exhibitions. The latter include hands-on activities such as building structures with KEVA wooden planks, testing agility, and solving a variety of puzzles, making this museum popular with children. In the Search: Sara Stern Gallery, you can touch fur, bones, and animal skins, crawl into a beaver lodge or look into a beehive. Kidspace, aimed at children aged six and under, has a huge kaleidoscope kids can crawl into, and a flying saucer. The Our World and Eureka! exhibits are especially educational, exploring themes of sustainability, motion, and energy.

Science World is renowned for its OMNIMAX Theatre, located in the dome and the world's largest dome screen. A five-story screen 88 ft (27 m) in diameter shows films on subjects ranging from bears to Sir Ernest Shackleton's epic 1914 Antarctic journey.

Vogue Theatre

C4 918 Granville St Vancouver City Centre Box office: 10am-6pm Mon-Sat, noon-4pm Sun voguetheatre.com

Designed in 1940 by Kaplan & Sprachman, the glamorous Art Deco Vogue Theatre was a defining architectural achievement for Vancouver at the time. With its symmetrical facades and 62-ft (19-m) neon sign topped by a silhouette of the Roman goddess Diana, the Vogue is a prominent landmark on busy Granville Street.

A National Historic Site of Canada, the Vogue has great acoustics and hosts theater, live music, and movie events, including the renowned Vancouver International Film Festival every fall.

BC Place Stadium

E5 777 Pacific Blvd Stadium Times vary, check website bcplace.com

This multipurpose stadium, consisting of enough cement to pour a sidewalk from Vancouver to Tacoma *(p205)*, can be converted in a matter of hours from a football field seating 54,000 to a cozier

Did You Know?

The Vogue is one of the last remaining theaters from the city's famous Theatre Row.

concert bowl seating 27,000. It has a fully retractable roof and is home to the CFL's BC Lions and the MLS team, the Vancouver Whitecaps FC.

---

11  

BC Sports Hall of Fame and Museum

E5 Gate A, BC Place Stadium Stadium 10am-5pm daily Dec 25 bcsportshall.com

Canada's largest sports museum, the BC Sports Hall of Fame and Museum is housed in 20,000 sq ft (1,858 sq m) of space inside the BC Place Stadium. Twenty galleries showcase BC's sports history, starting in the 1860s, and include a Vancouver 2010 Games Gallery that celebrates hosting the Winter Olympics. Among the artifacts on display are medals, trophies, uniforms, equipment, murals, and photos. Clever games test visitors' knowledge. Interactive displays provide fascinating details of the lives of famous athletes, such as Olympic medalists sprinter Harry Jerome and skier Nancy Greene. A series of videos on the 1990s tells the exciting stories of the Vancouver Canucks' skate to the Stanley Cup finals, the BC Lions' Grey Cup victory, and Victoria's Commonwealth Games, all held in 1994.

Children will particularly enjoy the Participation Gallery, where they can run against the clock, rock climb, and see how fast they can pitch.

One of the most touching displays is that honoring runner Terry Fox (1958–81), who lost his leg to cancer. His run across Canada to raise money for cancer research was halted only by his death. The feat of local wheelchair athlete Rick Hansen is also highlighted. To raise awareness of the potential of people with disabilities, he set out in 1987 to wheel 24,855 miles (40,000 km) around the world.

---

12  

Vancouver Central Library

D4 350 W Georgia St Vancouver City Centre, Stadium 10am-9pm Mon-Thu, 10am-6pm Fri & Sat, 11am-6pm Sun Major hols vpl.ca

Imaginative and daring, the design of the Vancouver Central Library was inspired by a Roman coliseum. The wraparound, sand-colored, precast concrete colonnade occupies a full city block. The nine-story library building features a dramatic concourse, the ceiling soaring six stories overhead. The top two floors are lovely community spaces and include a rooftop garden.

GREAT VIEW

Look out from the Library

Head up to level 9 of the Vancouver Central Library to the serene public rooftop garden. From here you'll be rewarded with a great view over Vancouver's bustling cityscape.

Designed by Moshe Safdie & Associates with DA Architects and opened in 1995, the building was decried by some as not fitting into the Vancouver cityscape. The negative opinions have been toppled by the unanimous support the building has since received.

More than 1.3 million items, including books, periodicals, DVDs, and CDs, are housed in the 350,000-sq-ft (32,500-sq-m) library space, which draws over 7,000 people daily.

On the concourse there are several cafes, where you can get a drink or a light snack.

↑ Impressive atrium of the Vancouver Central Library

A SHORT WALK DOWNTOWN

Distance 0.6 miles (1 km) **Time** 15 minutes
Nearest station Burrard

Although Vancouver is a relatively new city, it has taken care to preserve many of its divine historic buildings and apartment blocks, which gives the Downtown area a panache that is missing in other North American city centers. Nonetheless, the small Downtown area does have a number of new towers, built to accommodate inner-city dwellers. As you explore the area, keep your eyes peeled for the more historic and characterful buildings sidled up against over 100 shops in the city's premier shopping district.

A stunning, seven-story brushed-aluminum pendulum, created by BC artist Alan Storey, swings gracefully through the wonderful tree-filled atrium of the **HSBC building***.*

The elegant **Cathedral Place** (p240) *building is indicative of Vancouver's efforts to preserve the past with an eye to the future.*

Stained-glass windows inside **Christ Church Cathedral** (p240), *which was once a landmark for sailors, depict the lives of Vancouver heroes.*

START

A historic building and Vancouver landmark, the restored **Fairmont Hotel Vancouver** (p241) *dates back to the mid-20th century.*

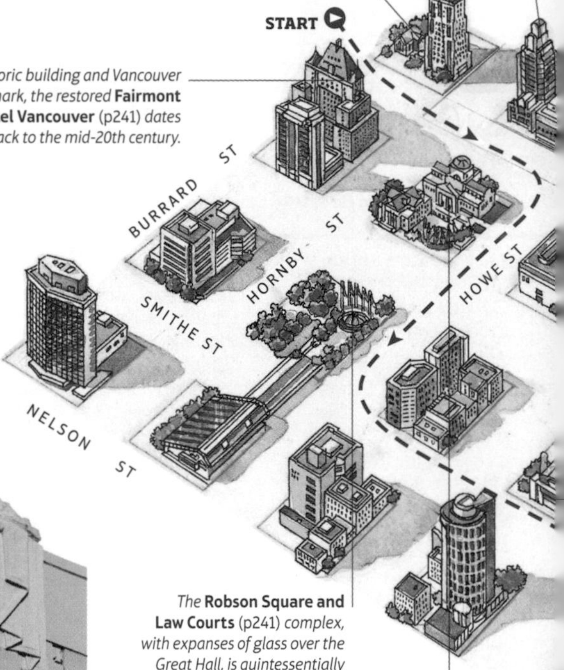

BURRARD ST

HORNBY ST

HOWE ST

SMITHE ST

NELSON ST

The **Robson Square and Law Courts** (p241) *complex, with expanses of glass over the Great Hall, is quintessentially West Coast in style.*

Work from BC's major artists is shown at the **Vancouver Art Gallery** (p241), *alongside exhibits by acclaimed international artists.*

←

Memorial depicting a World War I nursing sister on Cathedral Place

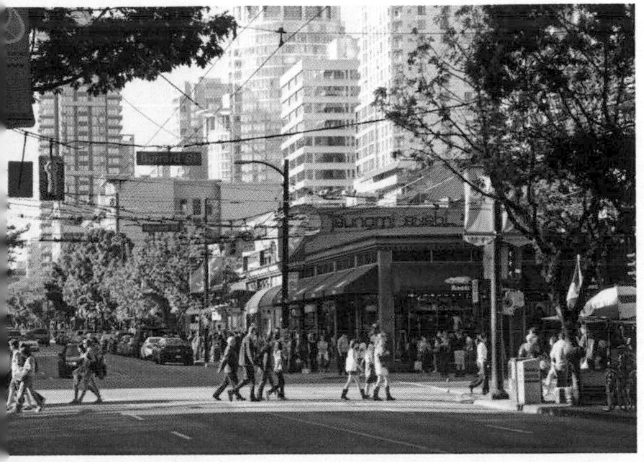

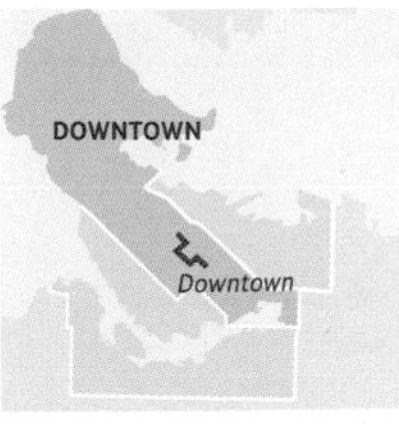

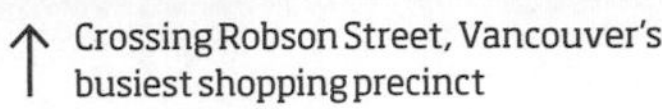

↑ Crossing Robson Street, Vancouver's busiest shopping precinct

DOWNTOWN
Downtown

Locator Map
For more detail see p236

Did You Know?

Fairmont Hotel Vancouver is known to residents as "the Castle in the City."

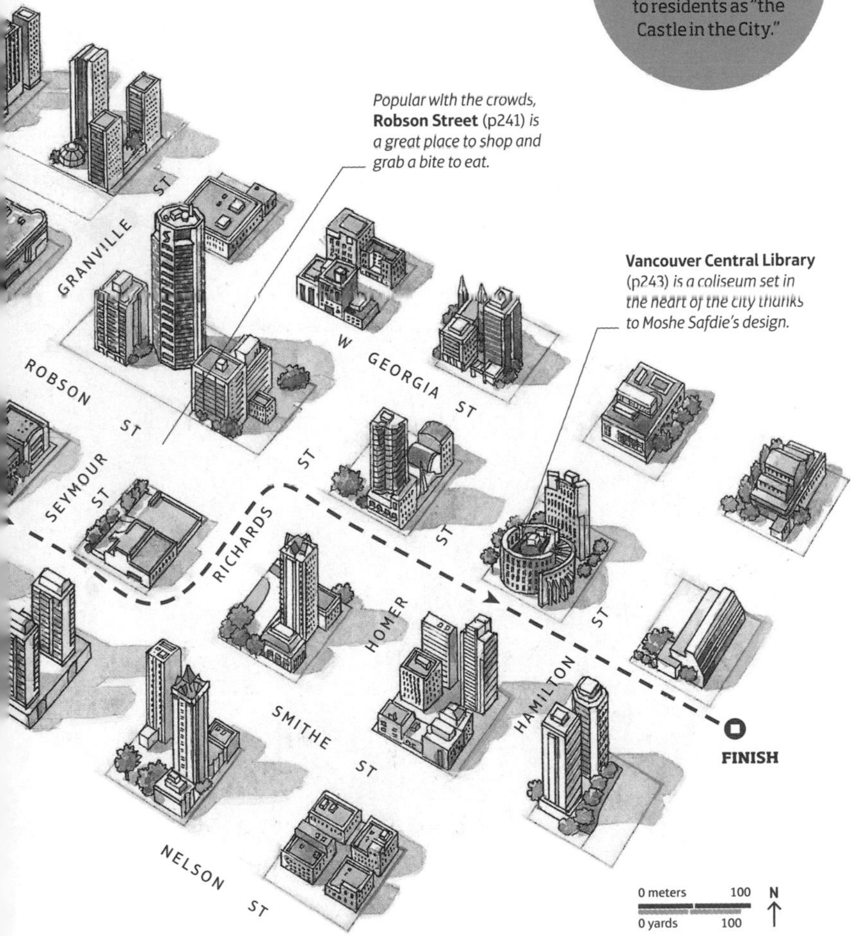

Popular with the crowds, **Robson Street** (p241) *is a great place to shop and grab a bite to eat.*
Vancouver Central Library (p243) *is a coliseum set in the heart of the city thanks to Moshe Safdie's design.*
GRANVILLE ST
ROBSON ST
W GEORGIA ST
SEYMOUR ST
RICHARDS ST
HOMER ST
HAMILTON ST
SMITHE ST
NELSON ST
FINISH
0 meters 100
0 yards 100
N

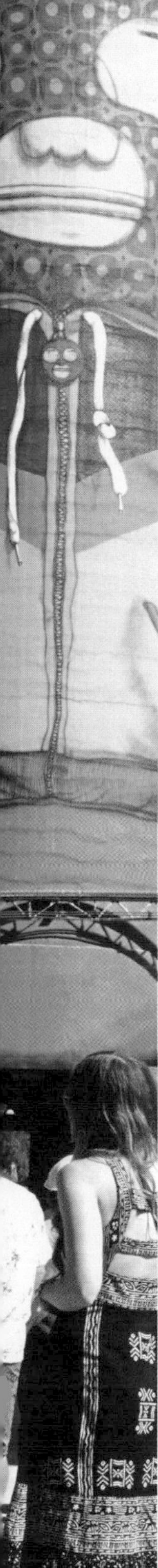

Giants mural by OSGEMEOS, adding vibrancy to Granville Island

SOUTH GRANVILLE AND YALETOWN

The neighborhoods of South Granville and Yaletown are separated by a drive across Granville Bridge or a nautical ride across False Creek. Yaletown was first settled by Canadian Pacific Railway (CPR) train crews and laborers. They arrived after the CPR closed its construction camp in Yale, BC, following the completion of the transcontinental railroad to Vancouver in 1887. Its location between the creek and the railway terminus made it an ideal area for rail yards, industry, and warehouses. As a consequence, the city grew in the late 19th and early 20th centuries. A development plan in the early 1990s started its full transformation into the lively urban area seen today.

South Granville, across False Creek, was originally forested, and as Vancouver's downtown area grew, people wanting more rural living began to settle here. With the building of the first Granville Street Bridge in 1889, it became inevitable that South Granville would also develop, and it officially developed as a real neighborhood in 1907. In 1931 the Stanley Theatre was built, and today the area is known for its thriving arts and culture scene, as well as its galleries, shops, and restaurants.

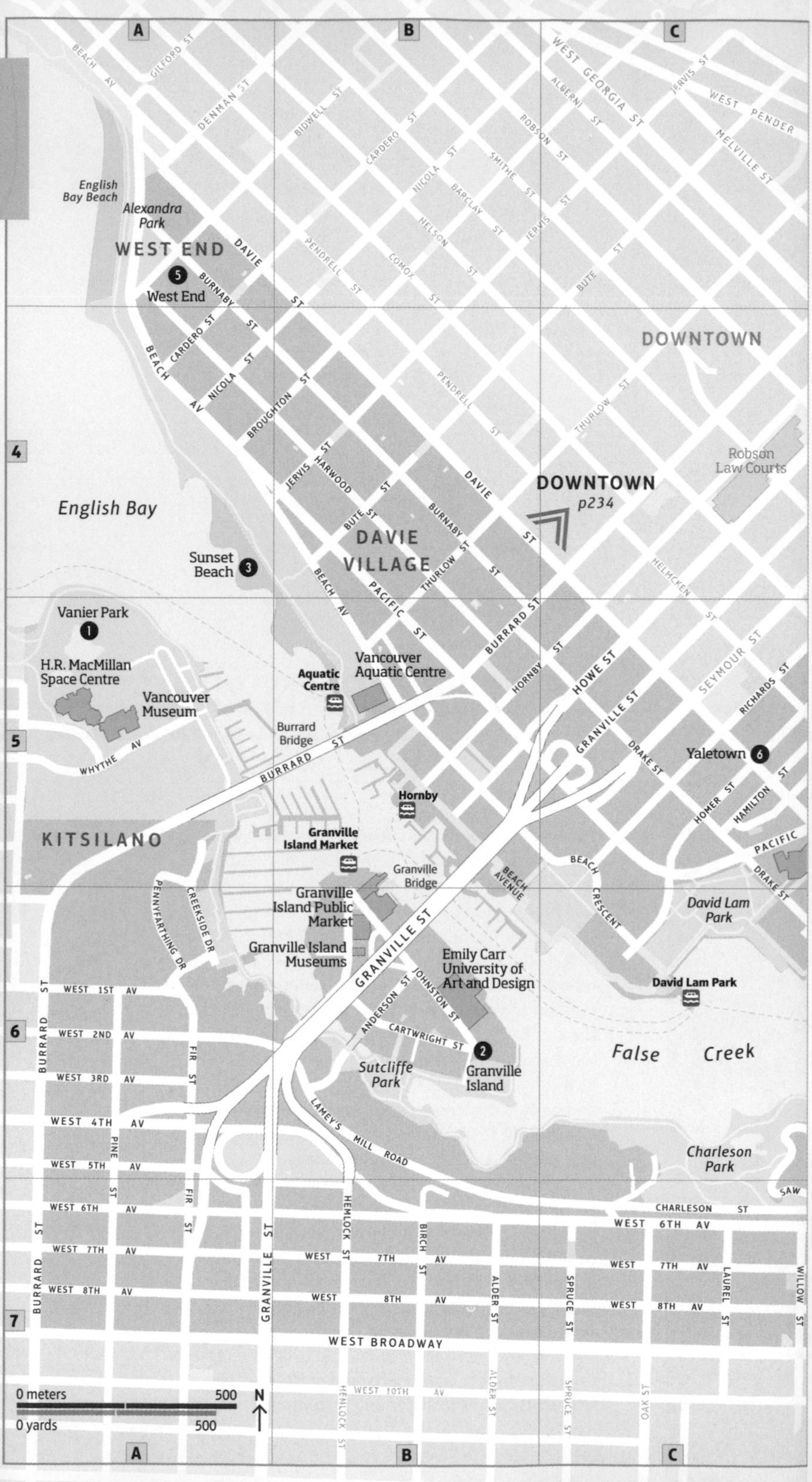

A
B
C
4
5
6
7
English Bay Beach
Alexandra Park
WEST END
West End
English Bay
Sunset Beach
DAVIE VILLAGE
DOWNTOWN
DOWNTOWN
p234
Robson Law Courts
Vanier Park
H.R. MacMillan Space Centre
Vancouver Museum
Aquatic Centre
Vancouver Aquatic Centre
Burrard Bridge
KITSILANO
Hornby
Granville Island Market
Granville Bridge
Granville Island Public Market
Granville Island Museums
Emily Carr University of Art and Design
Yaletown
David Lam Park
David Lam Park
Sutcliffe Park
Granville Island
False Creek
Charleson Park
WEST BROADWAY
0 meters
500
0 yards
500
N

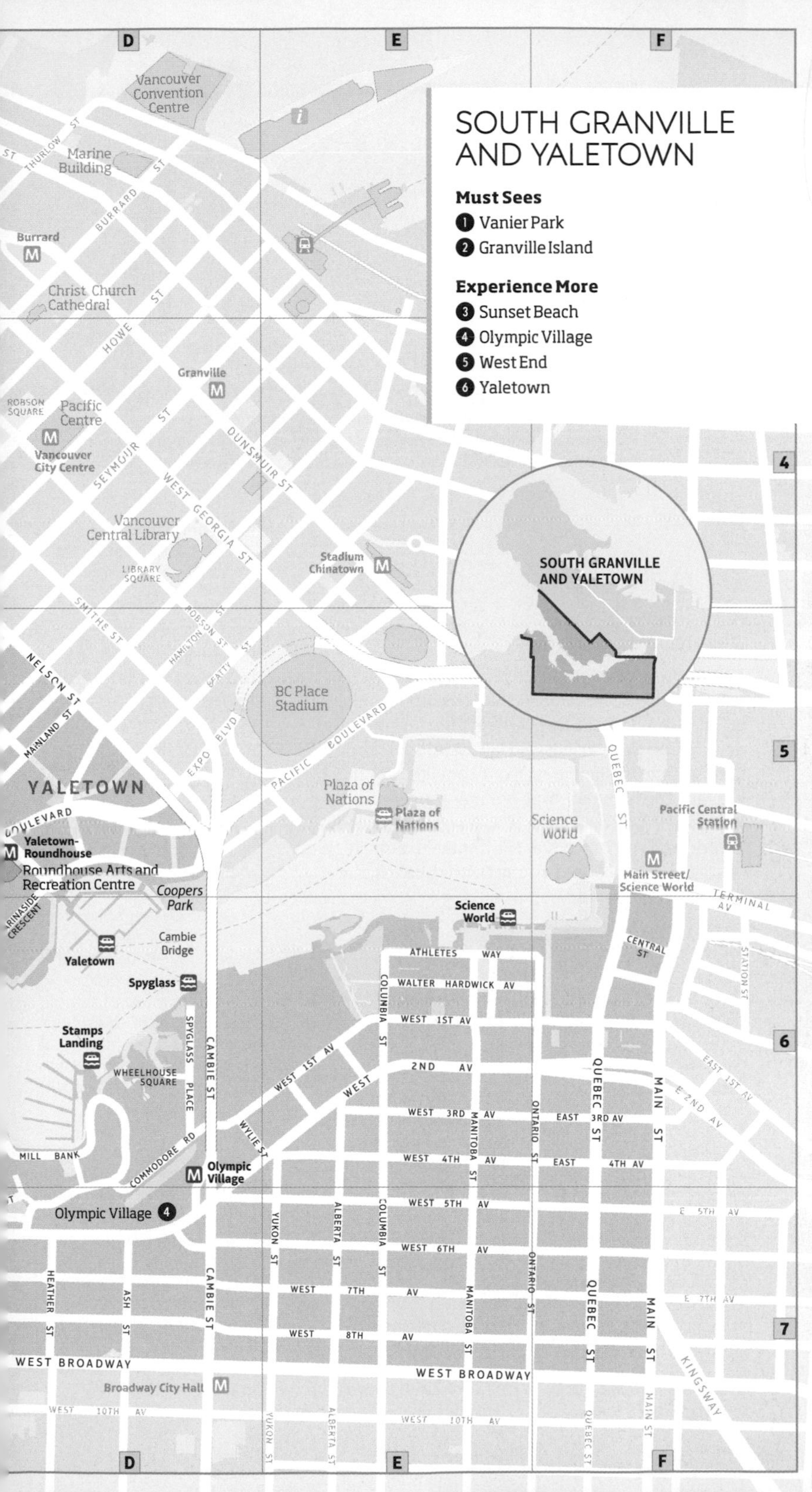
SOUTH GRANVILLE AND YALETOWN
Must Sees
1 Vanier Park
2 Granville Island
Experience More
3 Sunset Beach
4 Olympic Village
5 West End
6 Yaletown
D
E
F
4
5
6
7
Vancouver Convention Centre
Marine Building
Burrard
Christ Church Cathedral
Granville
Robson Square
Pacific Centre
Vancouver City Centre
Vancouver Central Library
Library Square
Stadium Chinatown
BC Place Stadium
Plaza of Nations
Science World
Pacific Central Station
Main Street/ Science World
YALETOWN
Yaletown-Roundhouse
Roundhouse Arts and Recreation Centre
Coopers Park
Cambie Bridge
Yaletown
Spyglass
Stamps Landing
Wheelhouse Square
Olympic Village
Olympic Village 4
Broadway City Hall
SOUTH GRANVILLE AND YALETOWN
Thurlow St
Burrard St
Howe St
Seymour St
Dunsmuir St
West Georgia St
Smithe St
Robson St
Hamilton St
Beatty St
Nelson St
Mainland St
Expo Blvd
Pacific Boulevard
Marinaside Crescent
Quebec St
Terminal Av
Central St
Station St
Athletes Way
Walter Hardwick Av
Columbia St
West 1st Av
2nd Av
West 3rd Av
Manitoba St
Ontario St
East 3rd Av
Main St
East 1st Av
E 2nd Av
West 4th Av
East 4th Av
West 5th Av
E 5th Av
West 6th Av
West 7th Av
E 7th Av
West 8th Av
Kingsway
West Broadway
West 10th Av
Spyglass Place
Cambie St
Wylie St
Commodore Rd
Mill Bank
Heather St
Ash St
Yukon St
Alberta St

↑ Flying kites on a clear day by the iconic Gate to the Northwest Passage

VANIER PARK

A5 False Creek Ferries

This calming oasis on the city's west side may be relatively small, but it feels spacious. Boats sail by on English Bay, kites fly overhead, ferries dock and depart, and pedestrians and cyclists pass through on their way to Kitsilano Beach or Granville Island *(p252)*. It is also the home of three popular museums: the Museum of Vancouver, the H. R. MacMillan Space Centre, and the Vancouver Maritime Museum. It also hosts the cultural Bard on the Beach Shakespeare Festival in the summer.

Gate to the Northwest Passage

Rust-colored and imposing, this large 15 ft (4.6 m) high steel sculpture forms a perfect frame for photo opportunities. It was created in 1980 by Alan Chung Hung, a Chinese-born Vancouver resident. Hung thought of it as a symbolic piece to commemorate the arrival of the city's namesake, Captain George Vancouver, a British explorer who arrived in the Burrard Inlet in 1792. Located next to the Vancouver Maritime Museum in the park, this unique, twisting sculpture overlooks English Bay.

Vancouver Maritime Museum

1905 Ogden Av Vanier Park 10am-5pm daily (to 8pm Thu; adm by donation) Mid-Sep-mid-May: Mon vancouvermaritime museum.com

Located on the waterfront in a spectacular A-frame building, this popular, family-oriented museum celebrates Vancouver's rich history as a port and trading center. Its star feature is the schooner St. Roch, the narrow corridors of which can be wandered on site. Built as a supply ship for the Mounties in 1928, St. Roch became the first ship to navigate the Northwest Passage in both directions between 1940 and 1942.

Other displays that are worth visiting include "Map the Coast," which tells the story of British Captain George Vancouver and the crews of the *Chatham* and the *Discovery*, who charted the inlets of the coast of BC in 1792. The Children's Maritime Discovery Centre has a powerful telescope, through which the busy port can be viewed. The museum also hosts a variety of workshops, where you can watch talented craftsmen construct model ships and sea vessels or even create sea glass jewelry.

INSIDER TIP
Behold the Bard

The park transforms every year from June through September into a theater-tent village for the Bard on the Beach Shakespeare Festival *(www.bardonthebeach.org)*, which sees various plays brought to life.

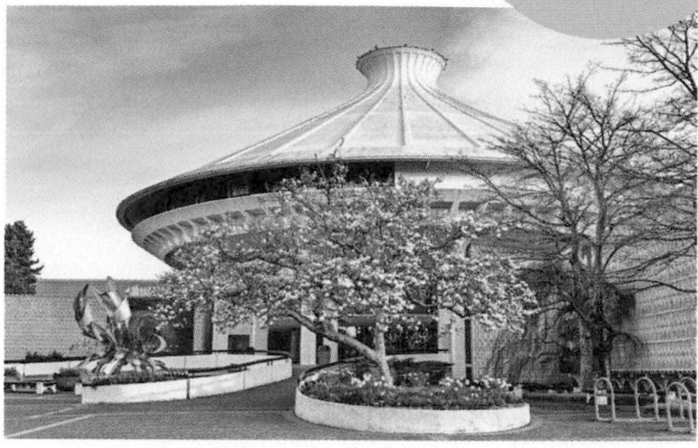

→ Pretty magnolia trees outside the distinctive Museum of Vancouver

Museum of Vancouver and H. R. MacMillan Space Centre

1100 Chestnut St, Vanier Park Times vary, check websites museumofvancouver.ca; spacecentre.ca

This structure is a distinctive addition to the city's skyline. Built in 1967, the museum's curved, concrete roof resembles a Haida woven hat. Outside, a stunning sculpture that looks like a giant steel crab (aptly called *The Crab*) by Canadian sculptor George Norris sits in a fountain on the museum's south side.

Canada's largest civic museum houses five brilliant re-creations of Vancouver's history, including an immigrant ship and a fur-trading post. Everything from Indigenous culture to recent everyday life is explored, with exhibits such as the 1950s gallery that houses a working jukebox. Other highlights include the Orientation Gallery, which re-creates BC's interior and rocky coastline.

At the same location as the Museum of Vancouver, the excellent H. R. MacMillan Space Centre is popular with both children and adults, who can explore the universe in the Planetarium and in the GroundStation Canada Theatre. The Cosmic Courtyard, an interactive gallery that focuses on space exploration, is another key highlight for curious children.

You can visit both museums, and the Vancouver Maritime Museum, at a discounted price with an ExplorePass (*www.spacecentre.ca/explore-pass*).

THE MIGHTY SEAWALL

Vancouver's vast Seawall is the longest uninterrupted waterfront path in the world at 17.4 miles (28 km), and extends far beyond Stanley Park *(p238)*. Walkers, joggers, and cyclists can continue on past English Bay, around False Creek, on to Vanier Park, and connect all the way west to Spanish Banks, Pacific Spirit Regional Park, and UBC. The scenic route is a great way to see the city.

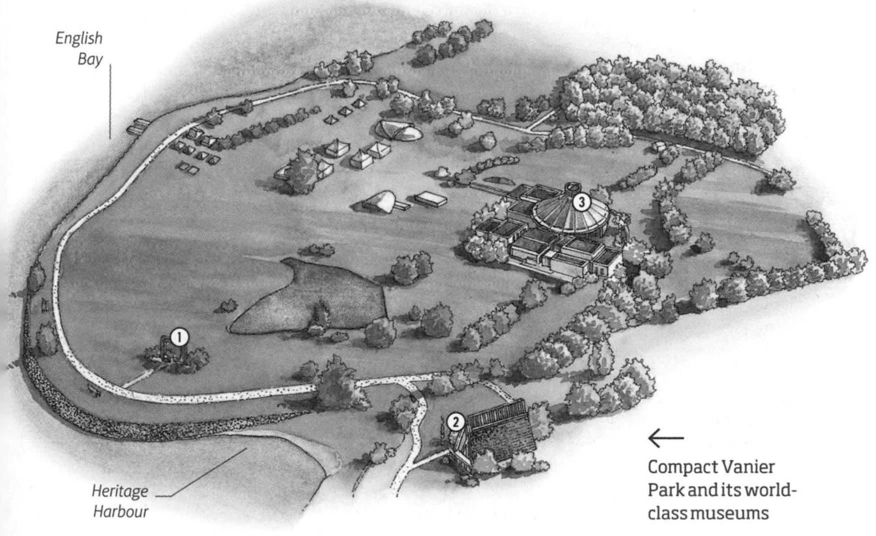

← Compact Vanier Park and its world-class museums

2

GRANVILLE ISLAND

B6  granvilleisland.com

This bustling peninsula in False Creek attracts millions of visitors every year, and rightly so. Where once heavy industries belched noxious fumes, there's now artisanal breweries, top comedy clubs, an array of street entertainment and a lively market overflowing with fresh and tempting local produce.

①

Granville Island Public Market

1689 Johnston St 9am-7pm daily Jan: Mon, Jan 1, Dec 25 & 26 granville island.com

Always colorful and buzzing, this public market opened in 1979 in a former industrial building. Best known for its irresistible cornucopia of foods, you can choose from locally grown blueberries straight from the Fraser Valley, or cherries and peaches picked ripe from Okanagan orchards. Fresh wild salmon, crab, scallops, and shrimp are piled high, while cheeses, charcuterie, and maple syrup products tempt you at every corner. The food court, too, has a dizzying array of choices, and a food fair on the market's west side offers a variety of multicultural cuisines. Throughout the market, vendors also sell the wares of local artisans and craftspeople – candles, custom jewelry, and hats.

From the benches outside on the wharf, you can take in one of the best views of the False Creek marina and docks, as well as a spectacular view of downtown and the North Shore mountains. Street performers – from musicians and stilt-walkers to magicians – entertain outside, adding to the market's eclectic ambience.

INSIDER TIP
Granville Island Ferries

A ride aboard one of the ferries that service Granville Island and the surrounding area is one of the best ways to see the sights of False Creek. Try False Creek Ferries or the Aquabus.

②  

Vancouver Studio Glass

1440 Old Bridge St Daily; times vary, check website Major hols vancouverstudio glass.com

Many famed glassblowers in BC have worked here since it opened in 1982. You can watch artists create vases, bowls, and artwork using techniques dating back hundreds of years.

The studio specializes in free-blown glass, made without molds using steel blowpipes and pontils. The other glass is fired as needed to heat and shape works in progress. The adjacent shop is one of the best-known glass galleries in Western Canada.

Granville Island Public Market is Vancouver's most popular attraction, brimming with food.

False Creek marina

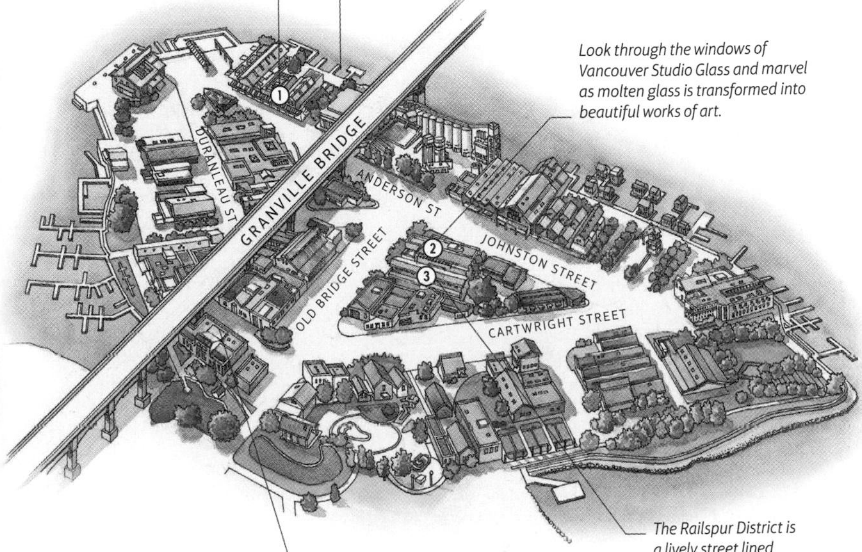

Look through the windows of Vancouver Studio Glass and marvel as molten glass is transformed into beautiful works of art.

The Railspur District is a lively street lined with quirky local stores, independent cafes, and thriving businesses.

The Kids Market is a child's fantasyland, with shopkeepers selling everything from toys to clothing.

The peninsula and its various bustling and unique sights ↑

Railspur District

Tucked away off Old Bridge Street on Granville Island, you can find the Railspur District, a quiet, charming street that has been remodeled and is filled with boutique shops and artisan businesses. A highlight is the cluster of artists' studios, where you can watch artists at work and browse the various items for sale.

Shops include Alarte Silks Studio Gallery in the Alley Gallery, which has beautiful, hand-painted and wearable silk art, and Sadryna Design, which sells custom leather fashions with European flair.

The Artisan Sake Maker is Vancouver's first fresh, premium sake producer, and offers tastings at its tasting counters between 11:30am and 6pm. Off the Tracks is a bistro that offers organic, fair-trade coffee and local wine.

Boats moored in False Creek and the colorful tin roofs of Granville Island

Kids Market

1496 Cartwright St
10am-6pm daily **Major hols** **kidsmarket.ca**

Children will be dazzled by the Kids Market: two floors filled with toys, games, gadgets, clothing, and jewelry. More than 25 retailers provide an eclectic shopping experience. Clownin' Around Magic is filled with puzzles and magic tricks, Knotty Toys features hand-made wooden toys, while The Hairloft offers spa treatments and haircuts. There is also the Adventure Zone, with a supervised play area, a picnic spot, and special events. Outside, Granville Island Waterpark is a joyful free-for-all of fountains and sprays.

EAT

Dockside

This chic restaurant has one of the best patios in the city. It also serves a legendary brunch every Sunday.

1253 Johnston St
dockside vancouver.com

$$$

Edible Canada

A casual spot using locally produced, sustainable Canadian produce, including crispy oysters and duck poutine.

1596 Johnston St
ediblecanada.com

$$$

EXPERIENCE MORE

Sunset Beach

A4 False Creek Ferries, Aquabus

The white sands of Sunset Beach, which marks the end of the English Bay seawall and the start of False Creek, make an ideal place to relax and do some suntanning or swimming. Summertime water temperatures rise to 65°F (18°C), and lifeguards are on duty from mid-May to Labor Day.

The western end of Sunset Beach provides a good view of the gray granite *Inukshuk*, which sits at the foot of neighboring English Bay Beach. This Inuit sculpture by Alvin Kanak, modeled on traditional markers used by the Inuit for navigation, is a symbol of friendship.

The Vancouver Aquatic Centre, at the beach's east end, has a 164-ft- (50-m-) long Olympic-size swimming pool, diving pools, a sauna, and a steam room. False Creek Ferries dock here, with routes to Vanier Park, Granville Island, Yaletown, and Science World.

JOE FORTES, THE HERO OF ENGLISH BAY

Vancouver's "Citizen of the Century" was a man named Seraphim "Joe" Fortes. Born in Barbados in 1865, he came to Vancouver in 1885 and was soon a regular at the English Bay Beach. He taught thousands of children to swim. As the city's first appointed lifeguard, he is credited with saving more than 100 lives. Joe's cottage was located by the beach at the site of today's Alexandra Park. The Joe Fortes Memorial Drinking Fountain in the park was designed by Charles Marega and installed in 1926.

Olympic Village

D7 vancouver.ca SkyTrain: Olympic Village

Originally built for the 2010 Winter Olympic Games, this neighborhood sits along the southeast section of False Creek. Rent a kayak, SUP, or canoe from Creekside Kayaks *(www.creeksidekayaks.ca)*, take the aquabus, or walk along the seawall for a scenic route to this sprightly area full of interesting green spaces. Hinge Park has unique and unusual art installations as well as an excellent children's playground, while the adjacent little Habitat Island's shores are home to starfish and crabs. Head to the village square for a great selection of craft breweries, restaurants, and the city's favorite dessert spot – Earnest Ice Cream *(1829 Quebec St)*.

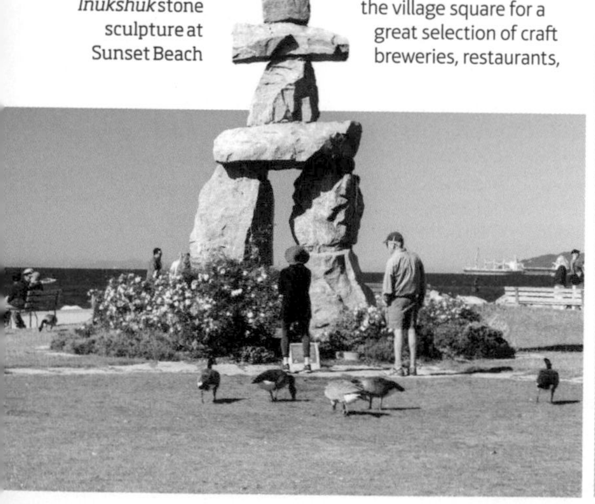

→ The interesting *Inukshuk* stone sculpture at Sunset Beach

West End

A3 Burrard

Vancouver's West End is the most densely populated residential area in Canada, yet it maintains a relaxed and spacious ambience, in part because of its proximity to Stanley Park and English Bay. Offering everything from beaches to urban streetlife, it is one of the best neighborhoods in Vancouver for strolling and taking in the delights of the city. It is also home to Western Canada's largest LGBT+ community.

The West End, as one of Vancouver's earliest neighborhoods, has preserved several historic buildings, such as the exquisite 1893 **Roedde House**, home to Vancouver's first bookbinder and now a museum, and the ivy-clad Sylvia Hotel, built in 1911.

West End streets tend to be busy with people at all hours of the day or night. Robson, Denman, and Davie streets are the main West End thoroughfares, with Burrard Street as its eastern boundary. Among the many shops and restaurants on Robson Street is the Robson Public Market. Denman Street reflects the

The condominiums of Yaletown, along Quayside Marina

beach culture of English Bay with its casual clothing boutiques and cafes. Davie Street is more residential, but also has many cafes and restaurants. Between Burrard Street and Jervis Street is Davie Village, Vancouver's LGBT+ district, a lively 24-hour strip with cafes, shops, clubs, and bars. Little Sister's Book & Art Emporium *(1238 Davie Street)* is a legendary shop selling books and pride gear.

Roedde House
1415 Barclay St
Times vary, check website
roeddehouse.org

Yaletown

C5 Yaletown-Roundhouse False Creek Ferries, Aquabus

Outdoor cafes have sprung up on old loading docks, warehouses have been converted into lofts, and high-rise buildings have filled in the horizon of Yaletown. The area was first settled by Canadian Pacific Railway (CPR) train crews and laborers after the CPR closed its construction camp in Yale, BC, on completion of the transcontinental railroad to Vancouver in 1887. Yaletown was the decaying heart of the city's industrial activity until the early 1990s, when a development plan began its transformation into a lively urban community.

A multitude of Yaletown condominiums now house a youthful, sophisticated crowd. Dirty and neglected industrial warehouses on Homer, Hamilton, and Mainland streets in Yaleton were given major face-lifts. The result is a landscape of bistros, cafes, restaurants, nightclubs, studios, galleries, hair salons, interior design stores, and international and local designer clothing outlets. On Beach Avenue, the **Roundhouse Community Arts & Recreation Centre** includes a theater, gallery spaces, and a host of community arts and athletics programs. It also houses the locomotive that pulled the first passenger train to Vancouver in 1887.

Roundhouse Community Arts & Recreation Centre
181 Roundhouse Mews
roundhouse.ca

LGBT+ CLUBS IN THE WEST END

Celebrities
1022 Davie St
celebritiesnightclub.com
This iconic dance club caters to a mixed crowd.

Numbers Cabaret
1042 Davie St
numbers.ca
Dance tunes seven nights a week.

1181 Lounge
1181 Davie St
(604) 992-9269
Sunday drag shows and weekend happy hour.

Cafes have sprung up on old loading docks, warehouses have been converted into lofts, and high-rise buildings have filled in the horizon of Yaletown.

Looking out from the observation deck at the Lonsdale Quay sign

Must See

1 Museum of Anthropology

Experience More

2 Capilano Suspension Bridge Park
3 Marine Drive
4 Lonsdale Quay Market
5 West Vancouver Art Museum
6 Grouse Mountain
7 Steveston
8 International Buddhist Temple
9 VanDusen Botanical Garden
10 Richmond
11 University of British Columbia

BEYOND THE CENTER

Beyond downtown Vancouver lie memorable attractions and outlying cities, easily reached by car or public transit. Lions Gate Bridge spans the First Narrows to West Vancouver, and also leads to North Vancouver and the physical wonders of Capilano Canyon and Grouse Mountain. At the mouth of the Fraser River is fast-growing Richmond, once an isolated farming community settled by Europeans in the 1880s. The riverside community of Steveston, meanwhile, was built on the salmon industry in the 19th century, and is still noted for its historic cannery.

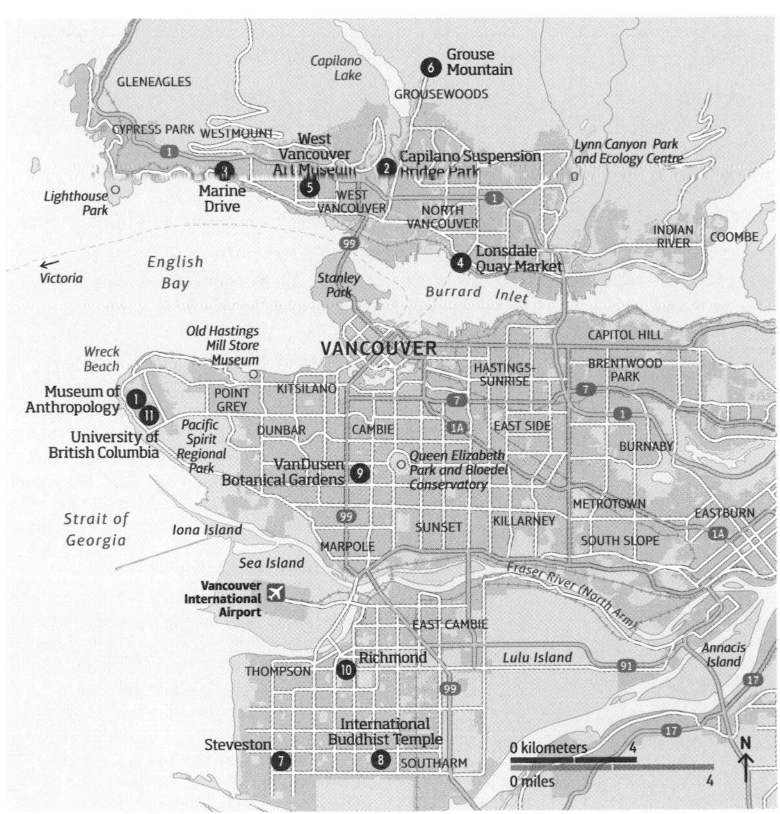

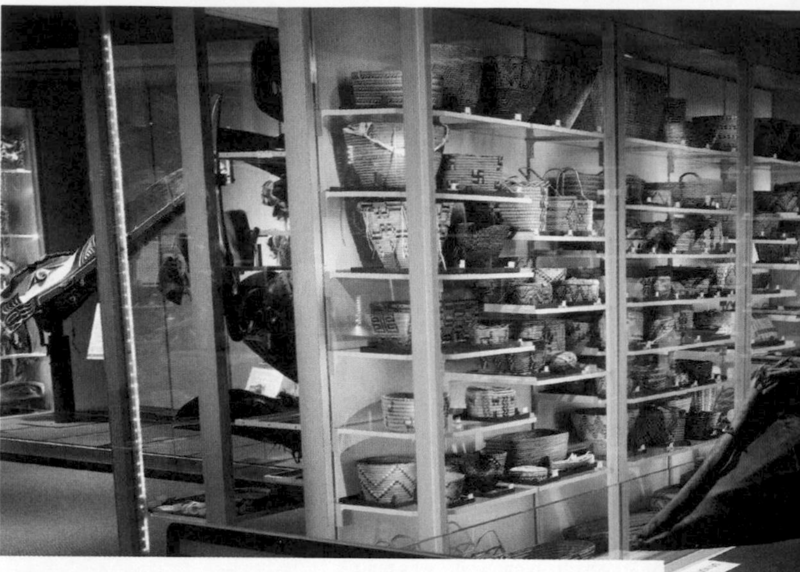

1

MUSEUM OF ANTHROPOLOGY AT UBC

6393 NW Marine Dr 10am-5pm Tue-Sun (to 9pm Thu; Jun-Sep: daily) moa.ubc.ca

Located at the University of British Columbia (UBC), this museum is home to one of the world's finest collections of Northwest Coast Indigenous Peoples' art. The outstanding building itself is a work of art, overlooking mountains and sea.

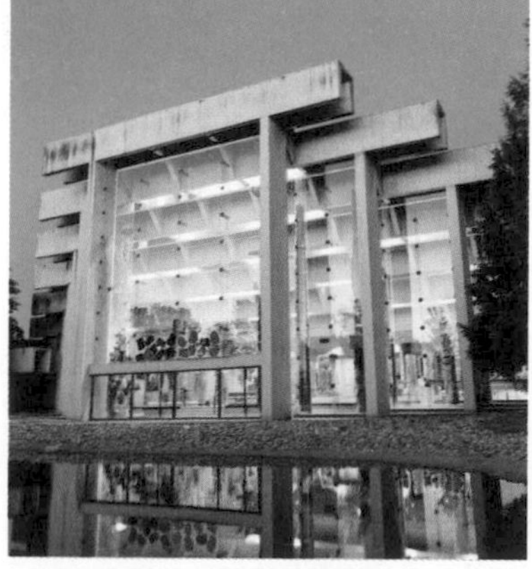

↑ The imposing glass walls of the museum's Great Hall, lit up at night

The Great Hall

After entering the museum front doors and walking down a short ramp, the space opens up to the light-filled, glass-and-concrete structure of the Great Hall. Glass walls that reach 50 ft (15 m) high are lined with full-size totem poles and carved figures, while traditional canoes and other works flank the surrounding walls.

Multiversity Galleries

Arranged in a labyrinth of glass displays, these spaces house more than 9,000 cultural objects from all around the world. From delicate Inuit bone carvings to West African tribal masks, Chinese opera costumes and Indonesian puppets, there's an almost overwhelming amount of diverse artifacts to admire. Below the display cases are even more pieces to browse through, hidden in drawers just waiting for an eager visitor to open.

ARTHUR ERICKSON

Canadian architect Arthur Erickson (1924–2009) designed the fine Museum of Anthropology in 1976, inspired by the post-and-beam architecture of the Northwest Coast Indigenous Peoples. Like much of Erickson's work, which includes the Vancouver Art Gallery, the Provincial Law Courts, and Simon Fraser University (to name just a few), the museum building is made primarily out of concrete and is modernist in style.

The museum's vast collection, which includes *(right)* Bill Reid's thought-provoking *The Raven and the First Men* ↑

Bill Reid Rotunda

The museum has the world's largest collection of works by local Haida artist Bill Reid, including his famous sculpture *The Raven and the First Men*. Carved out of yellow cedar in 1980, it is a modern interpretation of a Haida creation myth, depicting the Raven trickster trying to coax mankind into the world from a clamshell. It once featured on the Canadian $20 dollar bill.

Koerner European Ceramic Gallery

Shortly after World War II, fleeing the expansion of Nazi Germany, Walter C. Koerner moved his impressive collection of 16th- to 19th- century European ceramics from his native former Czechoslovakia to Canada, where it was eventually donated to the MOA. Now an award-winning gallery displays some 600 pieces of his unique collection, which thankfully survived the arduous journey.

The museum has the world's largest collection of works by local Haida artist Bill Reid, including his famous sculpture *The Raven and the First Men*.

Outdoor Haida Houses and Totem Poles

Modeled after a 19th-century Haida village are a Haida House and Mortuary House constructed by Bill Reid and 'Namgis artist Doug Cranmer. A reflecting pool, executed in 2010, adds drama to the site and is surrounded by memorial and mortuary poles dating from 1951 to the present.

EXPERIENCE MORE

Capilano Suspension Bridge Park

3735 Capilano Rd, North Vancouver SeaBus Times vary, check website Dec 25 capbridge.com

The first Capilano Suspension Bridge, not much more than a hemp rope and cedar planks, was built in 1889 by Scotsman George Mackay. Mackay was drawn by Capilano Canyon's wild beauty and built a cabin beside it. Access to the Capilano River below was almost impossible. It is said that Mackay built the bridge so that his son, who loved fishing, could reach the river.

The present bridge, dating to 1956 and the fourth to be built here, spans 450 ft (137 m). Secured by 13 tons of concrete, 230 ft (70 m) above the canyon floor, it is one of the longest such bridges in the world.

You will be treated to truly spectacular views, old-growth woods, trout ponds, and a 200-ft- (61-m-) high waterfall. Other highlights in the park include the totem poles at the Kia'palano Indigenous Peoples' cultural area; Treetops Adventure, a walk through the mid-story of 250-year-old Douglas firs; and Cliffwalk, a series of high and narrow cantilevered walkways attached to a granite cliff face.

Marine Drive

westvanchamber.com

Scenic Marine Drive winds through West Vancouver and makes for an ideal day trip. Park Royal Shopping Centre, with its 280 stores, is the area's major mall. The nearby seaside suburb of Ambleside offers a par-three golf course on the Capilano American Indian Reserve; a popular seawall walkway; and a park which includes tennis courts, a fitness circuit, skateboard park, and waterfowl pond. At the end of the Ambleside Sea Walk, Dundarave Pier offers a great view of Vancouver and the Strait of Georgia.

From here westward, Marine Drive clings to the rocky shoreline, buffered by some of Canada's priciest real estate.

INSIDER TIP

Building Bridges

The Lynn Canyon Suspension Bridge is smaller than the Capilano Suspension Bridge and free. Just 6 miles (9 km) east of the Capilano bridge, it is great for hikes along creeks and waterfalls.

At Lighthouse Park, a forest walk leads to the Atkinson lighthouse, built in 1912. Horseshoe Bay has a park, a marina, and an art gallery. Ice cream and fish and chips are specialties here.

Lonsdale Quay Market

123 Carrie Cates Ct, North Vancouver SeaBus 9am–7pm daily Jan 1, Dec 25 lonsdalequay.com

Opened in 1986, this striking building houses the Lonsdale Quay Market. The market has a floor devoted to food, as well as an array of cafes and restaurants that serve a variety of ethnic cuisines. On the second floor, you will find specialty shops selling hand-crafted products, such as jewelry, pottery, and textiles; and Kid's Alley, a row of child-oriented shops. The complex also includes a hotel, a pub, and a brewery. In the summer, music festivals are held outside on the Plaza Deck, overlooking the city and port. Musical offerings include jazz, African, folk, and Celtic performances.

West Vancouver Art Museum

680 17th St, West Vancouver 11am-5pm Tue-Sat Major hols westvancouverart museum.ca

Small and inviting, the West Vancouver Art Museum is housed in the stately former home of Gertrude Lawson, daughter of John Lawson, the first permanent white settler in West Vancouver. After Gertrude died in 1989, the District of West Vancouver acquired the property. The house was restored and then opened in 1995 as a museum.

The museum's exhibits relate to West Vancouver heritage and community interests, such as local sporting history and historic toys. Local communities are sometimes profiled and decorative arts are especially well represented. The gift shop sells arts and crafts by local artists and books on West Vancouver's history and architecture. Events include school programs as well as summer art and architecture programs for children.

The magnificent and daring Cliffwalk over the Capilano River

↑ Navigating the serene, snow-covered slopes at Grouse Mountain ski resort

Grouse Mountain

6400 Nancy Greene Way SeaBus 9am-10pm daily grouse mountain.com

From the summit of Grouse Mountain, on a clear day you can see as far as Vancouver Island in the west and the Columbia Mountains in the east.

The 2-mile (3-km) Grouse Grind trail, leading to Peak Chalet at 3,700 ft (1,128 m), lives up to its name. A less energetic option is the Skyride gondola. The breathtaking Peak Chairlift ride goes even further up to the peak of the mountain at 4,100 ft (1,250 m).

Popular activities include skiing, snowboarding, skating, snowshoeing, and sleigh rides in the winter; hiking, forest walks, zip-lining, and tandem paragliding in the summer. Ski and snowboarding schools, 33 ski runs, and equipment rentals are among the amenities here.

During the day, the World's Greatest Lumberjack Show takes place at the top of the mountain. At the Refuge for Endangered Wildlife, home to orphaned grizzly bears and wolves, wildlife rangers give daily talks, while the Eye of the Wind is a 360-degree observation pod set at the top of a wind turbine.

STAY

O Canada House

This restored 1897 house has a wrap-around porch and a beautiful garden. The breakfast is divine.

1114 Barclay St ocanadahouse.com

Sylvia Hotel

A landmark 1912 brick and terra-cotta building, favored for its old-world charm. The restaurant serves excellent food.

1154 Gilford St sylviahotel.com

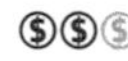

SHOP

The Boardroom

Locally owned ski, snowboard, skate, and surf shop, that also offers repairs.

2057 Lonsdale Av, N Vancouver boardroomshop.com

7

Steveston

visitrichmondbc.com

The village of Steveston, in Richmond, offers a peek into British Columbia's fishing and agricultural past. Steveston dates back to the turn of the 19th century. The **Steveston Museum** is housed in the last of the original 350 Northern Banks that once operated in Western Canada. The **London Heritage Farm** features a restored 1890s farmhouse.

Steveston's waterfront is home to Canada's largest commercial fishing fleet. On Fisherman's Wharf, shoppers can purchase the catch of the day directly off the fishing boats. Restaurants overlooking the water serve up equally fresh fish and seafood dishes. Harbor cruises meander up the Fraser River. A block away, on Moncton Street, art shops and souvenir galleries mingle with local businesses. A short walk away is Garry Point Park, whose sandy beaches offer vistas of Vancouver Island.

A highlight is the **Gulf of Georgia Cannery National Historic Site**. The salmon canneries were at their height in the 1890s. This site includes an icehouse, a lead foundry, and an artifact collection.

Steveston Museum
3811 Moncton St
9:30am-5pm Mon-Sat, noon-4pm Sun Major hols

London Heritage Farm
6511 Dyke Rd
Grounds: dawn to dusk daily; house: Jul-Sep: 10am-5pm Sat & Sun london heritagefarm.ca

Gulf of Georgia Cannery National Historic Site
12138 4th Av
10am-5pm daily gulfof georgiacannery.org

EAT

With origins as a salmon canning center, it's no wonder Steveston is still a hotspot for fresh seafood. Check out these eateries for the best fish and chips:

Pajos
12351 3rd Av
pajos.com
$$$

Dave's Fish & Chips
3460 Moncton St
davesfishand chips.com
$$$

Blue Canoe
3866 Bayview St
bluecanoe restaurant.com

8 

International Buddhist Temple

9160 Steveston Hwy, Richmond 9:30am-5pm daily buddhist temple.ca

The grace of Richmond's huge International Buddhist Temple, completed in 1983, is evident in the curved roof of golden porcelain tiles and the marble lions guarding the entrance. The interior is richly adorned with sculptures of the Buddha, ornate murals, and sumptuous painting, woodwork, and embroidery. You may even encounter one of the daily ceremonies that take place.

Outside, a majestic stone path lined with Tang Dynasty lanterns and marigolds leads to the statue of the Maitreya Buddha. The shade of twin gazebos and the sound of fountains offer a soothing respite from the bustling city.

Fall colors over a pond in the VanDusen Botanical Garden

VanDusen Botanical Garden

5251 Oak St Times vary; check website van dusengarden.org

This 54-acre (22-ha) garden was opened in 1975. In 1960 the land was under threat, and it took a campaign by locals and a donation from a local wealthy businessman, Mr W. J. VanDusen, to save the site. Today, the garden is home to over 7,500 families of plants, set amid lakes and sculptures. Roses fill the grounds in summer, while September has the colors of fall. In December, the garden hosts a Festival of Lights, when the grounds are lit by a million twinkling lights.

Richmond

Canada Line SkyTrain
3811 Moncton St; www. visitrichmondbc.com

Built on a group of islands, Richmond was a farming community in the 1880s. Today it is a busy metropolis. Lulu Island, the largest island, is the site of the city.

Richmond is home to the second-largest North American Asian community. Yaohan Centre *(3700 No 3 Rd)*, sells everything from traditional Chinese herbs to gadgetry.

Richmond also offers varied dining, art galleries, and live performances at the Gateway Theatre. Outdoor activities include golfing, and visiting the **Richmond Nature Park**, with its trails through forests. Walking or cycling the West Dyke Trail is also popular.

Nearby is **Terra Nova Adventure Play Environment**. This huge park has trails, zip-lines, swings, slides, and mazes.

Richmond Nature Park
11851 Westminster Hwy
7am-dusk daily
richmond.ca

Terra Nova Adventure Play Environment
2340 River Rd Dawn till dusk daily richmond.ca

HIDDEN GEM
UBC Farm

Visit the little farmers' market on Saturday mornings at the UBC Farm *(3461 Ross Dr)* and check out the chickens, beehives, and apple orchards. There's a great playground, Nobel Park, just around the corner.

University of British Columbia

ubc.ca

The University of British Columbia (UBC), founded in 1915, is one of Canada's leading medical universities. A 30-minute drive from the heart of downtown Vancouver, the campus is an eclectic mix of architecture. Campus highlights include the **UBC Botanical Garden**, with over 8,000 species of rare plants, and the Greenheart TreeWalk, where you can walk on suspended canopy walkways amid the treetops in the rainforest. For stunning ocean views, head to the serene UBC Rose Garden. The Chan Centre for the Performing Arts hosts theater, opera, and classical and contemporary musicians. Works by leading Canadian artists are shown at the **Morris and Helen Belkin Art Gallery**. UBC's Museum of Anthropology *(p258)* is world-renowned. The Pacific Museum of Earth is a treasure chest of minerals and fossils, including an impressive collection of BC jade. The cedar-and-glass First Nations Longhouse resembles a traditional longhouse. The Asian Centre hosts a photographic exhibit of Asian Canadians and one of North America's largest collections of rare Chinese books.

UBC Botanical Garden
6804 SW Marine Dr 10am-4:30pm daily
botanicalgarden.ubc.ca

Morris and Helen Belkin Art Gallery
1825 Main Mall
10am-5pm Tue-Fri, noon-5pm Sat & Sun Major hols belkin.ubc.ca

The beautifully landscaped UBC Rose Garden, and *(inset)* the impressive Chan Centre interior

BRITISH COLUMBIA

Thousands of years before the first Europeans arrived, the 366,254-sq-mile (948,600-sq-km) area that is now British Columbia (BC) was home only to its Indigenous Peoples. Spanish and British ships explored the province's coastline from 1774 onward, which led to the arrival of fur traders, and the setting up of fur-trading posts: the start of the desire for the area's natural resources. In 1792, Captain George Vancouver – for whom the province's largest city was later named – was impressed, describing "innumerable pleasing landscapes." BC joined the confederation of Canada in 1871, and the Canadian Pacific Railway (CPR) arrived in Vancouver in 1887, joining the new West Coast province to the already established eastern ones and bringing waves of new settlers. By 1891 the population was almost 100,000. Further rail routes opening up the center and north of the province ensured further development of logging and farming. BC was built on logging, mining, and fishing, and while these industries have seen hard times over the years, they continue to support many communities today.

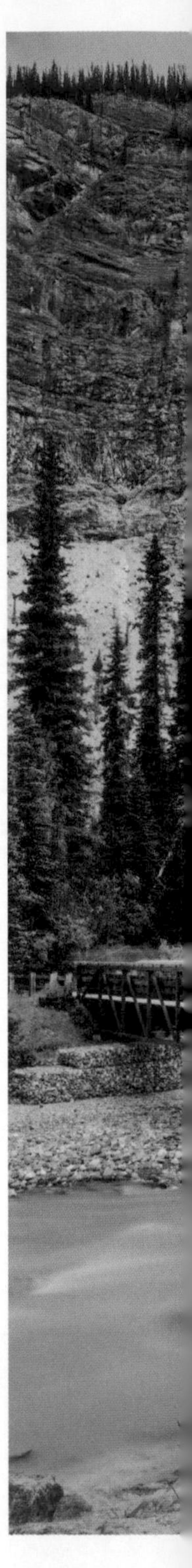

Takakkaw Falls and auburn foliage at Yoho National Park

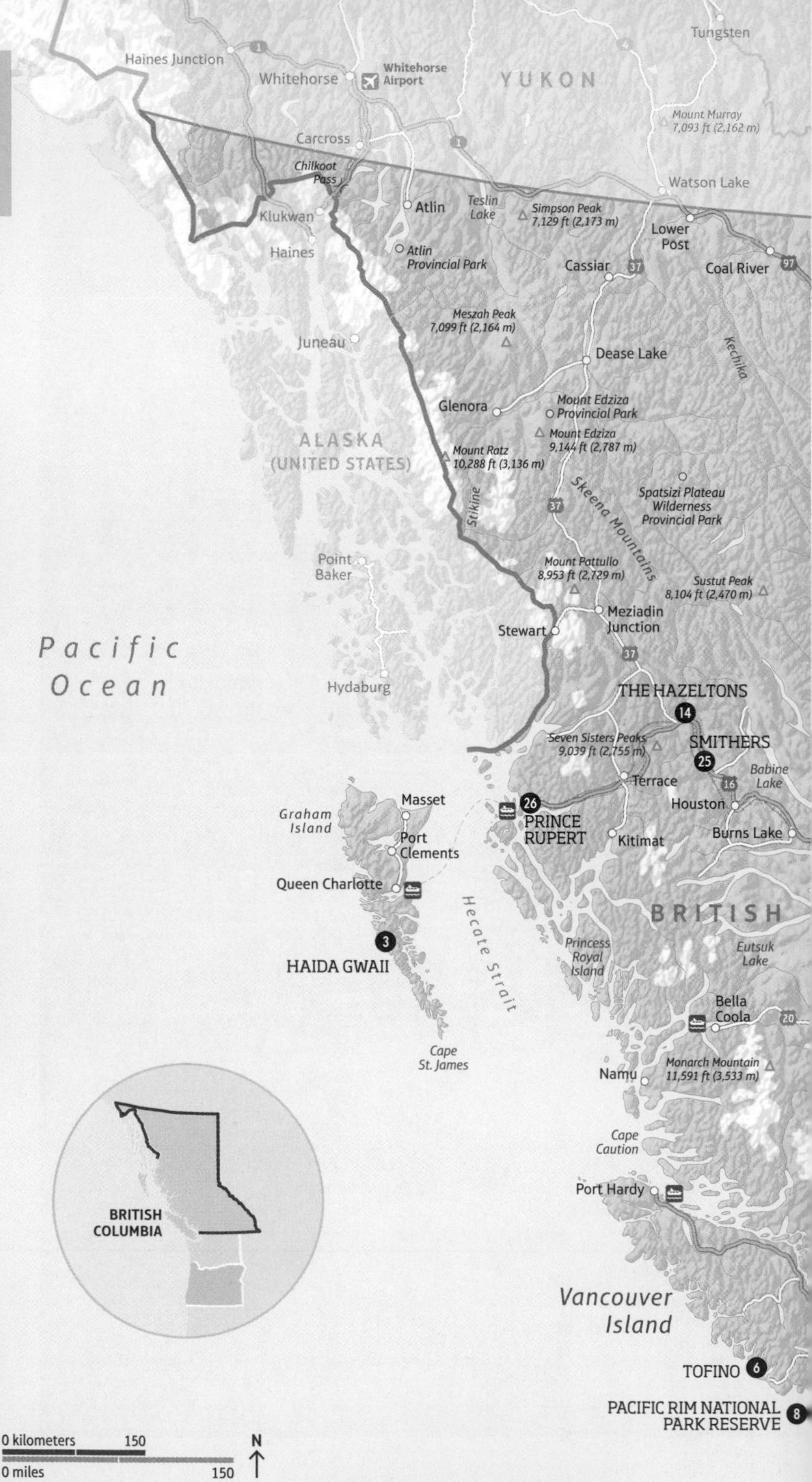

Haines Junction
Whitehorse
Whitehorse Airport
YUKON
Tungsten
Mount Murray
7,093 ft (2,162 m)
Carcross
Chilkoot Pass
Watson Lake
Atlin
Teslin Lake
Simpson Peak
7,129 ft (2,173 m)
Klukwan
Haines
Lower Post
Atlin Provincial Park
Cassiar
Coal River
Meszah Peak
7,099 ft (2,164 m)
Juneau
Dease Lake
Kechika
Glenora
Mount Edziza Provincial Park
Mount Edziza
9,144 ft (2,787 m)
ALASKA
(UNITED STATES)
Mount Ratz
10,288 ft (3,136 m)
Stikine
Skeena Mountains
Spatsizi Plateau Wilderness Provincial Park
Point Baker
Mount Pattullo
8,953 ft (2,729 m)
Sustut Peak
8,104 ft (2,470 m)
Meziadin Junction
Stewart
Pacific Ocean
Hydaburg
THE HAZELTONS
14
Seven Sisters Peaks
9,039 ft (2,755 m)
SMITHERS
25
Babine Lake
Terrace
Masset
Graham Island
26
PRINCE RUPERT
Houston
Port Clements
Kitimat
Burns Lake
Queen Charlotte
Hecate Strait
BRITISH
3
HAIDA GWAII
Princess Royal Island
Eutsuk Lake
Bella Coola
Cape St. James
Namu
Monarch Mountain
11,591 ft (3,533 m)
Cape Caution
BRITISH COLUMBIA
Port Hardy
Vancouver Island
TOFINO
6
PACIFIC RIM NATIONAL PARK RESERVE
8
0 kilometers 150
0 miles 150
N

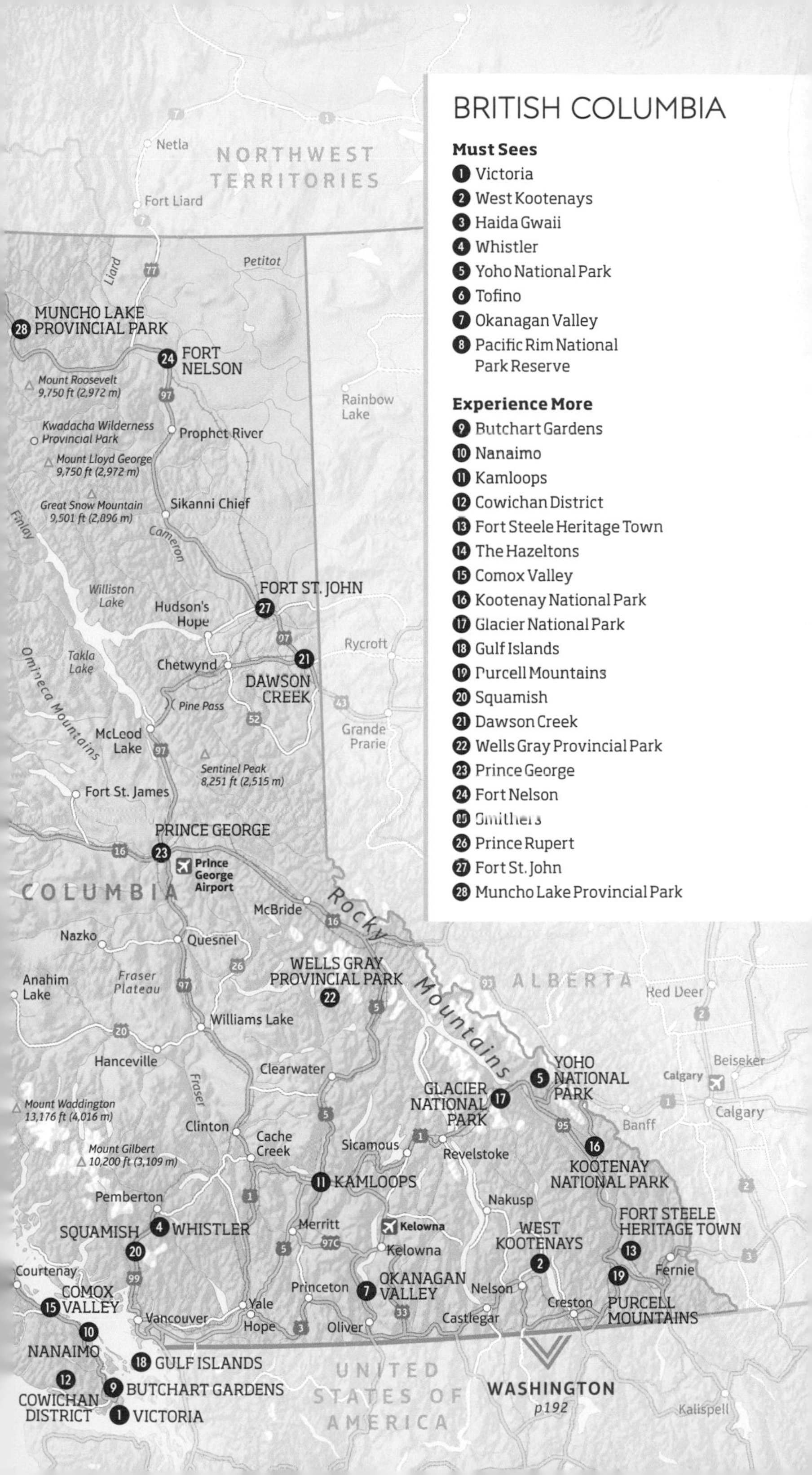

BRITISH COLUMBIA

Must Sees

1 Victoria
2 West Kootenays
3 Haida Gwaii
4 Whistler
5 Yoho National Park
6 Tofino
7 Okanagan Valley
8 Pacific Rim National Park Reserve

Experience More

9 Butchart Gardens
10 Nanaimo
11 Kamloops
12 Cowichan District
13 Fort Steele Heritage Town
14 The Hazeltons
15 Comox Valley
16 Kootenay National Park
17 Glacier National Park
18 Gulf Islands
19 Purcell Mountains
20 Squamish
21 Dawson Creek
22 Wells Gray Provincial Park
23 Prince George
24 Fort Nelson
25 Smithers
26 Prince Rupert
27 Fort St. John
28 Muncho Lake Provincial Park

NORTHWEST TERRITORIES
Netla
Fort Liard
Liard
Petitot
28 MUNCHO LAKE PROVINCIAL PARK
24 FORT NELSON
Mount Roosevelt 9,750 ft (2,972 m)
Rainbow Lake
Kwadacha Wilderness Provincial Park
Prophet River
Mount Lloyd George 9,750 ft (2,972 m)
Great Snow Mountain 9,501 ft (2,896 m)
Sikanni Chief
Finlay
Cameron
Williston Lake
Hudson's Hope
27 FORT ST. JOHN
Rycroft
Takla Lake
Chetwynd
21 DAWSON CREEK
Omineca Mountains
Pine Pass
McLeod Lake
Grande Prarie
Sentinel Peak 8,251 ft (2,515 m)
Fort St. James
23 PRINCE GEORGE
Prince George Airport
COLUMBIA
McBride
Rocky Mountains
Nazko
Quesnel
Anahim Lake
Fraser Plateau
WELLS GRAY PROVINCIAL PARK 22
ALBERTA
Red Deer
Williams Lake
Hanceville
Clearwater
Fraser
5 YOHO NATIONAL PARK
Beiseker
Calgary
GLACIER NATIONAL PARK 17
Mount Waddington 13,176 ft (4,016 m)
Banff
Clinton
Cache Creek
Sicamous
Revelstoke
16 KOOTENAY NATIONAL PARK
Mount Gilbert 10,200 ft (3,109 m)
11 KAMLOOPS
Pemberton
Nakusp
FORT STEELE HERITAGE TOWN 13
SQUAMISH 20
4 WHISTLER
Merritt
Kelowna
WEST KOOTENAYS 2
Fernie
Courtenay
15 COMOX VALLEY
Princeton
7 OKANAGAN VALLEY
Nelson
19 PURCELL MOUNTAINS
Yale
Vancouver
Hope
Oliver
Castlegar
Creston
10 NANAIMO
18 GULF ISLANDS
UNITED STATES OF AMERICA
12 COWICHAN DISTRICT
9 BUTCHART GARDENS
1 VICTORIA
WASHINGTON p192
Kalispell

The impressive Neo-Classical Parliament Buildings, set among leafy grounds

1

VICTORIA

F6 16 miles (25 km) N of city 450 Pandora Av 700 Douglas St Victoria Clipper/Black Ball Transport 812 Wharf St; www.tourismvictoria.com

With outstanding historic and cultural sights, pretty Victoria makes a great base for trips around Vancouver Island. The city was established as the capital of British Columbia in 1871. Though it was soon outgrown by Vancouver, it remains the political center of the province, and its leafy parks and gardens, museums, and buzzing harbor area continue to draw in the crowds.

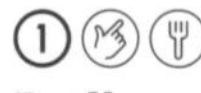

Parliament Buildings

501 Belleville St 9am-5pm Mon-Fri leg.bc.ca

Victoria's many-domed Parliament Buildings are an impressive sight, particularly at night, when the facades are illuminated by thousands of lights. Designed by Francis Rattenbury, the grand Neo-Classical buildings were completed in 1897, with a statue of explorer Captain George Vancouver perched on top of the main dome. Visitors can explore the extensive grounds, or take guided and self-guided tours of the interior, where exhibits tell the story of British Columbia and its parliamentary process. You can also observe the Legislative Assembly in action from the Public Galleries, visit the Legislative Library, or make reservations to eat in the Parliamentary Dining Room.

Thunderbird Park

Cnr Belleville & Douglas sts 8am-11pm daily

This compact park lies at the entrance to the Royal BC Museum *(p274)* and is home to an imposing collection of plain and painted giant totem poles. During the summer months it is possible to watch artists in the Thunderbird Park Carving Studio working on similar totems. The carved mythical figures tell stories of traditional Coast Salish cultures. Included are Gitxsan memorial poles, a Cumshewa pole, and Kwakwaka'wakw heraldic poles, as well as a traditional Kwakwaka'wakw "big house" built in 1952.

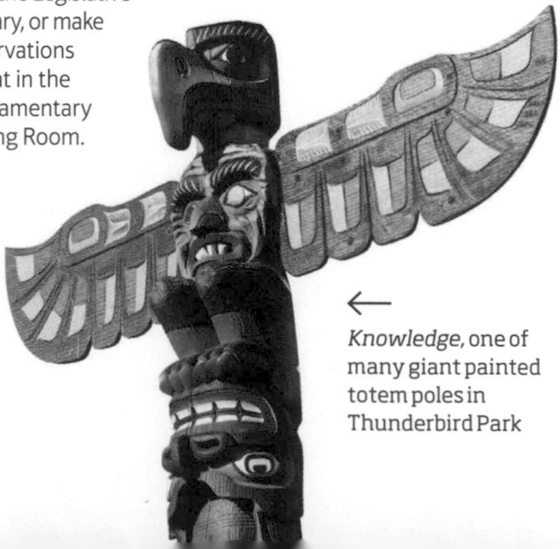

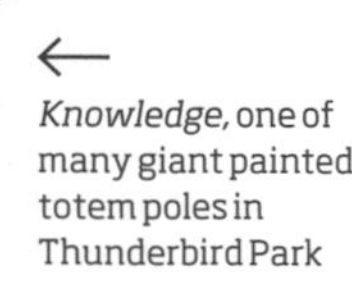

Knowledge, one of many giant painted totem poles in Thunderbird Park

Fairmont Empress Hotel

721 Government St Daily fairmont.com/ empress-victoria

Completed in 1908 to a Francis Rattenbury design, the Empress is one of Victoria's best-loved sights. Close to the Parliament Buildings, the hotel overlooks the Inner Harbour and dominates the skyline with its ivy-covered Edwardian splendor.

St. Andrew's Cathedral

740 View St 8am-5pm daily standrews cathedral.com

Built in 1892, this is the oldest Roman Catholic church in the area. The Victorian Gothic-style cathedral, made of stone, slate, and brick, features a 175-ft- (53-m-) tall spire and stained-glass windows. Works of local Indigenous artists were introduced in the 1980s, and the altar was designed by Charles Elliott, of the Coast Salish Nation; the candles beside the pulpit are decorated with Indigenous designs.

Market Square

560 Johnson St 10am-5pm daily marketsquare.ca

Market Square has some of the finest Victorian saloon, hotel, and store facades in Victoria. Most of the buildings were built in the 1880s and 1890s, during the boom period of the Klondike Gold Rush. After decades of neglect, the area received a face-lift in 1975. The square is now a shoppers' paradise, with stores selling books, jewelry, and arts and crafts.

Helmcken House

638 Douglas St Times vary, check website royalbcmuseum.bc.ca

The home of Hudson's Bay Company employee Dr. John Sebastian Helmcken was built in 1852 and is thought to be one of the oldest houses in British Columbia. The young doctor, who later helped negotiate BC's entry into the Dominion of Canada, built his house with Douglas fir trees felled in the surrounding forest. The elegantly designed clapboard dwelling contains many of its original furnishings, including the piano, which visitors are permitted to play. Among other exhibits are a collection of antique dolls and the family's clothes, shoes, and toiletries.

FRANCIS RATTENBURY

Born in Britain, Francis Rattenbury (1867-1935) traveled to Canada after working as an architectural apprentice for six years. Shortly after arriving, the 25-year-old won a provincial competition to design the new Parliament Buildings. He went on to design several important structures, including the Fairmont Empress Hotel in Victoria, and the Burns Manor in Calgary. After returning to Britain, he was brutally murdered by his wife's chauffeur and lover.

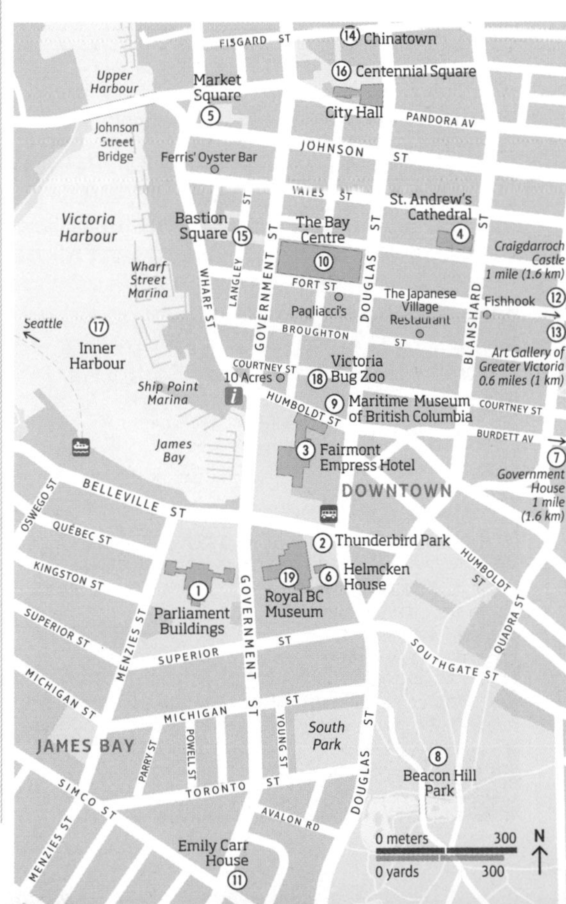

GREAT VIEW
Woodland's Trail

This hiking trail in the Government House estate weaves through 22 acres (8.9 ha) of oak forests blanketed with wildflowers. At the Woodland's Viewpoint and towards the edge of the estate, you can take in spectacular views of the Salish Sea.

Government House

1401 Rockland Av Gardens: dawn to dusk daily ltgov.bc.ca

The present Government House building was completed in 1959 after fire destroyed the 1903 building, which was designed by renowned architect Francis Rattenbury.

As the official residence of the Lieutenant-Governor of British Columbia, the Queen's representative to the province, the house is not open to the public, but you can view 14 acres (5.5 ha) of stunning grounds, including beautiful lawns and a lovely Victorian rose garden.

Beacon Hill Park

Douglas St 24 hrs daily victoria.ca

In the late 19th century this delightful park was used for stabling horses, but in 1888 John Blair, a Scottish landscape gardener, redesigned the park to include two lakes and initiated extensive tree planting. Once a favorite haunt of artist Emily Carr, the peaceful 184-acre (74.5-ha) Beacon Hill Park is now renowned for its lofty Garry oak trees and picturesque duck ponds.

 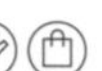

Maritime Museum of British Columbia

634 Humboldt St Times vary, check website mmbc.bc.ca

A fascinating collection of model ships, historical records, maps, and architectural plans for vessels is on display at this small but informative museum. During the summer months, the museum offers daily walking tours of the Inner Harbour with explanations on Victoria's maritime heritage and culture. The museum also hosts fun festivals throughout the year.

The Bay Centre

1150 Douglas St 10am-6pm daily (to 9pm Thu & Fri) thebaycentre.ca

The Bay Centre is a shopping mall within walking distance of the Inner Harbour and was constructed behind the elegant facades of several historic buildings on Government Street. The fronts of the 1892 Driard Hotel, the 1910 Times Building, and the 19th-century Lettice and Sears Building were all, after a campaign by locals, saved from demolition to make way for the mall.

Once a favorite haunt of artist Emily Carr, the peaceful 184-acre (74.5-ha) Beacon Hill Park is now renowned for its lofty Garry oak trees.

↑ Dale Doebert's *Moss Lady* sculpture in the foliage of Beacon Hill Park

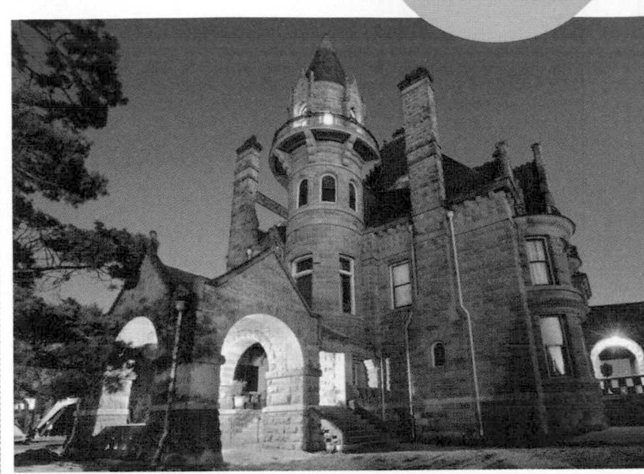

→ The grand exterior of Craigdarroch Castle lit up at dusk

11  

Emily Carr House

207 Government St May-Oct: 11am-4pm Tue-Sat emilycarr.com

Emily Carr, one of Canada's best-known artists, was born in 1871 in this charming, yellow clapboard house. The attractive house was built in 1864 by prominent architects of the time Wright and Saunders, under instruction from Emily's father, Richard Carr. Both the house and its English-style garden are open to visitors. All the rooms are appropriately furnished in late 19th-century period style, with some original family pieces. You can see the dining room where Emily taught her first art classes to local children, and Emily's drawing of her father still sits on the mantelpiece in the sitting room, where, as an eight-year-old, she made her first sketches.

12   

Craigdarroch Castle

1050 Joan Cres Jun-Sep: 9am-7pm daily; Oct-May: 10am-4:30pm daily Jan 1, Dec 25 & 26 thecastle.ca.

Completed in 1890, this building was the pet project of respected local millionaire Robert Dunsmuir. Although it is not a real castle, the design of this large manor home was based on that of his ancestral home in Scotland and mixes several architectural styles including Scottish Baronial, Romanesque Revival and French Gothic.

When the castle was threatened with demolition in 1959, a group of local citizens formed a society that successfully battled for its preservation. Today, the restored interior of the castle is a museum that offers a fascinating insight into the lifestyle of a wealthy Canadian entrepreneur.

The castle is noted for having one of the finest collections of Art Nouveau lead-glass windows in North America, and many of the rooms and hallways retain their patterned-wood parquet floors and intricately carved paneling in white oak, cedar, and mahogany. Every room is filled with opulent Victorian furnishings from the late 19th century and decorated in its original colors, such as deep greens, pinks and rusts. Several layers of the paint have been painstakingly removed from the drawing room ceiling to reveal the original hand-painted and stenciled decorations beneath, including wonderfully detailed butterflies and lions.

Did You Know?

After Dunsmuir's wife died, the Craigdarroch estate was subdivided and the castle offered up as a raffle prize.

13

Art Gallery of Greater Victoria

1040 Moss St 10am-5pm Tue-Sat (to 9pm Thu), noon-5pm Sun & most hols aggv.ca

This popular gallery is housed in an 1889 mansion located in the heritage neighborhood of Rockland, a few blocks west of Craigdarroch Castle. Inside, you will find a diverse range of works on display, including Canadian contemporary and heritage pieces, an excellent Asian art collection, and temporary exhibitions.

A superb collection of work by British Columbia's premier artist, Emily Carr, is always on display. Highlights include paintings of the British Columbian coastal forests and depictions of the lives of Indigenous Peoples, as well as photographs and excerpts from her writings.

The gallery is also home to one of Canada's most important collections of Asian art. Look out for the Chinese Bell (cast during the Ming dynasty and presented to the City of Victoria in 1903) and the only original Japanese Shinto shrine in North America (on display amid bamboo and Japanese maple trees in the museum's quaint courtyard garden).

FROM FORT TO CAPITAL

James Douglas fell in love with Camosack, known now as Victoria, when he sailed into its harbor in 1842. As chief factor of the Hudson's Bay Company (HBC), he was there to establish a fur-trading post and fort, in part to thwart American expansion into the region. He was welcomed, and in 1843, Fort Camosack (later Fort Victoria) was established. By the end of the decade, the Indigenous Peoples of the area had signed treaties, selling much of their land to the HBC. Small farms sprung up, and the harbor became a busy stopping-off point for prospectors in the 1858 Gold Rush. Victoria incorporated in 1862.

Chinatown

Bounded by Pandora Av & Store, Government & Herald sts

Victoria's Chinatown, the oldest in Canada and once its largest, is now the country's smallest, yet its vegetable markets, curio shops, and restaurants provide hours' worth of exploration. The ornate Gate of Harmonious Interest (Fisgard and Government streets) leads into the two-block-square area that was at one time home to Chinese railroad laborers and their families *(p241)*.

Fan Tan Alley, possibly the world's narrowest street, was once filled with opium dens and gambling houses. Today, you will find an eclectic mix of shops here. From the alley, enter through the back door of Chinatown Trading Co. *(551 Fisgard Street)* to see impressive artifacts from the district's earlier days, including those from a 19th-century gambling house.

  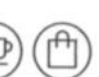

Bastion Square

Government St
bastionsquare.ca

This beautifully restored square faces Victoria's picturesque harbor and contains some of the city's oldest 19th-century buildings. What were once luxury hotels and offices, built during the boom era of the late 1800s, now house several eclectic restaurants. Restoration began in 1963, when it was discovered that the Hudson's Bay Company's fur-trading post Fort Victoria, established in 1843, once stood on this site.

Centennial Square

Bounded by Fisgard, Douglas & Government sts & Pandora Av

Created in 1963, Centennial Square is part of an effort to revitalize the city's downtown. Its centerpiece is a fountain with concrete "totems" adorned with mosaics by a local artist. Surrounding the public space are specialty shops, McPherson Playhouse – which opened in 1914 as the first Pantages Theatre and which has a beautiful Baroque interior – a knot garden, and the renowned City Hall.

The Second Empire-style south wing of City Hall – its redbrick facade and tin mansard roof exemplifying this style – was built in 1878. In 1880, a fire station was added, and the clock, installed in the tower in 1891, is still wound once a week.

Bustling Inner Harbour with an imposing view of the Parliament Buildings

A popular gathering spot, Centennial Square offers something for every season. In the summer, the square hosts a series of free lunch-time and evening concerts performed by local musicians, with food trucks selling local produce and brews. The winter sees an ice-skating rink accompanied by Christmas lights and a ferris wheel.

17

Inner Harbour

Foot of Government St

Home to the Songhees, of the Coast Salish Nation, between 1850 and 1911, the Inner Harbour today is vibrant with boats, pedestrians strolling along the promenade, and street performers. Plaques along the walkway pay tribute to those who shaped the harbor's history. The promenade offers excellent views not only of the harbor but also of the Parliament Buildings and the iconic Empress Hotel, particularly in the reflecting sunlight of late afternoon.

The opulent and vibrant Gate of Harmonious Interest on Fisgard Street in Chinatown

Did You Know?

Victoria Bug Zoo is home to glow-in-the-dark scorpions.

18   

Victoria Bug Zoo

631 Courtney St
10am-5pm daily Jan 1, Dec 25 victoriabugzoo.ca

This unusual mini-zoo occupies only two rooms. Here, you can get up close and personal with some of the world's most exotic insects. The Victoria Bug Zoo exhibits more than 50 species of insects, arachnids, and myriapods; it also has the largest ant farm in Canada, comprising a colony of leaf-cutter ants. You can wander around the zoo independently or join a free tour during which the knowledgeable guides share a series of fascinating facts on their charges. It is also possible to hold one of the zoo's friendly tarantulas, a surefire way to get over a fear of spiders. The small gift shop stocks insect collecting kits and edible bug snacks.

EAT

Ferris' Oyster Bar
Convivial, rustic eatery with three rooms - the original grill, a tapas and wine bar, and a refined seafood space.
536 Yates St
ferrisoysterbar.com
$$$

Pagliacci's
Fill up on fresh-baked bread and delicious pastas at this long-standing favorite.
1011 Broad St
pagliaccis.ca
$$$

10 Acres
Seasonally focused restaurant with three rooms - a casual bistro, a pub-style spot, and a romantically lit room.
611 Courtney St
10acres.ca
$$$

The Japanese Village Restaurant
Reservations are recommended for this busy restaurant, where chefs cook teppan-grill-style in front of you.
734 Broughton St
Mon japanesevillage.bc.ca
$$$

Fishhook
An eclectic fusion of Indian and French cuisine perfect for a casual lunch. Try the tuna melt tartine (an open-faced sandwich).
805 Fort St
fishhookvic.com
$$$

19

ROYAL BC MUSEUM

675 Belleville St 10am-5pm daily (May-Oct: to 10pm Fri & Sat) royalbcmuseum.bc.ca

Regarded as one of the best museums in Canada, the Royal BC Museum houses a spectacular collection of exhibits tracing the natural and human history of British Columbia. Its superb selection of Indigenous Peoples artifacts and art is second to none.

Founded in 1886, the Royal BC Museum has an engaging and immersive way of presenting BC history. Stand close to a furry and tusked woolly mammoth and see live crabs scuttling inside a tidal pool in the Natural History Gallery. Stroll through an authentically re-created scene from 19th-century Chinatown in the Modern History Gallery and get a chance to peek inside a 3,000-year-old Indigenous Peoples pit house. The traveling exhibits, too, are remarkable, and cover topics such as the Vikings, Ancient Egypt, and the Mayans. Outside, a dozen replica totem poles carved with colorful mythical figures preside over Thunderbird Park *(p268)*, and you can step inside the 1852 Helmcken House *(p269)*, one of the oldest houses in BC.

Did You Know?

The museum's Carillon (bell tower) was a gift from the Dutch to honor Canada's 100th birthday in 1967.

Totem pole standing outside the exterior of the Royal BC Museum

Brightly colored replica totem poles, carved in the Coast Salish tradition, standing tall in Thunderbird Park

Natural History Gallery

Located on the second floor, this gallery contains dioramas re-creating the sights, sounds, and even smells of areas such as the seashore, the ocean, and the coast forest. A Victorian-era mock submarine is also on display.

Becoming BC

On the third floor, you can walk along wooden sidewalks and cobblestone streets, passing through Victoria as it was from the 1870s to the 1920s. Excellent displays include a variety of storefronts, a replica silent movie theater, a grand hotel, a dress-maker's studio, a train station, a saloon, and a busy Chinatown street.

First Peoples Gallery

This gallery is dedicated to the First Peoples of BC, with many of the fascinating artifacts belonging to the Haida. The central exhibit is the Totem Hall, featuring huge carvings, startling masks, and a ceremonial longhouse belonging to Chief Kwakwabalasami.

Thunderbird Park

This park, established in 1941, surrounds the museum. Exhibits here include some outstanding totem poles, a traditional Indigenous Peoples big house, the Helmcken House, and St. Ann's Schoolhouse, one of the oldest structures (built in 1844) still standing in Victoria.

STAY

Halcyon Hot Springs
The luxurious lakeshore chalets and hot-springs spa here offer views of gleaming-white peaks.

Hwy 23, Nakusp
halcyon-hotsprings.com

$$$

Hume Hotel & Spa
This landmark hotel dating back to 1898 features heritage details and modern rooms.

422 Vernon St, Nelson
humehotel.com

$$$

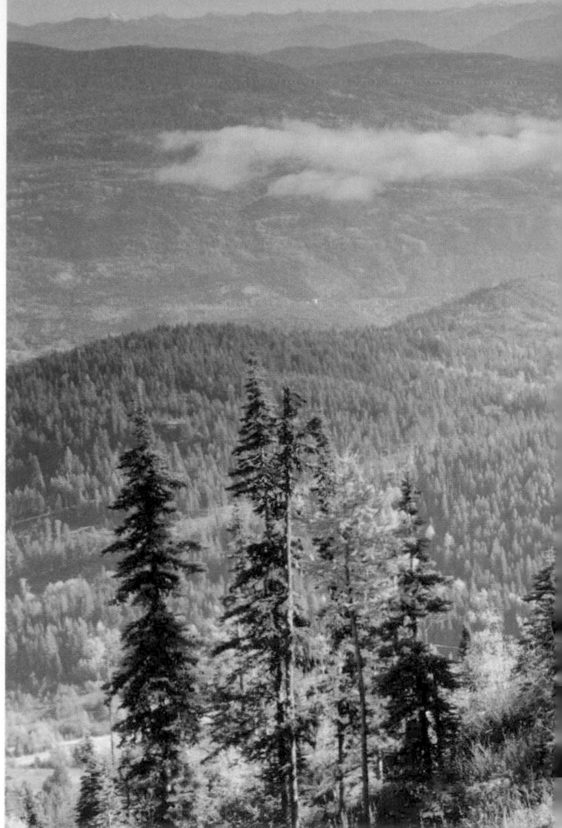

→ Mountain biking through larch forests in Rossland's Red Mountain

WEST KOOTENAYS

H5 Nelson Visitor Information Centre, 91 Baker St, Nelson; www.nelsonkootenaylake.com

A picturesque region of dense forest and snowy peaks, the West Kootenays is dotted with historic mining towns set on the shores of glacier-fed lakes. Hike, bike, and ski the endless slopes here, explore deep caves, soak in hot springs, or cosy up inside a snug cabin after a long day sightseeing in this remote mountain playground.

Nelson

Nestled into the side of the Selkirk Mountains along the West Arm of Kootenay Lake, Nelson is an attractive former mining and lumber town with an easy-going outdoor-lifestyle vibe. The eateries here are top-notch, as is the locally roasted coffee. The restored downtown core is full of heritage buildings dating back to the 1890s. Take a scenic ride along Nelson's pleasant waterfront and soak up the relaxed atmosphere on Car 23 – a streetcar that operated in the town between 1924 and 1949, before being restored in 1992.

Rossland

This mountain resort village comes alive in the winter months, when the nearby Red Mountain Resort attracts professional skiers and snowboarders for its excellent powder. Old railroad beds, whiskey-running routes, and miner's trails crisscross the area and are perfect for mountain biking and hiking in the summer.

Nakusp

Located on the shores of Upper Arrow Lake, this small town is famous for its mineral hot springs, three of which are close to town,

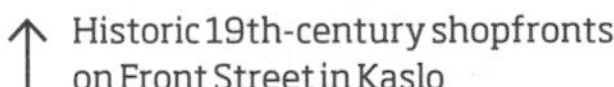

↑ Historic 19th-century shopfronts on Front Street in Kaslo

and two of which have been developed into comfortable resorts: Nakusp Hot Springs and Halcyon Hot Springs. Up in the nearby Selkirk Mountains are dozens of hiking, mountain biking, and snowmobiling trails. Roughly 25 miles (40 km) south of Nakusp, in the Slocan Valley, are several abandoned silver-mining "ghost" towns – the most fascinating is Sandon, once the unofficial capital of the mining region.

Kaslo

Dominated by the peaks of the Selkirk and Purcell mountains, this charming lakefront village is often referred to as Canada's Little Switzerland. A former sawmill and mining boom town, its picturesque, colorful streets are lined with frontier-style storefronts and flower-filled gardens. The village's main attraction is the beached SS *Moyie*, a sternwheeler that worked on Kootenay Lake from 1889 until 1957.

HOT SPRINGS

The West Kootenays is peppered with geothermal hot springs, ranging from fully developed spa-like resorts to wilderness backcountry pools. They provide therapeutic bathing in hot waters, rich in sulfates, calcium, sodium, lithium, and magnesium - all said to be good for everyday aches, as well as arthritis.

A DRIVING TOUR THE WEST KOOTENAYS

Length 340 miles (550 km) **Departure point** Nelson **Stopping-off points** Nakusp has good restaurants

Vast, remote, and spectacularly beautiful, the West Kootenays is a region best explored by car. This driving tour should ideally be spread out over several days or more in order to thoroughly enjoy the sights. Keep your eyes peeled for wildlife en route – it's not uncommon to see wild turkeys, deer, and bears crossing the roads in this region. Between October and March, winter tires are required and some high mountain passes may be temporarily closed.

The upscale resort of **Halcyon Hot Springs** *(p276) is set in some truly spectacular scenery. You can stop here for a relaxing soak in the mineral-rich waters.*

↑ Sunset in the Red Mountain Resort near Rossland

In winter, day passes are available at the **Red Mountain Resort** *(p276), and the resident snow hosts will be able to direct you to the best ski runs. Non-skiers can take guided tours of the picturesque snow-covered scenery.*

Trout Lake *is a pretty lake renowned for its excellent fishing, and the site of a former mining boom town.*

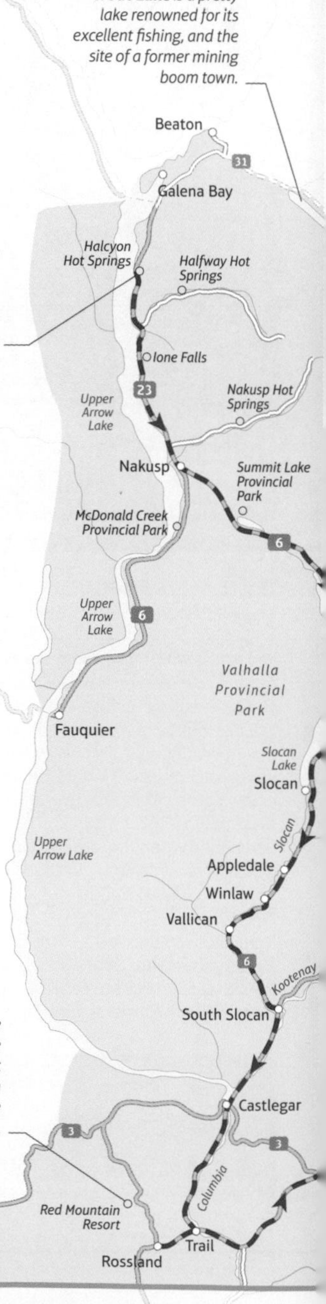

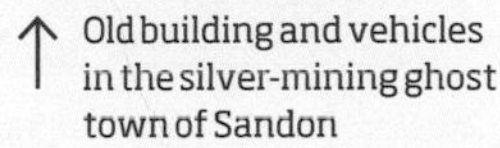

↑ Old building and vehicles in the silver-mining ghost town of Sandon

BRITISH COLUMBIA

The West Kootenays

Locator Map

GREAT VIEW

Buchanan Fire Tower

Follow the Blue Ridge Forest Services Road, a rough dirt track, to a retired fire tower on the top of Mount Buchanan. At 6,272 ft (1,912 m), the 360-degree views from the peak here are stunning. Picnic tables are dotted around near the former lookout.

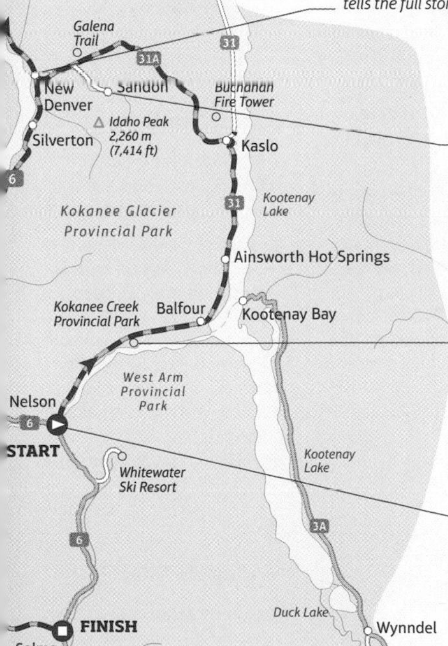

The small village of **Meadow Creek** *is the gateway to the Lardeau Valley, a gorgeous, if remote, stretch of backcountry with great hiking trails and several rafting tours.*

New Denver *was the site of an internment camp for the Japanese during WWII. The Nikkei Internment Memorial Centre (306 Josephine St) tells the full story.*

Sandon *(p277), a former silver-mining town, had a population of 10,000 during the boom years. Now a ghost town, you can explore its empty buildings and abandoned streetcars.*

Kokanee Creek Provincial Park *has beautiful sandy beaches, several playgrounds, and plenty of mountain-biking trails to explore.*

The vibrant town of **Nelson** *(p276) has a pretty historic center, with many buildings dating back to the 19th century.*

0 kilometers 25

0 miles 25

N ↑

↑ Verdant islands dotted along the north coast of the vast Haida Gwaii archipelago

3 HAIDA GWAII

**E4 BC Ferries from Prince Rupert Gwaii Haanas National Marine Conservation Area Reserve and Haida Heritage Site; www.gohaidagwaii.ca**

Haida Gwaii, formerly known as the Queen Charlotte Islands, is an archipelago of about 150 islands, many with unique ecosystems that nurture distinctive species. For thousands of years they have been home to the Haida Nation, a people renowned for their carvings and sculptures made of silver, gold, cedar, and argillite.

① Masset

**Graham Island 1686 Main St; www.masset bc.com**

The oldest fishing community in Haida Gwaii, Masset is located on the largest island in the archipelago. Its Delkatla Wildlife Sanctuary, an intertidal wetland and bird-watcher's paradise, is refuge to more than 140 recorded species, including large flocks of migrating shorebirds. In the nearby Haida village of Old Massett, traditional jewelers, carvers, and weavers work in home studios that you can visit.

Did You Know?

Referred to as Canada's Galapagos, the rainforests here are home to some of the world's oldest cedar trees.

② Naikoon Provincial Park

**Graham Island env. gov.bc.ca**

According to Haida legend, the Raven first brought people into the world at the northern border of this vast park by tempting them out of a clamshell. It's fitting, then, that the North Beach is a perfect spot for clam digging, as well as crabbing. On the East Beach, accessed by a 3-mile (5-km) hiking trail, is the 1928 *Pesuta* shipwreck. There are also two year-round developed campgrounds.

③ Queen Charlotte

**Graham Island 3220 Wharf St; www.queen charlottevisitorcentre.com**

This quaint fishing village, also known simply as Charlotte, is a good base from which to explore the islands and take an ecotour. Its tiny downtown offers cafés, hotels, and shops that sell a variety of goods including Haida carvings and pottery. You can also rent bicycles to explore the area.

④ Skidegate Inlet

**gohaidagwaii.ca**

This area comprises the three communities of Skidegate, Queen Charlotte, and Sandspit, and is one of the prime fishing

locations on the islands. In the spring, gray whales can sometimes be seen resting and feeding here. Once a thriving Haida village, Skidegate is now the site of the ferry and plane terminals to the islands. Try to time your visit to coincide with the Skidegate Days in July, a family-friendly festival that sees exciting canoe races.

SGang Gwaay (Ninstints)

Anthony Island **gohaidagwaii.ca**

A UNESCO World Heritage Site since 1981, this spiritual Haida settlement has more totems standing on their original sites than any other village. Many of the totems and remains of longhouses are succumbing to the natural decaying process as a result of their temperate rainforest environment. Official Parks Canada Watchmen guide you around this area, sharing their knowledge of the structures.

⑥  

Haida Heritage Centre

2 Second Beach Rd, Skidegate 9am-5pm Mon-Sat haidaheritagecentre.com

These longhouses, comprising a museum, artists studios, workshop spaces, and an amphitheater, celebrate Haida culture, past and present. Highlights include totems dating to 1878 and Loos Taas, a 49-ft- (15-m-) long canoe carved by Haida artist Bill Reid.

↑ Imposing, elaborately carved totem poles at Haida Heritage Centre

STAY

Jags Beanstalk
Modern and cosy guest rooms and a wonderful bistro on site. A quick walk along the beach takes you to the Haida Heritage Centre.

1 Hwy 16, Skidegate
jagsbeanstalk.com

Highwater House
Set within Naikoon Provincial Park, this secluded, treehouse-like home is equipped with modern amenities.

1 Limberlost Place, Tow Hill Rd, Masset
highwaterhouse.ca

$$$

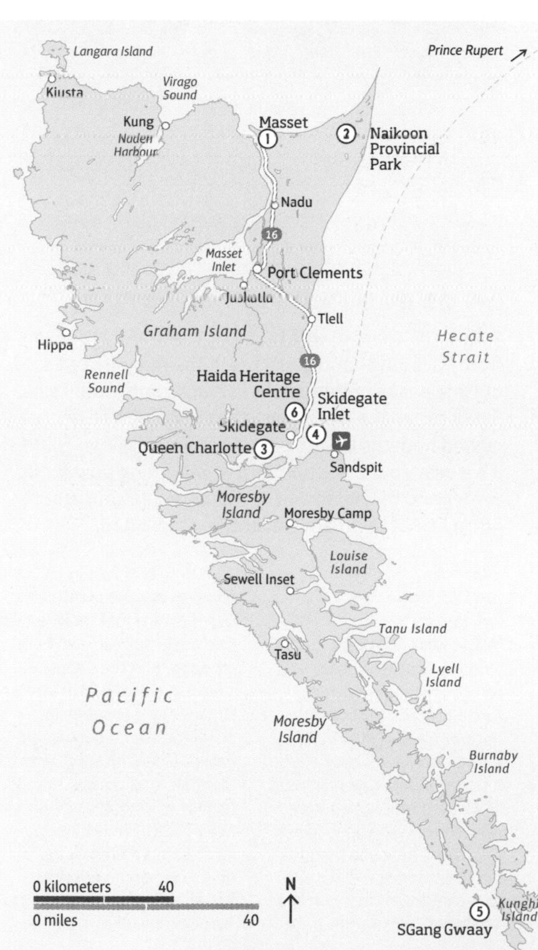

WHISTLER

F5 4230 Gateway Dr; www.whistler.com

Follow the coastal, cliff-hugging Sea-to-Sky Highway from Vancouver and you'll reach the magnificent side-by-side peaks of Whistler and Blackcomb mountains. Set between the mountains, the village of Whistler has hosted both the Olympic and Paralympic Winter Games. It's a year-round destination, where riding powder in winter and biking down the mountain in summer are just a few of the many adventures to be had.

Whistler Village

Once a stopover along a fur-trading and gold-rush route, the village of Whistler became a resort in 1914, when a rural fishing lodge opened its doors at Alta Lake, just west of where the village is today. Now, the cobblestoned Village Centre is where you'll find a range of lodges and hotels, shops selling winter gear and souvenirs, restaurants, pubs for après-ski, and nightclubs. Dog-sledding and snowmobile-tour outfitters can also be found among the shops.

Vestiges of the 2010 Winter Olympics are proudly on display in the Upper Village, notably the Whistler Olympic Plaza. Here you'll find the most luxurious of hotels, top-notch health spas, dimly lit cocktail lounges, and skiers lining up for one of the gondolas and chairlifts heading up Blackcomb Mountain.

Whistler Museum

4333 Main St 11am-5pm daily (to 9pm Thu) whistlermuseum.org

Beginning with the early pioneers, this museum tells the fascinating story of Whistler Blackcomb. Highlights include a section on the 2010 Winter Olympics and a great exhibit on local wildlife. For those wanting to delve more into Whistler's history, several guided walking tours are offered by the museum.

GREAT VIEW
Peak 2 Peak Gondola

For thrilling views, take a ride on the record-breaking Peak 2 Peak Gondola or dare to walk across the vertiginous Cloudraker Skybridge suspension bridge that sways 6,650 ft (2,000 m) above sea level.

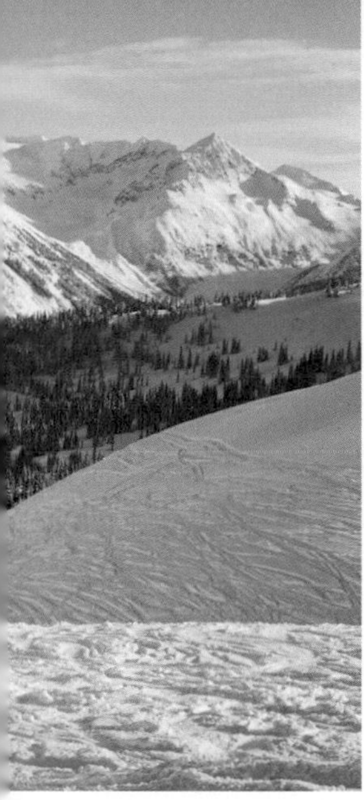

↑ Skiers enjoying the famous powder on Whistler Mountain

③

Whistler Mountain

Skiers and snowboarders can enjoy over 7 sq miles (19 sq km) of thrilling terrain with more than 100 marked trials, while the Whistler Village Gondola offers superb views of Whistler Valley during the 20-minute ride to the top. During the summer months, Whistler Mountain becomes a mecca for mountain bikers, with over 155 miles (250 km) of trails suitable for all skill levels.

④

Whistler Olympic Plaza

Village Stroll

A legacy of the 2010 Winter Olympics, this plaza has a state-of-the-art outdoor performance facility that hosts an array of shows throughout the year, including concerts, sporting events, and cultural festivities. The Olympic Rings are a favorite spot for photos.

⑤

Blackcomb Mountain

With a top elevation of 7,992 ft (2,436 m), this mountain is one mighty playground. A combination of 17 chairlifts and gondolas whisk skiers and snowboarders up to a winter wonderland. Also on offer are zip-trekking opportunities, snowcat tours, and helicopter rides to spot glaciers.

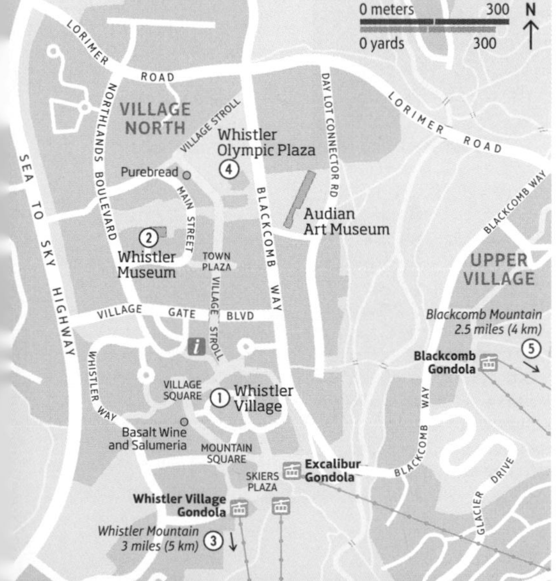

EAT

Basalt Wine and Salumeria

The heated patio at this eatery in the heart of Whistler Village is one of the best around and it's always buzzing, especially during happy hour. Try the excellent charcuterie platters or the grea-value seasonal set menu. The selection of wines and cocktails on offer is superb.

4154 Village Green
basaltwhistler.com

Christine's on Blackcomb

Set at 6,102 ft (1,860 m), you'll experience real mountain-top fine dining here, with incredible 360-degree views of the resort below and the surrounding mountain ranges. The food, wine, and service are as sublime as the scenery.

4545 Blackcomb Way
(604) 938-7437
For lunch only

$$$

Purebread

This is a true local gem of a bakery, with an amazing, piled-high assortment of sweet and savory croissants, hearty breads, scones stuffed with delicious fillings, picnic-ready sandwiches, pizza tarts, and good strong coffee that never runs out.

4338 Main St
purebread.ca

5

YOHO NATIONAL PARK

H5 Park Visitor Centre, Hwy 1, Field; www.pc.gc.ca

Set against the stunning backdrop of the snow-draped Rocky Mountains, Yoho National Park is a mecca for outdoor enthusiasts. You can peacefully canoe on jewel-blue lakes; gaze up in awe at veils of pounding waterfalls; or discover remote alpine meadows sweetened with the scent of wildflowers.

Inspired by the beauty of the park's mountains, lakes, waterfalls, and distinctive rock formations, this area was named Yoho, for the Cree word meaning "awe and wonder." Highlights include the Natural Bridge – a rock bridge gradually eroded over the centuries by the icy Kicking Horse River rushing below it – and the Emerald Lake, named for the intense color of its waters.

If the weather allows, don't miss the Takakkaw Falls. Scramble right to the base and feel the mist and thunderous power as glacial meltwater plunges down 1,260 ft (384 m), making it the second-tallest waterfall in Canada. On the way back, watch as trains snake through the Spiral Tunnels in the depths of the aptly named Cathedral Mountain.

Book a visit well in advance to see Lake O'Hara, southeast of Field. Surrounded by hanging valleys and jagged peaks dotted with hiking trails, this picturesque lake is an astounding shade of impossible blue, but it is only accessible by reservation.

STAY

Takakkaw Falls Campground

This is a basic, walk-in campground, with little more than a spot for your tent and some firewood. But it's all you'll need. Panoramic vistas of the roaring falls and glacier-clad mountains are shared only with the local wildlife here.

Takakkaw Falls, Yoho National Park (250) 343-6783 Mid-Jun-mid-Oct

A rock climber ascending the steep Takakkaw Falls route in Yoho National Park

BURGESS SHALE

This UNESCO World Heritage Site in Yoho National Park was set up to protect an extraordinary group of perfectly preserved marine creatures dating to the Cambrian period, over 500 million years ago. It is one of the few places on earth where both hard body parts and soft tissues have been fossilized, contributing much to the understanding of the origins of life on our planet. Access to the fossil beds is by guided hike.

Did You Know?

There are more than 250 miles (400 km) of hiking trails within Yoho National Park.

↑ The scenic shoreline of Lake O'Hara, set below majestic Mount Huber

↑ Tofino's stunning coastal scenery, seen from above

6 TOFINO

E6 Tofino/Long Beach Airport 1426 Pacific Rim Hwy; www.tourismtofino.com

Once an isolated logging outpost, and named for a hydrographer by a Spanish explorer, Tofino is now a busy resort town that attracts surfers, families, and Vancouverites who avoid the long road journey by taking the floatplane. It's home to picturesque sandy beaches, delightful woodland trails, and a celebrated foodie culture.

① Tofino Clayoquot Heritage Museum

331 Main St May-Aug: 11am-4:30pm Wed-Sun; Sep-Apr: 12:30-4:30pm Thu-Sun tofino museum.com

Interesting artifacts, such as whaling harpoons and canoes, are on display at this free museum. It tells the story of the Nuu-chah-nulth traditional territory and peoples' history, and of the pioneering families and subsequent local timber and fishing industries that developed in the area over the decades. The museum also offers walking tours on a variety of themes, such as the Japanese-Canadian heritage in the area, and the history of Tofino.

② Roy Henry Vickers Gallery

350 Campbell St 10am-5pm daily royhenryvickers.com

Award-winning artist Roy Vickers of the Tsimshian Indigenous Peoples welcomes you to his longhouse-style art gallery, where he exhibits his carvings, original prints, paintings, books, and jewelry. His contemporary, boldly colorful work represents the magnificent natural beauty of the west coast. The longhouse was built by Vickers and his family, along with the late local carver Henry Nolla.

③ The Whale Centre

411 Campbell St 8am-8pm daily tofinowhale centre.com

Both a hub for organized excursions – including whale-watching, bear-watching, and hot-springs tours – and a free museum, this center showcases artifacts from local shipwrecks and Indigenous Peoples' history. On display are cedar baskets, whaling equipment used by Indigenous Peoples, canoe paddles, and marine specimens, including a complete gray whale skeleton.

HIDDEN GEM
Natural Spa

For an amazing day trip, try the Hot Springs Cove Sea-to-Sky tour *(www.tofinowhalecentre.com)*. After a short seaplane flight, walk through old-growth forest to geothermal rock pools on the edge of the Pacific.

Mackenzie Beach

A family favorite, this lovely, sheltered beach has calm waters and gentle waves. It's ideal for paddle-boarding and skim-boarding, with rental gear available on site. During low tide, small islets are exposed and tidal pools can be seen in the rocky coves.

Chesterman Beach

Mainly a residential area lined with quaint and quirky homes, this white sandy beach has lovely tidal pools that are home to sea stars, anemones, and tiny crabs. At the north end at low tide, you could almost walk out to the Lennard Island Lighthouse, but the stroll to the privately owned Frank Island is easier. Over at the Wickaninnish Inn, check if the yellow welcome sign is on the Carving Shed door, in which case you can watch wood-carvers busy with their art.

Cox Bay Beach

Originally named False Bay, the beach here was renamed Cox Bay in 1934 in honor of the British fur trader and explorer John Henry Cox. Driftwood logs are piled high on the beach but there's still plenty of fine, white sand to sink your feet into. Several resorts are based here and professional surfers practice on the big waves in the winter months, getting ready for the competitions that are hosted here in the spring each year.

↑ Surfers tackling the waves on Chesterman Beach

EAT

1909 Kitchen

This gorgeous, marine-inspired restaurant has a large patio perched out over the water. The Pacific Rim-focused menu features such items as cedar-roasted black cod and shrimp-topped pizza, all cooked in a huge Italian wood-fired oven.

634 Campbell St, Tofino Resort and Marina **W tofino resortandmarina.com**

$$$

Tacofino

This is the original orange Tacofino food truck that started the popular franchise in 2009. Its bursting burritos and tasty tacos are still the best in all of BC, especially when stuffed with freshly sourced lingcod, chipotle mayo, and crispy cabbage.

1184 Pacific Rim Hwy **W tacofino.com**

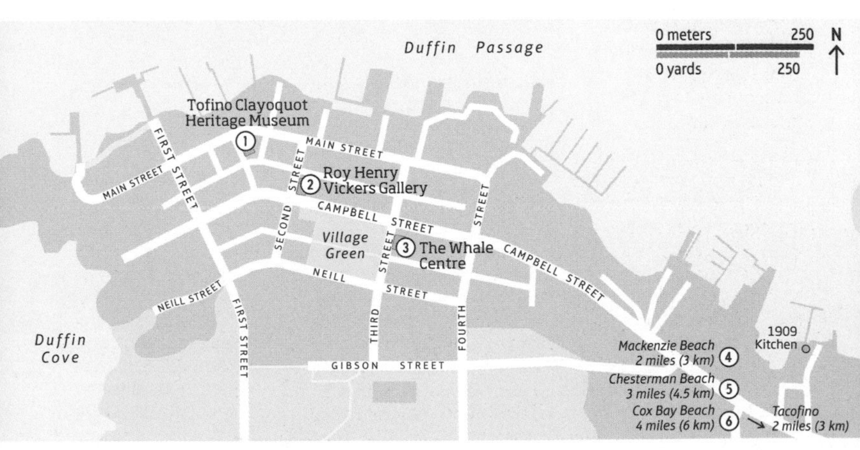

7

OKANAGAN VALLEY

G5 238 Queensway, Kelowna; www.tourismkelowna.com

Tucked away behind gently sloping mountains and linked by a string of deep, lengthy lakes, the Okanagan Valley is a five-hour drive east of Vancouver. Dry grasslands, ribbons of grape vines, and orchards full of peach and cherry trees fill the beautiful landscape.

↑ Chong Fahcheong's *The Romp* sculpture at Penticton

Vernon

Cattle ranches sprang up here on the flats early on in the 1800s, one of which, the **O'Keefe Ranch**, still exists. Today, Vernon is surrounded by farms and orchards. It is a popular summer spot for watersports on either Lake Okanagan or the teal-colored Kalamalka Lake. Come winter, ski bunnies flock to the excellent Silver Star Mountain Resort to make fresh tracks in the champagne powder.

O'Keefe Ranch
9380 Hwy 97 N
May-Sep: 10am-5pm daily
okeeferanch.ca

Kelowna

The biggest city in the valley, Kelowna lies neatly on the shores of Lake Okanagan and is at the center of the wine- and fruit-growing industries. Wine-tastings and fruit-stand-stops aside, Kelowna's sun-kissed beaches are perfect to play and picnic on. Myra Canyon, a short drive away, makes a great day-trip from the city. This thrilling portion of the historic Kettle Valley Rail Trail network is a spectacular spot for hikes and bike rides.

Summerland

This small but charming lakeside town is home to several 19th-century buildings and stunning views from the top of Giant's Head Mountain,

Did You Know?

The Valley's Syilx Indigenous Peoples gave Okanagan its name, which means "place of water."

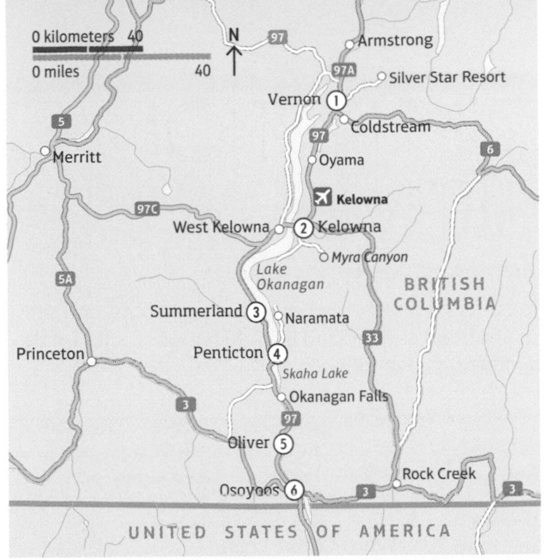

an extinct volcano. You can also ride a locomotive here along a preserved section of the Kettle Valley Railway.

Penticton

Laid-back and friendly, this popular destination has two lakefronts – Okanagan Lake and Skaha Lake. Beach life is, understandably, a big focus here. Other activities include gently floating the channel between the two lakes on a comfy tube, hopping from one vineyard to the next on scooters – with a designated driver – over in neighboring Naramata, or daring to scale the towering Skaha Bluffs, just a short drive south of town.

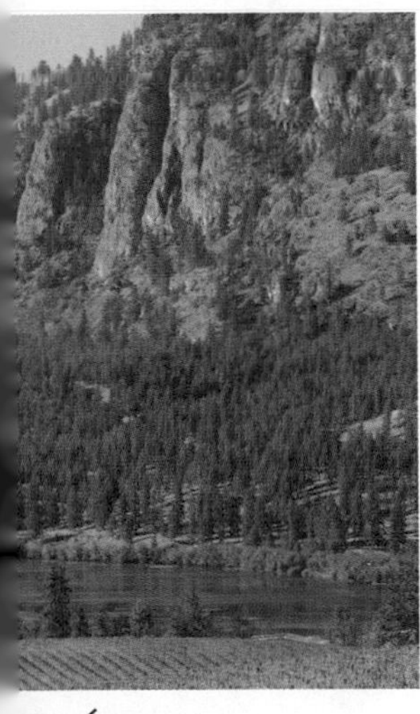

←

Vineyards in Okanagan Valley, with the Mcintyre Bluff in the distance

Oliver

Officially labeled as the Wine Capital of Canada, the area around Oliver is home to over 40 wineries. Many of these offer excellent dining and accommodations options, so it's worth stopping over.

Osoyoos

Kitschy but thoroughly enjoyable, this resort town experiences some of the driest and hottest summer temperatures in the country, and Osoyoos Lake is the country's warmest freshwater lake; a winning combination that draws many visitors to the beaches along the lakefront every summer for sunbathing and watersports.

TOP 6 LOCAL WINERIES

Burrowing Owl Estate Winery
500 Burrowing Owl Pl, Oliver
Chic, premium winery with a top restaurant and a series of luxurious guest rooms.

Elephant Island Orchard Wines
2730 Aikens Loop, Naramata, 8.6 miles (14 km) N of Penticton
Family-run estate known for its fruit wines, in particular its Apricot Dessert Wine.

Mission Hill Family Estate
1730 Mission Hill Rd, West Kelowna
This modern winery has a sculpture garden within its stunning grounds. Make sure you sample the Pinot Noir.

Nk'Mip Cellars
1400 Rancher Creek Rd, Osoyoos
Indigenous-owned winery and resort selling top Chardonnays and Rieslings.

See Ya Later Ranch
2575 Green Lake Rd, Okanagan Falls, 11 miles (18.5 km) S of Penticton
Tastings are held inside a beautifully restored early 19th-century hilltop home with spectacular views. Try their Gewürztraminer.

Covert Farms Family Estate
300 Covert Pl, Oliver
The perfect spot to sample a range of organic wines, tasty charcuterie, and delicious pick-your-own produce.

8

PACIFIC RIM NATIONAL PARK RESERVE

A F6 i Kwisitis Visitor Centre, 485 Wick Rd, Ucluelet; www.pc.gc.ca

Composed of three distinct areas – Long Beach, the Broken Group Islands, and the West Coast Trail – this vast and untamed strip of land is world famous for its whale-watching, surfing, kayaking, and hiking adventures.

Long Beach

The rugged, windswept sands of this seemingly endless beach, 15.5 miles (25 km) long, are renowned for their wild beauty. The crashing Pacific waves offer unbeatable year-round opportunities for surfers, both amateur and professional, while beachcombers can explore the beach's numerous rock pools, filled with marine life and scattered with driftwood. Hikers can choose from several scenic trails, including the 1-mile (1.5-km) Schooner Trail, which weaves through lush rainforests bordering the beach.

Broken Group Islands

A mecca for sea kayakers and scuba divers, the Broken Group Islands are an archipelago of some 100 islets clustered close enough for exploring one by one. Discover secret coves for a private picnic, or peer through crystal-clear waters revealing sea stars and other critters scuttling along the ocean floor.

West Coast Trail

Explore 47 miles (75 km) of ancient paths and paddling routes used for trade and travel by the Indigenous Peoples, following the southwestern edge of Vancouver Island. Built up in 1907 to aid in the rescue of shipwrecked survivors along the coast, this trail is now

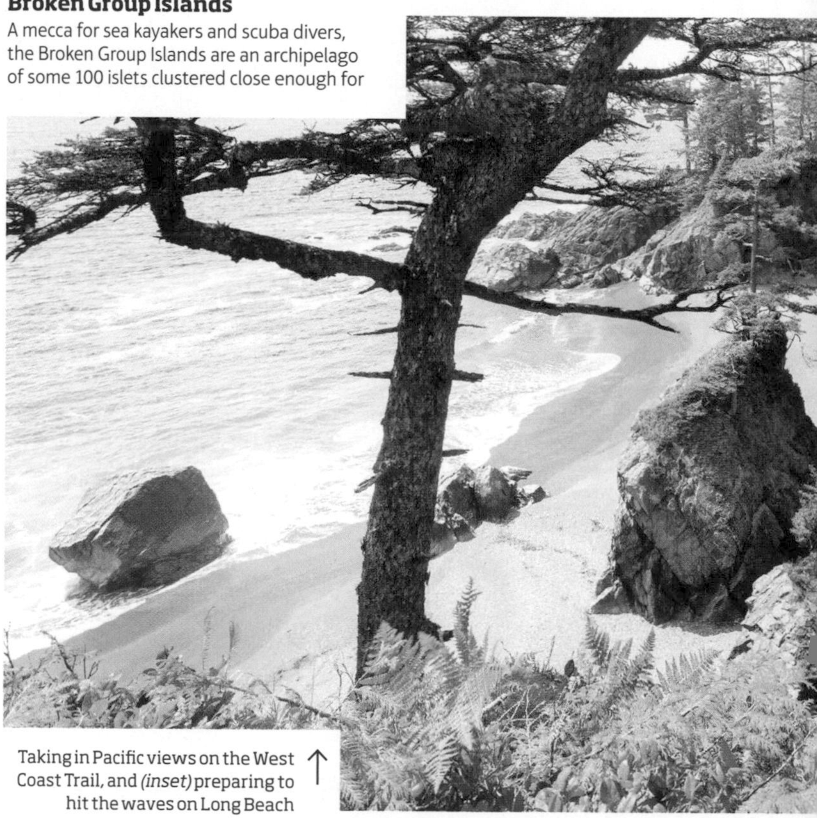

Taking in Pacific views on the West Coast Trail, and *(inset)* preparing to hit the waves on Long Beach ↑

WHALE-WATCHING

More than 20 species of whale are found in British Columbia's coastal waters, and around 22,000 gray whales migrate annually from their feeding grounds in the Arctic Ocean to breed off the coast of Mexico. The whales tend to stay near to the coast and are often close enough to Vancouver Island's west shore to be seen from land. From March to August there are daily whale-watching trips from Tofino, Ucluelet, and Bamfield.

rated as one of the world's best hiking routes. Taking approximately seven days or more, it passes through stunning natural scenery, including moss-draped rainforests, roaring waterfalls rushing down onto the shores of pebble beaches, and deep, rocky gullies hidden by groves of towering cedar trees. Hikers embarking on this once-in-a-lifetime adventure must be experienced and well prepared. The trail is only open in the summer months between May and September and requires a permit and reservations.

EXPERIENCE MORE

9 

Butchart Gardens

F6 800 Benvenuto Av, Brentwood Bay, Vancouver Island 9am daily; closing times vary, check website butchartgardens.com

These beautiful botanical gardens were established in 1904 by Jennie Butchart. The site, home to thousands of rare plants, is arranged into distinct areas, including a formal Italian garden, a Japanese garden, and a rose garden. There are also ponds, statues, fountains, a boat tour, and a carousel. In summer, the gardens are illuminated and play host to a variety of musical entertainment, and fireworks displays are held on Saturday nights.

Nanaimo

F6 2450 Northfield Rd; www.tourismnanaimo.com

Originally the site of five Coast Salish villages, Nanaimo was established as a coal-mining town in the 1850s. Nanaimo has plenty of malls and businesses along the Island Highway, but it is the Old City Quarter on the waterfront, with its fine 19th-century buildings, that visitors enjoy the most. To discover the city's history, head to the **Nanaimo Museum**. One of the highlights is the replica coal mine, allowing you to see what it was like to work underground. Also part of the museum is the bastion located on the waterfront, North America's only freestanding Hudson's Bay Company Bastion. Cannon firings take place here at noon.

Nanaimo Museum

100 Museum Way
10am-5pm daily (Labor Day-Victoria Day: Mon-Sat)
nanaimomuseum.ca

Kamloops

G5 1290 W Trans-Canada Hwy; www.tourismkamloops.com

Kamloops – which means "where the rivers meet" in the language of the Secwepemc, or Shuswap, people – is situated at the confluence of the North and South Thompson rivers. Nestled amid mountains and lakes, the city offers hiking, biking, skiing, and golfing.

European settlement began in 1812, when fur traders started doing business with the Secwepemc. Remains of a 2,000-year-old village at the **Secwepemc Museum and Heritage Park** reflect the people's history.

US train robber Bill Miner arrived in Kamloops in 1904, on the run after committing a robbery. Kamloops and trains have been linked ever since, and it's possible to ride along the Kamloops Heritage Railway on a 1912 steam locomotive, one of the few

INSIDER TIP

Don't Sweat It

For an authentic souvenir from the island, seek out the thick-wool and cosy Cowichan sweaters that are traditionally hand-knitted by the Cowichan Indigenous Peoples of this region.

←

The incredible colors and lush greenery of Butchart Gardens

remaining operational steam engines. There are also train rides at **BC Wildlife Park**, home to threatened animals.

Secwepemc Museum and Heritage Park
330 Chief Alex Thomas Way 8am–4pm daily Sep–May: Sat & Sun secwepemcmuseum.ca

BC Wildlife Park
9077 Dallas Dr, Kamloops 9:30am–5pm daily bcwildlife.org

Cowichan District

F6 2896 Drinkwater Rd, Duncan; www.tourism cowichan.com

The south-central coast of Vancouver Island consists of the Chemainus and Cowichan valleys. The main freshwater lake on the island, Lake Cowichan is great for cycling, swimming, canoeing, whale-watching, and fishing. Another favorite local activity is tubing down the Cowichan River. The warm climate here also favors grape-growing. The Cowichan Valley is BC's second-highest wine-producing region, after Okanagan, and you can take a self-guided or escorted tasting tour along country back roads.

Between the town of Duncan and the lake lies the Valley Demonstration Forest, which has scenic lookouts. Duncan is known as the City of Totems, as it displays more than 40 magnificent totem poles in the downtown area. The town of Chemainus is also noted for its giant murals.

A short drive from Duncan is **The Raptors**, where you can learn about a variety of birds such as hawks, owls, falcons, and eagles.

The Raptors
1877 Herd Rd, Duncan Times vary, check website pnwraptors.com

Fort Steele Heritage Town

H5 9851 Hwy 95 Times vary, check website fortsteele.ca

Fort Steele is a re-creation of the mining supply town that was established at this site in 1864, when gold was discovered at Wild Horse Creek. By the early 1900s, though, Fort Steele was a ghost town. Today, there are more than 60 reconstructed or restored buildings, staffed by guides in period costume, including the general store and North West Mounted Police officers' quarters, where items such as family photographs, swords, and uniforms create the illusion of recent occupation. Demonstrations of traditional crafts such as ice-cream-making and quilting are also held here. "Living history" dramas and musical comedy shows are staged in the Wild Horse Theater, and tours at the nearby Wild Horse Creek Historic Site include a chance to pan for gold.

TOP 3 GHOST TOWNS IN BC

Fort Steele
H5
Once a booming Gold Rush town and now an open-air museum.

Barkerville
G4
Another boom-and-bust Gold Rush town with a restored village exhibit.

Copper Mountain
G5
A copper-mining town that was abandoned in the late 1950s.

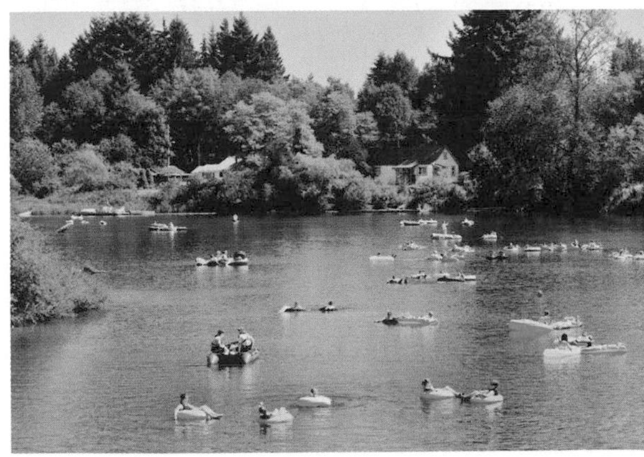

→

Tubers drifting down Cowichan River on a warm summer's day

14

The Hazeltons

E3 9th Av, New Hazelton; www.hazeltons tourism.ca

In the 1860s, bustling pioneer communities were established at the confluence of the Skeena and Bulkley rivers, 180 miles (290 km) east of Prince Rupert. Today, the three villages at this location – Old, New, and South Hazelton – are known collectively as the Hazeltons. The villages are named for the hazel bushes covering the area's river-carved terraces.

Old Hazelton is particularly charming, with its old-fashioned storefronts. The Old Hazelton walking tour shows remnants of a Victorian steam engine, Skeena River paddlewheelers, St. Peter's Anglican Church, and the **Hazelton Pioneer Museum and Archives**, which portrays the early days of the initial settlement.

The highlight of the area is the **'Ksan Historical Village**, a replica of a Northwest Coast-style Gitxsan village. Skilled in carving and painting masks, totems, and canoes, Gitxsan elders are teaching new generations these skills at the 'Ksan village. Within the complex are seven longhouses, a carving school, totems, and a museum.

A 70-mile (113-km) driving tour winds through many indigenous villages where you can see dozens of totem poles. The Hazeltons are known as the "totem pole capital of the world."

Hazelton Pioneer Museum and Archives

4255 Government St, Hazelton (250) 842-5961 11am-5pm Tue-Fri, 1pm-4pm Sat

Besides the many hiking, paddling, and biking trails, the highlight of the Comox Valley is Mount Washington Alpine Resort.

'Ksan Historical Village

High Level Rd, Hazelton May-Oct: 10am-5pm daily ksan.org

Comox Valley

F5 Tourist Office: 101-3607 Small Rd, Cumberland; www. discovercomoxvalley.com

Overlooked by the Comox Glacier, this valley region comprises the historic city of Courtenay, the seaside town of Comox, and the artsy village of Cumberland. Besides the many hiking, paddling, and biking trails, the highlight of the Comox Valley is Mount Washington Alpine Resort, which offers year-round outdoor activities and one of the deepest snowpacks in North America. Down in the valley there are also festivals, wineries, oyster tastings, and farmers' markets.

Kootenay National Park

H5 7556 Main St E, Radium Hot Springs; www. pc.gc.ca

Kootenay National Park covers 543 sq miles (1,406 sq km) of the most diverse terrain in the Rockies. Much of this scenery can be seen from the Kootenay

Two impressive totem poles at 'Ksan Historical Village, Hazelton

↑ Hikers taking a rest in the scenic Glacier National Park

Parkway (Highway 93 South), which cuts through the park from north to south following the Vermilion and Kootenay rivers. Most of the park's attractions can be seen from the many short trails that lead from the highway.

The road winds eastward through Sinclair Pass, where the high red walls of Sinclair Canyon, a limestone gorge, lead to the Sinclair Falls and the Redwall Fault.

17 

Glacier National Park

A G5 i Rogers Pass; www.pc.gc.ca

Not to be confused with the park of the same name in the US, Glacier National Park covers 520 sq miles (1,350 sq km) of wilderness in the Selkirk Range of the Columbia Mountains. The park was established in 1886, and its growth was linked to the expansion of the railroad, which was routed through Rogers Pass in 1885. Trails here offer spectacular views of the park's many glaciers, including the Great Glacier, now known as the Illecillewaet Glacier.

Glacier National Park contains rainforests, glacial lakes, streams, and waterfalls. During winter, snow falls almost daily, totaling as much as 75 ft (23 m) per season. The threat of avalanches is serious; skiers and climbers should obtain information about conditions before visiting.

Did You Know?

The Gulf Islands are made up of 15 islands as well as many smaller islets and reef areas.

Gulf Islands

A F6 Strait of Georgia W hellobc.com

Their tranquility and beauty draw visitors to the Gulf Islands, where sightings of eagles and turkey vultures are common. Fishing charters and kayak tours provide views of otters, seals, and marine birds.

The largest island is Salt Spring, which is renowned for its vineyards, organic produce, and markets. Saturna, the smallest, most remote island, hosts a lamb barbecue each Canada Day. Ganges Village is a pretty spot to stroll around in summer, while Galiano has many hiking trails that are great year-round.

EAT

Tree House Cafe

Eclectic local hangout for sandwiches, curry bowls, and nightly live music.

A F6 106 Purvis Ln, Ganges, Salt Spring Island W treehousecafe.ca

$$$

Blackfin Pub

Modern and refined pub on the marina serving fine food. Try the bacon-wrapped scallops.

A F5 132 Port Augusta St, Comox W blackfinpub.com

$$$

Locals

Indulge in a locally sourced brunch at this fine riverside spot.

A F5 1760 Riverside Lane, Courtenay, Comox Valley W localscomoxvalley.com

$$$

Hastings House

Housed in a beautiful manor hotel, this restaurant serves local, organic food.

A F6 160 Upper Ganges Rd, Salt Spring Island W hastingshouse.com

$$$

The Twisted Cork

Enjoy delicious tapas and comfort food in a relaxing atmosphere.

A F4 1157 5th Av, Prince George W twisted-cork.com

$$$

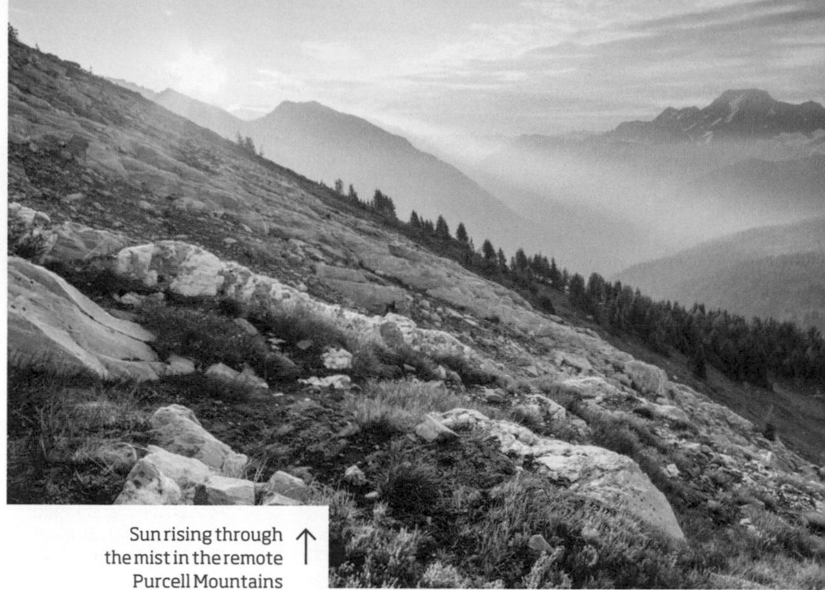

Sun rising through the mist in the remote Purcell Mountains

19

Purcell Mountains

**H5 270 Kimberley Av, Kimberley; (778) 481-1891**

The rugged and beautiful Purcell Mountains face the Rockies across the broad Columbia River Valley. The region is one of the most remote in the Rockies and attracts hikers and skiers from around the globe. A high range of granite spires, called the Bugaboos, also draws mountain climbers. In the north of the Purcell range, the Purcell Wilderness Conservancy covers a vast 500,900 acres (202,709 ha).

From the nearby town of Invermere, it is possible to access the Earl Grey Pass Trail, which extends 35 miles (56 km). It is named after Earl Grey, Canada's Governor General from 1904 to 1911, who built a vacation cabin for his family here. The trail he traveled was a route used by the Kinbasket peoples of the Ktunaxa Indigenous Peoples. Today, the trail is notoriously dangerous; bears, avalanches, and fallen trees are some of the hazards hikers may encounter. Hiking here requires skill and should not be attempted by novices.

Did You Know?

There's another group of hidden granitic peaks in the Purcell Mountains, called the Leaning Towers.

20

Squamish

**F5 38551 Loggers Lane; www.explore squamish.com**

The town of Squamish is surrounded by vast provincial parks, and lies halfway between Vancouver and Whistler, along the scenic Sea-to-Sky Highway. Once a sleepy logging town, Squamish has grown into a playground for adventurous outdoorsy types, earning itself the nickname "Canada's Outdoor Recreation Capital." The town's towering landmark, the Stawamus Chief Mountain, is a favorite for rock climbers, and hikers can also take one of several trails to reach the top. Next door is the Sea-to-Sky Gondola, which takes visitors even farther up behind the Chief. From there are several dining options, plus year-round hiking trails and incredible views of the Howe Sound below, crowned by the surrounding Coast Mountains. The Squamish Spit, on the west side of town, is a top kiteboarding destination, and Squamish's northernmost neighborhood, Brackendale, is home to North America's largest concentration of wintering bald eagles. Just north of town is Alice Lake Provincial Park, and beyond it is the Garibaldi Provincial Park, home to glacier-capped Mount Garibaldi, a dormant volcano and a dream for snowmobilers and off-piste skiers in winter.

21

Dawson Creek

G3 **900 Alaska Av; www.tourismdawson creek.com**

The formerly quiet town of Dawson Creek was transformed by the construction of the Alaska Highway, which began in 1942 and swelled the town's

Wells Gray Provincial Park, in the Cariboo Mountains, is one of the largest and also one of the most beautiful wildernesses in British Columbia.

population from 600 to 10,000. Designated as historic Mile Zero on the road to Fairbanks, 1,486 miles (2,391 km) to the north, the city recognizes this distinction with the Mile Zero post at 10th Street and 102nd Avenue. Located at the corner of Highway 97 and the Alaska Highway, the 1931 Northern Alberta Railway station is now a park and information center. The site includes the Mile Zero stone cairn marking the official start of the Alaska Highway. Next to the railway station is a 1948 grain elevator annex that is now an art gallery. Shows include the work of local artists.

At **Walter Wright Pioneer Village**, restored buildings and farm machinery re-create the agricultural community of Dawson Creek before the highway was built.

Walter Wright Pioneer Village
1901 Alaska Hwy
Mid-May–Aug: 9am–7:30pm daily Sep–mid-May
mile0park.ca

Wells Gray Provincial Park

G4 416 Eden Rd, Clearwater; www.wellsgray.ca

Wells Gray Provincial Park, in the Cariboo Mountains, is one of the largest and also one of the most beautiful wildernesses in British Columbia, offering wonders comparable to the Rockies. The park is distinguished by alpine meadows, thundering waterfalls, and glacier-topped peaks that rise as high as 8,450 ft (2,575 m). The Canadian National Railroad and Highway 5 follow the Thompson River, and both routes provide stunning views.

From the Clearwater Valley Road, off Highway 5, there are several trails, from easy walks to arduous overnight hikes. A short trail leads to spectacular 450-ft (137-m) Helmcken Falls. Nearby Mushbowl Bridge provides the best view of the fast-moving Murtle River and the giant holes it has carved into the surrounding rock.

Four lakes within the park provide excellent opportunities for canoeing and angling.

Prince George

F4 1300 First Av; www.tourismpg.com

The traditional home of the Lheidli T'enneh and Carrier Sekani Indigenous Peoples, and the largest town in northern British Columbia, Prince George is a bustling supply-and-transportation center for the region.

Prince George has its own symphony orchestra, several art galleries, and a university. **Exploration Place** lies within the Fort George Park, and contains a small collection of artifacts from Indigenous cultures, European pioneers, and early settlers of the region.

An important center for the lumber industry, the town of Prince George offers a range of free tours of local pulp mills, which take you through the fascinating process of wood production.

Exploration Place
333 Becott Pl
9am–5pm daily
Jan 1, Dec 25 & 26 theexplorationplace.com

→ Exhibits in the fascinating Exploration Place museum in Prince George

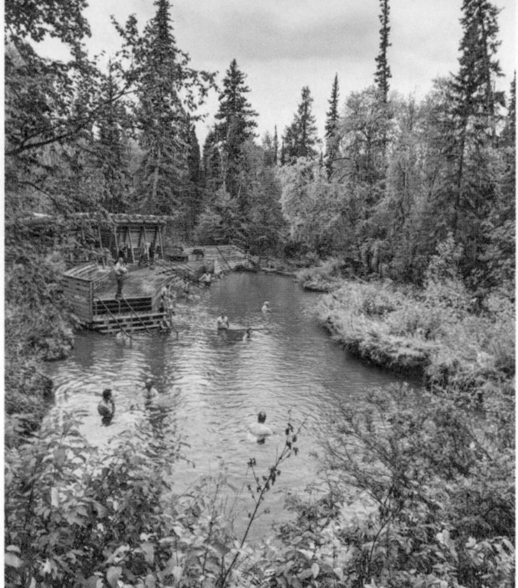

↑ People relaxing in the hot springs of Liard River Provincial Park, Fort Nelson

INSIDER TIP
Grizzly Bears

If visiting May to July, join a Prince Rupert Adventure Tour *(www.adventuretours.net)* to the Khutzeymateen Grizzly Bear Sanctuary, home to the highest concentration of grizzly bears on the continent.

Fort Nelson

F2 5500 Alaska Hwy; www.tourismnorthernrockies.ca

Despite the growth of the oil, gas, and lumber industries in the 1960s and 1970s, Fort Nelson retains the atmosphere of a northern frontier town. Until the 1950s, Fort Nelson was without telephones, running water, or electricity.

This town at Mile 300 of the Alaska Highway has an air and bus service, a hospital, motels, restaurants, and gas stations. Locals are known for their friendliness, and during the summer they run free talks, describing life in the North.

The small Fort Nelson Heritage Museum displays photographs and artifacts that tell the story of the building of the highway, and has a frontier-town general store and blacksmith's forge.

The region has over a dozen parks, including Liard River Provincial Park; its hot springs are open year-round. The area is a world-class cross-country skiing destination.

Smithers

E3 1411 Court St; www.tourismsmithers.com

The picturesque town of Smithers, located in the center of the fertile Bulkley Valley, is surrounded by the scenery of local mountain ranges over which the snow-crested 8,599-ft (2,621-m) Hudson Bay Mountain presides. Smithers is a year-round outdoor center where Babine Lake is known for its plentiful rainbow trout, and rafters on the Bulkley River twist past pine-lined shores. A hike along the forested 8-mile (13-km) Perimeter Trail may offer sightings of moose, deer, and grouse, while black bears and caribou live higher on the slopes. In winter, downhill, cross-country, and telemark skiing are popular.

Prince Rupert

E4 215 Cow Bay Rd; www.visitprincerupert.com

Prince Rupert is a vibrant port city, and the second-largest on BC's coast. Located on Kaien Island, the city is encircled by forests and

→ Fall colors surrounding Hudson Bay Mountain in Smithers, and *(inset)* a resident black bear

mountains, and overlooks the fjord-studded coastline. The harbor is the access point for Haida Gwaii and Alaska.

Like many of BC's major towns, Prince Rupert's development is linked to the growth of the railroad. The Kwinitsa Station Railway Museum tells the story of businessman Charles Hay's big plans for the town.

Tsimshian Indigenous People were the area's first occupants. The **Museum of Northern British Columbia** focuses on Tsimshian history, and tours showcase the culture over the past 10,000 years.

Museum of Northern British Columbia

100 1st Av W
Times vary, check website
museumofnorthernbc.com

Fort St. John

G3 9324 96th St; www.fortstjohn.ca

The city of Fort St. John, at Mile 47 of the Alaska Highway, is among the rolling hills of the Peace River Valley. The city is the oldest non-Indigenous settlement in BC. At nearby Charlie Lake Cave, 10,000-year-old artifacts have been found, making it the site of the earliest-known human activity in the province.

The area around Fort St. John is a unique ecosystem in which moose, deer, elk, and black bears abound. When completed, the Alaska Highway turned Fort St. John into a busy supply center catering to visitors and supporting the agriculture industry. The town boomed in the 1950s, when oil was found here. The city's pride in its industrial heritage is reflected in its museum, which has a 140-ft- (43-m-) high oil derrick at its entrance and exhibits telling the story of the local oil industry. Other activities include cross-country skiing at Beatton Provincial Park in winter. Watching the northern lights, which are visible here, is also a draw.

Muncho Lake Provincial Park

E2 Daily (campsites May-Oct) env.gov.bc.ca

One of three provincial parks that were established after the building of the Alaska Highway in 1942, Muncho Lake occupies the most scenic section of the road. The park envelops the bare peaks of the northern Rockies, whose stark slopes incorporate rock formations created by thousands of years of glacial erosion. The highway skirts the eastern shoreline of the Muncho Lake before crossing the Liard River, where the Mackenzie Mountains begin. The park is particularly popular with botanists eager to see the rare yellow Lady's Slipper orchid. The deep waters of Muncho Lake offer a good supply of trout for anglers.

STAY

To stay overnight in Muncho Lake Provincial Park, choose between vehicle-accessible campgrounds or a privately owned lodge:

Strawberry Flats Campground
Mile 438 Alaska Hwy
$$$

MacDonald Campground
Mile 460 Alaska Hwy
$$$

Northern Rockies Lodge
Mile 462 Alaska Hwy
$$$

NEED TO KNOW

Driving through British Columbia

BEFORE YOU GO

Forward planning is essential to any successful trip. Be prepared for all eventualities by considering the following points before you travel.

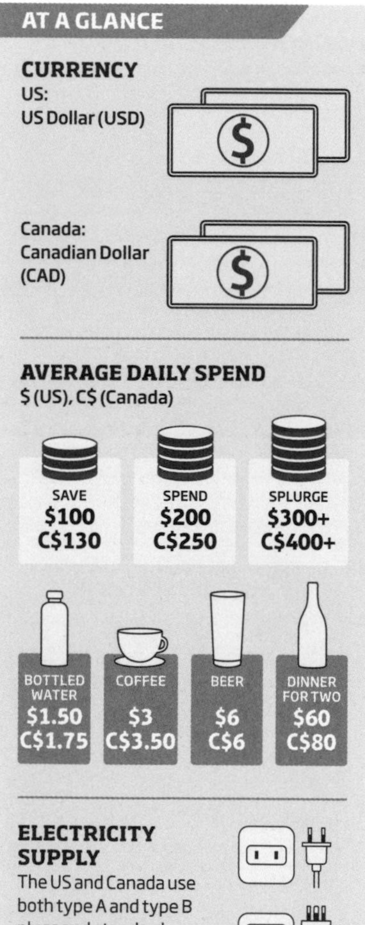

Passports and Visas

For entry into both the US and Canada, citizens of the UK, Australia, New Zealand, and EU do not require a visa for stays of up to 90 days. These citizens must fill in an **ESTA** (US) or **eTA** (Canada) form online at least 72 hours before travel.

For up-to-date visa information specific to your home country, check with your local embassy, or consult the **US Customs and Border Protection** or **Canadian Government** websites.

Canadian Government
W cic.gc.ca/english/visit/visas.asp
ESTA
W esta.cbp.dhs.gov/esta
eTA
W etacanada-application.com
US Customs and Border Protection
W cbp.gov

Travel Safety Information

Visitors can get up-to-date information from the **US Department of State**, the **UK Foreign and Commonwealth Office**, and the **Australian Department of Foreign Affairs and Trade**.

Australia
W smartraveller.gov.au
UK
W gov.uk/foreign-travel-advice
US
W travel.state.gov

Customs Information

An individual is permitted to carry the following within the Pacific Northwest for personal use:

Alcohol 1 liter for each person over 21 (US), 1.5 liters of wine or 1.14 liters of liquor for each person over 19 (Canada).

Cannabis It is illegal to take any amount of cannabis across the US or Canadian border.

Cash If entering or leaving the US or Canada with more than $10,000 in cash (or the equivalent in other currencies) it must be declared.

Tobacco products 200 cigarettes or 100 (US) or 50 (Canada) cigars.

No meat products, plants, fruits, or firearms.

Insurance

It is important to take out insurance covering health problems, accidents, trip cancelation, and interruption, as well as theft and loss of valuable possessions. A minimum of $1 million medical coverage is recommended, especially if you are traveling to the US.

Vaccinations

No inoculations are required to visit the region.

Money

Major credit and debit cards are accepted almost everywhere, while prepaid currency cards, Apple Pay, and American Express are accepted in many shops and restaurants. ATM machines are widely available, though most charge a fee per transaction. It's a good idea to bring a small amount of dollars with you for tipping, transportation, and other necessities. US currency is accepted in Canada, but you will get a better rate exchanging US dollars at a bank.

Reserving Accommodations

The Pacific Northwest offers a variety of good lodgings, from luxury five-star hotels to budget hostels. Camping, Motorhomes or RVs, and Airbnb are popular alternatives. In the summer months (June to September), accommodations are snapped up fast, and prices are often inflated. Sales Tax must be paid on accomm-odations (and on goods and other services), though it varies in each state, county, or city, and some levy additional taxes. These are usually paid on top of the advertised rates. A comprehensive list of accommodations to suit any budget can be found on the official Oregon, Washington, and BC tourism websites *(p309)*.

Travelers with Specific Needs

The Pacific Northwest has some of the world's best facilities and recreational opportunities for travelers with specific needs. Most public buildings, hotels, public transit, and entertainment venues provide wheelchair facilities with ramps and wide doors. However, some older buildings and smaller venues may not have these facilities, so always check in advance. Taxi services are available for people with wheelchairs, and parking spaces closest to the entrance of most buildings are reserved for persons with disabilities (note that permits may be required). The **Society for Accessible Travel and Hospitality** in the US and Tourism BC in British Columbia are excellent sources of information.

Society for Accessible Travel and Hospitality
W sath.org

Language

English is the official language in the Pacific Northwest. Although French is Canada's other official language, it isn't widely spoken in BC.

Closures

Mondays Some museums and tourist attractions are closed for the day.
Sundays Smaller shops and some restaurants are closed for the day.
Major holidays Schools, government offices, and banks close all day. A handful of shops and attractions close early or all day.

MAJOR HOLIDAYS

Martin Luther King, Jr. Day (US)	Jan 18 (2021) Jan 17 (2022)
Presidents' Day (US)	Feb 15 (2021) Feb 21 (2022)
Victoria Day (Canada)	May 24 (2021) May 23 (2022)
Memorial Day (US)	May 31 (2021) May 30 (2022)
Canada Day	Jul 1
Independence Day (US)	Jul 4
Labor Day	Sep 6 (2021) Sep 5 (2022)
Columbus Day (US)	Oct 11 (2021) Oct 10 (2022)
Thanksgiving Day (Canada)	Oct 11 (2021) Oct 10 (2022)
Veterans Day (US) and Remembrance Day (Canada)	Nov 11
Thanksgiving Day (US)	Nov 25 (2021) Nov 24 (2022)
Christmas Day	Dec 25

GETTING AROUND

Whether you are visiting for a short city break or a rural country retreat, discover how best to reach your destination and travel like a pro.

AT A GLANCE

TRANSPORTATION COSTS

PORTLAND
$2.50
Bus, light rail, and commuter rail for 2.5 hours

SEATTLE
$2.75
Single King County Metro bus service

VANCOUVER
$3.00
Travel within any one zone for 1.5 hours

SPEED LIMIT

OREGON INTERSTATE
65/70 mph (105/113 km/h)

WASHINGTON INTERSTATE
70 mph (113 km/h)

BC FREEWAY
62/80 mph (100/120 km/h)

BC URBAN AREAS
31 mph (50 km/h)

Arriving by Air

The main airports into the Pacific Northwest are located near the three major cities. Washington's Sea-Tac International Airport (SEA) is based between Seattle and Tacoma. In Oregon, Portland International Airport (PDX) is 13 miles outside the city proper. Most major carriers fly into these airports, though international passengers may need to transfer in Seattle to fly into Portland. United Airlines offers flights to the major cities, while Alaska Airlines and Horizon Air fly to these as well as to regional destinations. San Juan Airlines and Kenmore Air fly between Seattle and the San Juan Islands.

The point of arrival for most international visitors to BC is Vancouver International Airport (YVR), which is served by Canada's major carrier, Air Canada, as well as other national airlines. WestJet is a low-cost national alternative that links up with other major airlines. Air Canada's regional division flies to most major BC destinations; smaller airlines, such as Harbour Air, serving the Gulf Islands, connect the province's smaller communities.

All of the Pacific Northwest's international airports are well served by bus and taxi services, and rented cars, while smaller airports depend more on taxis. The table opposite lists the main transportation options to and from the region's major city airports.

Train Travel

Trains are a good way to get to the Pacific Northwest and to travel within it. All long-distance passenger train routes in the US are operated by **Amtrak**, the national rail system, and tickets should be reserved well in advance to avoid pricey fares. Amtrak offers daily services to Washington and Oregon from the Midwest, and California and has daily runs between Vancouver, Seattle, Portland, and Eugene. In BC, **VIA Rail**, Canada's national rail service, links Vancouver to Alberta and the rest of Canada. VIA Rail offers discounts for groups, families, and senior-citizens. Customs inspections occur at the Canada-US border (not upon boarding).

GETTING TO AND FROM THE AIRPORT

Airport	Distance to city	Taxi fare	Public Transportation	Journey time
Portland (PDX)	13 miles (21 km)	$35	Bus	35 mins
Seattle (SEA)	14 miles (22 km)	$45	Bus/rail	20 mins
Vancouver (YVR)	9 miles (15 km)	$35	Rail	15 mins

Privately run regional train companies offer scenic journeys. **Rocky Mountaineer®** takes a stunning route to Whistler or Kamloops, continuing along the coast to Seattle. Reserve seats through a travel agent or directly.

Amtrak
W amtrak.com
Rocky Mountaineer®
W rockymountaineer.com
VIA Rail
W viarail.ca

Long-Distance Bus Travel

Although buses may be the slowest way of getting to and around the Pacific Northwest, they are the most economical. **Greyhound** has bus routes throughout the region, while **Gray Line** and **Pacific Coach Lines** offer sightseeing tours. Discounts are available on Greyhound for children (2–16 years), students, and seniors (aged 62 and older). In BC, **Wilson's Transportation** runs an express service between Vancouver and Kamloops, and provides charter buses on Vancouver Island, as well as cross-ferry transportation between Vancouver and Victoria.

Gray Line
W grayline.com
Greyhound
W greyhound.com
Pacific Coach Lines
W pacificcoach.com
Wilson's Transportation
W wilsonstransportation.com

Boats and Ferries

Ferries are an important and scenic mode of transportation in the Pacific Northwest. **Washington State Ferries** travel regularly between Washington's mainland and the Puget Sound and San Juan Islands. **BC Ferries** travel 25 routes along the Sunshine Coast, in the Gulf Islands, Haida Gwaii, and between the mainland and Vancouver Island. The **Victoria Clipper** also provides a route to Washington, and from Victoria and Seattle to the San Juan Islands. BC and Washington ferries carry both foot passengers and vehicles, and offer discounts.

BC Ferries
W bcferries.com
Victoria Clipper
W clippervacations.com
Washington State Ferries
W wsdot.wa.gov/ferries

Public Transportation

Seattle, Portland, and Vancouver all have good public transportation systems, making it easier to explore them and leave the car behind.

In Seattle, **King County Metro Transit** operates bus services in downtown and the surrounding neighborhoods. **SoundTransit** runs the single-line Link Light Rail System north-south through the city, from the airport to Husky Stadium. It also operates the Sounder Train, which has two routes running north or south from King Street Station, and the ST Express Bus, which has several routes from the center.

Portland's excellent public transportation system is run by **TriMet** and includes light rail, bus, and streetcar lines, as well as a LIFT para-transit service for those who are less mobile.

The Vancouver system is operated by **TransLink** and covers transportation within the city and the nearby areas. There is an extensive bus network, the SkyTrain underground and overground rapid transit system, the SeaBus ferry service, and commuter rail networks.

King County Metro Transit
W kingcounty.gov
SoundTransit
W soundtransit.org
TransLink
W translink.ca
TriMet
W trimet.org

Taxis

Taxis are plentiful in Seattle, Portland, and Vancouver. They can either be flagged down outside major attractions as well as on main streets, outside hotels or at taxi stands, or pre-ordered by phone. Note that in Portland, taxis do not cruise the streets looking for fares as they do in other major cities.

Driving

Driving is a great way to explore the Pacific Northwest, especially if you want to enjoy the spectacular beauty of more remote areas. Oregon, Washington, and British Columbia maintain an extensive network of highways. The major interstate through Oregon and Washington is I-5, running north to BC and south to California. The best route to eastern Washington from Seattle is I-90; the most accessible route to eastern Oregon from Portland is I-84. The Trans-Canada Highway traverses BC, linking it to the rest of Canada. There are no tolls on roads leading into Portland and Seattle, and all US interstate highways are free.

Car Rental

Many car rental companies have offices within the cities and towns, as well as at airports, and rentals are easily arranged before arriving in the US or Canada. To rent a vehicle, you must be 21 years of age and have a valid driver's license. If you are younger than 25, you will likely have to pay a higher insurance premium. When picking up your rental car, you may be asked to show your passport and return airline ticket; you will also need a credit card (debit cards may be refused). Most rental companies offer GPS (SatNav) for an additional daily fee, and child seats with advance notice. Recreational vehicles (RVs) can also be rented but are more expensive and usually need to be reserved well in advance.

Crossing the Border

Travelers driving across the Canada–US border can choose from 16 crossings. Bring your passport and a current driver's license. In some cases an International Driving Permit will be required. Rules governing border crossings are subject to change; check with the authorities before traveling.

Insurance and Driver's Licenses

In the US, you do not need an International Driving Permit if you are carrying a valid driver's license from the country in which you live. You must, however, carry proof of auto insurance, vehicle registration, and, if renting a car, the rental contract. In BC, a valid driver's license from your own country entitles you to drive for up to 6 months. It is advisable to carry an International Driving Permit as well, in case you run into problems.

Insurance coverage for drivers is compulsory in the Pacific Northwest. Before leaving home, check your own policy to see if you are covered in a rental car. Most rental agencies offer damage and liability insurance; it is a good idea to have both. Insurance can be purchased on arrival through the **BCAA** (British Columbia Automobile Association); in the US, contact the **AAA** (American Automobile Association).

AAA
W aaa.com
BCAA
W bcaa.com

Rules of the Road

Everywhere in the US and Canada you drive on the right-hand side of the road. Right turns on red (unless otherwise indicated) are allowed after coming to a complete stop. Distances and speed limits are posted in miles in the US, and in kilometers in Canada. Speed limits vary from 25 mph (40 km/h) on neighborhood streets to a maximum of 80 mph (120 km/h) on major highways. Speed limits are strictly enforced. On most major highways, carpool lanes are available for vehicles with two or more passengers, to reduce pollution and traffic. Four-way stops are common in the Pacific Northwest. The first car to reach the intersection has the right of way. At intersections with no stop signs, drivers must yield to the car on their right.

Seat belts are compulsory, and cyclists and motorcyclists are required to wear helmets. Driving while intoxicated (which is defined as having a blood alcohol content of more than 0.08 percent) is a criminal offense. If you are involved in an accident, contact the local police. (In Canada, local policing may be carried out by the Royal Canadian Mounted Police, or RCMP, depending on where you are.)

Parking

On city streets, parking meters offer between 15 minutes and 2 hours of parking. Be sure to put money into the meter and to read all signs, since parking enforcement officers are especially active within city limits. Parking in the downtown core of major cities is expensive: for instance, parking from a meter in downtown Vancouver can cost up to $10 per hour. Illegally parked drivers run the risk of getting their vehicle towed with a substantial fine.

Safety on the Road

The Pacific Northwest experiences heavy rainfall and road surfaces become very slippery when wet, which increases the risk of hydroplaning. Other potential safety hazards for drivers

JOURNEY PLANNER

This map is a handy reference for travel on some of the Pacific Northwest's major roads. Journey times given below are for average traffic conditions.

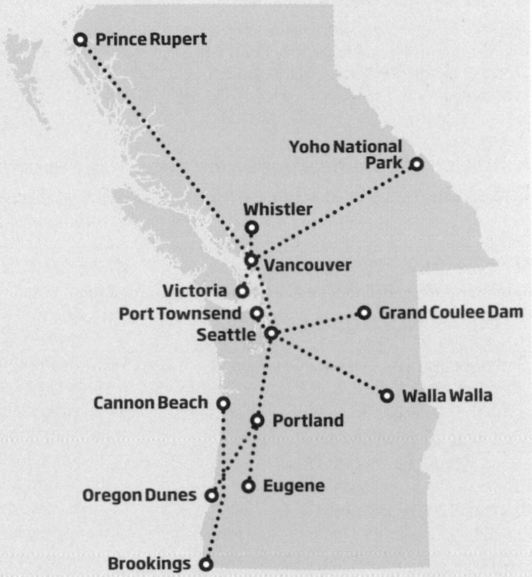

Route	Time	Route	Time
Brookings to Cannon Beach	7 hrs	**Seattle to Vancouver**	2 hrs 30 mins
Portland to Eugene	1 hr 45 mins	**Seattle to Walla Walla**	4 hrs 30 mins
Portland to Oregon Dunes	3 hrs	**Vancouver to Prince Rupert**	17 hrs
Portland to Seattle	3 hrs	**Vancouver to Victoria**	3 hrs
Seattle to Grand Coulee Dam	4 hrs	**Vancouver to Whistler**	1 hr 30 mins
Seattle to Port Townsend	2 hrs	**Vancouver to Yoho National Park**	8 hrs 30 mins

include heavy snowfalls, black ice, and fog, which can be particularly thick along the coast. To be safe, always carry a spare tire, and salt or sand in winter, a flashlight, jumper cables, blankets, water, some emergency food, and a shovel.

Before venturing out onto back roads, be sure to inquire about road conditions and weather forecasts and to have a full tank of gas. Refill the tank fairly often along the way as an extra precaution. If you know you will be driving on dirt roads or in treacherous conditions, you may want to rent a vehicle with 4WD. During the spring and summer, wildlife such as deer, bear, elk, and moose have been known to rush out of the woods onto the roads. Signs will indicate where wildlife is most likely to appear; take extra care in these areas.

Emergency road service is available 24 hours a day, 365 days a year, anywhere in the US or Canada. Members of the AAA and BCAA can call (800) 222-4357. Be prepared to give your name, membership number and expiry date, phone number, vehicle type, license plate number, exact location, and tow destination.

Cycling

Cycling is an inexpensive, healthy, and sustainable way of traveling around the cities and countryside of the Pacific Northwest. Most of the parks in the region have designated cycling trails as well as rental outlets for equipment; Portland, Seattle, Vancouver, and many other large cities have cycling paths.

Several companies offer long-distance cycling tours in the region. **Bicycle Adventures** offers tours through Oregon, Washington, and Western Canada. The **Washington State Department of Transportation** and **Cycling BC** provide maps of cycling trails. Most local tourist offices and bike rental shops will also have information about cycling.

Bicycle Adventures
W bicycleadventures.com
Cycling BC
W cyclingbc.net
Washington State Department of Transportation
W wsdot.wa.gov

PRACTICAL INFORMATION

A little local know-how goes a long way in the Pacific Northwest. Here you will find all the essential advice and information you will need during your stay.

AT A GLANCE

EMERGENCY NUMBERS

GENERAL EMERGENCY

911

TIME ZONE

The Pacific Northwest spans two time zones. All of Washington and most of Oregon and BC use PST; parts of Oregon and BC use MST. DST is observed from the second Sunday in March to the first Sunday in November.

TAP WATER

Unless stated otherwise, tap water throughout the Pacific Northwest is safe to drink.

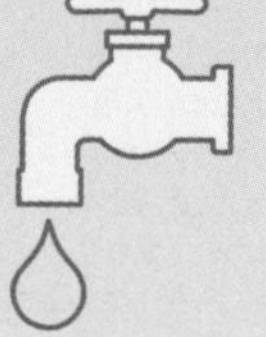

TIPPING

Waiter	15-20 percent
Hotel Porter	$1-2 per bag
Housekeeping	$3-5 per night
Concierge	$5-10
Taxi Driver	10-15 percent

Personal Security

The Pacific Northwest is generally a safe area to travel in. Most places are safe during the day and pickpocketing and muggings anywhere are rare, but it's still advised to avoid unknown parts of the major cities at night. Visitors should nonetheless take safety precautions: carry only small amounts of cash, wear a money belt under clothing, and always carry valuables and electronic devices securely.

If anything is stolen, report it as soon as possible to the nearest police station, and bring ID with you. Get a copy of the crime report in order to claim on your insurance. Contact your embassy if you have your passport stolen, or in the event of a serious crime or accident.

Health

Most major cities in the Pacific Northwest have walk-in medical clinics, which are sufficient for minor injuries and ailments. Non-prescription painkillers and other medicines can be obtained from drugstores, many of which are open 24 hours a day. Prescription drugs can only be dispensed from a pharmacy. If you take a prescription drug, pack a copy of the prescription.

Medical services are not free of charge in the Pacific Northwest, and it is important to take out health insurance prior to visiting. Even with insurance, you may have to pay upfront for the medical treatment and seek reimbursement from your insurance company later.

A first-aid kit is recommended when camping or trekking into remote areas. Seek local advice about wild animals, dangerous plants, and insects (including mosquitoes). If you are bitten or scratched by an animal, seek help immediately.

Smoking, Alcohol, and Drugs

You must be 21 to drink or purchase alcohol in Oregon and Washington and 19 in BC; expect to show photo ID. Drinking alcohol in non-licensed public places is illegal, as is driving with an open bottle of alcohol. The legal limit for drivers is 80 mg of alcohol per 100 ml of blood or

0.08 percent BAC (blood alcohol content). This is roughly equivalent to a small glass of wine or a pint of regular-strength beer.

You must be 18 to smoke in the US and 19 in BC. It is illegal to smoke in public buildings and on public transportation, and it is banned in restaurants, pubs, bars, and shopping centers.

Marijuana/cannabis has been legalized for both medical and recreational use for anyone over the age of 21 in Oregon and Washington, and over the age of 19 in BC. However, there are still strict regulations on the purchase and use of marijuana, so check local regulations. Taking any amount of cannabis across state lines or country borders is illegal, and being caught in possession of any other drug will likely result in jail time.

ID

There is no requirement for visitors to carry ID, but due to occasional checks (especially at Federal sites) you may be asked to show a picture ID. When driving, you must carry your license with you at all times.

Cell Phones and Wi-Fi

Visitors who wish to use their cell phone in the region will need a SIM card that has been set up for roaming. However, it is essential to check with your phone provider what charges you may incur while abroad. Cell phones can also be rented or purchased locally in many places. US residents can usually upgrade their domestic cell phone plan to extend to Canada, and vice versa.

Free Wi-Fi spots are generally available at major airports, libraries, and most hotels. Cafes and restaurants generally permit the use of their Wi-Fi on the condition that you make a purchase.

Post

Post offices generally open weekdays from 9am to 5pm, and also on Saturdays in the US. Stamped, addressed mail can be dropped into roadside mailboxes, which are blue in the US and red in Canada. Mail sent within the US or Canada takes from 1 to 5 business days for delivery; overseas mail, up to 7 business days. Courier companies and the priority services of the **USPS** (US Postal Service) and **Canada Post** offer speedier delivery.

Canada Post
W canadapost.ca
USPS
W usps.com

Taxes and Refunds

Sales taxes vary depending on which state or province you are visiting, and in the US they can vary depending on where you are within a state. In Washington, taxes are in the 8–9 percent range, though groceries are exempt. Visitors to Seattle who have no sales tax at home are exempt, provided they show ID. Oregon has no state sales tax. In BC, a 7 percent provincial sales tax (PST) and a 5 percent federal Goods and Service Tax (GST) apply to most goods. Visitors to BC may be eligible for a tax rebate; details can be found on the **Revenue Agency** website. In the US, as none of the taxes are levied at a national level, tourists cannot claim sales tax refunds.

Revenue Agency
W canada.ca/en/revenue-agency

Discount Cards

The Seattle **CityPASS** and **City Passport** in Vancouver offer savings on admission to major attractions; Portland doesn't offer an equivalent discount card. Washington's **Discover Pass** provides entry to the state's many national parks.

CityPASS
W citypass.com
City Passport
W citypassports.com
Discover Pass
W discoverpass.wa.gov

WEBSITES AND APPS

Washington State Travel and Tourism
The official travel website for the state of Washington *(www.experiencewa.com).*

Travel Oregon
Oregon's official travel information website *(www.traveloregon.com).*

Destination BC
British Columbia's official tourism website *(www.hellobc.com).*

INDEX

Page numbers in **bold** refer to main entries